Facing West from California's Shores

Facing West from California's Shores

*A Jesuit's Journey into
New Age Consciousness*

DAVID TOOLAN

CROSSROAD • NEW YORK

1987

The Crossroad Publishing Company
370 Lexington Avenue, New York, N.Y. 10017

Printed in the United States of America

Library of Congress Cataloging in Publication Data

Toolan, David.
  Facing west from California's shores.

  Bibliography: p.
  Includes index.
  1. New Age movement. 2. Toolan, David. I. Title.
BP605.N48T66 1987   291'.09' 04   87-6664
ISBN 0-8245-0805-X

To my parents, for the feast they threw

Facing west, from California's shores,
Inquiring, tireless, seeking what is yet
    unfound,
I, a child, very old, over waves
    towards the house of maternity,
    the land of migrations, look afar,
Look off the shores of my Western
    Sea — the circle almost circled;
For, starting westward from
    Hindustan, from the values of
    Kashmere,
From Asia — from the north — from the
    God, the sage, and the hero,
From the south — from the flowery
    peninsulas, and the spice islands;
Long having wander'd since — round
    the earth having wander'd.
Now I face home again — very pleas'd
    and joyous;
(But where is what I started for, so
    long ago?
And why is it yet unfound?)

                              Walt Whitman

Contents

Preface   xi

Part I: Initiation Rites   1

  1. Mother Esalen Gives Permission   3
  2. Cognitive Dissonance and Rising Expectation   26
  3. Psychedelic Telescopes   55

Part II: Thickening the Plot: India's Time Machine   85

  4. Pilgrim's Regress: The Eternal Return of the Oral World   87
  5. Pilgrim's Egress: A Genesis of Consciousness Story   116
  6. India's Leaky Grail   148

Part III: Recovering a Genesis Story   177

  7. Waking Mother Nature   179
  8. Holonomic Mind Fields   206
  9. Tantric Thermodynamics   229

Part IV: Resurrecting the Body   255

  10. Narcissists and Meditators   257
  11. Jean Houston's Ritual Theater   285
  12. End Notes   308

Bibliography   319

Index   331

Preface

In late July 1969 I signed up for a week-long "sensitivity session" — much in vogue at the time but quite new to me — in St. Louis, Missouri, sponsored by the National Training Laboratory of Bethel, Maine. That was my first introduction to the human potential and consciousness movements. Thereafter, in episodic fashion, I became something of a fellow-traveler of the movement in its various metamorphoses. Why I did was no mystery after my first experience in St. Louis. Out of encounters with extreme human fragility and confusion the event had sparked something like a communion feast for me. The ostensibly secular group therapists of the session were doing priest's work. From the outset, my hypothesis has been that, consciously or not (and in some cases it was quite conscious), the new humanistic growth therapies were tacitly renewing and amplifying the ascetical and contemplative traditions that church and synagogue in America had virtually forgotten. They were addressing the *how to* question which moral exhortation always blithely — and mistakenly — assumes is a question of muscular will power.

During most of the time which this book covers, I was either teaching at a Catholic college in upstate New York or working as a journalist and editor in New York City. I was and remain a member of a Roman Catholic religious community, the Jesuit order.

Following the consciousness movement would take me to places, geographical, intellectual, and psychological, which I would never have anticipated at the beginning — to India, Nepal, Thailand, and Japan, to study of the "new physics," to a variety of domestic growth centers, ashrams, zendos, conferences, and meetings with Buddhist monks, Hindu gurus, Sufis, Gurdjieffians, psychics, and far-out scientists. Only a fraction of all that will be narrated in the pages which follow — enough of a sample to get a reflection started. Above all, this book represents my effort *to understand*, to make some sense of where I've been and what happened — to me and to many others. It represents the witness of a participant, not a bystander. Yet it is not a witness in the first rush of events but a reflective phase, with some critical distance.

Taken together, this is the story of a pilgrimage, a rite of passage, and this book's four parts follow the wayward trek, trying to discern its significance. The various turning points of this journey—the human potential phase, psychedelics, the pilgrimages East, the new physics, and the efforts, against charges of narcissism, to initiate a new cultural act for Americans to pursue—present topics of interest in themselves, quite apart from their relevance to the American consciousness movement which is my theme. I try to take them both ways, using their pertinence to the cultural movement as a limit and a restraint.

Part I deals with the Esalen Institute, the epistemological revolution triggered by psychedelics, and the transition from humanistic psychology to transpersonal psychology. Polymorphous India, the subject of Part II, is endlessly fascinating in its own right. I try to treat it as such, while at the same time turning it to my own purposes, a reflection on the history of consciousness, the continuities between East and West, and the pluses and minuses of a literate mind. Seeing East in terms of West and West in terms of East, provided inscape into the way plot thickening, an intensification of experience, occurs in both traditions. Playing them both against each other, over against the differences literacy makes in assimilating each, turned into a way of diagnosing and understanding not only deficits in Hinduism but fractures in the Western narrative line.

In turn, reflections on the differences between oral and literate cultures prepare ground for the issues raised by new scientific paradigms which revise the picture of nature, the subject of Part III. Like Hinduism, this topic could easily have run away with the book—if the preeminent question had been, say, the permanent validity or truth of the new physics. But I am no physicist, much less a professional philosopher of science. The pertinence of the new physics to the consciousness movement is its contribution to an image of nature, its mythic dimension if you will, which, given the honorific place hard science possesses in our culture, shapes the collective psyche and a cultural world view. Right from the start, the leaders of the consciousness movement were intent on overcoming C. P. Snow's "two culture" split by means of a revisioned conception of nature. It was inevitable, then, that the movement would mix its psychological, aesthetic, and religious searches with an interest in new scientific paradigms, and accordingly express a concern with developments in brain research, cognitive science, biology, and physical chemistry. In the three chapters of Part III, I consider a sample of these developments in the natural sciences. In relation to the cultural shift I am tracking in these pages, they form part of a search for a new cosmology in the largest sense.

Part IV weaves together new images of nature and contemplative disciplines. In chapter 10 I take up the issue of narcissism in relation to meditative practices. If you want to get to the heart of the Judeo-Christian tradition, to something more than the "guilty conscience" recommended recently by Christopher Lasch, then I argue that it may pay to be more than a little Buddhist. Chapter 11, which pulls together many of the book's motifs, focuses on the work of Jean Houston. It provides a way of exemplifying where a significant part of the movement is in the eighties, and its distinctive American style. Chapter 12 is epilogue.

The irregular terrain which this book covers is, I believe, fairly representative of many American spiritual journeys during the last few decades. Yet the tour is selective and omits much. I do not consider what has been a conspicuous feature along the way, namely, the discovery of psychic abilities: clairvoyance, telepathy, and healing powers. Nor, though I advert to the implications often enough, do I examine movement politics — which even in this green, budding stage surely deserves closer, critical scrutiny. Only in a very partial sense is it my project to sketch a history of the consciousness movement. Rather, certain aspects of this history are examined, not just for the insight they afford into the movement but in order to reflect on the human situation and, on the meaning of time. I make no claim that my particular way of understanding the trip is at all typical of my fellow-travelers. The reflections which follow are my own, and perhaps idiosyncratic. They represent an effort, born of my own background, to relate the consciousness movement to the Western tradition, specifically to the Judeo-Christian tradition.

That has not always been easy. Generally speaking, especially in its early period, the movement has been framed by its advocates in terms of Eastern religions. When it has been read in Western terms, it has been associated with gnosticism or other marginal, if not heretical currents of thought such as esoteric alchemy. If one looks at a cross-section of movement literature, running, say, from *The Whole Earth Catalog* to the books of as articulate and intelligent a spokesman as Ken Wilbur, one often finds dismissive caricatures of Western religious traditions — a polemic often tinged with old-fashioned bigotry. Rarely has the movement been understood in terms of mainstream Western orthodoxy, either Jewish or Christian. I think that can be done. It is what in part I propose to do, or begin to do, in these chapters.

PART I

Initiation Rites

ONE

Mother Esalen Gives Permission

How is it possible for the man who designed Voyager 19, which arrived at Tatania, a satellite of Uranus, three seconds off schedule and a hundred yards off course after a flight of six years, to be one of the most screwed up creatures in California — or of the Cosmos?

Walker Percy

Patient: I dream of an erupting volcano.
Fritz: All right, talk to the volcano.
Patient: You're just sitting inside . . . and most of the time I don't even know you're there . . . .
Fritz: Be the volcano.
Patient: Well, I'm waiting. I may erupt any time, you'd better watch out.
Fritz: Say this to me.
Patient: I may erupt any time — you better watch out.
Fritz: Huh? . . . I don't hear you yet.
Patient: (loud) I may erupt at any moment — you better watch out.
Fritz: Okay, I'm ready. . . . Can you allow your shaking to develop? . . . Decontrol yourself?

Frederick Perls, *Gestalt Therapy*

Ah, but I was so much older then
I'm younger than that now.

Bob Dylan

3

California: a place where the American expansionist ethos once reached its geographic outer limit. In the sixties and seventies it became a state of mind, a mythic medium for charting inner space and untried human potentials. The heart of this new frontier, its laboratory center, was the hanging garden about fifty miles south of Carmel along the Big Sur coast named after an extinct Indian tribe. It was called the Esalen Institute. Poised on a cliff overlooking the Pacific below Route 1, where mountains rise steeply behind, the place, with its craggy cypresses etched against the ocean, is staggeringly beautiful. Banks of flowers around the buildings, lush spongy lawns, Zen-like plantings, vegetable and herb gardens, added by its celebrated gardener, Selig Morgenrath, enhance the natural beauty. Morgenrath is now dead but his labor of love, and his legend, lives on. Through all the years of acrimonious dispute over who was the institute's presiding genius, a consensus endures on one thing: Selig Morgenrath, who never formally offered a workshop there, was an authentic wise man. I had no trouble believing it. It wasn't jet lag or the trials of reaching this secluded spot that always left me slightly dizzy on arrival. It was the air of the place, what God had planted, and Morgenrath cultivated, there—a garden of Eden.

"Mother Esalen gives permission," ran one of the axioms of the place. It was Great Mother country, sensual and nurturing. People were encouraged to drop their false fronts, to relax, trust their own spontaneity, and try out new behaviors. The effect was often marvelous to behold. Macho men became suddenly softer, lighter, more elastic and approachable. On the opposite side, timid souls allowed their strength and sensuality to show. All sorts of new faces, voices, and secrets manifested themselves. The place floated on a sea of eroticism so broad and many-fathomed that, despite appearances, sexual gamesmanship was at a minimum. With the spectrum of affect so wide, beyond at least what I was used to, there were multiple alternatives to the either/or of avoidance or bedding down. For all its nudity, the strange thing is that Esalen was a celibate's dream. But then, of course, I went there after the bacchanalian 1967 "summer of love." By the time I arrived, the place was more like early American utopian communities—New Harmony, Oneida, and Brook Farm.

Liberals like me who came to Esalen and other "growth centers" like it spreading throughout the nation in the late sixties and early seventies were refugees from Camelot, from the shattered promises awakened by Lyndon Johnson's Great Society and Martin Luther King's civil rights campaigns. For liberals just celebrating the "end of ideology" and blinkered to the covert contradictions of our society, the thought that there might be virulent, poisonous blood in the body politic came as a shock. The magic chemistry began to dissolve—as in quick succession came ghetto burnings (Watts, Detroit, Chicago, the South Bronx), the escalating war in Vietnam, protest marches, Robert Kennedy's assassination, the 1968 Democratic National Convention in Chicago, the Pentagon Papers, and finally Watergate. The customary pep talks and half-time breaks would not do to close the fissures which had opened up an abyss in the American psyche. Esalen was a refugee camp and fast-food monastery.

From the outset traumatic public events of the sixties and seventies triggered a crisis of soul, essentially religious and probably always latent. It has been said that places like Esalen simply ministered to everyday alienation, the stress and strain of the corporate state and faceless bureaucracies. I just don't believe that was all there was to it. The droves of beautiful people, of tenured academics, and prosperous professionals would never have swarmed to Esalen if all they had been looking for was a "moral holiday" from the rat race of high-tech society and its misbegetting obligations. The wells feeding a sense of promise embodied in the American system—call it the *novus ordo saecularum*, the new time for humankind, that it had been our manifest destiny as a people to implant in the planet—had dried up. Liberals, in particular, aren't prone to speak out loud about it, but nonetheless dwelt within this current of promise, lived on it, took it for granted—and social trauma opened the abyss of life without it. The event was also an opportunity, what Paul Tillich called a *kairos*, a hazardous, precious, fluid moment of truth.

CRITICS TO THE RIGHT AND LEFT

It's not exactly true, then, that Esalen gave birth to the human potential movement, to the "consciousness revolution," and finally, to transpersonal psychology. Rather, it seized the day (or the dark night of soul) and provided search tools, the kind of ascetical means of recovering from a fall from grace that Protestant America, following on the word of the sixteenth-century Reformers, had repudiated as papist priestcraft. It's amazing how the judgments Esalen evoked differ. To its conservative critics, sure that the American kingdom of righteousness had not fallen, Esalen appeared a den of iniquity, Babylon West, a hedonistic Shangrila bent on subverting the work ethic of corporate America. For its aficianados, of course, the place was a three-ring therapeutic circus, a nurturing womb, a haven of healing, and a sanctuary. Like a Kali temple I once visited in Calcutta, it offered all-forgiving refuge for the offscouring of the earth, including thugs and bandits. Well not quite; the Kali temple had been free of charge. At Esalen you had to be able to afford the freight, and it wasn't cheap. Well-tenured professionals, corporate thugs and bandits had a distinct edge over the less well-heeled variety from Watts and Bedford-Stuyvesant. Which is part of what got the goat of Esalen's critics from the Left.

According to the Left, old and new, the trouble was that places like Esalen weren't subverting corporate America enough. All this "touchy feely" business, it was said, ignored the social and economic determinants of consciousness. The self-realization motto of responsibility to and for oneself, which prefaced every Esalen catalogue, was nothing new. For well over a century it had been the jingle, incessantly replayed, of the complacent self-made individualist's success story. Centers like Esalen had simply refined the means of teaching their clientele to forget their conflicted subconscious, to bliss-out on "peak experience" as if genuine liberation-now were possible without the sweat of social change. Humanistic psychology of the post-Freudians, of Karen Horney, Erich Fromm, Abraham Maslow, and Carl Rodgers, the charge proceeded, ignored the socially critical metapsychology of Father Sigmund, which had stressed the sediment of history, and of oppressive institutions, in the formation of the subconscious. Therefore the "growth movement" was repeating the postcritical original sin of neglecting the real causes of the "sigh of the oppressed, the heart of a heartless world, and the soul of soulless conditions." This was not enlightenment but "social amnesia" (see Jacoby, 1975). Or as another critic put the political implications: it spelled "complacency for those who have succeeded; resignation or self-blame for those who have not" (Schur, 1976: 4).

Such criticism cannot be dismissed. From what I could observe, at least in the early days, the pathologies of Esalen guests were scarcely ever translated into the material and social conditions outside the family network. Class divisions were hardly mentioned. On top of that, as critics rightly saw, the stress on perception rather than work as the primary way of relating to the world could well simply aggravate the modern self's position of spectator and passive viewer. Given how much human activity is preempted by the action of markets and investment, the focus on heightening perception might encourage a surrender to the way things are and lose all sense of social critique. And it's true: for a period the absence of a theoretical perspective on the social goals of therapy, the way in which Esalen and places like it emasculated practice by stripping it of philosophic underpinnings, constituted a serious defect—and a defection from the political philosophy of most of the European originators of these "new" growth therapies. The same thing happened later with oriental imports; for popular American consumption, they were deodorized to smell like sandalwood.

It was not a time when anyone was doing very much homework. The New Left thought it knew what had to be done at the barricades, and accordingly neglected the question whether the revolutionary was a fit instrument of service. Resentment of "flower children" and self-realizers assumed a version of the "noble savage" myth: since all our ills stem from social and economic conditions, capitalist conditions in particular, once these are overturned, the innocent, prelapsarian Adam will reemerge. Meanwhile, Old Lefties, whose moment had come and passed, sputtered reminders (in vain) of the "god that failed" in the Stalinization of the Russian Revolution. They (people like Irving Howe and Michael Harrington) had read their Theodor Adorno, Max Horkheimer, and Walter Benjamin—the neo-Marxian Frankfurt School—and recognized that the authoritarian personality was a menace on the Left as well as the Right, knew that Marx without something like Freud was an empty illusion. If anyone had been listening, if the critics had actually gone to Esalen rather than sitting in an ivory tower, they might have seen that despite its early reluctance to theorize, Esalen's growth therapies, its psychodrama, gestalt therapy, and even its body work had origins in radical European political philosophy. Even as expurgated for the American quick-fix market, the stuff had revolutionary implications and intended institutional change. A critical and reformist spirit was still evident at Esalen in the late sixties and early seventies. Esalen served as the inspiration and testing center, for instance, for Stuart Miller's campaign for humanistic medicine, for educator George Brown's efforts to integrate the emotional factor with cognitive training at an early period (so adults wouldn't be driven to growth centers to unlearn or relearn what they had failed to acquire as children), and for women's consciousness-raising groups. Because of the difficulty of getting major funding if the Esalen name were attached to a program, both Miller and Brown quickly moved their efforts to the more respectable university; but the point is that these significant movements had their start at Esalen. Equally important at this time were the interracial encounter groups spearheaded by George Leonard and black psychologist Price Cobbs; for several years, until black power rage ruined their chances, these efforts to heal white prejudice and black anger achieved some remarkable successes.

THE VISION TAKES OFF

When Michael Murphy and Richard Price arrived in the spring of 1961 to take over the Murphy family property from the then lesee, the charismatic Church of the God of Prophecy, the place was already accustomed to speaking in tongues—and to anarchy. One of the first things they had to do was purge the site of bohemians (Henry Miller's crowd), San Francisco homosexuals, and Big Sur motorcycle gangs, all of whom used to congregate (and fight) in the baths and bar at what, till then, was known as Slate's Hot Springs. Murphy and Price, the new management, were about to open a cosmic motel. They had been talking up a vision-storm, had been encouraged by Aldous Huxley, Alan Watts, and Gerald Heard to believe that an amorphous "great evolutionary leap forward" was brewing in the Western psyche. All it needed was a launching pad. They would provide one.

Both then thirty, the two had not known each other as undergraduates at Stanford University, but both had been introduced there to oriental philosophy by Frederic Spiegelberg. In 1961 Price was just getting his life together again after a postgraduate breakdown and brutal insulin and electric shock treatment. From the outset, he would put Esalen in the forefront of the movement for patients' rights and humanistic medicine. And anyone who witnessed him practice his Taoistic mode of gestalt therapy (so different in its gentle nonintrusiveness from that of Fritz Perls) saw a genuine contemplative in action. Until his death in a rock slide in 1985, his quiet, behind-the-scenes presence in the daily running of Esalen was like that too. The man did not preside, but was instantly there, a steadying hand when things got stuck.

Murphy presides. Though today retired from an active managerial role, he has been Esalen's circus impresario, up-front promoter, constantly brimming with fresh ideas. Following graduation from Stanford, military service, and already a serious meditator, he spent time at Shri Aurobindo's ashram in Pondicherry, India. There he absorbed this ex-revolutionary's remarkable synthesis of body-mind polarities, inner growth and species evolution, mysticism and political action. The influence has been permanent, evident in Murphy's dithyrambic career. He was especially taken with Aurobindo's practice of "spiritual sports"—and not at all pleased with the master's authoritarian successor, Mira Richard (known as "the Mother"). In the late sixties, Esalen would sponsor a major conference on the problem of tyrannical gurus and therapists. Later, unleashing a great publishing wave of sports-as-yoga books, Murphy wrote *Golf in the Kingdom* (1972) and then the "speculative fiction" *Joseph Atabet* (1977), which envisions what it might be like to live in this world in a resurrected body. To get human potential ideas into the mainstream of American culture, in the early seventies Murphy founded the Sports Center in San Francisco. These days he frequently commutes to Russia to further a budding human potential movement there.

In its first seasons, Esalen fielded itself as a think-tank, a birthplace for "the Vision." The roster of seminar leaders reads like a Who's Who: Arnold Toynbee, Paul Goodman, Linus Pauling, S. I. Hayakawa, Gardner Murphy, Gregory Bateson, Joseph Campbell, Bishop James Pike, Ansel Adams, Harry Bridges, Norman O. Brown, Virginia Satir, Rollo May, Ashley Montagu, and Paul Tillich. By its third year, however, the transition had begun to the participatory, experiential workshop, and by 1964 this was in full swing. In that year, after an all-night bull session with *Look* editor George Leonard, Murphy was ready to redo the American revolution. "George," he exclaimed, "let's fire a shot heard round the world!" With that, what had barely received the name "human potential" movement upshifted to the "consciousness revolution." Militant activists may not have approved of the psychological approach, but there is no doubt that from the beginning Murphy and his friends were out to change the world.

THE ALCHEMICAL MIX

From the outset providence, or in California argot, "synchronicities," smiled on the project. Quite fortuitously in the summer of 1962, a vacationing Abraham Maslow, champion of "third force" humanistic psychology, was driving along Route 1 and spotted the Esalen sign. Curious, he dropped in, heard what was going on, and came away a staunch supporter. He had found allies for the case he was trying to make to his behaviorist peers; at the same time, the long-suffering Maslow would become the intellectual conscience of the human potential movement. "It becomes more and more clear," he had written in 1954 (in Anderson, 1983: 66), "that the study of crippled, stunted, immature, and unhealthy specimens can yield only a cripple psychology and a cripple philosophy."

Seeking to revise the outlook, Maslow was studying the phenomenon of "peak experience," powerful moments of clarity, joy, or religious ecstasy that occur in the lives of people he called "self-actualizers" (a term deriving from German gestalt psychologist Kurt Goldstein). Not only was it possible for people to live out of something other than "deficiency motivation," Maslow's studies concluded, but more commonly than thought, a considerable number actually did so; that is, lived out of "being motivation." But a healthy society needed more of them. In *Toward a Psychology of Being* (1962) he had put the social need this way (in Anderson, 1983: 66):

> Every age but ours has its model or hero. All these have been given us by our culture; the hero, the gentleman, the knight, the mystic. About all we have left is the well-adjusted man without problems, a very pale and doubtful substitute. Perhaps we shall soon be able to use as our guide and model the fully growing and self-fulfilling human being, the one whose inner nature expresses itself freely, rather than being warped, repressed, or denied.

Something of a model himself to those who knew him, Maslow was a solid family man, rarely apart from his wife Bertha. His self-actualizers were typically scholars and intellectuals. The vision of optimal human development required the use of mental ability in the service of some beneficial social purpose. In the crucible of the self-fulfillment ethos, the point would often be lost.

"Esalen's law," Dick Price observed, "is that you always teach others what you most need to learn yourself." For Esalen in particular and the growth movement in general, this functions as a hermeneutical law, a guiding rule for the interpretation of ensuing events both fortunate and disastrous.

Body work, gestalt therapy, and encounter were the staples at Esalen. Nineteen sixty-four was a banner year. It brought into residence Frederick ("Fritz") Perls, founder of gestalt therapy, and Charlotte Selver's and her husband Charles Brooks's "sensory awareness" exercises. Sensory awareness practice derived from a Berlin calesthenics teacher, Elsa Gindler, who in 1910 had been struck by tuberculosis. She had taken an active part in the curative process by learning how to control her breathing so that she could rest her diseased lung. Selver, who had studied with her, brought the method to New York in the 1930s, and there Erich Fromm, Perls himself, and Alan Watts (who pronounced it the essence of Zen) had discovered her. Sensory awareness training was one of a long line of body therapies that would become an Esalen trademark. The first had been T'ai Chi Chuang movements (introduced by Gai-fu-Feng), followed by Ida Rolph's strenuous "rolphing" massage, Alexander technique, and Moshe Feldenkrais's supple body movements ("functional integration"), along with various forms of dance movement such as Gabrielle Roth's. At one time or another, I have tried them all, and Feldenkrais and T'ai Chi have stayed with me.

As for the brilliant, insatiable, cantankerous Fritz Perls—a burly mass of deficiency motive and self-assertion—he surprised Price and Murphy by asking to move in to stay. Gestalt therapy, his creation, distilled a gypsy career spanning three continents. Perls grew up in the avant-garde, bohemian Berlin of Kurt Weil, Bertolt Brecht, and Walter Gropius's Bauhaus. Later in Frankfurt, he had closely studied Paul Tillich's early existentialism and Martin Buber's *I and Thou*, both responses to the depersonalizing effects of massive modern institutions. As a psychologist he worked with gestalt psychologist Kurt Goldstein and became a patient of maverick Freudian Wilhelm Reich. Reich had talked of "body armor" as a way of protecting oneself from reality and paid more attention to *how* people spoke than to *what* they said; Perls incorporated both features in gestalt therapy. (By all accounts he was a genius at reading "body language.") Emigrating to South Africa in the thirties to escape Hitler, Perls revisioned Freud, arguing ([1947] 1969) that neurosis was equivalent to the avoidance of contact, to experience never tasted, hunger never filled. Moving to New York in 1946, Perls eventually came in touch with the group psychodrama therapy of Jacob Levy Moreno—a method perfectly designed for a person (or a country) replete with contradictory voices. As Perls adapted Moreno's work in his own one-on-one gestalt work, "acting out" the multitude of conflicted internal voices would become central (see Perls, 1971b).

As the Austrian Moreno conceived it (1966), psychodrama provided a form of group therapy whose goal is not only insight (as with Freud) but catharsis, self-expression, and spontaneity. The therapist acts as a director and members of the group enact dreams and real or imagined life scenes, reversing roles frequently. The thing is not dissimilar to Actors Studio method. For Moreno himself, however, spontaneity had religious significance. It was the life force, the creative spirit of the cosmos; in consequence, psychodrama was at once therapy, social ritual, and religious ceremony—and an antidote to the dehumanization of large organizations. (In the 1940s Moreno had used the method to train groups, teachers and social workers mostly, to work in behalf of fair labor practices.) Stripped of its spiritual overtones, Moreno's work filtered into Perl's more one-on-one gestalt method. In turn, stripped of the element of revolt against large-scale organizations, it formed the matrix for the National Training Laboratory's "sensitivity sessions" and "T-groups," (training groups) for the gray flannel corporate elite in the sixties. The latter in effect removed the therapist-director from a position of dominance, leaving the process and evaluation to the group participants themselves. (If that message were carried back to the front office, as it occasionally was, it would have to mean some form of work-place participatory democracy.)

In any event, Fritz Perls moved to Big Sur to stay, until a little before his death in 1970. From that time forward intellectual analysis came in for little but abuse. It was not that gestalt theory is opposed to rational thought as such, but that rationalizing is so often a disguised form of avoidance, a "head trip." Perls considered himself an expert "shit detector." His slogan was "lose your mind and come to your senses"—and he was a master at making that happen. His Gestalt Prayer took the place (and arguably the country) by storm:

> I do my thing, and you do your thing.
> I am not in this world to live up to your expectations
> And you are not in this world to live up to mine.
> You are you and I am I,
> And if by chance we find each other, it's beautiful.
> If not, it can't be helped.

Most reproductions in glossy omitted the bleak last line. Perls had not grown up in Germany between the wars, nor had he fled Hitler, for nothing. He was Esalen's irascible Jewish Hemingway, insisting that the high flyers stay earth bound, implacably opposed to visionary big words, scornful of empathetic helpers. Maslow's high "being motivation" and "peak experience" were so much "elephantshit." If people (e.g., like himself) had to be relieved of the irrational catastrophic expectations by which they escape reality, Esalen itself in his view suffered from the opposite syndrome, "anastrophic expectations," a pox of visionary fantasy. As for himself, "I teach people to wipe their own ass." At which point, in 1967, Michael Murphy moved north to open up the San Francisco Esalen on Union Street, where he could pursue something closer to Aurobindo's ecumenical religious orientation. Esalen was expanding in all directions and would soon become a literary movement as well.

Meanwhile, at the Big Sur campus, Will Schutz and his "open encounter" arrived to stay. "Joy boys!" Perls snapped. The two titans, both assured that the universe revolved around them, did not mix. The rivalry between Perls and Schutz and the Maslow contingent could be hilarious—and ugly. Former professor at Harvard, the University of California at Berkeley, and the Albert Einstein School of Medicine in New York, Schutz was probably at the time the nation's leading expert in group therapy. He had assimilated everything. The cornucopia of what he named "open encounter" included elements of Alexander Lowen's emotion-releasing bioenergetics, Moreno's psychodrama, gestalt, sensitivity T-group methods, nonverbal "trust" exercises, "high noon" showdowns, body wrestling, nudity, and psychosynthesis exercises in imagery. The open encounter therapist was not so much director as ringmaster, constantly introducing new acts. With Schutz's free-associative method, the line between therapy in the strict sense and personal growth method, always cloudy, began to disappear. The point was no longer to take people from minus to coping zero, but to shoot for the moon. The new word was "expansion"—as in Schutz's 1967 book *Joy: Expanding Human Awareness.*

Schutz in practice, I'm told, was better than the salesman in print. The latter was a perfect candidate for satire. The point was to feel good, better, best (Schutz, in Anderson, 1983: 158):

> The theme of this book is joy. The theories and methods presented here are aimed at achieving joy. Joy is the feeling that comes from the fulfillment of one's potential. Fulfillment brings to an individual the feeling that he can cope with his environment; the sense of confidence in himself as a significant, competent, lovable person who is capable of handling situations as they arise, able to use fully his own capacities, and free to express his feelings.

Schutz reformulated the Cartesian "I think, therefore I am." Hereafter it would be "I feel, therefore I am" (a graffiti logo still plastered to a downtown Berkeley building wall as of 1985). A little narcissism, like a little antiintellectualism, goes a long way. If understood dialectically as a corrective to a pervasive disembodied rationalism, the thing makes eminent sense. Out of context, however, it was another matter. The film *Bob and Carol and Ted and Alice* satirized Esalen's growth psychology, and not without some accuracy.

FLYING HIGH

For what was actually a rather brief period (by my estimate about three years) psychedelics, primal scream, and the tyranny of "hold nothing back" ruled at Esalen. Rollo May protested the orgiastic atmosphere, the fact that not a soul seemed sober. The conscientious Maslow begged for "more reading, more research, a stronger philosophical base." But to little avail. Until Perls died and Schutz left over a management (or control?) dispute in 1973, sage restraint went unheeded. The frenzy of the time should doubtless be understood in connection with ancient rites of orgy, wherein oral tribal societies sought to compensate for the poverty of their self-understanding by deliberately setting aside the regulative forms and laws of social life. The person had to regress, the self die. The idea was to destroy the old creation, along with its limits and boundaries, in order to return to the *seed* state of biocosmic unity, of primeval chaos preceding creation. It was the way people tapped in again to the primordial excess, whose boundless overflow makes possible a new creation. The degraded forms of the thing should not put us off. As Mircea Eliade remarks (1958: 359), "every feast of its nature involves something of an orgy."

The risks and hazards of course ran high, were themselves part of the Esalen mystique, of its *kairos*. Nothing illustrates that better than the intensive, "residential" programs which Esalen staged throughout 1967 and 1968 for a select group of hardy souls who stayed a year or more and were initiated into the gamut of reeducational blow-outs. Years later, encounter leader John Heider summed it up (in Anderson, 1983: 177):

> There may be one of us for whom that was *not* the most significant time of our lives, but for most of us this was the crucible. This was our World War II. This was our place of coming of age. I don't know anybody, even those of us who were badly hurt, who would wish they'd been at a place of safety that year.

Yet this experiment and others like it of reduced scale demonstrated the perils of a fast-food monastery—and the need for taking sociological reference points seriously. In several cases toward the end of the sixties, shooting for more than the moon, flying too close to the sun proved fatal. In 1969 Esalen was deeply shaken by three suicides in quick succession. There were others later. As Walter Truett Anderson (1983: 289), Esalen's biographer, tells the story:

> Through all the residential programs there had been a frequently expressed sense of incompleteness, a general belief among the residents that they were getting too much of something and not enough of something else. They talked of the need for "grounding." In search of it, they tried yoga and meditation. . . . They worked on the buildings, and in the garden . . . liter-

ally digging into the ground in search of that missing something outside themselves. The more conventional things that people used as foundations for their personal lives—families, jobs, communities, organized religion— were often the very things the residents had abandoned when they set out for Esalen along the path of self-development.

After the "peaks" came the bottomless letdowns.

COMING DOWN

A while before Jane Howard of *Life*, Peter Marin writing for the *New York Times Magazine*, and other reporters descended on the place to worry about excesses and narcissism, eclectic bacchanalian Esalen had already begun to change, tone down, go slower. Thereafter, this central headquarters actually functioned as a steadying influence on the beserk tendencies of the growth movement throughout the country. The place had always been selective about who was let through the doors to lead workshops, and few cult entrepreneurs passed muster. As a participant, Werner Erhart (of *est*) simply ripped off and repackaged what he could. Others, like Leonard Orr, who arrived with a team to lead "rebirthing" workshops in the late seventies when I was present, violated the rule against proselytizing and were never invited back to exploit the Esalen name.

Tragedy brought a measure of sobering up, revealed the need of greater connections than the suppositions of humanistic psychology or the philosophy of personalism could supply. The magnification of personal life, looking to other people for redemption, seizing on them, clinging to them—as encounter groups, sensitivity sessions, and gestalt sometimes seemed to imply—proved insufficient, often enough spoiled actual friendships, marriages, loves, and families. Esalen had cloned itself across the country, had spawned the anarchic human potential movement, a big, messy target like a church. Selig Morgenrath created a garden of Eden; the noble savages who inhabited and visited the place promptly replicated the Fall. Critics were sure of pointing this out, and did. But Esalen was also a moving target, rather like a snake shedding its skin annually. Metamorphosis was its business.

Maslow died in 1970, the same year as Fritz Perls. Already sniffing the winds of transition, Michael Murphy had led a trip of Esalen heavies to Europe in 1969. After holding court in London, he and Stuart Miller had proceeded to visit Roberto Assagioli, then in his eighties, in Florence, Italy. Assagioli (1971), who trained under Freud, had founded the so-called psychosynthesis approach to development, a comprehensive theoretical and practical system, which relies heavily on active fantasy and imaging to sort out the many "subpersonalities" we contain within us (one of which usually tyrannizes over the others). But the method also speaks of a "higher self" in touch with a spiritual dimension that is capable of orchestrating and sorting out (the "synthesis" part) our internal multiplicity. The wise old man was receptive to the gamut of Esalen experiments, in fact, excluded no plausible technique, but thought that the higher self, if a therapist were in touch with it, would know what technique fit in a particular case. For Miller, meeting Assagioli occasioned something of a religious conversion, and for both him and Murphy, the "higher self" approach was a possible check on the one-sidedness of encounter and gestalt. Moreover, they saw psychosynthesis as providing a framework, as Miller wrote, "for the *synthesis* of Esalen's techniques."

As the seventies began, then, Esalen shifted toward subtlety and greater balance. It moved from the exclusively interpersonal to the *trans*-personal (which I shall explain in greater detail in the next chapter). This also meant more California Hinduism and Buddhism, the beginning of a more multitudinous raid on oriental riches and esoteric contemplative traditions generally.

LIMINALITY

In 1972, straight from a civil disobedience "action," I made my first pilgrimage to Esalen for a week-long meditation workshop—which was perhaps representative of Esalen's new direction in the seventies. In leaving behind my work world and the conspiracies, scenarios, and actions of the Catholic Left in which I was then involved, I was quite literally on pilgrimage. Though it was a season for "retreats" organized around the theme of political street-theater, and my movement friends were tolerant of my idiosyncrasy, this kind of retreat drew disapproval; to them it was something of a betrayal of the cause—and a trip to a country club no less. But the thing made sense. Given my professional drop-out status and what my life was supposed to be about, I had more reason to be at Esalen than most of the others there. I was stepping out of ordinary structured time into another space.

Let me explain. It relates to the orgy business as a rite of regeneration. What is a pilgrimage? Historically, it was the way more complex, feudal societies reprogrammed the compulsory, collective rites of passage of more primitive, oral societies. Rites of passage marked a transition process, a ritual death leading to change in a person's or group's social status or psychic state. Classically, as Arnold van Gennep described them, rites of passage involved three stages: (1) separation or seclusion from ordinary secular relationships, (2) symbolic rebirth, and (3) reincorporation into society with enhanced vision and functions. No longer hedged about with taboos, feudal societies invented the pilgrimage to carry out this process over an extended time and in a heightened individual and voluntary manner (a personal vow). Pilgrimages provided a mode of extending freedom, of releasing a person from the manifold guiles, guilts, and anxieties which conventional role-playing entails. The idea, said the late anthropologist Victor Turner ([1969] 1977: 95–130; [1974] 1975: 166–230) is to create an "anti-structure" over against the rules, routines, and divisions of the usual social contract and its obligations—and thus to find out who you are at root, independent of those structures and roles. Withdrawing from multiplicity did not mean the elimination of diversity but aimed at a realization of nonduality, of common membership. Turner calls it a "liminal" phase, a threshold time-out betwixt and between periods of intense social involvement.

Liminality is what "on the road" dharma bums, beatniks, and hippies were instinctively after. It is exactly what ancient orgiastic rites of the *hieros gamos*, the marriage of earth and sky, aimed to achieve. As the ritual association suggests, access to liminal space requires performance, if you will, psychodrama. Traditionally, it involved the kinetic reenactment of the lives of incarnate gods, saints, and seers. Rather than merely looking *at* the ritual of temple, mosque, church, and synagogue from outside, as a passive spectator, one became their central symbols of re-membering—as an *inside participant in the action*. And dwelling in-between, neither one thing nor another, again as orgy suggests, entails danger-time, the high risk of a vacuum. For liminal antistructure annuls the classifications upon which order depends. One deliberately sets up an antinomian pole, a wide-open space, thus creating a charged field of tension between it and business as usual. The old evaluative frames and gestalts cease to apply; the indicative mood of everyday is sacrificed, deconstructed, reduced to ground zero. For someone dwelling in this imaginal desert, emptiness enacts a symbolic death. The idea is to generate meditative, contemplative space, where everything can fall into the subjunctive mood. What happens then? No telling. Depending on the group or person, it can mean grace or force. If it's the latter, you get totalism—scapegoating pogroms, crusades, holy wars. Such fallout may be the underlying reason Western rationalists, for the last several centuries, find mysticism suspect, have maintained contemplation off-limits.

So what's the point? Strictly, the question is inappropriate, for utilitarian queries belong to the differentiated social order left behind. But we can approach the thing obliquely. First, liminality is a culture's subjunctive mood, its space for unbound might-have-beens, as-ifs, what-ifs, maybes, should-bes. Functionally, it represents a culture's way of declaring that conservation does not suffice, that qualitative growth is also essential. The *limen* spells release from and protection against the stasis of a petrified monoculture. As such, it is organized on aesthetic, poetic principles rather than those of law and ethics. It creates space for reverie, dream, wild imagination; time for new options and recombinations, utopian blueprints or models. Though currently functionless, these imaginings may become functional in the future. In this sense, the arts, scientific research, and hypothesis framing are what Turner calls "liminoid" activities, by which he means posttraditional, posttribal modes of in-betweenness, characterized by the optative mood rather than the obligation of sheer social pressure. Authorship in a liminoid situation is individual rather than collective, and the setting is secular rather than that of sacred ritual. In the sixties, perhaps the capital example of what liminoid subjunctivity can do was supplied by Malcolm X's pilgrimage to Mecca. "What I have seen and experienced," Malcolm X wrote (1966: 340), "has forced me to *rearrange* much of my thought patterns previously held and to *toss aside* some of my previous conclusions. . . . We were truly all the same."

Secondly, there is the aspect of unity or communion. Orgiastic rites aim to dissolve boundaries and replicate a seed state of biocosmic unity with primordial excess. The case is identical with the performative process of being pilgrim. Turner calls this feature of anti-structure *communitas*. Such communion does not necessarily mean antithesis, that is, the regulative social structure with its signs reversed. Of course it can mean that, and if it does, the result displays itself in a heterodox, esoteric, antinomian sect. But that result is not predestined. Confucianism, for instance, saw complementarity between *li* (propriety, rite, ceremonial) and *jeu* (love, goodness, humanness). Similarly, the great religious systems of love proposed a tensive harmony, a kind of Yin-Yang relationship, between *communitas* and structure. The rule is: no dualisms. Without the inspiration of love, law degenerates into legalism; conversely, without law, boundless love withers into vacuous sentimentality or anarchy. If the performative pilgrim process works, liminal communion comes across as the *fons et origo* of all structure, and, at the same time, its critique. The very existence of *communitas* puts all structure in question, allows for healthy iconoclasm, and suggests new possibilities.

In fact, as medieval pilgrimages show, extended liminal conditions breed new types of secular liminality and communities—fairs, fiestas, marketing systems, new forms of wayfaring literature, and intercourse of all kinds. The thing strains toward universality and is something other than Durkheim's "mechanical solidarity" (which hinges on in-group/out-group oppositions). As in Chaucer's *Canterbury Tales*, the different orders of society mingle without submerging into each other; before God, with God, all are equal and social stratification doesn't count. They are members of each other, of one cosmic body (which still allows them to tell ribald stories). Those jointly undergoing this ritual transition, a symbolic rebirth, frequently reverse roles and status, or hold them in suspense. Relationships are reconceived in liminal time in an anti-structural mode—as undifferentiated, egalitarian, immediate, nonrational, and spontaneous I-Thou encounter. Pilgrimages are meant not only to free the individual but, in broadening parochial horizons, to initiate a radical cosmopolitan outlook. Again, Malcolm X's testimony is classic (1966: 330, 339):

> All ate as One, and slept as One. Everything about the pilgrimage atmosphere accented the Oneness of Man under God . . . .Never have I witnessed such sincere hospitality and the overwhelming spirit of true brotherhood.

Unlike the comraderie of everyday, or its divisions, this kind of concrete meeting is "serious" or sacred.

It's probably evident that a good deal of the above analysis—separation, seclusion, psychodramatic ritual elements, liminal fluidity, and subjunctive mood—can be applied to Esalen. To any meditator, it will be equally evident that the scheme applies to meditation. For whether performed outdoors or in a closet or prison, meditation condenses a rite of passage or pilgrimage to anti-structural liminality. I didn't have these categories the first time I went to Esalen, but acted on instinct. Members of renunciatory religious orders—be they Buddhist monks and nuns, Sufi dervishes, or Catholic Jesuits—vow themselves to embody a condition of *permanent liminality*. In coming to Esalen, I was looking for ways of sustaining my vow.

SUBJUNCTIVE MOOD: STONE FACES

My first exposure to Esalen magic did not precipitate any states of exalted *communitas*. (It took me a while to get over the penchant for ecstatic "highs.") But it did bring me down to a less tense, subjunctive earth. The leader of that first workshop I attended at Esalen was Claudio Naranjo. He had studied gestalt under Fritz Perls, and was the author (with Robert Ornstein) of *On the Psychology of Meditation* (1971). He was also soon to publish *The One Quest* (1972), the best integration of growth therapies and spiritual disciplines I have yet come across. The Chilean Naranjo had lately returned from intensive esoteric training in Chile under Oscar Ichazo. Ichazo's Arica method combined elements from G. I. Gurdjieff and the Islamic Sufi tradition, the specialty being a rather remarkably complex character typology that divides the world into nine types of human beings (which was a lot more than the two, us and them, I was used to). From one angle, the types discriminate nine varieties of neurotic fixation, and from another view, nine virtues, faces of God, or divine energies. Though obviously but a part of a whole spiritual culture, the thing in itself offers a major tool for self-knowledge and understanding others.

As you might expect, Naranjo's meditation exercises mixed freely with psychodrama, encounter, and gestalt work. I recall one exercise in particular that illustrates the subjunctive atmosphere. It resembled a game of charades. Everyone in the room, according to character type, was given a piece of paper instructing him or her to act out a certain behavior before the group, in most cases a performance which ran against the grain of self-image. For instance, an amicable "nice guy" like me could hardly imagine himself going about the room loudly correcting and admonishing everyone. (I was supplied with a voice-monitor who made sure the free advice came in a shout.)

Agonizing in anticipation, I performed on cue. Then, with mounting energy, fluency, and much to my surprise, I found that I got "off" on it, came alive. By the time I got round to the last few targets, I had spent most of the venom I'd saved up—and had left something approaching detached, fearless lucidity! Who was that lucid one? Who had been agonized? Who unable to imagine? It was very confusing at first. At the same time, I felt like one of Michelangelo's unfinished marbles at the Academia in Florence, a human figure emerging from shapeless rock. The "act" enabled me to see through my everyday act. At Esalen, anything seemed possible.

And ambiguous. To some extent, it was still the season of Schutzian unmasking, tearing down, exposing naked, disagreeable truth. In terms of the classical mystical way, at the time Esalen featured the purgative element without much input from the illuminative and unitive ways. Sample: at one juncture Naranjo set up a "hot seat" where members of his team took turns at receiving brotherly and sisterly correction to assist them in the "Work" (the Sufi term for the preeminent action of God in human life). The tactic is well known (or used to be) in Catholic religious orders. But in this case, charity being mostly absent, the demonstration turned into a bloody shredding machine—and after it was over I suspect there was little "team" left.

Still, thereafter, I signed up for Claudio's extension course (SAT, pretentiously, Seekers After Truth), which was his way of following through on the transient, glancing shocks and wakenings at a place like Esalen. (The growth movement had been under constant attack, rightly so, for its lack of follow-up.) This correspondence program lasted about two years, helped many of us to process our confused, tattered states of mind during that open moment, but eventually the thing folded. Again, because something was missing—perhaps the kind of heart-opening that had been absent in the "hot seat" demonstration.

SUBJUNCTIVE MOOD: A FISH STORY

The show on that first Esalen visit wasn't over. I got as much out of observing the other participants—and my roommate. He was, like me, a college professor, a behavioral psychologist in the mold of B. F. Skinner, teaching in Minnesota. He told me at the start of our week together that he didn't take all this emotivism, much less the talk of inner depths or peak experience, to heart. Yet this stuff, and some of the techniques, provided a "kick," sold well on campus, helped his student ratings. As I recall, American Airlines was then sending personnel to Esalen with a similar if less cynical idea; better than Dale Carnegie it would polish images, teach people the arts of "impression management." But if such motives were fishy, Esalen was even fishier—a sly catcher of souls.

Even from the first, I didn't believe my professor friend. His superior pragmatism looked to me like a ruse, a protective feint for the benefit of his hard-boiled professional colleagues, to throw them off his scent. As the week wore on he grew less glib, quieter, more pensive—as if something had set off a severe case of self-doubt. But the account he gave of himself was implausible from the outset. Hardly naive, he had chosen a neo-Reichian workshop, scarcely the kind of workout one signs up for if the motive is kicks or self-promotion. I didn't know this at the time; it was only years later that I would experience a version of Reichian body work in the form of Radix therapy. It's an ordeal. Worth doing only if you're willing to surrender all your ego's poised popular fronts, all the controls and tricks that hide your deepest fears and fault lines from yourself and the world in which you would pass incognito as a slick customer. No, this is no place for the surface image-polisher — unless subconsciously he wants to get caught out.

I know almost nothing of the theory behind it, but nonverbal Reichian work involves ordeal by aeration. Similar to bioenergetic calesthenics, the exercises intentionally build up energy tensions, palpable heat, in the body-system, and expand breathing. If these warm-ups work — and I can testify, at least in the case of the strenuous Radix version, they do — then some of the psychic blocks, all those defenses and resistances carefully crafted into your muscle and tissue, can come tumbling down around you. The citadel falls, "body armor" collapses; the lie, the facade (say, of the authoritarian personality Reich was so concerned with) stands exposed — and often the vulnerable flesh, some primal scene, truth. I have witnessed torrents of deadly pride, bitter anger, and fear streaming from the woundings of such primal scenes. Dangerous places to get stuck. Imitating Reich's heretical dissent from Freud, Reichian therapists do not usually engage in extended verbal processing after the shock waves. No interpretive follow-through — which strikes me as missing an opportunity — and there's little question but that in its nonverbal heyday Esalen tended to revel in this premature expressive closure.

But that's not the end of it. In the hands of a skilled therapist, and if one stays with the deep breathing, I have seen another sort of bottoming out. The bottlenecks broken, rages subsided, something like bliss bursts forth in the flesh: empty fullness, blessed mourning, awesome longing, rich simplicity, reconciliation that passes understanding. In the language game of my cultural form of life (i.e., Catholic), we call these oxymorons the beatitudes — and there they were, come to our senses. My activist friends and I had a lot to learn here. Far from encouraging the passive spectator immured in the status quo, the dismantling of ego controls could often uncage a lion much more likely to demand more of itself and the social system. But my theological peers might also learn something — like the art of oxymoron, a reconciliation of opposites; lion lying down with lamb. Liberating the animal in people, the caged tiger, fox, fish, bird, Esalen rediscovered, began to recover animation, potency, spirited soulfulness that cross-connected more than insulated individualists dreamed. My whole experience of the human potential movement has been that one passed from the psychological into the spiritual as through an unmarked door, *the deeper one penetrated the flesh.* By his own account Wilhelm Reich was not a religious believer. Despite that, I'm willing to believe he tripped upon a physical method that, carried far enough, discloses the experience behind the principle that spirit is the life of the body seen from within, and the body the outward manifestation of the life of the spirit.

My jaded behaviorist roommate did not ostensibly profess any religious faith either, was no churchgoer. Had he been, I wonder if he would have found any rite powerful enough to penetrate his defenses. A good sermon? But talk was cheap for this man. He made his living by words, was expert at it, and like many an academic was immunized against words, especially, I'd guess, high-toned clerical rhetoric. He knew perfectly well (hadn't his graduate education assured him of it?) that all of us were nothing but stimulus-response organisms destined to rot. Then why was he here, voluntarily submitting himself to anything but a placebo or narcotic, on the contrary to an ordeal which might put himself and his settled biologism at such risk? Which might ironically expose that he (and I) did not really know what it felt like to be animal, but only rational. Which could, for all he knew, display his philosophy as a hideout from despair—stemming, let me arbitrarily say, from one of those primal scenes of abandonment or loss. Why indeed? Unless this is either a covert trickster or fishy story in which this fish, my professor friend, wanted to be caught and found anew.

Wittingly or not, I think that's what we all wanted: all of us fishy folk who impulsively came to Esalen's boundless liminal space for a rite of symbolic death and transformation. Something was sorely missing. It was a pitiless season; without apology, we owed ourselves some self-pity, grief at loss, maybe even compassion. From childhood I knew more than I could say, knew I was a missing person. Only as a wayward adult, there were twists. In this case, the person we brought along with us to places like Esalen was only too well found, known, oversocialized, monotonous. The thing was to defamiliarize the familiar, dismember the old configurations, displace ourselves, flip out into the unknown, get lost. That's what you do, or some did, when the culture fissures, begins to break apart. At the time, it was the theme, the story line of Stanley Kubrick's film *2001: A Space Odyssey*. Instead of resisting, holding on, fighting the derelict or escape artist in your dreams, you go with the flow, return to ground zero — a seed condition, a moment of truth. That's the way grail quests begin.

There were, of course, severe problems when you returned from getting lost and/or found in outer, liminal space. Either way, but particularly if you had just reached the deep confusion part (as perhaps my pensive roommate had), and came back to earth, your family, friends, and job, more profoundly lost than ever you were on setting out. "In the middle of life's course, lost in a dark wood . . . " — without Dante's Virgil! Where, to whom, to turn? "Abandon hope, all ye who enter." Growth junkies crashed in more ways than one, or grew bitter at cashing in on more than they'd bargained for. This is part, I think, of the current backlash of the eighties, the country's inertial determination to call wastelands paradise. On the other hand, there were those whose getting lost, whose descent into hell, preceded a finding in liminal space: however transient, illumination. Relanding has been no less difficult. Whom can you talk to about that "other thing" — a kind of risen body — in order to reinforce it, sustain it, reassure you that it isn't a pipe dream, that you can own the experience, do something with it? Sociological erosion has been severe in this quarter too. The country, however, is currently a mass of new networks. Could they be ablaze? Burning midnight oil? What's up? Or going down?

The next question is not, as some insist: Where will it all end? To ask that prematurely is to stop the process. The right question for travelers on a tacit grail quest is rather: Where's the next thicket, the next damsel in distress, the next figure of *anima* or soul — and of course, the next caravansarie, the next hospice, for one still has to eat and sleep? Whatever else it was, Murphy's and Price's "great evolutionary leap," envisioned in 1961, had been premonitory. They anticipated the psychic fissures which public events would later open up — and effectively cloned a network of refugee centers across the country. Esalen was one of those. For all I know (not having been there since 1977), the place still serves that function.

In contrast to its early wild days, I'm told the place is relatively tame today, still doing its core body work, gestalt, and encounter, providing hospitality for the new physics to get together with psychology and religion — and welcoming children, families. No longer inhabited by that "on the road" feeling, there's now a grammar school there for the children of staff members. The atmosphere has the slightly musky smell of ripe fruit — or delayed dreams — like early Christians settling down after expecting there would be no tomorrow. The surviving original Esalen co-hort is today somewhat uncertain of the success of its "great evolu-tionary leap forward." The falls have come; they've run through a successsion of disillusionments: to mention a few, the distortions of open encounter, Ron Hubbard's scientology, Oscar Ichazo's Arica training, gurus like Baghwan Rajneesh, and that shameless raider of Esalen's and everybody else's pot of gold, Werner Erhart. (None of the above was ever permitted to run seminars.) Today many early Esalen enthusiasts ac-knowledge that it would have been more successful if it had had a healthier respect for the vastness and difficulty of the task. Amen. In the abandon of Esalen's early experimentation there was something of the recklessness that marked nuclear testing. Like as not, if cautious foresight had been there at the start, nothing would have happened. The place's promise, its contribution to an American spirituality of substance, would have died stillborn.

Since pioneer days, California has served as the test range for America's mythic boundaries. The state has no doubt also teased its current inhabit-ants to imagine they ought to look and feel as good as the scenery and weather. For a while there, such dream space took flesh on Esalen's cliffside. Perhaps now, having served its mothering, generative purpose, Esalen is going the way of its precedents, Oneida and Brook Farm. Or were the antecedents the mobile sanctuary of Great American Awaken-ings and their circuit riders? No question, Esalen seeded the U.S. land-scape with its catalogue of body, mind, and soul arts that other networks and institutions with firmer sociological roots and longer historical mem-ories continue to harvest. And I am grateful.

TWO

Cognitive Dissonance and Rising Expectation

The course of liberation . . . is thus not aimed at facilitating somnolence or generalizing the pleasurable. . . .The goal . . . is this: to give every human not just a job but his own distress, boredom, wretchedness, misery, and darkness, his own buried, summoning light; to give to everyone's life a Dostoevskyan touch.

Ernst Bloch

Dark and cold we may be, but this
is no winter now. The frozen misery
of centuries breaks, cracks, begins to move,
the thunder is the thunder of the floes,
the flaw, the flood, the upstart spring.
. . . .
Affairs are now soul size.
The enterprise
is exploration into God
where no nation's foot has ever trodden yet.

Christopher Fry, *A Sleep of Prisoners*

For my own part I doubt whether man can support at the same time complete religious independence and entire public freedom. And I am inclined to think, that if faith be wanting him, he must serve, and if he be free, he must believe.

Alexis de Tocqueville, *Democracy in America*

"We tell ourselves stories," Joan Didion wrote in *The White Album* (1979: 11), "in order to live." It was only in retrospect that I began to realize

26

that getting a handle on this story business—in a rather big way—set the contours of how to understand the consciousness movement and my own participation in it. As I will define it, the essential problem to which the consciousness movement addresses itself is the thinning or loss of the Western plot line. (The provision of a larger reference system, a historical context, for this movement will be the function of Part II of this book. Here, I only want to get the process started by setting the theme.) In the eighties all the hoopla about "the greening of America" and a definable "consciousness movement" has become an already faded memory. Most cultural commentators today speak of it in the past tense, as another one of those flashes in the cultural sky, no more lasting than a passing summer storm. Moreover, at this juncture, it is questionable whether consciousness movement isn't misleading as an appellation; certainly many of those who carry it on will not recognize themselves by that title. Notification that the movement, though off the front page, is still alive arrived in 1981 with Marilyn Ferguson's *The Aquarian Conspiracy: Personal and Social Transformation in the 1980s*. Perhaps "Aquarian Conspiracy" or the less provocative "transformation movement," more accurately conveys the current status of the thing. In fact, the name changes accurately point up the sequence of metamorphoses the movement has passed through in the past several decades.

Whatever one chooses to call it now, what started out as the human potential movement made a difference. If Daniel Yankelovich's figures can be trusted, some 17 percent of Americans were strongly affected and 63 percent weakly so, by what, for lack of a better term, I will generally call the consciousness movement (in a variety of therapeutic forms). Only 20 percent remained unaffected. I can only say, then, that I must number myself among those 17 percent affected in a "strong form."

In retrospect, the question raised by this movement comes down to this: What might be the wider, deeper historical and spiritual currents that run in our veins whether ego is aware of them or not? The consciousness movement was—and is—no passing flash in the cultural sky because it was triggered by an awakening to these larger connections to time and history. Perceived publicly as a demonstration-case of our therapeutic culture's habitual solipsism, I shall maintain that for many it was just the opposite, an inward turn that ended up outdoors, laden with ontological and positive social implication. At root, *the movement was after a new cosmology*; not cosmology as a subbranch of physics, that is, as the kind of speculation that astronomers engage in about the origins of the physical universe. I mean cosmology as it was understood before 1600 and the scientific revolution. Prior to that time, as understood, for instance, by the Stoic legacy, the conception of an ordered whole (*kosmos*) hospitable to human life involved not only the input of the natural sciences but anthropology and political theory as well. By contrast, the Greek word for the physical universe was not *kosmos* but *ouranos*. From that perspective, what modern science studies is not cosmology but, as Stephen Toulmin says (1984: 28), "ouranology." Prior to 1600 the basic assumption was that in a well-ordered universe the cosmos would be reflected in the *polis*, the political order in the most general sense, and that together the two form a single, integral *kosmopolis*. At the center of the consciousness movement's problematic, it seems to me, lies the scourge of C. P. Snow's "two cultures," the division between the exact sciences and the humanities, which makes a cosmopolitan outlook nearly impossible. Conversely, at the center of its agenda lies the project of healing this cultural schizophrenia and making a cosmopolis possible. From the outset, the movement has thus been implicitly social and political.

Then how is it that by the seventies the thing was being excoriated as the "triumph of the therapeutic," "narcissistic," and the godfather of the "me decade"? The confusion here rests with failing to differentiate between a "transpersonal" reorientation, which as I indicated in the last chapter began to occur in the early seventies, and the heavy legacy of humanism in the movement—and thus the overlay of a *humanistic/human potential psychology* which invariably does get trapped in a solipsistic, psychologizing turn. In the following chapters, I will focus on the former, the transformative transpersonal dimension, which is implicitly social, political, and, in a sense that will take some space to articulate, religious. Admittedly, the borderline between these two orientations is fuzzier in practice than in theory, and the two often overlap; nonetheless, the distinction is important to keep in mind. For the transpersonal dimension means little else than remedy for the hyperintrospective consciousness locked up in a skull and forbidden entry to, or exit from, the hard scientist's world of nature.

In the sixties, when the movement was preoccupied with the liberation of the "self," with what was called "human potential," the absence of firm sociological roots and long historical memories obviously did constitute a severe deficiency. This is hardly a weakness unique to the consciousness movers. Neither historical memory nor local communitarian affiliation is particularly conspicuous in mobile, postindustrial America. Are we not, most of us, escapees from all that, the old worlds we left behind? At least for those living in metropolises like Los Angeles, Dallas, and New York (granted, they're not the world), who really possesses an excess of rootedness, sense of place and history such as Shakespeare had, or "regional" writers like Eudora Welty evidently still have? Already in the nineteenth century Baudelaire called the Paris of his day a "moving chaos." It's almost a definition of the modern urban ambience. Today's market economy, as Henry Ford recognized ("history is bunk!"), keeps very little of the past in stock. Early on, that great admirer of bourgeois culture, Karl Marx, caught the spirit exactly. "All that is solid," he says in the *Communist Manifesto*, "melts into air." Contemporary electronics culture simply intensifies this molten, dissolving quality. Strangely, the sensory overload, the wrap-around sound and be-there-now speed of the present communication revolution, has broken the cultural hegemony of the Book. It has brought us closer to the oral sensorium of our ancestors (see chapter 4).

For the moment, it is enough to notice that though the consciousness movement has been accused of being ahistorical, what this often comes down to is the charge that it partakes of a general antimodernist sentiment. There's some truth in that, but it's complicated. The conservative/liberal dichotomy breaks down here. A conserving strain goes deep; the movement qualifies as an ally of what the German philosopher Hans-Georg Gadamer calls a "hermeneutics of restoration." These people have been engaged in an archeological dig, a nonacademic retrieval of beliefs and ancient spiritual disciplines that are characteristic of premodern, traditional societies. The "ethnic others," as Victor Turner expressed it, have provided a new path to reflexivity, a "metacommentary on our own ways of life." It's a way of "making visible," as primitive ritual was, what the subconscious is up to in the ego's overt projects, a way of getting beneath the surface "white noise" of current life. On the other hand, the mentality here is revisionist, an Aquarian Conspiracy racing, sometimes half-cocked, sometimes with postcritical suspicion, toward the postmodern — whatever that may be. At its best, the movement is not a repudiation of the Enlightenment's critical agenda, but a new way of carrying on that agenda — with a fresh appreciation of the "inner light" out of which critical reason grew. In fact, once the consciousness movement is seen within context, what emerges, it seems to me, is a protest against psychological one-dimensionality, and conversely, a search for psychological complexity.

CHARACTERS IN SEARCH OF PLOT THICKENING

The context of Didion's remark about stories will help amplify the point that solipsism, or a sickly individualism, represents exactly what transpersonalists sought liberation from. Even when we know our family history, are familiar with the Western history of ideas, very often these things have a detached, uninvolving quality—like sex on the brain. They do not resonate biologically or act as real connective tissue. Hence the stories, the traditions, do not yield up vital spirits. The quote from Didion I began with goes on (1979: 11):

> We look for the sermon in the suicide, for the social or moral lesson in the murder of five. We interpret what we see, select the most workable of the multiple choices. We live entirely . . . by the imposition of a narrative line upon disparate images, by the "ideas" with which we have learned to freeze the shifting phantasmagoria which is our actual experience.

The context of these remarks? Didion had been living a journalist's life close to the traumas of the seventies: the Sharon Tate murders, Huey Newton and the Black Panthers, San Francisco State riots, Soledad prison, and the rock-group Doors' salvation through sex-equated-with-death. Too much. It led to some kind of breakdown. Reported one of her doctors: "In her view she lives in a world of people moved by strange, conflicted, poorly comprehended, and, above all, devious motivations which commit them inevitably to conflict and failure." Was Didion's "reality principle" awry, as the doctor seems to have assumed? I suspect the description exactly fits the company Didion had been keeping. Moreover, in my suspicious Freudian moments, the account appears to fit the very "civilized" company that I keep, that most of us do. We all suffer from what I would call a galloping case of the Enlightenment epistemology I shall speak of in a moment. We feel cut off from nature, forlorn *individualists*. Passively, we stand *outside* our world, the thread of meaning slipping through our fingers.

Notice the telling images of the position. The story lines are matter of "multiple choice," ideas a question of "imposition." For the original tellers and hearers of the cultural myths which set our society's goals, Didion's free-wheeling multiple-choice attitude would have been unthinkable. Were the pilgrims' vision of a *novus ordo saecularum*, the myth of progress, the doctrine of Manifest Destiny, the inaugural dreams of Western culture items on a shopping list? Had the world turned into Bloomingdale's? The tales issued from unbidden dream, from the flesh and bone of pioneer and immigrant sweat and tears, from a prophet's belly-full of words. Where great earth-moving symbols are concerned, the rabbi of Nazareth's words are still apposite: "You did not choose me; no, I chose you." You can freely formulate a concept, not a symbol. Like the scientist's "fact," a symbol is given, not imposed.

And when no inspiration comes, when the symbol is not given, what happens then? Didion describes it (1979: 13):

> I was supposed to have a script, and I had mislaid it. I was supposed to hear cues, and no longer did. I was meant to know the plot, but all I knew was what I saw: flash pictures in variable sequence, images with no "meaning" beyond their temporary arrangement, not a movie but a cutting-room experience . . . .I wanted still to believe in the narrative's intelligibility, but to know that one could change the sense with every cut was to begin to perceive the experience as rather more electrical than ethical.

Once upon a time, the world-story was not the screenwriter's random choice. Nor was sensation a Humean flux to be imposed upon. Didion's attitude is distinctively modern. It is the mind of a detached spectator suddenly aware of a lack of participation in events—and consequently aware of spinning in a loose orbit. It's a little as if the mind had tried Plato's prescription for liberation from the "prison body" and succeeded only too well. (In no small part because of centuries of literacy, as I shall suggest in chapter 5, this is exactly what has happened.)

On the other hand, one could say that subconsciously we have simply assimilated the message modern physics fairly shouts at us: that the human sensorium is the interpreter through which amorphous nature is transmuted into the ordinary world of color, odor, sound, taste, and touch; that therefore nature *represents us*—and without us, our nervous systems, memories, imagination, and thinking, the whole blooming, buzzing expanse would mean nothing. The recognition of this epistemological situation raises, in acute form, the question of who we are, who the primal poet (in the Greek sense of "maker") in us is, who must take a piece of the physicist's empty stuff and breathe spirit (or smog) into it. Aristotle could never have imagined "saving the appearances" in this fate-laden, creative/destructive way. What shall we make of the world? Since Francis Bacon's *Novum Organum*, that has been the nerve-wracking question for a Western psyche that wonders whether it is up to the task— and shows as much by speaking of "imposing" on things. But who are *we*? What's our plot line? What kind of world we make hinges on that prior question. And the atomized modern individualist will have enormous problems, and may well break down under the pressure of being equal to the creative task. Creation from ground zero is sheer play, the ancient genesis stories tell us, but for a human being it's no mean feat.

For me, Didion is a representative figure, a type. She is scarcely alone in reporting that the encompassing plots, the metaphysical stories that crystallize for our imaginations and will what existence is about, that these "narrative lines" often fail to register for many of us. Is it that they are no longer deep-set, or that *we* are not set deep enough to receive them? Or to receive them in anything but a shallow way? A good deal of the anomalous experience we shall point to in the following chapters suggests that below, behind, and around the shallow consciousness of the individualist in us, the ontogeny of the race—and a good deal more—still pulses. The unfinished story line is already there, in our nervous systems, if we could just remember it, perhaps as Saint Augustine deconstructed himself in the "remembering" of his *Confessions*. The allusion is suggestive. Since Rousseau's *Confessions*, the art of autobiography has tended to be the crafty product of resentment, an act of triumphing over one's enemies (who would efface you from memory) by a *construction* of the life-story that imprints itself ineffaceably on posterity's memory. The thing is to get the last word in, and thus immortalize one's own self. In contrast, Augustine's confessing runs in an almost Buddhist direction: he empties himself in order to remember his true identity in God. The subject of his story is not himself. Psychedelic initiation, traveling to India, I will claim, could often trigger something like self-forgetful Augustinian anamnesis.

The problem Didion articulates lies at the heart of the consciousness movement—in some ways got it going. Well connected in one sense, indeed perhaps oversocialized, one sometimes feels in a more basic way disjoined, like Turgenev's "superfluous man" without a passport to public space. The deeper disconnection behind a facade of competency means all the more self-preoccupation, a nagging recitative of "how am I doing?" In the Middle Ages it wouldn't have been so embarrassing or unnerving. Dutiful creatures of Renaissance and Enlightenment images of selfhood, we know well enough that we are supposed to be agents in history, participants in shaping our own destiny by shaping a world. And there we are footless, ground gone, the wind somehow knocked out of us. It's a specifically modern kind of metaphysical vertigo: on the one hand, a provocative sense of hardly having any other choice but to create the world—as God did on the first day. On the other hand, to paraphrase Yeats, the best lack energy and the worst lack any scruple.

Didion supplies at least a partial diagnosis of the problem: the loss of narrative line, of thickened plot. The trouble arises from the absence of roots and cross-connection—epitomized by some symbolic tale like the grail legend, an ancestral tale of Moses or Judith, Socrates or the Cumaean Sibyl. This incapacity to resonate with figures who implicitly embody ontological vision may encapsulate the dilemma of much of modern freedom: an almost unlimited field of choice, and yet minimal impulse to invest much of self in any direction, in part because the blood of one's ancestry doesn't seem to run any longer in the veins. To de Tocqueville ([1850] 1944: II, pt. 2, chap. 2), more than a century ago, the problem was already evident:

> Amongst democratic nations new families are constantly springing up, others are constantly falling away, and all that remain change their condition; the woof of time is every instant broken, and the track of generations effaced . . . . As each class approximates to other classes, and intermingles with them, its members become indifferent and as strangers to one another. Aristocracy had made a chain of all members of the community, from the peasant to the king: democracy breaks that chain and severs every link of it . . . . They owe nothing to any man, they expect nothing from any man; they acquire the habit of always considering themselves as standing alone, and they are apt to imagine that their whole destiny is in their own hands. Thus not only does democracy make every man forget his ancestors, but it hides his descendants and separates his contemporaries from him. It throws him back forever upon himself alone and threatens in the end to confine him entirely within the solitude of his own heart.

The condition has been aptly termed the disinherited mind. From this point on, then, I shall be concerned with releases from solitary confinement by means of thickening plots, reweaving "the woof of time."

Part of a cure might be learning to reconnect with the *mystery* of earth, something that had often been lost in the madding crowds and urban sprawl of the post–World War II prosperity boom. As I shall try to indicate in what follows, the sense of disconnection has far older origins and has been growing for centuries. But in this regard, places like the Esalen Institute, where so much of the consciousness movement began, become a bit more comprehensible. If the sense of disconnection bordering on pathological dissociation is as epidemic as I tend to think it, then an American variation on the ancient Greek Eleusis, a site for the healing rituals of Mother Earth, was not a bad idea. The birth process which life is about, it would seem, has typically gotten fixated along the way. Hence the many shapes of "burn-out." A retreat to the symbolic blissful womb might supply renewed energy, a new start. Moreover, if it's true, as Christopher Lasch argues, that long-term commitments are problematic in American culture because we suffer from an epidemic of narcissistic or "borderline" personality disorders, then the focus on rebuilding the self from the ground up makes sense. The strained heroes and heroines of the corporate ladder evidently required "regressions" in service of deeper and richer connection.

In this regard, the human potential movement's promotion of "regression in service of the ego" was highly problematic. For since the scientific revolution, the correlate of neutered nature has been the omniverous ego, gobbling up and imposing upon everything in its Faustian wake. The self is the idol of our times, the twin of Newton's hollow nature. Much of the criticism of the consciousness movement was on target; the human potential wing, at least, continued nineteenth-century romanticism's apotheosis of the imperial self that was only too glad to "own" everything in and out of sight. As psychologist James Hillman (1975b: 110) would put it, the enlighted, decisive, controlling ego is today problematic:

> *Ego consciousness as we used to know it no longer reflects reality.* Ego has become a delusional system. "Heightened" consciousness today no longer tells it from the mountain of Nietzsche's superman, an overview. Now it is an underview, for we are down in the multitudinous entanglements of the marshland, in anima country, the "vale of Soul-making." So heightened consciousness today now refers to movements of intense uncertainty, moments of ambivalence.

Consequently, it is extremely unlikely that simply learning to express one's personality, such as is accented in the human potential orientation, will do much lasting good. It is likely to unleash the mean spirit of someone like Nietzsche's "last man"—as ineradicable as the flea-beetle, "who makes everything small" (in Kaufmann, 1954: 128–31).

One of the dangers, in fact, of highlighting the neutrality of nature as a field for human imagination is that it invites horror shows like Hitler and Pol Pot. The trick calls for wisdom in the imagination, something that recalls Kierkegaard's formula ([1848] 1954: 147) for the condition of the self in whom despair has been overcome:"By relating itself to its own self and willing to be itself the self is grounded transparently in the Power which posited it." Owen Barfield (1965: 131–32) perhaps puts the thing less elliptically.

> If I know that nature herself is the system of my representations, I cannot do otherwise than adopt a humbler and more responsible attitude to the representations of art and the metaphors of poetry. For in the case of nature there is no danger of my fancying that she exists to express my personality. I know in that case that what is meant, when I say she is my representation, is that I stand, whether I like it or not, in . . . a "directionally creator" relation to her.

But I know also that what so stands is not my poor temporal personality, but the Divine Name in the unfathomable depths behind it. And if I strive to produce a work of art, I cannot then do otherwise than strive humbly to create more nearly as that creates, and not as my idiosyncrasy wills.

The plot thickening I was looking for through the consciousness movement was of the sort Barfield refers to — again, a kind of Augustinian "memory."

The therapies, then, which concerned me most were those which seemed to pose a very unmodern question, one of T. S. Eliot's overwhelming ones. In what way does the great world outside us, which the ancients called the macrocosm, live in my microcosm? And how does *that* express itself through and in us? The consciousness movement took on that question. It is one that goes back to the foundations of the world religions in the first millennium B.C. and the possibility of a new form of human existence. But as I say, this needs a context, some history, a narrative line. To make a beginning at that, let me return to the California grail questers. When the legendary Percival leaves his mother's home, he's a naive Natty Bumpo. Fascinated on encountering knights, he's quickly educated in their heroic ways of upward mobility, only to learn, with the first mysterious apparition of the grail castle and its wounded fisher-king, that his education inhibited him, prevented him from asking: What does the grail mean? Whom does it serve? Which might have delivered the land from waste. As the story indicates by linking spiritual condition with the state of the land, psychology and cosmology are two sides of one plot. From this point on, the adventure required some unlearning — the acquisition of a "learned ignorance." In the early and mid-seventies, that's about where the leaders of the consciousness revolution stood.

MANIFESTOS

Steamrolled by Gerald Heard, Maslow, and others, the movement had something more in mind than the light coat of eighteenth-century deism with which Washington and Jefferson had varnished the Declaration of Independence and the Constitution. They were out for something like the whole shtick, another Great Awakening. The "civil religion," sociologist Robert N. Bellah was assuring us at the time, ran deep; America, after all, had the "soul of a church." The new awakening reincarnated that peculiarly American mixture of extraordinary organizing ability and love of something like anarchy. Once again, it was the antinomian pioneer spirit impatient with the settler's banal stamina and stability. "Americans," Sidney E. Mead (1963: 5, 6) had once written, "have never had time to spare. . . . It is not too much to say that in America space has played the part that time has played in the older cultures of the world."

But by mid-twentieth century we had run out of geographical space; the wilderness was disappearing. So it was either moon shots, outer space, that captivated our dreamers or (though the term is finally misleading) "inner space." For the consciousness-raisers I speak of here, this inner soul-space constituted the new call of the wild, the unknown open territory to light out for. George Leonard (in Anderson, 1983: 117–18) stated this in the prologue of Esalen's 1965 brochure:

> Within a single lifetime, our physical environment has been changed almost beyond recognition. But there has been little corresponding change in how we, as individuals, relate to the world and experience reality. Such a change is inevitable, however—indeed, it is imminent. New tools and techniques of the human potentiality—generally unknown to the public and to much of the intellectual community—are already at hand; many more are presently under development. We stand on an exhilarating and dangerous frontier—and must answer anew the old questions: "What are the limits of human ability, the boundaries of the human experience? What does it mean to be a human being?"

Lest the reader miss the point, Leonard's salvo was captioned by lines from Christoper Fry cited as epigraph for this chapter. Make no mistake, "The enterprise is exploration into God . . . " The venture was to prove as much outward-bound as inward. This is a point critics accustomed to disjoining psychology and physics never adequately understood. John Calvin or Julian of Norwich would have. For inward psychological and spiritual change alters the way the world appears, how it stands for us with reality.

Yes, the whole thing was incorrigibly American. The antiseptic technical term for the new frontier of "exploration into God" was "transpersonal." Transpersonal—it is one of those deliberately neutral neologisms of the specialist, in this case invented by restless "pioneers" disguised in the clothing of the psychoanalytic tradition who wanted to stress that a human life amounted to more than the conflicts of the nuclear family. Human potential, they would assert, involves more than the expression of one's little skin-enclosed personality; we are more than our chemistry, more than automatons responding to stimuli, more than our family history and socialization process. These psychologists wanted to leave room for more than the standard schools of psychology—medical pharmacology, the psychoanalytic model, behaviorism, and cognitive development theory—were likely to deal with. Transpersonal psychology aspires a grand synthesis that would locate the legitimate therapeutic functions of all these other models, and yet set them within a larger theoretical frame that would have a place for extrasensory psychic phenomena and strictly spiritual experience. Under certain conditions, the *persona* may express the macrocosm, mirror the universe. *Tat tvam asi*, as the Hindus say, "thou art that." The idea is ancient, no more Eastern than Western. The New Left, no less than the Old Left, couldn't stand it that these disillusioned bourgeois liberals were calling "time out" from the political struggle to indulge in such follies.

TRANSPERSONAL PSYCHOLOGY

The Association of Transpersonal Psychology was founded in 1969 by Anthony Sutich, an arthritic and almost legendary therapist who rarely left his bed. Earlier, Sutich had been a prime, creative mover behind new methods of group therapy. He had also been instrumental in the organization of the Association of Humanistic Psychology in which Maslow had played such a central role. But now, with Maslow's blessing, the ceiling of humanistic psychology was felt to hang too low. Human closeness no longer seemed the be-all and end-all. Among other things in the late sixties, high psychedelic states were disclosing possibilities beyond humanism's ken, amazing connections with our phylogenetic origins, affinities with foreign cultures and primitive histories, and visions that elicited a religious reading from even the most dyed-in-wool skeptic or atheist. The schismatics found themselves impelled, with new eyes, to reread Emerson, Whitman, and William James. They plunged into Eastern mysticism—encouraging, in the process, that spate of publishing primary Eastern texts and popularizations that so marked the following decade.

All of this had the most shady bohemian beginnings in drop-out hippiedom. In the mid-sixties the human potential movement and the hippie movement had virtually fused, forming a united front against the Apollonian mind. It was the bacchanalian "flower child" phase, hungering for the perfect chemical hit, for transitory euphoric "altered states" of consciousness. As one Esalen resident put it, "We believed that if we could find the right combination we could get the permanent Sanforized satori."

One-time transpersonal association president James Fadiman acknowledged, "we made all the mistakes as soon as possible." The greed and jazz-style is visible in Sutich's rambling definition of transpersonal psychology in the premier issue (1969: 13) of the association's journal.

> Transpersonal psychology is interested in those *ultimate* human capacities and potentialities that have no place in positivistic or behavioristic theory, classical psychoanalytic theory, or humanistic psychology. The emerging Transpersonal Psychology is concerned specifically with the *empirical* scientific study of . . . becoming, individual and species-wide meta-needs, ultimate values, unitive consciousness, peak experiences . . . mystical experience . . . transcendence of self, spirit and species-wide synergy . . . and related concepts, experiences, and activities.

It took some time before fascination with transient, ecstatic "states" began to sober up, before the grail questers would discover the Sufi distinction between "states" and "stations," the contrast between passing "highs" and relatively permanent, character-informing conditions of being. And some time before instant nirvana was replaced by a recognition of the need for long-term spiritual discipline. When spiritual discipline did arrive, of course, it was mostly of Eastern provenance. The people who flocked to Esalen might have gotten some pointers a few miles down the road, from Camaldolese monks perched high on a mountain above Route 1. But few in Esalen's sulphur baths even knew the monks were there. And if they had known, for most anything smacking of the Christian church was, in the late sixties, suspect, a part of the problem not the solution. It was thought that few of the "tools and techniques of the human potentiality" Leonard spoke of could be found in the family attic. Better to defamiliarize the familiar by heading for the Orient.

JOYOUS COSMOLOGIES

In effect, you could travel East without leaving the borders of the United States. The "Zen boom" of the fifties, heralded by Jack Kerouac, Gary Snyder, and Allen Ginsberg, had been mostly a literary phenomenon. By the sixties authentic gurus like Shunryu Suzuki (*Zen Mind, Beginner's Mind*) of the San Francisco Zen Center were holding forth; serious Zen practice had settled in. Theravada Buddhism (with "insight meditation") and Tibetan Vajrayana Buddhism would arrive in the seventies—not to mention assorted Hindu sadhus and Sufi teachers, serious and spurious.

But there is no question in my mind but that the new psychedelic medicine cabinet (mescalin, psilocybin, and diethylamide of d-lysergic acid (LSD), et alia) opened the doors for such disciplines. "If the doors of perception were cleansed," William Blake had written, "every thing would appear as it is, infinite. / For man has closed himself up. . . . " Sixties air was charged with the chemical ecstasies of Aldous Huxley's *The Doors of Perception* and Alan Watts's *The Joyous Cosmology*. And this had nearly everything to do with Anthony Sutich's rediscovered conviction that mystical experience could be the subject of "empirical" study. It should also be said that, by a wayward path, the drug culture eventually got the presses running for the classics of the Western contemplative tradition. Not to mention myself, some surprisingly "straight," orthodox folk were tripping in the early seventies and finding a renewed interest in the classics of Western spirituality. If for no other reason, we needed new translations of Gregory of Nyssa and John of the Cross to chart where we had been. Or where we might still go.

In fact, history was repeating itself. The ingestion of nitrous oxide had once had a lot to with William James's study of mysticism. His famous remark would be much cited in the sixties and seventies (James [1903] 1919: 388):

> One conclusion was forced upon my mind at that time. It is that our normal waking consciousness, rational consciousness as we call it, is but one special type of consciousness, whilst all about it, parted from it by the filmiest of screens, there lie potential forms of consciousness entirely different. We may go through life without suspecting their existence; but supply the requisite stimulus, and at a touch they are there in all their completeness, definite types of mentality which probably somewhere have their field of application and adaptation. No account of the universe in its totality can be final which leaves these other forms of consciousness quite disregarded . . . .

Well, for many, LSD supplied the "requisite stimulus" for an eye-opener. Serious research, however, showed that the screens are often anything but filmy. But on a wide scale LSD also begot an epistemological revolution, exactly as nitrous oxide had once done for James.

Consider the case of Huston Smith, in the early sixties professor of philosophy at MIT. One evening in 1961 he stopped by the home of his Harvard friend, Dr. Timothy Leary, in Newton. After coffee and an exchange of pleasantries with Leary's guests, Smith took two capsules of mescaline and went into the living room adjoining the study where Leary and his friends carried on their conversation. He lay down on a couch, and after a while, this is what happened (Metzner, 1968: 72–73):

The world into which I was ushered was strange, weird, uncanny, significant, and terrifying beyond belief . . . .The mescaline acted as a psychological prism. It was as though the infinitely complex and layered psychological ingredients which normally smelt down into a single band of weak, nondescript sensation-impressions were now being refracted; spread out as if by a spectroscope into about five layers. . . . I was experiencing the metaphysical theory known as emanationism, in which, beginning with the clear, unbroken and infinite light of God or the void, the light then breaks into forms and decreases in intensity as it diffuses through descending degrees of reality. My friends in the study were functioning in an intelligible wave band, but one which was far more restricted, cramped and wooden than the bands I was now privileged to experience. . . . The emanation theory and elaborately delineated layers of Indian cosmology and psychology had hitherto been concepts and inferences. Now they were objects of immediate perceptions. . . .I found myself amused, thinking how duped historians of philosophy had been in crediting those who formulated such world views with being speculative geniuses. Had they had experiences such as mine they need have been no more than hack reporters.

Smith's statement is interesting on several counts. On its face, it illustrates a breakthrough into that "widened empiricism" the work of William James had championed. With the requisite stimulus, Smith sees himself breaking out of a habit of thought that was "restricted, cramped, and wooden"—in effect, out of the "limits of reason" given canonical expression by Immanuel Kant at the close of the eighteenth century. To that reason, which has enjoyed cultural hegemony ever since, spiritual reality, the numinosity of nature, has been off limits in the West to *cognition*. To a degree, this has been true not only for religious skeptics but for believers as well. Even in the universities of the Catholic ghetto in which I grew up, where metaphysical speculation was highly approved, the general assumption was that the noumenal order of things could not be perceived. One got to it only by subtle argument, by "transcendental reductions" and other such inferential, speculative acrobatics. (The ordinary pious Catholic who prayed before the Blessed Sacrament may have known otherwise, but such pedestrian experience was typically ignored by professors of "natural theology" and theology.) But metaphysics a matter of "immediate perceptions"? Without argument? The eyewitness of a hack reporter? If true, this would be first-order cultural news. Psychedelics provided the gate-opener for just this announcement. Such news would prove significant to the extent that it could be connected, as it was, to those nondrug "new tools and techniques" of metamorphosis that George Leonard knew most Americans were ignorant of.

The Hindus who originally proposed the doctrine of divine emanation, Huston Smith had implicitly realized, were not theorizing in our sense of the detached spectator gazing upon "nondescript sensation-impressions." They did not dwell in a Humean world. They were witnessing, confessing, what their minded senses were telling them — the different grades of vibratory energy (once known as the Great Chain of Being) existing behind and within the scenes around them. Further, they were crediting each other's testimonies publicly. In other words, they were sorting out "truth" from private delusion and hallucination in the only way human beings, then or now, can differentiate "what I *think* is so" from "what *is* so." In which case, their version of reality stands on a par with ours. Except in their case, and now in Smith's, what the mind took in of the objective world seemed immeasurably richer than our updated Newtonian brand of nature, a brand that Alfred North Whitehead did not hesitate to judge a "severely edited version." Could it be that Smith had come across not so much another culture's mysticism, but its common sense? Was that perspective, moreover, somehow already engraved in our nerve fibers' landscape long before we began, in droves, to travel East physically? Stranger things have happened. After all, the primitive images of Africa and Oceania irrupted, occasionally, without any direct influence, in the designs of Kandinsky and Joan Miró. What to make of all this?

COGNITIVE MAJORITIES/DUPED HISTORIANS

For some, such news was not fit to print. The heirs of Schleiermacher's "cultured despisers of religion" had an explanation ready to hand. For them, Feuerbach, Marx, and Freud had sealed this book. It was another case of pie in the sky, a self-alienating projection, compensatory flight from reality, infantile need overwhelming rational judgment. Such continuing symptoms of incurable human frailty and the refusal to grow up should surprise no one. Even MIT professors have their lapses, moral weaknesses, and failures of nerve. The line was familiar, at this point the equivalent of the "dogmatic spell" from which Hume had awakened Immanuel Kant. Besides, it was all a pharmacological effect, was it not? For at the time, the scientific consensus held that drugs like mescaline, and more so LSD, mimicked schizophrenic symptoms, triggered a "model psychosis."

I shall come to the "model psychosis" problem in the next chapter. For now consider popular common-sense empiricism which finds Smith's emanationist perceptions incredible. The point is important because it controls the way in which we have construed, or misconstrued, the story of evolution and the history of consciousness—from Darwin, Max Müller, and T. H. Huxley to H. G. Wells, Jacques Monod, and Carl Sagan. It is important because this evolutionary account of ourselves and the nature we are sprung from is arguably the principal way in which the modern West has mythologized itself. And the consciousness movement would revise it, ultimately casting the story of evolution in a form reminiscent of ancient cosmic Logos doctrines. An odd way this, a valid way I am inclined to think, to change the course of Western society.

In what way have we been "duped"? Briefly, the duping derives from the West's great romance with modern physics as *the* exact science and *hard* truth-giver of reality par excellence. (Of course I have in mind "scientism" rather than science itself.) Over several centuries, this infatuation has inscribed in our language and our psyches the common assumption that nature stands independent of mind; further, that the relation between subject and object, between human consciousness and Greek *physis* ("nature," from the verb, "to bring forth," "to give birth"), remains fixed and asymmetrical throughout time. That is, according to canonical Enlightenment epistemology, consciousness changes; the objective world of nature doesn't. The *physis* of classical modern physics could not give birth, was no longer *natura naturans*. On the contrary, it is that reified expanse, the *natura naturata*, which Whitehead ([1925] 1958: 56) called that "dull affair, soundless, scentless, colourless; merely the hurrying of material, endlessly, meaninglessly." The life, the inner kinesis, had gone out of it.

Where once, well up to the Renaissance, our ancestors lived in a semantic gold mine, a riddling qualitative universe pregnant with signs ready at any moment to turn into hierophanies, we have exchanged all that for empty space which signifies nothing. Medieval people, for instance, felt themselves connected by extrasensory links to the invisible influences of the planets and spheres which hummed subtle, audible music. Their wits, they knew, were "humored" by bodily fluids. But those fluids were not, as they are for us, enclosed in a bag of skin. They were perceived, rather, as a tidal estuary, an inner reservoir of the wide seas, which themselves rained down from the heavenly waters above the crystalline spheres. It was the cosmic water of life itself, they felt, that tided them with common sense, imagination, fantasy, memory, and conjecture—the five wits. From all that we are cut off. For our nature is a neutral, utterly prosaic world in which the human mind cannot, except in a reductionist sense, participate. From five wits we are reduced to one: instrumental reason.

And thus the schism. Psychology is disjoined from cosmology. The order of nature, instinct, and eros is severed from culture's order of meanings; fact is divorced from value, reason from imagination. In short, Lord Snow's "two cultures."

> The fundamental division [wrote Lancelot Law Whyte] is between deliberate activity organized by static concepts and the instinctive and spontaneous life. The European dissociation of these two components [reason at war with impulse] of the system results in a common distortion of both. The instinctive life lost its innocence, its proper rhythm being replaced by obsessive desire. On the other hand rationally controlled behavior was partly deflected towards ideals which also obsessed the individual with their allure of perfection. . . . Bewitched by these illusory aims which appear to promise the absolute, man is led away from the proper rhythm of the organic processes to chase an elusive ecstasy. [in Wilber, 1981: 208]

In such a world the psyche must figure itself a disinherited stranger, all its dreams, reveries, musings, trances, and meditations regarded as *fanciful*, or denigrated as reversions to preenlightened, subhuman superstition. Cut off from its organic roots, idealism goes rancid. As Whyte says, "morbid religiosity, hyperintellectualism, delicate sensuality, and cold ambition are some of the variants of the dissociated personality's attempt to escape its own division." But then twisted, disgraced idealism debases the coinage of the language. The referents of language must appear superficial — as indeed to an A. J. Ayer or the early Wittgenstein they did. For by theoretical fiat in the first place, and cultural habit in the second, normative sense reaches only skin deep, and so the sensible no longer delivers sense. "The ancient covenant is in pieces," Jacques Monod wrote (1972: 167) "man knows that he is alone in the unfeeling immensity of the universe out of which he emerged only by chance."

MISPLACED CONCRETENESS

Whitehead ([1925] 1958: 52) called it the "fallacy of misplaced concretion," the mistake of taking an abstraction, a selective excision from the thick body of experience of nature for the whole. But the error is much more than a philosopher's conceptual one; its proportions are the size of culture. The archetypal premises of Apollo — the scientist's ascetic detachment, exclusive masculinity, his preference for clarity, formal beauty, and farsighted aims — are converted into a breach, as if we the observers were not part of nature, and not party to what we know of it. Then by a slip of attention, Galileo's and Newton's legitimate isolation of the mechano-morphic aspect of nature gradually, over several centuries of scientific triumph, preempted the West's collective representation, its common sense, of what nature discloses. Instead of the "lived world" of nature experienced with a full complement of senses and imagination (dismissed as subjective, "secondary qualities"), the quantifiable atoms usurped the place of primary reality. In effect, Newton's abstracted world became mythic for our culture, seeped into the dictionary meanings of our words, and thus into our subconscious modes of perception.

Observe the usage of the word *subjective* in the Oxford English Diction-ary. At the dawn of the scientific revolution, it meant "pertaining to the essence of the reality of a thing; real, essential." By the early eighteenth century, the meaning had shrunk to "having its source in the mind." By the late eighteenth century, the climate of opinion in which Kant worked is evident: "pertaining to an individual subject or his mental operations . . . personal, individual." By the late nineteenth century, the retreat of the subject before triumphant mechanism is one of full flight; the term has come to mean exactly the reverse of what it meant earlier: "existing in the mind only, without anything real to correspond with it; illusory, fanciful." Such an exhibit from the dictionary, which captures the cultural common sense, graphically documents an acute crisis in Western self-esteem. But it also illustrates the reason: that it is through our under-standing of nature that we form our own self-consciousness — and a na-ture full of sound and fury signifying nothing erodes our own substance. (Naturally, there's an inverse spin to all this, a heightened concern for the subject in jeopardy, increased pressure on imagination.)

In such a world artists can no longer "imitate" nature, by definition spiritless; they must draw what inspiration they can from expressing their personalities. When it comes to interpreting history, the consequence is that whether the object of study is modern or ancient, all minds are set down like blank film — or now, xerox copiers — before the *same data*, the scientifically filtered world of dead repetition and deterministic law in which entropy rules supreme. It then follows that the reality of primitive and archaic peoples is put down as metaphorical personification or pro-jection. We are told they are animists, that they are "anthropomorphiz-ing" or committing the pathetic fallacy — terms which betray the episte-mological imperialism of the modern Western outlook. Even Jungians, who might be expected to know better, typically honor the preestablished schism between mind and matter. The agricultural myths they delight in, which ostensibly refer to nature, are explained away as exclusively intra-psychic. They erupt, we are told, from that curious modern limbo, the no-man's-land of the unconscious.

The explanation for this evasion is not far to seek. Like phenomenologists prescinding from questions of reality or truth, Jungians are observing a cultural prohibition, an epistemological taboo. And the taboo here wreaks havoc with our understanding of evolution and the history of human thought. Evolution is charted in terms of a Cartesian split of mind from matter, the more explained by the less. Inexorably, consciousness must appear as an epiphenomenon conjured magically out of a strictly material substrate. Mind rates as a cosmic anomaly. For by definition, nature can have no inside, no inner dynamic form below the threshold such as the Greek mind of Aristotle took for granted. Nature is dead. *Pace* the Greek tragedians and Shakespeare's *King Lear*, no pathos within nature links up with our passions and pathologies. No *movement within nature* can be taken as having implications for sea changes in consciousness such as we witness in the rise of Greek speculation, the Renaissance, the scientific revolution itself, or the sudden emergence, in our own time, of depth psychology.

It might be otherwise if the unconscious were apprehended as another name for our link to nature's inside. But as things stand, the history of human thought, of consciousness, is turned into an exclusively intrapsychic and intersubjective affair, skating over the icy surfaces of a nature we are predestined to look *at*, as outsiders, never to apprehend from *within*. The development of consciousness thus appears as if it were exclusively a discursive process. One generation simply displaces the ideas of a former one in a process that resembles nothing so much as a syllogism. The history of ideas, accordingly, is presented as if Australian aborigines, Lao Tzu, the Presocratics, Plato, Descartes, Adam Smith, and Bertrand Russell were all posing questions to the same immutable "givens."

The other way around to understand what has been going on in our world over time arises from recognizing that nature, the nature we know, is a system of our collective representations, and that we receive our own self-understanding in terms of these representations (see Barfield, 1965). Neither the subject nor the object pole remains fixed; each changes concomitantly. Or to put it more straightforwardly, you can't study natural history or the history of science without simultaneously getting a fix on the history of consciousness, and vice versa. The history of consciousness is never just the story of intrapsychic events, but equally the story of transformations in the objective world. Socrates, the author of Job, Clement of Alexandria, Pascal, and Newton were not simply sending ideas from their brains like Athena from the forehead of Zeus. They were expressing something, responding to a depth or surface movement of nature that wanted saying, and which the less articulate others of their time were also collectively sensing. "When we study consciousness historically," writes Owen Barfield (1981: 18),

> contrasting perhaps what men perceive and think *now* with what they perceived and thought at some period in the past, when we study long-term *changes* in consciousness, we are studying changes in the world itself, and not simply changes in the human brain. We are not studying some so-called "inner" world, divided off by a skin or a skull, from the so-called "outer" world stuck on to the rest of it. It is the inside of the whole world . . . . Or . . . it is part of the whole world.

Consciousness, then, is not something apart from nature. It *is* nature, part of the inside of nature — or nature more or less awake and cognizant of itself, wondering what to make of itself. Barfield adds the qualification that human consciousness is "part of the whole" on the assumption, agreed upon by nearly everyone who thought about the matter up until the Renaissance, that our wakefulness is only possible because we participate in the cosmic wisdom ingredient in all things. Something much bigger than finite mind awakes, expresses itself.

THE WILL TO BELIEVE

When it comes to common-sense empiricism, a collective consciousness that is inscribed in the very dictionary meanings of our words, arguments are probably futile. For the arguments will be conducted with words that contain the offending premises, and thus opposing contentions, whether from literature, sociology, theology, or politics, amount — as Owen Barfield once put it — to "ways of occupying ourselves in prison." You have to tunnel under fixations at the preconscious level — or blow a hole in them experientially. Which is where psychedelics come in.

Nevertheless, by the sixties the fallacy I have just referred to was beginning to be softened up on a wide scale — by the liminoid state of flux of intellectual culture. Experiences like Huston Smith's, though they might still be deemed "far out," could not be so easily dismissed intellectually. A maverick elite stood by, a cognitive minority, that was ready to relativize the relativizers of religion. This is not to say they were ready yet to find nature numinous. But something else, closer to a Jamesian "will to believe" reading of the data, was conceivable. This more positive interpretation received plausibility from the sociology of knowledge. The work of Karl Mannheim and his successors had reached our shores. As an anthropologist, Gregory Bateson had been playing for years with the idea of cultural definitions of reality. The recognition grew that all official versions of reality are the products of social interaction. The human animal is plastic, instinctually undetermined to a large degree. What we call "reality" is consequently a complex of habits of action and power arrangements that, in the process of handing them on to another generation, become institutionalized. Enlightenment secularist orthodoxy was no exception, and thus not immune to relativizing. In the hands of a Michel Foucault, for instance, the sacred cows of the Faustian bourgeois self *and* its objective world were being archeologized, traced back to their power-grab roots, and deconstructed.

Nor was this demythologization limited to the social world. The work of Michael Polanyi and, in particular, Thomas S. Kuhn's *The Structure of Scientific Revolutions* (1962) showed that even hard science involved acts of faith, an incorporation of social rules and paradigms where major development occurs less by methodical "reason" than by visceral intuition and educated guess. (I shall come back to this in chapter 7.) In short, science could no longer be conceived as objective (i.e., independent of mind) in the old way. The subject's participation in the object was a *sine qua non* for meaning of whatever kind. Whether sociological, theological, or hard-scientific, our belief systems were, in the words of the title of Peter L. Berger's and Thomas Luckmann's influential book (1966), a "social construction of reality." As such, world views could be challenged and undone. By the late sixties, with the Vietnam War in full, bloody flush on the evening TV screen, there were many ready for a thorough revision.

On at least intellectual grounds, the suspicion grew that the collective Western consciousness — prohibited from knowing noumenal depths and oriented to measurable, visual surfaces by Immanuel Kant's Enlightenment epistemological settlement — did not possess a monopoly on reason. Such reason consisted of no more, and no less, than a historically and socially conditioned narrowing of the human "wave band." The frequency on which we were receiving nature's data might be accurate, even eminently useful, so far as it went (especially if you were interested in crossing streets, building dams and aqueducts, and converting crude ore to steel and aluminum wrap). But maybe the available cognitive aperture repressed as much of the spectrum as it let in, if not more. Perhaps other cultures, including other historical eras than our own, perceived with infrared lenses—or at least selectively saw things that we, in overreacting to obscurantism and ecclesiastical corruption, edit out. Less and less could reason or realism be taken in the singular; there were, it seemed, as many worlds as modes of perception.

THE GENESIS OF SHRINKAGE

Then there was Ernest Becker's psychological account of the correlative editing of reality and the shrinking of self. Becker was a social scientist much affected by what he saw and felt around university campuses in those days, and a somewhat heartsick secular humanist *thinking* his way back to a Judaism that made sense. Becker himself was obviously no optimistic "peaker" in the Abraham Maslow school. The overall tone of his last two books, *The Denial of Death* (1973) and *Escape from Evil* (1975), is one of gloom and Jeremiah-like lament. The premises of Becker's books are overtly and strictly those of Enlightenment orthodoxy (of "duped historians"), but his private letters (Bates, 1977: 219, 220), for instance, to a Protestant pastor friend, suggest the proper way to read him. "I celebrated the day of Atonement this year," he wrote to his friend, Harvey Bates, in October 1965, "for the first time since adolescence. . . . It was really a very genuine experience for me." Or again, in December 1965, "I am reading from the Bible . . . .Psalm 10:17–18 and Psalm 11 ["Yahweh, you listen to the wants of the humble, / you bring strength to their hearts, you grant them a hearing." And "In Yahweh I take shelter."]. Does any other prayer make sense?" His books are to be understood, I think, as exercises in prophetic iconoclasm—in this case as a frontal attack on modern idol worship of the hollow heroic self. The voice here is that of a Jew made in the image of Jeremiah or Job.

The shrinkage of the self, argued Becker, was no temporary hiatus in the long-term march of progress. On the contrary, *The Denial of Death* proposed to summarize the results of the whole psychoanalytic tradition's depth-insight into the heroic climb of the Faustian modern self. The data in, the mountain-top adventure of the self-made man is a fraud. Depth psychology's severe scrutiny exposes the self as a futile passion to play god. The program is built on the terror, the denial of death. Taking his cue from Otto Rank and Norman O. Brown, Becker claimed the self builds, and embeds itself into, a culture of enduring institutions as vehicles of its own *causa sui* project. It's the ingenious way of pretending to live "supernaturally," and thus of avoiding mortality and creatureliness. All understandable: the hero can't tolerate being a passive object of fate, a mere appendage of mothering, smothering earth. So courageously, he sets out to become an active center within himself, controlling his destiny with his own powers. But finally, as Rank had it, the whole mythos of self-realization is a "vital lie." And to recognize the self-deception, to strip away the successive layers of glib talk, the social role-playing, the character defenses against unconscious anxiety—in short, to dismantle the self as humanistic "human potential" advocates wished—ought to result in the "real probability of the awakening to terror and dread, from which there is no turning back." Esalen's suicides seemed to bear out the thesis that liberation of the "authentic self" brought you first to Kierkegaard's world of existential despair.

And perhaps to the verge of his "leap of faith" as well. *The Denial of Death* gave no indication that Becker could or would make any such leap (not a very Hebrew notion, I suspect), but insistently the book posed the question of whether the "beyond" of religious faith wasn't, expecially in contrast to all the cramped secular ideologies and utopias of the past century, a "legitimate foolishness." Becker devised a new legitimacy test for necessary illusions: human beings require grandeur and perfection with which to be nourished, mystery, power, and majesty to expand in. It's the condition of our freedom. How much freedom, dignity, and hope, then, does a given illusion provide? Meticulously, he examined the alternatives, the way the infant sets the pattern for adult trade-offs, repressing, partializing itself, surrendering feeling and instinct, and losing its earliest sense of the *mysterium tremendum* of existence. The payoff consists in the manageable security blankets provided by parents. The bargain, the bribery, means that instinctively at first, and then with increasing deliberateness, we construct our own prisons.

The prison is built by Freud's one-two combination of repression and transference. The *numen*, especially for the child, is too much to take in. So it is transferred and thereby reduced to controllable proportions. What the transference relation is all about, first with parents, later with the corporate institutions of the cultural fathers, with a lover, or with the creative person's work of art itself (such as psychoanalysis was for Freud), is a process of taming the wonder of the cosmic mystery, confining its range to the "visible god" where a person can establish footing, gain esteem, keep order. The dissociation Lancelot Law Whyte declaims against, Becker shows, begins early and builds with the self's momentum to get to "the top" of the social pyramid which is to preserve it from death. For at each step in the ladder there is a binding over to a limited "beyond" which involves corresponding contraction, a self-forgetting, a condemnation of a part of us to oblivion.

Nor, Becker argues, is the "cosmology of two," the romantic solution, any way out—for it puts too much pressure on the partner to be an angel, "my salvation," god—and an unqualified "I'm OK, you're OK" rooter for the other's hero status. Freud's solution, the archetypal creative person's solution, on the other hand, consisted of making a self-justifying fetish, a "private religion," out of one's own opus. But if we have no one to give our gift to, argues Becker, it becomes a trap. The work of art becomes god, beyond criticism precisely because it is the covert means to immortality. Carl Jung mentions death in Freud's presence, and he faints. The famous incident reflects on us lesser mortals, shows the almost universal fix subjects are in when, as is customary, we identify ourselves with our objects.

So Becker paints the Oedipal self into a no-exit corner, shows its self-serving social contract to be founded on a series of self-reducing give-aways to a set-up that cannot possibly deliver on the promise we have invested in it. "Your gods are empty." Where have we heard this before? Becker's whole argument is that of a son of that peculiar deity who tolerates no image, or rather idol, to stand before him.

By Becker's original criterion, the test of freedom, however, the theistic "beyond" begins to gain intellectual respectability. A "will to believe" is possible just because God—as Becker puts it—in being hidden and intangible, allows unlimited expansion.

A GUIDED TOUR OF HELL

Our brains, scientists had been telling us for years, contained vast, unused equipment. Could it be that our potential was far more complex, hid more possibilities, than we were bringing into play? Was not the longing for transcendence entwined with our creative and moral powers? Was not a great deal of modern pathology traceable to the self-diminishment due to a suppression of the sublime? In the sixties, disciples of Freud such as Italy's Roberto Assagioli and England's heterodox Ronald Laing were suggesting as much. Always the spokesman, Alan Watts argued (in Anderson, 1983: 70) that authentic religious experience let grandeur into the cosmos that exposed the narrowness of the establishment view.

Such experiences imply that . . . our normal perception and valuation of the world is a subjective but collective nightmare. They suggest our ordinary sense of practical reality . . . is a construct of socialized conditioning and repression, a system of selective inattention whereby we are taught to screen out aspects and relations within nature which do not accord with the rules of the game of civilized life.

The soul needed wonders. But if the epistemological deadlock was to be broken, the soul also needed something to blow the lid off.

Caution advised. The condition of the body-mind system mattered. Huston Smith is well known as the author of the immensely popular *The Religions of Man* (1958). By years of study arising out of a felt affinity with Hinduism, he had effectively prepared himself for his revelation-experience of emanationism. In many another case, however, the culturally conditioned resistance to disclosures of this sublime kind were too vigorous. In which case, a psychedelic drug might simply shove the nose into one's own belief system. It was then anything but an academic matter to discover that ideation had sunk into the nerves and tissue, that one's secularist epistemological embargoes had severe biological consequences. Thus, to take an example, when in 1968 dolphin researcher John Lilly ingested one hundred milligrams of pure Sandoz LSD, he met up with agony — the agony of the standard brand scientific world view he'd absorbed from his elite education at Cal Tech. The doors of perception opened to a "guided tour of hell."

Suddenly I was precipitated into what I later called the "cosmic computer." I was merely a very small program in somebody else's huge computer . . . . I was being programmed by other senseless programs above me and above them others. I was programming smaller programs below me. The information that came to me was meaningless. I was meaningless . . . . Everywhere I found entities like myself who were slave programs in this huge cosmic conspiracy, this cosmic dance of energy and matter which had absolutely no meaning, no love, no human value. The computer was absolutely dispassionate, objective, and terrifying. The layer of ultimate programmers on the outside of it were personifications of the devil himself and yet they too were merely programs. There was no hope or choice of ever leaving this hell. I was in fantastic pain and terror. [Lilly, 1972: 87–88]

The experience shook Lilly from head to foot. Like many who took psychedelics at the time, he found that his body was amazingly mindful. The body, normally overshadowed by the imposing brain, had its own wisdom. And among other things, it alerted him to the empty environment into which his "education " had deposited him—a place of "fantastic pain and terror." But that did it. Lilly was shaken loose from what had been, up until then, his basic assumptions about reality. His Big Bang Darwinian materialism, the studied literalism of our culture, shattered. For those who ride high on the remarkable three-hundred-year achievements of mechanistic natural science, and who allow its regulative assumptions to blur over into an unexamined metaphysical outlook, something like the extreme shock therapy of LSD was virtually a necessity. Positivistic presuppositions are simply sunk too deep for dialectics to dislodge. We require a crash program, something just like LSD's rocket-impact; and above all something experiential, that a seeing-is-believing mind would have to respect. On occasion LSD provided that for the most determined agnostic or atheist. They could at least entertain the thought of religious faith. While debriefing himself in the days following his "tour of hell," John Lilly (1972: 91) felt a major paradigm shift taking place in himself:

> I was to experience and feel love of the intensity that I had felt earlier in my childhood. I was to go through grief, through all sorts of emotions that I had been blocking off and refusing to recognize because of my "scientific knowledge." For the first time I began to consider that God really existed in me and that there was a guiding intelligence in the universe.

For Lilly, then, psychedelics provided release from a spell; it enabled him to see through the Enlightment pretense to be *the* enlightenment. In the classic Western three-stage distinction of the mystical journey—the purgative way, the illuminative, and the unitive—Lilly's tour amounted to an accelerated purgation, a first venture in unlearning. It also gave him his first taste of the *docta ignorantia*, the "learned ignorance" of the medievals, which he was later to formulate as a basic epistemological axiom (Lilly, 1972: 5):

> In the province of the mind, what is believed to be true is true or becomes true, within the limits to be found experientially and experimentally. These limits are further beliefs to be transcended. In the province of the mind, there are no limits.

The course correction was not untypical, nor were psychedelics the only means of its happening.

TWICE BORN AGAINS

In the theologian company I also kept at the time, "self-realization" was generally understood pejoratively; it meant ego tripping, selfishness, narcissism. Places like Esalen were dismissed as "Pepsi-generation Marienbads." In contrast to the self-seekers, the folk who stayed home, kept their hands to the plow, presumably my academic friends themselves, were praised for adhering to (more or less) selfless duty, were responsible, self-transcending. "Self-transcendence" was the eulogistic term. The distinction has applications, admittedly, and I have no intention of disparaging silent laborers in the vineyard (who include most of the self-seekers, who also held jobs).

In real life, however, the distinction between self-realizers and self-transcenders was not so neat. As I say, Calvin and Julian of Norwich would have understood how easy it is, in quest of missing persons, to slide unobtrusively into being a religious seeker without missing a beat. In my workshop experience, religious language or awed silence kept displacing humanistic talk, kept erupting from participants, often to their amazement — and there was no stopping it. It should have come as no surprise. Many of the growth therapies targeted the false self. Once that gave way, the "rushes" which followed often filled the room with radiance.

Let me cite one example. On another visit to Esalen in 1977 I was involved in a month-long program, titled "Birth, Sex, and Death," which featured a spectrum of exercises designed to enable participants to enact a process of birth analogous to that of obstetric delivery. Among these was one technique used by British psychologist Ronald Laing. The group simulates a tight birth canal, webbing themselves together in a line to form a pressurized tunnel wall. The candidate for birthing, stripped and oiled, then elbow-crawls, squirms through.

One candidate for birthing was a recent medical school graduate on his way to psychiatric specialization. Good looking and athletic, you could tell he had been an overachieving winner all his life. He relished challenges, excelled at performance; tight squeezes were his metier. Resistance, opposition, just drove up his energy. Like greased lightning, he plunged in, stormed through our ten or fifteen encircling, contracting bodies — the ultimate athlete flushed with adrenalin. The part of the process he hadn't figured on, which caught his defenses off-guard, was the finish, the moment of delivery and yielding up as a neonate into caressing, loving care. The rules of the game were that he had to rest there, be

helpless, allow himself to be held and admired for just being, not doing—
and at that point the assertive all-American independent, the Pelagian in
him, came apart at the seams. He was out of control.

His fright was visible. His chest heaved, he began to hyperventilate.
Our two Laingian guides gently insisted that he permit himself to be
nurtured, and to stay with his feelings and breathing. Finally, tears came,
and he was asked to look into the faces of those around him, few of
whom did not see their own sore hearts in his confusion, his resistance to
being loved for no ulterior purpose, few of whom were not teary themselves. You had to hear his phlegmy voice at that moment after the tears;
it possessed an eerie, earthy strength I had not heard before. You had to
see his face. It was if a cloud on his features had cleared; a certain
handsome granite was no longer there. His face was softly radiant, beautiful, transfigured—and so was the quality of energy filling the room. If I
had not known that it was late in the day, about 11 P.M., I would have
said the sun had just risen, bathing us all in its glow. The thing had
turned into a communion rite, the liminal *communitas* Victor Turner
speaks of in pilgrim rites of passage. It had been, I thought, one of those
ground zero moments of truth, a genuine unveiling. I still think so.

The medieval grail quest was neither monastic not clerical. Nor was its
language overtly religious in the conventional sense. It was conducted by
noncelibate, this-worldly knights and ladies who abandoned their courts,
who temporarily dropped out of secular functions, to pursue the quest at
great cost and with many casualties along the way. Its religious language
was coded in terms of wounded fisher-kings, wastelands, mysterious cups
and lances, seductions, drops of blood on the snow, strange apparitions
of castles, hags and elusive virgin-sisters. In short, religious research was
conducted incognito. And so here. The consciousness movement did not
broadcast its religiosity, in part because it was seeking a new form unen-
cumbered by conventions that might only mislead, in part because many
of its leaders were alienated from organized religion and for the most part
couldn't have found there, if they had tried at the time, the disciplines and
maps they sought. In its own way, however, it was breaking through
frozen secularist dogma. The epistemological ice had begun to crack.
"The flaw, the flood, the upstart spring" was happening.

THREE

Psychedelic Telescopes

How can we contrive to be at once astonished at the world and yet at home in it? How can this queer cosmic town . . . give us at once the fascination of a strange town and the comfort and honour of being our own town?

G. K. Chesterton

Heaven lies about us in our infancy!
Shades of the prison-house begin to close
Upon the growing Boy. . . .

William Wordsworth

I tell you solemnly, anyone who does not welcome the king-dom of God like a little child will never enter it.

Jesus (Mark 10:15)

Now that my ladder's gone,
I must lie down where all the ladders start,
In the foul rag-and-bone shop of the heart.

W. B. Yeats

Modern psychology grew out of nineteenth-century scientism and philo-sophical rationalism. If one takes William James and Freud as the pioneer representatives of modern psychology, we can see them as ambivalently trying to assimilate the individual to a case illustrative of impersonal, biological laws—stimulus-response arcs for instance, or the thermody-namics of libido. The result was the standing joke of the field: a "psychology without psyche." At the same time, thanks to the ambivalence, James and Freud opened the way to the unconscious and "depth psychology." They stand uncomfortably astraddle a more ancient conception of psyche and modern, reductionistic biologism. Reacting against the latter, we have the ego psychology of Karen Horney, Harry Stack Sullivan, Erich Fromm, Gordon Allport, and Maslow; and bidding to extend the depth approach of the former we have Freud's dissident disciples, Carl Jung, Alfred Adler, Roberto Assagioli, and Otto Rank. Rank's last book (1941), never finished, called for a step "beyond psychology," that is, a step surpassing the "destructive ideology" of psychoanalysis which he thought had arisen to fill the vacuum left by collapsing religious faith. What was demanded, Rank believed, was a new program and style of psychology more aware of its larger cultural task, its attention not focused on the self-conscious analysis of the personal past, but on the development of human capacities by means of which the meaning of existence could be plumbed anew. In the early seventies, somewhat confusedly, Rank's farewell message landed at places like Esalen. Maslow's "being psychology" was part of it, and psychodramatic happenings signaled it. I have been calling this new style transpersonal psychology. It involved the reappearance, intact, of *anima* or soul.

But Rank's *envoi* also came flooding through the back door, in the form of rocketing psychedelics. It was not, of course, that drugs like mescaline or LSD programmatically guaranteed that a person would, as it were, retrieve the perceptual mode of a fifth-century B.C. Hindu—as Huston Smith apparently did. It is also another question whether that perceptual mode is desirable. And to be sure, for all too many, psychedelics simply formed another episode in the American sociopathology of the quick fix. Or they were soporific escapes, like soap operas. Or worse, they were anything but escapes. In many cases, certainly, the drugs flushed out Medusas from the closet that the tripper was unprepared to deal with, and he or she got stuck, petrified on the spot. All this is true. Here, I would simply stress that other quite extraordinary cultural sea change that I have already adverted to. I mean Huston Smith's discovery of what he calls "empirical metaphysics." For almost two hundred years in the West, this wasn't supposed to be possible.

But if such a possibility is to be plausible we ought (1) to dispose of the misconception that psychedelics necessarily produced a "model psychosis." (2) Then I want to examine some of the reasons for thinking that, carefully used, these drugs unearth important information about the structure of the psyche—and the frame of our life-stories. Which will bring us (3) to the subsequent spin-offs in nondrug experiment, that is, the heightened interest in spiritual disciplines, rites of passage, and so on. Initiated by psychedelics, consciousness-raisers would meet the very old idea that the worlds we encounter are a function of the disposition of our minds, and thus point up the role of nondrug spiritual disciplines in transfiguring the world by altering consciousness. "Eyes and ears," said Heraclitus, "are bad witnesses to those with barbarian souls." At the same time, (5) for the first time in the following explication, there will surface a major difference of style in the movement which has to do with different governing myths, in a sense the differences between East and West.

AN UNSPECIFIC CATALYST

The term "psychedelics" means "manifestation of psyche." Or revealer of soul. And as such, in the form of psychedelic plants like peyote, psyche-delics have been in human use for thousands of years. Yet the notion persists that when synthesized in a laboratory, the results of ingestion somehow denature the recipient, are "drug induced." But the evidence, so far as I am able to tell, does not sustain this verdict.

Take rocketing LSD. It was found that it had no uniform pharmacolog-ical effect. The most striking thing about its use, independent of dosage, was the variable impact upon its users. Contrary to the popular impres-sion, the chemical did not perform as a causal agent but as a catalyst. This was not a case of Pavlovian or Skinnerian stimulus-response. Serious psychedelic research, it turned out, had little to do with the study of psychoactive substances. It rendered porous those "filmiest of screens," the culturally derived mental sets, filters, and defense systems of the subject. After some three thousand sessions with clients in psychedelic therapy, Dr. Stanislav Grof (1976: 6), the director of the government-sponsored Maryland Psychiatric Center at Spring Grove Hospital in the sixties, concluded that the drug acted as a "unspecific amplifier of mental processes that bring to the surface various elements from the depths of the unconscious." Depending then on the aesthetic quality of the setting in which taken, the subject's background, and the quality of the therapist or sitter, LSD accelerated the release of normal defense mechanisms and body armor. A typical session would dramatize in condensed symbolic form the psychological, emotional, intellectual, and spiritual issues of an individual at the time of ingestion. The drug itself was neutral, a mere surfacer; in effect, it externalized and magnified "the conflicts intrinsic to human nature and civilization." For the clinician, then, psychedelics provided a powerful diagnostic tool and an extraordinary insight into the structure of the human mind; for the serious subject, they offered a way of taking the whole organism's pulse, checking where you stood. "It does not seem inappropriate and exaggerated," Grof concluded, "to compare their potential significance for psychiatry and psychology to that of the microscope for medicine or the telescope for astronomy." (Grof's judgment received essential confirmation in 1979 from two Harvard medical professors, Lester Grinspoon and James B. Bakalar, in their *Psychedelic Drugs Reconsidered*.)

I shall come to the problem I have with Grof's larger interpretation, his ontology, in due course, but for the moment he gets us started.

TOO MUCH, CAN'T STAND IT

What's behind Grof's analogy with the microscope and telescope? R. C. Zaehner, Spalding Professor of Eastern Religions and Ethics at Oxford (and a Catholic), was arguing at the time that psychedelics could only induce those monistic dissolution states common to certain poets and, say, Shamkhya Hinduism. His book, *Mysticism, Sacred and Profane*, attempted to refute the quickie-mysticism of Aldous Huxley's *The Doors of Perception*. Huxley, we were to think, had obviously been seized by a "profane" kind of oceanic regress. Genuine theistic experience, Zaehner maintained, remained off-limits through chemical means. This judgment is understandable; being a member of a cognitive minority, a believer at Oxford is to be on the defensive. As a generalization, however, Zaehner's caustic judgment is also wrong.

I'd tried LSD, and knew Zaehner didn't know what he was talking about. In every one of my five trips, I left ego control behind rather rapidly. To mention just my first incidence, after about a half hour, the walls of the room and the house where two friends and I were experimenting simply fell away — and I was navigating about in a space something like Stanley Kubrick explored at the end of *2001: A Space Odyssey*. It was a wonderland of sensory distortion and synesthesia, solid objects turning liquid, colors and sounds vibrating and fusing; the ordinary empirical world assumed all the charged panpsychism of a Van Gogh painting. But I didn't spend long with this epicurean feast. Before I knew quite what was happening, I felt my body shrinking. With all the physical sensations of it, I was catapulted back to infancy; further, into the womb. I had to gct born again. Don't ask me whether this was the resurgent memory of my biological birth, an anticipation of death-as-rebirth, or some kind of symbolic, spiritual rebirth—all common enough in LSD experience I was later to discover. It was probably multidimensional, a condensation of all three in one. At a certain point, then, I assumed a fetal position, and with the cooperation of my cohorts who simulated a birth canal, I pushed and shoved my way—twice as I recall—from uterine darkness into light and autonomous breathing. And felt wounded, stricken in the right shoulder. Whereupon a tussle with radiant energy ensued.

The energy had the quality of ethereal dazzling light, sheer, glorious golden splendor. At the time it did not occur to me to think of the Hebrew tradition's *Shekhinah*, God's effulgent "glory"—but I would now understand it in such terms. (More subtly, it would occur to me it was the "color" I felt when, as a child, I saw my father greet my mother when he came home from work.) There was also a sound attached to it, a dynamo whirring with electricity. I had to stand up and move, at the same time coordinating my thoughts, to get "with it," sense it coursing through my psychophysical system—and it wasn't easy. I kept slipping in and out of its field, sensing the blockages in my body, the knots in my anatomy, and the fears and suspicions in my mind that prevented its circulation through me. A few years later, under similar circumstances, I found myself spontaneously doing T'ai Chi (which I had learned in the meantime) to dance my way through the blocks (which felt like severe stomach cramps and inhibitions of breathing) into a clear flow.

This first time, I found myself both moving and playing with ideas that somehow not only enabled me to plug into this high-altitude energy without short-circuit but also rendered it intelligible, even familiar. As if I had my hand on a theater lighting panel, I was switching buttons in my mind labeled Upanishads, Buddhism, and Christianity. The rocketing speed of what was happening made it difficult to discriminate more exactly. But in a rough way, all these big-idea schemata more or less fit and charted the charged space I was in, and exorcised its strangeness, made me feel I could get about, find my way here. These were not simply symbolic images on a screen, but firsthand experience, the *Ding an sich*, the *numen* or pneumatic energy out of which, it seemed, I—all of us, I felt—had come. And to which we all still belonged. "Good vibes," as the saying of the time went. I suddenly realized "where I was coming from." Yes, I was remembering in a double, almost comical sense: who I was, and at the same time re-membering *us*. For all the while I was urging my companions to join me, "taste and see," and issuing orders that they configure themselves physically so that we could move in this radiance together—commands which met with bewilderment and incomprehension on their part. "You won't believe this," I kept saying, "but it's so good."

After a while (what was time here?), the radiance subsided. But not until it had left me with a stupendous mythic vision. It was as if the whole human race were flooding into Yankee Stadium, admission free. And inside, perhaps like a descending Goodyear blimp hovering in the midst of the throng, the glory of God blazed forth, inundating, inseminating all. "For nothing!" I remember shouting incredulously to my friends, "you won't believe this, but it's all free, no charge." They looked at me quizzically—as if to say, either that I was perfectly mad or that they knew quite well that there's no free lunch.

Later, walking across a snow-blanketed city, coming painfully down, I had a bad case of amnesia. Only by inches did my life, year by year, creep back into memory. And in some ways the most powerful impact of the trip, I realized how much of that life and the people in it I had been unwilling to say yes to. It was as if, as each set of circumstances returned, all my secret ambivalence stood exposed. Every "yes, but . . . so what else is there?" of mine. The difference was that I had a choice this time around. In retrospect, this was a painful, blessed event. It was like being given Nietzsche's test of a worthy life: Can you say, when it's done, "once more!"? Nietzsche had in mind the acceptance of an exact repetition, eternal return without wanting an iota altered. His was a "classic" Greco-Roman mind (had he not also said the best is not to be born, the next best to die soon?). I had something else in mind, closer perhaps to Kierkegaard's sense of repetition, a once-again with a twist, with the old familiars made new, fresh minted—not by any change in them necessarily, but by a different attitude in me. A grateful yes to events might do. Since then, a good part of the agenda of my life has involved learning to utter that yes.

But this first psychedelic experiment, which I was not to repeat again without more sober guardians in attendance, taught another lesson as well. On reflection, it occurred to me that part of my trouble in standing the "glory," or for that matter communion with anyone or anything at high intensity, was the catastrophe mentality I carried around in my head. To see God, I knew—or thought I knew—is to die. It would be like sticking your finger into the main high-voltage line of the Niagara Mohawk Power Generator. Life at a safe distance, even at a crouch, was preferable. And I was attached to that low profile's security and familiarity even if, in other respects, it was killing me with monotony. Liminal *communitas* was hard to bear, "too much." When it hit me in the racing whorl of psychedelic propulsion, it was largely an "out of body" experience. Apparently, I did not have the body to sustain it, keep my feet on the ground. The lesson: I needed psychophysical tune-up, athletic conditioning. In my tradition, levitation is *not* a positive sign.

A few years later, Fr. Andrew Greeley and William McCready wondered aloud in the *New York Times Magazine* (26 January 1975), "Are We a Nation of Mystics?" In a survey of fifteen hundred respondents, they reported that five out of ten Americans seem to be occasional mystics. Forty percent of their sample at least once in their lives had experienced "ecstasy," a spiritual force that lifted them out of themselves. By the respondents' own reckoning the experience had been one of the most important things that ever happened to them, and it had significantly reshaped their decisions and behavior thereafter. Yet according to Greeley and McGready, "no one to whom we spoke wants such an experience again." Why? Such experiences were too disconcerting, disruptive, disturbing. The typical reaction: "I couldn't stand it."

I sympathize, understand. When the golden thread you search for is given, the door you want opened swings wide—what then? Do you take hold? Step through? Or freak out, hide in the crevice of a rock, go cold? The early consciousness-raisers may have been overenamored of euphoric "peaks," overviews, harmonic "highs," and conflict-free synergy, but one thing they did notice: the need to build up a psychophysical system that can tolerate a high degree of intensity and sustained tension. Perseus, we're told, could only slay Medusa if he had a mirrorlike shield—quick-witted mindfulness.

Medieval alchemical wisdom, if not literalized into metallurgy, furthered the insight. If you're on a grail quest, the first thing you require is a container, a dish, cup, or crucible which, as alchemists maintained, is able to take a lot of heat in order to transform leaden states, the "shadow side," into the white silver of imagination. Silver is the subtle body, the place of flashes of insight. And since the journey costs much, you need lots of this kind of silver. It enables an exchange, commerce in energy, and the transformation of energy into new form—perhaps even gold.

EXPLORING LIMINAL COUNTRY

In 1966 Robert E. L. Masters and Jean Houston, husband and wife, published a best seller, *The Varieties of Psychedelic Experience*. As the title suggests, Masters's and Houston's work, observations of 206 drug sessions and interviews with another 214 subjects who had taken the drugs on their own (extending over fifteen years), had been an attempt to carry on the legacy of William James. Significantly, the subjects of their experiments were not severely disturbed individuals, but the comparatively normal, "average person" (though some might not consider Jean Paul Sartre, one of their interviewees, quite the man-in-the-street). The book's pages are filled with the stuff of the psychiatric couch. They are also dense with accounts of the sort of experience which for the most part only Lucien Lévy-Bruhl's primal peoples, Czeslaw Milosz's Eastern European peasants, or the figures of my childhood Catholicism dealt with: preternatural clairvoyance and clairaudiance, phylogenetic regressions, previous incarnations, animal metamorphoses, telepathy, angels, demons, angry and benign deities, and more.

For all that, by the authors' strict criteria, only six of their 206 research subjects under LSD attained what they were willing to call an "integral religious" experience, which they defined as a "direct and unmediated encounter with the source level of reality, felt as Holy, Awful, Ultimate, and Ineffable"—and which had a permanently transforming impact on self. Unlike Timothy Leary, Richard Alpert (later Ram Dass), and Huxley at the time, Masters and Houston did not claim that psychedelics induced an instant, painless nirvana. Their conclusion was far more sober—more sober, I think, than Zaehner's, which was based on secondhand evidence and his own one-shot experiment with mescalin. Thus Masters and Houston (1966: 259):

> It is frequently funny, if also unfortunate, to encounter young members of the Drug Movement who claim to have achieved a personal apotheosis when, in fact, their experience appears to have consisted mainly of depersonalization, dissociation, and similar phenomena. Such individuals seek their beatitude in regular drug-taking, continuing to avoid the fact that their psychedelic "illumination" is not the sign of divine or cosmic approval they suppose it to be, but rather a flight from reality.

To attain the depths or heights—and even then perhaps not the habits—of a Teresa of Avila or John of the Cross, Masters and Houston argued, one had to take into account extrapharmacological factors. Their six religiously "successful" subjects were all mature, creative adults over forty. As Stanislav Grof had found, what above all seemed to count was the subject's background, belief system, and long tacit if not explicit preparation. Huston Smith had not come cold to Hindu emanationism, nor was he unfamiliar with the fact that it was a standard experiential feature for Dionysius the Areopagite, the Kabbalists, Dante, and John of the Cross. My "Yankee Stadium" experience amounted to a variant of the same thing, and was, furthermore, a parochial school's common image of a grandstand heaven.

Masters and Houston also noted that in each case, before entering into the religious phase of the drug experience, the subject normally passed through several preliminary stages, an excavation of the psyche's archeological strata as it were. These identifiable stage-layers offered the basis for an ideal typology corresponding to a hierarchy of psyche and its correlative, overlapping worlds. Stanislav Grof's larger sample of cases, many of whom were also in the "normal" category, suggested a roughly similar, though more fine-grained, stratification. As I can testify, however, in the concrete these planes of being are much more interpenetrating and synchronic than a linear presentation would indicate. The texture of these experiences is polysemous, a multiweave of meanings operating at several levels — somatic, psychological, and spiritual — at once. A tapestry effect: the most trivial event of memory ramifies with double and triple entendre. Toilet training is easily forgettable, but it may contain our whole life-story, a slant on the history of the world. Huston Smith's image of wave frequencies or "bands" is also appropriate.

At one level, the Masters-Houston schema follows the ontogenic explanatory pattern of depth psychology, accounting for a person's present manifestations (or symptoms) in terms of antecedent life history. The child is father to the man. Therapy ostensibly turns back the clock, consists of reversal whereby key events that have skewed or arrested development are remembered and worked through with an adult's heart and mind in the transference relation to the analyst. The presence of the analyst/therapist keeps the working-through in the present, reminds us that the hermetic interaction does not literally turn back the clock so much as spiral inward (and laterally, back and forth) to unlock a core process-presence that has been interrupted. But it usually goes only so far — to the traumas of infancy — and further, it tends not to challenge a secular culture's worship of success, off-hours pleasure, and adjustment to the social order as is.

What psychedelic experience did was to go much further in opening up origins, but again in an even more explicitly mythic way than psychoanalysis; that is, attuning the subject to beginning times, the eminently "strong" *in principio* time of nonliterate cultures, the time-out-of-time before the separation of heaven and earth. Vividly and powerfully, it rendered worlds soluble, restored the seed time of primitive orgiastic rite, where you could often discern the seed of latent futures. The thing was often so "mind blowing" that people could not stand it, lost their way, mistook the out-of-body trip for realization, turned it into ego inflation, got stuck in a labyrinth. And hence the need for a sure-footed, wise guide, a Hermes (or Joseph Campbell) for the trip. For you could not so easily get off this roller coaster, stop with family familiars. The gyre here was likely to bore both deeper vertically and wider horizontally. Which is to say that, potentially, these space-trips were not simply intrapsychic. Masters and Houston at this early stage of research still speak misleadingly of "inner space." But that is only the half of it.

These inner trips were full of ontological implication; the further "in" you reached, the farther "out" you got—into a circumambient Being whose center is nowhere and whose circumference is everywhere. In practice if not quite yet in theory, religion and psychology—or the transpersonal and the cosmological—were making contact in the overlap border realm of liminality. "Tripping out" traced lost persons in a direction much closer to Bonaventure's *itinerarium mentis in Deum*, a journey of remembrance back to God. Or closer to the Buddha's unraveling of "dependent origination" in those feelings, perceptions, forces, ideas that ruptured interconnection and started off the bottled-up self in its bid for an independent, self-fulfilling career set against the whole. Psychedelics sometimes exposed what the Buddhists call *dukkha*, the imprisoning limitations of the self's small mindedness.

Hence the connection, perceived rather quickly, between what was happening in psychedelic experience and traditional spiritual disciplines—and a host of contemporary nondrug analogues such as sensory deprivation, shock therapy, bioenergetics, gestalt therapy, and so on. Through all these methods people occasionally came in touch with those archetypal and spiritual forces which psychedelic trips "speeded" you into ready or not. Either way, to those who had such openings, life and the material world itself began to appear as a crystallization, a dumb epiphany, of those more subtle archetypal patterns and spirit realms. But it was especially to the inner-space age, psychedelic explorers that their laminated inner spaces began to appear as corresponding to a hierarchical ontological order. Their "common sense" sense of the literal was being reversed; instead of imagining mind anomalously growing out of dumb matter, they began to suspect that dumb matter was but an apparition of cosmic mind. The planet bloomed the way it did—into life and finite mind—because aboriginally the whole universe bloomed out of nameless mystery. Before you knew it, if no one (like the U.S. government) put a stop to it, the physical cosmos was going to regain its medieval texture as psychophysical, as a potential hierophany of Aquinas's prime Poet-Maker. But the consciousness movement preferred to think of it as Shiva's dance or the *Tao*. That was probably a tactical mistake, needlessly offensive to straight, Bible-reading legislators.

The thing was highly ironic. At just the time in the late sixties when theologians like Rudolph Bultmann, Harvey Cox (*The Secular City*), and Bishop John A. Robinson (*Honest to God*) were abandoning the Great Chain of Being as embarrassingly prescientific (the embarrassment being self-induced by their crudely literalistic ways of taking spatial metaphors), ivy-league professors (like Timothy Leary, Richard Alpert, and Huston Smith) and "flower children" were resurrecting the notion. Then careful psychedelic researchers like Masters, Houston, and Grof stumbled into it too, and rather than finding a four-storied universe a pale, obsolete idea, they found it vitally and energetically alive, and began to elaborate their own versions of the scheme in a distinctly more dynamic and less dualistic mode than Plato's. It looked less like a footnote to Plato than a major revision, closer in style to that of Alfred North Whitehead's *Process and Reality*. The revision did not encourage a spirituality of withdrawal and retreat from involvement with the world. As Masters and Houston (1966: 313) summed it up:

> The beneficial effect of the psychedelic mystical experience, then, was to take the subject through a process of experiencing Essence in such a way that it illuminated all of existence, making him more interested in and responsive to the phenomena of existence than he had been before. Thus instead of retreating from the phenomenal world, as often occurs with the traditional mystic, the psychedelic subject was inspired by the process of his experience to a kind of flight *toward* reality.

REMEMBERING THE PLOT LINE

Whether the catalyst is a drug, school of hard knocks, or concerted spiritual discipline, there is no uniform psychedelic, or soul-manifesting trip. Yet, say the psychedelic researchers, nature's madness has method, and psychedelic drugs provided insight into ontological outer space. The territory can be mapped in a four-stage ideal typology. In order, the four stages proceed from (1) the aesthetic-sensory plane to (2) the recollective-analytic or psychodynamic to (3) the symbolic or mythic-ritual level and, finally (4) what Masters and Houston call the integral-religious level. The rule is: the further "in," the further "out." The gyre widens, thickens. The first level reveals only Kierkegaard's "immediate man," the philistine embedded in daily routine but seeking bread-and-circus entertainment. The second psychodynamic level of strictly "personal" history widens and deepens to include the length and breadth of the individual lifetime, the familiar company it keeps, its fit into society—and what's stopping it, currently, in getting on with its aspirant ambitions (usually a career, a family). With this third level, however, the issues of individual struggle take on a larger, more mythic context, as if one had finally reckoned death in the offing and began to wonder of one's place in the story of the race. The "who" in the "Who am I?" query reaches the question of generativity in the larger sense. How do I fit into the larger course of time, beyond the individual life span, across the generations? The subject's life takes on the dimensions of historical and prehistorical density. Gregory Bateson called it, "the pattern that connects." But connections do not stop there. At the fourth level, through a process of death-rebirth, there's more to come.

Since the latter two planes, the symbolic and strictly mystical, are less familiar and more strictly liminal in our culture, I shall dwell on them at greater length. Finally, I shall reweave this hierarchy in Grof's birth-process schema. But first, Master's and Houston's typology.

1. *Aesthetic-Sensory*: The first and most superficial level of soul-manifestation, according to Masters and Houston, consisted of a purely sensory kaleidoscope. As I indicated in my own case, the empirical world turns into a perceptual feast or "sensory goulash." It is an aesthetic plane that many fun-trippers never passed beyond. Yet, for Masters and Houston (1966: 177), this phase is not exactly idle:

> Its purpose . . . is to free the subject from the limitations of his old ways of perceiving, thinking, and feeling. It would seem that only when the consciousness has been freed from these limitations is the unconscious free to release.

It is the world of common-sense empiricism which this level of psychedelic experience turns into a beam in the eye, dissolves and relativizes.

EVERYDAY UNHAPPINESS

2. *Recollective-Analytic*: The second level, which Masters and Houston refer to as the recollective-analytic, consisted of one's personal history, the psychodynamics explored by Sigmund Freud—important memories,

emotional problems, unresolved conflicts, and repressed material — all the forgotten detritus of Becker's hero in a lifetime on-the-make. Grof refers to such material as "COEX systems," specific constellations of memory consisting of condensed experiences and related fantasies from different periods of a life. Operating relatively autonomously, these subpersonalities collect events in a life around similar basic themes that carry an equivalent emotional charge (like helplessness, anxiety over self-esteem, guilt, deprivation, sex, or rejection). John Lilly's "hell" experience, my own experience of internal blockage, or while "coming down," of being dragged through life by circumstance rather than willingly leading a life, will serve as examples of this recollective level. But these are episodes; the thing to get at is the "core," the oldest event in the chain that forms the memory matrix and sets the prototypical pattern. (The rebirthing aspect I referred to is crucial to this "core" phenomenon, but I shall come to this in a moment since it is more complex.)

Psychedelic research, in fact, confirmed Freud's and Breuer's thesis that insufficient emotional and motor response during early traumatic episodes induces a jamming of affect that later supplies energy for neurotic symptoms. When psychedelic subjects relived and integrated these events into consciousness, the symptoms disappeared. As Grof put it, psychedelics provided "laboratory proof of the basic premises of psychoanalysis." But personal history is only part of our lives. Or, more accurately stated, the pressure in our small drama is likely to overwhelm, appear too much, because there's more going on there than meets the eye. No wonder we find it hard to settle down, are continually discontented even when otherwise so well adjusted to profitable functioning in the economy.

WOVEN INTO THE WOOF OF TIME

3. *Symbolic*: The subject had to "work through" the preceding second-level biographical material before penetrating to (or more accurately, being penetrated by) the third, *trans*personal level, which Masters and Houston called the "symbolic/mythic-ritual" stratum. The material surfacing here can be very weird and disconcerting until you realize that what is becoming manifest is your multiple cross-connections with time and history. Jungians refer to it as collective archetypal experience. Unfortunately, however, they incline to make it seem strictly intrapsychic, which it is not. On the contrary, the opening at this level stretches consciousness beyond the span of the individual lifetime; it shows us to be major intersections for the traffic patterns of the cosmos and history. Sociality is

extended beyond our immediate face-to-face encounters, to remote forebears and the generations that will come after. Par excellence, it seems to
me, the awareness of this stage creates a "historical being." And yes, the
traffic patterns may be strange. For instance, many psychedelic subjects
undergo experience that suggests previous incarnations.

Previous incarnation experiences form part of this thickening historical
awareness and give a retrospect, as it were, on highly charged areas of
harmony or conflict in the individual. The "law of karma" operating here
does not appear to respect genes or ethnic heredity. An American laborer
may find himself in India; a management consultant in an Ameroindian
torture rite. The point is not necessarily that one was a Sioux Indian in
some prior lifetime. At a minimum, the point is that, for one's unconscious being, what may be transpiring in an entirely "civilized," well-lit
insurance office today has the pattern of a flesh-rending torture rite.
Those trivial office battles are not so trivial; they have an aristocratic
genealogy, a certain grandeur. And if you can figure it out, instead of
being simply sado-masochistic, maybe there's a way to transfigure the
arrangement into a blessing. Some of these overdetermined experiences
can of course be very positive. One may suddenly recognize that current
friendships and loves involve one in patterns reminiscent of Rama and
Sita, or going back to Dante and Beatrice. The plot of one's small drama
thus does thicken, gathers richness. Other revelations will darken a small
plot ominously: bitterness at a crippling disease or an accidental death; or
again, murderous aggression arising from a master-slave relationship.
The latter, "bad karma" experiences keynote a fixation or unfinished
gestalt in a person's life that will repeat until worked through and resolved. Both master and slave, these experiences seem to suggest, must
emotionally and spiritually relive the oppressor-victim symbiosis in order
to transcend it—to forgive and be forgiven.

Equally disconcerting are encounters with the "nonhuman." For instance, Grof refers to remarkable identifications with animals, plants, the
microscopic world—what he calls "phylogenetic" experience. I experienced this phenomenon on one of my own trips, a spiraling free-fall into
what seemed like subatomic chaos. After that I metamorphosed into a
slippery paramecium (which I rather enjoyed), only to turn into a crusta-
cean (which I did not). The thing should be understood in terms of
ancient rites of orgy, a regenerative regression to protoplasmic unity, to
the chaos preceding all form. This chaos is the stuff of nothing less than
nuclear energy and nuclear bombs, which runs in our veins. It is all there,
subconscious. For speedy seconds, psychedelics could make the connec-

tion suddenly conscious—that you are that—waiting to explode or to be put to productive use.

These evolutionary memories can be very specific. Reports Grof (1976: 172):

> The individual can have, for example, an illuminating insight into what it feels like when a snake is hungry, when a turtle is sexually excited, when a hummingbird is feeding its young, or when a shark breathes through its gills. Subjects have reported that they have experienced the drive that sustains an eel or a sockeye salmon on its heroic journey against a river's flow, the sensations of a spider spinning his web, or the mysterious process of metamorphosis from an egg through a caterpillar and chrysalis to a butterfly.

One of Grof's subjects even identified with a large reptile extinct millions of years ago, and proceeded to act the part, right up to being sexually attracted by the scales on the head of a handsome male reptile opposite her (who thought he was a therapist!). The lady had been quite ignorant of the relevant paleontology, but when Grof later checked with a zoologist, it turned out that at least contemporary female reptiles do find colored areas on the male's head highly erotic.

What one encounters at this level, often of a grim, ordeal character, seems to be the "existentials" of suffering nature and humanity at large— but in detail. The effort of the fish to move to land as a reptile, of Neanderthals to make tools and speak, the sufferings of victims of war, natural disaster, and concentration camp, it began to dawn, are somehow woven into our bones. Hence the struggle, the pathos, of a lifetime are not individualistic but planetary.

In addition, this is the archetypal level of those highly overdetermined psychic constellations of Jung's collective unconscious, his inner company of "little people" who figure organic links to a wider ecology than the philistine or careerist can imagine. These connective patterns, often appearing in psychedelic sessions (as in dreams) as titans and gods, typically "live us" rather than we them; our personalities personify them rather than the reverse. Full of vinegar, grotesquerie, and above all energy, these animating figures from the shadow world surprised many a psychedelic tripper—as if the drug had released the denizens of Plato's cave along with the whole Olympian pantheon. That is, when they were not Tibetan wrathful deities, specters out of Dante's hell, or the spirits of Plains Indians. For the collective unconscious did not honor ethnic boundaries or background. As often as not, the subject had no prior conscious acquaintance with these mythological figures. But after their apparition, it was worth learning the stories. They were clues, condensed information in code—to entrapment, and to a way out of tight squeezes, impasses, blocks.

Just as frequently, subjects would find themselves reliving ancient historical events, the Black Plague, the Thirty Years' War, bull-leaping at Knossos, the building of the pyramids or a medieval cathedral, the westward march of Genghis Khan or the Battle of Hastings. Beneath the facade of the modern American ego, psychedelics revealed, these great thematics of myth and history were still being acted out as ever, their blind spots, tragic flaws, and occasionally, their visions of reconciliation repeated in contemporary idiom and dress. As most good novelists and poets know.

A sense of participating in primordial rites of passage was equally common. A twenty-seven-year-old bookkeeper, a high school graduate whose reading never extended beyond the daily newspapers, found himself, in sequence, a participant-observer at the rites of Dionysius, at a Greek drama, and then involved in the rites of Eleusis, Osiris, Attis and Adonis, and the Roman Catholic Mass. "Are you at Eleusis?" the guide asked the young man at one point. He nodded "yes," whereupon the guide suggested he enter the great hall and witness the rite. "I can't," he answered, "it is forbidden . . . I must confess . . . I must confess." Eleusinian initiates could seek enlightenment only after confessing, making reparation, and being absolved of their sin. Masters and Houston (1966: 219–20) commented as follows:

> The sequence began with the Dionysian rites, an early Greek form of the celebration of the vegetation god's struggle, death, and rebirth, linked to the yearly triumph of spring over winter. There next appeared the ancient Greek drama which had in fact evolved out of the Dionysian sacrificial ritual. (In the artistic transformation of this ritual in tragedy the audience no longer consumed the body and blood of the god, but instead experienced a spiritual and psychological ingestion of the body of the tragic hero, and in so doing, found a new community and solidarity within itself.) The sequence then found a sublimation in the Eleusinian Mystery, the great ritual of catharsis and spiritual rebirth which itself grew out of Dionysian rites. After this there followed a proliferation of many myths and rituals bearing upon the themes of the eternal return and culminating in the sophisticated expression of this theme in the Roman Catholic Mass. Finally, the subject himself identified with the god-thyrsus and evoked the mystic words of renewal. The entire sequence told the same story—the drama of redemption seen on all levels at

once; the redemption of the vegetation cycle and the redemption of the human consciousness—each seen through the prism of the tree-man dying to live and yielding, by death and resurrection, life to those of his cult or his cultivators.

Such psychedelic initiations, like their originals, frequently had a profoundly transformative effect upon the participant. They often delivered the person from a shallow adolescence, enhancing his or her capacity to identify with the sufferings of others—usually groups of others like famine victims or prisoners in Nazi extermination camps. At the same time, sessions often extended the mental horizon to include a sacred, multidimensional sense of reality that evoked a new sense of adult obligation and responsibility. Participants afterward often declared themselves "dead" to their old self and "reborn" into a bigger life-project.

HIEROPHANY

4. *Integral Religious*: In turn, the prior level of archetypal imagery served as a warm-up, a bridge to a fourth level of strictly mystical experience— to "Essence, Ground of Being," cosmic unity, communication with the "God beyond God," the Buddhist Void, the Hindu Brahman "without qualities," the unutterable Name of the Hebrews.

Is this simply crawling back to the protective womb, a regression to some predifferentiated oceanic condition? Psychedelic experience actually suggested a rather sharp distinction between two types of monism: the undifferentiated biocosmic seed state (nature mysticism) to which I referred above, and quite a different matter, merger with God-as-Mother. In either connection, however, it is important to note that psychedelic experience is very different from a narcotic fog. Though temporarily peripheralized, your normal waking consciousness stays with you, a kind of "double" or platform to leave or return to at will. Moreover, on "coming down," the trip is not shrouded but vividly recallable. Phenomenologically, the analogy is not with sleepiness or being "drugged," but rather the opposite, the awakening and alertness associated with advanced practitioners of meditation. If you reach the symbolic or religious level, there's another kind of sight available—probably what medieval Scholastics referred to as "interior senses." On two occasions myself, I recall weeping at suddenly "seeing through" the occluded faces of my sober sitters to the unspeakable beauty that lay behind, and in one case, actually shaking my companion by the shoulders to "wake up" to that beauty. At such junctures, you are "seeing" with new eyes in multiple directions, your own old empirical and blocked self as well as your real potential, the old face your friend wears and the "new" face he or she hides within. The thing is utterly unlike either seeing the world dejectedly through bitter realism or through rosy glasses which deceive. One sees both sides simultaneously — arguably with equal objectivity — and, for once, you don't have to pretend that the world is *not* a mess, or so benighted as to be unredeemable.

If one attained the religious dimension Masters and Houston speak of, then, it was not so much atomizing as both expanding and humbling at once. And one major criterion by which Masters and Houston judged the authenticity of a person's attaining this fourth level lay in the question of whether they absorbed a powerful new sense of *intentionality* that got them up and out — doing — when they returned to earth. In a later book, Houston (1982: 146) puts the integral religious experience this way:

> When experienced, it is felt as an entelechy — a kind of structuring, dynamic energy rising up from the depths and informing and energizing the other three levels. What this four-stage typology suggests is that this energizing fundamental reality [the entelechy] rises first to the third level and there assumes its universal paradigms, reinforcing and invigorating the mythic structures, and then, moving upward, energizes the personal, historical, and psychological structures of the second level, and finally intensifies the sensory levels by cleansing the doors of perception both within and without.

Hence the "flight *toward* reality."

UNDERSTANDING THE TRANSITION

At this point, Stanislav Grof's analysis offers helpful qualification. What seems to trigger such religious experiences, interestingly enough, is *not* so much the psychological dimension of the prior archetypal level, but specifically, the experience, whether biographical or not, of threats to *physical*, bodily survival. That is, it is the recollection of actual injuries, severe diseases, painful operations, incarceration and physical abuse, thickened by identification with archetypal historical examples of such trauma, that does three things. First, as Grof puts it, the shocks precipitate an ontological crisis. They crystallize basic values, worldly ambitions, cravings for status, power, wealth, and prestige — and remind one that all this, in the face of death, will have to be relinquished. So the individual must question the meaning of existence and its value. Secondly, it seems to be the confrontation with death that precipitates a descent to the aboriginal prototype in our lives for death's agony: *the event of biological birth*. And thus all the compulsion to be "born again," not simply biologically but psychically and spiritually. Thirdly, the symbolic, psychodramatic enactment of the stages of birth, according to Grof, if actually "worked through" and integrated, opens the way to spiritual experience.

The insight here, the result of observing thousands of therapeutic psychedelic sessions, is Grof's distinctive contribution to what the world looks like from the bottom up, or inside-out from "the foul rag-and-bone shop of the heart." A "descent into hell" or the underworld was common in psychedelic sessions, as it had been in shamanic vision quests, as it was in the literature of the world religions. In an aesthetically pleasant surrounding (usually with carefully chosen music), in the company of a trusted sitter or therapist, the agony began to assume a recognizable form. If the person could "go with" the claustrophobic damnation-experience rather than resisting it or collapsing, this phase seemed to give way to another, of titanic struggle against certain death and for life. It was as if, yes, as if the cervix were opening! And as if that pedestrian biological event were symbolic of how it is with the astonishing universe itself. Exactly.

Grof, who started out a convinced Freudian skeptic, began to map this process as an analogue of delivery in childbirth. To be sure, there was some evidence that at one level these experiences did involve reliving actual biological birth. At times, Grof reports, specific aspects of that event could be independently verified: nausea from a mother's hangover or smoking, abortion attempts, the hospital room setting, breech position, umbilical cord wrapped around the neck, the use of forceps, resuscitation efforts, and so forth. The process fell into definite stages, what Grof called "perinatal matrices." They are basically four: (1) interuterine union with the mother; (2) the onset of contractions and antagonism toward the mother; (3) synergistic struggle with the mother to pass through the birth canal; and (4) birth and separation from the mother. Grof calls these stages "matrices" because the crucial events and cross-references of a lifetime constellate, stack up around them (hence "perinatal," literally "around birth").

For the literal-minded, Grof's scheme offered an open invitation to perform reductionistic surgery, as Carl Sagan would be quick to do. Riddling enigmas were not to be tolerated. In an *Atlantic* essay titled "The Amniotic Universe" (later a chapter of *Broca's Brain*, 1978), he reacted to Grof's *Realms of the Unconscious* with biologistic lockjaw: all this perinatal memory suggested, Sagan argued, was that religious experience was a throwback to the womb.

But for Grof himself, each stage of the process was visibly multireferential, biological, psychological, and spiritual. To the subject and witness, the process constituted a figure, an enigma in the alchemical sense. That is, it was an expression of transcendence, an allusion of macrocosmic process immanent in microcosmic process. And the most conspicuous aspect of such enactments was not reference backward to the past, but the forward thrust, and the fact that the issues raised were the psychological and spiritual ones of current adult existence. Regardless of background or cultural programming, says Grof (1977: 276), spiritual experience manifested itself as an intrinsic part of human being at its core:

> The only way to resolve the existentialist dilemma . . . is transcendence. To escape this crisis, the individual has to find referential points that are beyond the narrow boundaries of his or her perishable physical shrine and the limitations of the individual life span. It seems that everybody who experientially reaches these levels develops convincing insights into the utmost relevance of the spiritual dimension in the universal scheme of things. Even positivistically oriented scientists, hard core materialists, sceptics and cynics, uncompromising atheists and antireligious crusaders . . . become interested in the spiritual quest after they confront these levels in themselves.

BIRTH TRAUMAS: PROTOTYPES AND ANTITYPES

What is "the oldest event that forms the matrix and sets the prototypical pattern" of a human life? Some pages back, I let that question drop in order to take it up here. Symbolic death-rebirth, I observed in chapter 1, constituted the core of rites of passage and their pilgrim analogues in patronomial feudal societies. Modern industrial culture has all but dropped such practice. If psychedelic experience is an index, however, the unconscious was not pleased, felt deprived. In one sense or another, all the reversions to the birth process I have previously touched on—the Laingian and my own, as instances—express the lure to be regenerated at a richer, deeper level, as consciousness-raisers might put it, in a wider ecology. That's what we have already observed going on in the way Masters and Houston schematize the process. Now we have Grof's way of handling the same material. "The similarity between birth and death," he remarks, "is the major philosophical issue that accompanies the perinatal experience."

What we confront in these four matrices is a bottom for a concatenation of memory, somehow racial and even phylogenetic, which cast shadow and light the length of a life, deciding the basic feel for existence and how we deal with issues like dependency, sexuality, physical pain and suffering, effort and aging, dying and death. The point is not that psychedelic subjects, much less shamans, devotees of Osiris, Buddha, or Christ, are literally crawling back into the womb to reenact biological birth — though reliving that as a prototypical event, prefiguring how we subsequently respond to ecstasy and agony in life, may be a part of it. The point is the symbolic (but very real) nature of the act, its antitypal relation to biological birth. It is a "second birth" at a spirited level, an event which follows the structure of biological birth but discloses it as figure and premonition. Our end is like our beginning, with a twist: our true beginning the end, death the end of our beginning.

AMNIOTIC HEAVEN

The key to getting through the hell and purgatory of the second and third stages of the death-rebirth rite which is life on earth rests, I think, with Grof's first matrix, the prototypical womb experience and its antitypes — other events and memories of nurturance, other subtle levels of being, which gather around it. That is, the "to be or not to be" question, Hamlet's question of how to ignite and get going, rests on the "good" or "bad womb" experience. If the actual embryonic state has been positive, generative of "basic trust" as Erik Erikson would phrase it, it serves as the memory matrix for recording all subsequent experiences of relaxation, freedom from need, of natural and aesthetic beauty, of harmonious episodes and relationships. The basic characteristics of the psychedelic good womb are transcendence of the subject-object dichotomy, strong positive affect, a special feeling of sacredness and pure being which exceeds time, space, and words. Aristotelian logic need not apply. Are you resting in your biological mother's womb again? Yes of course. And every other experience in one's life of being effortlessly held, fed, and bountifully loved is also present, implicated. But simultaneously you float in an archetypal pattern of energy, biocosmic unity *and* the Earth Mother of Hindus, the cosmic "Wisdom, mother of all the living" of the Jews, and the Virgin Mary, coredemptrix of humanity according to Catholics. The "oceanic ecstasy" here can be described as contentless and yet all-containing, a loss of ego and still an expansion of consciousness that includes the whole universe—that identifies with God-as-Mother. Typically, this kind of bliss opens up the gate to vast ancestral and phylogenetic connections reminiscent of totemistic cultures. Or again, one will feel simultaneously insignificant, humbled—and yet an enormous achievement, a cosmic prize display. One is back in oxymoron country, the land of paradox, where opposites coincide. Paradigmatically, this is the matrix of "eternal return" myths, returns to a golden age, to Eden.

On the other hand, problems can arise here if, biologically, one has had a "bad womb" marked by distress stemming from the mother's health or behavior during pregnancy—or a shocking early trauma which destroys or severely occludes basic trust, the kind of faith without which, as Luther knew, good works are impossible. Was I wanted? What's wrong with me? Am I any good? Does the center hold? Will anyone, anything hold me, cherish me? Can I accept all that I am, especially my embarrassingly earthy, death-bound body? Such self-doubt, particularly suspicion of the body, filled psychedelic sessions. One could understand why chronic psychosis or "borderline" personality problems, which typically reflect contamination at the nonverbal, somatic level, are the despair of psychoanalytic method. Grof's scheme suggests that if there is any healing for such cases, it would have to lie in the direction of radical regression, in somehow reenacting the embryonic experience in a positive (and very physical) way. As I understand it, this is in fact the direction contemporary therapy for schizophrenia and borderline cases has taken. One has to start over, and go very deep into the tissue with unconditional love.

HELL AND DAMNATION

It was rare that psychedelics surfaced this rebirthing process in neat chronological order. The psychological condition of the organism acted as the selector and scene-changer. The more typical first step was something like Lilly's "guided tour of hell," in effect the second matrix which simultaneously recalled the paradigmatic event just before or at the onset of birth contractions. The second matrix links with every comparable claustrophobic experience in one's life, and the lives of others back into the far reaches of time. It serves as the recording device for every conceivable experience of being helpless against destructive force: operations, diseases, injuries, imprisonments, extreme hungers, thirsts, sieges, traps of all kinds. At the same time, all those situations that mean abandonment, deprivation, emotional rejection, and constriction gather here. "Hell is other people." One has been cast out into the cold (Heidegger's *Geworfenheit*), or into destructive apocalypse.

John Lilly's experience is representative: the world feels "cardboard," dehumanized, run by demonic automata bereft of meaning. Taken together, it's the archetypal situation of cosmic engulfment, of the doldrums, and paranoid "no exit." A person characteristically feels the disproportionate guilt of the victim, of an oppressive absurdity from which there is no escape. Has anyone called me out of the Ur-Mother's womb, the prized firstborn? Do I have a chance? Grounds for hope? One can understand some of the figures that emerge here: Sisyphus, Ixion, Tantalus, Prometheus, the Furies, Dante's inferno, the world of Hieronymous Bosch, Francisco Goya's images of war, Gethsemane, the mystics' dark night. If stuck in this stage—and it is paradigmatically the "stuck" place—one's philosophy of life will tend to be caustic, cynical, or nihilistic.

But a word needs to be said about the god-figures which appear here and the subsequent stage. They are passports out of "no exit" stuck-places. Rather than taking such apparitions as exclusively intrapsychic phenomena, I suspect it is wiser to take them in the way primitive and archaic peoples do—as no less stubbornly objective than our nuclear energy. In fact, it *is* "psychized" nuclear energy premoderns are talking of with their fabulous powers and gods. Equivalently, they accurately acknowledge the titanic and godlike proportions of the energies that surround them and run in their nervous systems, their unruly instincts. In naming such titanic, destructive-creative forces—of sea, storm, sun, and earth—"gods," they enter into a participatory relationship with cosmic chance and necessity. In thus exorcising the terror of anonymous energy to which otherwise they would have to remain passively subject, they deliver themselves from those subtle possession states that our more sophisticated culture, with its ban on "personifying," suffers from but refuses to acknowledge. But in dialoging with anarchic cosmic energy, our less sophistic and wiser ancestors gained a measure of understanding and freedom. In this respect, Jung understood. "It is not a matter of indifference," he wrote, "whether one calls something a 'mania' or a 'god.' To serve a mania is detestable and undignified, but to serve a god is full of meaning" (in Hillman, 1975b: 14–15).

PURGATORY

But it gets worse, at least more intensely dramatic, with the third perinatal matrix, propulsion and struggle through the birth canal. The infant, remember, knows nothing of what lies ahead; so far as it is concerned, it is being forced to abandon the only life it has known for a whirling vortex that can only mean an utter unknown and death to all it has known. It is not true that no one experiences death until it happens. For everyone who comes into the world, biological birth was death's rehearsal and prefigured the analogues: failures, losses, plunges into the unknown of a lifetime. For the adult the death-rebirth struggle involves ego death. The third matrix represents the bottom line, as it were, of the crucial transition, noted above, to authentic spiritual experience. As a memory matrix, this stage connects with intense sensual and sexual experience; also with all wild, hazardous, risk-taking adventure (gymnastics, high diving, parachuting, stunt-man feats, and the bestiality of war).

Phenomenologically, the atmosphere here is of titanic, sado-masochistic struggle thick with orgiastic sexual and scatological imagery — all suspended before imminent catastrophe. Hence the elemental imagery: of earthquakes, volcanoes, hurricanes, tornadoes, electric storms, meteors, supernova explosions, thermonuclear energy; or of Pompeii, Herculaneum, Sodom and Gomorrah, Armageddon, H. G. Wells's "war of the worlds." Or of tyrants and bloody sacrifice: Nero, Genghis Khan, Pizarro, Cortes, Hitler, Stalin, Dracula, Caesare Borgia, the Inquisition, and Aztec hecatombs. The person typically oscillates between destructive/aggressive feelings (sadism) and severe inhibition, the will to shrink, burrow safely into the staging (masochism). He or she is Becker's hero, seized by the dilemmas of either standing out too much or too little from the framework of life. Such ambivalence, if accepted, is often followed by a streaming, purging fire that induces "volcanic ecstasy." In religious terms, this stage is not so much hell as purgatory. For the person is neither helpless nor hopeless, but actively involved in a kind of suffering which, potentially at least, has direction, goal. Above all, it exposes and dismantles the *causa sui* project.

DELIVERANCE/RESURRECTION

The resolution of this death-rebirth struggle comes in the phase related to the clinical stage of delivery, an apex of agony followed by enormous decompression and relief. Suffering hits "cosmic bottom," meets absolute failure and defeat. As a memory matrix, this bottoming out serves as a crossing point for all similar events of a lifetime and history. The secular symbols within this matrix involve images of the end of an exhausting war, the overthrow of a despot, or the disintegration of a totalitarian political regime. The scatological element arises with experiences of swallowing filth and excrement, crawling in cesspools and sewage systems, drowning in blood, phlegm, and urine. Willingly, at this stage, the god-self must descend into all the mess which it has spurned and denied in the vain quest to gain self-made immortality. Religiously, the symbols are frequently of sacrificial holocaust: immolation to a bloody goddess Kali or Moloch, being crushed in the dance of Shiva the Destroyer, sacrifice to the Aztec sun god Huitzilopochtli or the pre-Columbian serpent god Quetzalcoatl. Or the Egyptian Osiris's dismemberment by his evil brother Set. Or Orpheus torn apart.

Such images portend what a creaturely unconscious understands: the annihilation of experience at all levels, physical, emotional, intellectual, ethical, and even transcendental. But physical death, like biological birth, is but figure; the essential transaction at this stage, though the body is implicated, is a spiritual death-rebirth. The self-serving, death-avoiding ambitions of the self for status, wealth, prestige, and power must go, but so too must one's standard-brand images of remote, self-preserving deity, of a God who will not, cannot really participate in earthly suffering and death. The release entailed in ego death may trigger new images of God: as the taste of nectar, pure spiritual energy, a transcendental sun, atman-Brahman union, or union with the Great Mother Isis of the Egyptians. "Probably the most common symbolic framework for this experience," however, reports Grof (1976: 142),

> . . . is Christ's death on the cross and his resurrection, the mystery of Good Friday, and the unveiling of the Holy Grail. These are typically associated with intuitive insights into the fundamental significance and relevance of this symbolism as the deepest core of the Christian faith. . . . *The perinatal roots of Christianity* are clearly revealed by its simultaneous emphasis on agony and death (Christ on the cross), the perils of the newborn child (Herod's killing of the children), and on maternal care and protection (the Virgin Mary with little Jesus). [italics mine]

Apparently, it's just this renunciation, a complete letting-go, that springs the great decompression and expansion, and begets a sense of having been purged of all "garbage," guilt, and aggression—a risen body essentially social. For the releasing experience begets as well, says Grof (1976: 139), "an atmosphere . . . of liberation, redemption, salvation, love, and forgiveness. The individual . . . experiences overwhelming love for his fellow men, . . . solidarity, and friendship. Such feelings are accompanied by humility and a tendency to engage in service and charitable activities." The outgoing, activist thrust here deserves note. Deliverance, a resurrected body, evidently releases what early Christians called *charis*, the strictly theological strength of "charity." It is what I surmise the Buddhist tradition names "compassion."

Phenomenologically, however, there are remarkable parallels between this kind of awakening and the experience associated with the first interuterine matrix, whose spiritual counterpart is that of cosmic unity, and a sense of relaxation and serenity. Is the end the same as the beginning? Grof's own verdict, if I understand it, is that it is—full circle. Throughout his exposition of the life/history cycle in terms of perinatal matrices, the stress falls on relationships—unity, antagonism, synergy with, and separation from the mother/Great Mother. There is little accent on the archetype of mature sexual relations of husband-wife, or the role of father/Father in the process—as the one who calls forth "firstborns" from blissful darkness into moving daylight, who entrusts with worthy work, who passes on the blessing of generativity. In short, though Grof may perform an enormous service in focusing attention on the bedrock of "basic trust" in unity with a Mother-Universe, and that precisely because without such bonding we will be without reserves to overcome "separation anxiety," his scheme, it seems to me, needs to be amplified by something like Erik Erikson's schedule of psychosexual maturation—and perhaps more, some lessons from Western history. In Grof's cosmology, we are the spray of waves in a vast ocean of Being; ultimately, we return, are predestined for reabsorption in that ocean. What then has happened during the interim of a human life, the in-between time of human history and evolution? I am tempted to say, nothing; the meaning of time and history evaporates.

So let me repeat: Is the end-time identical with beginning-time? It is impossible to ask that question without smuggling in basic assumptions, a world view. If one asks it from the standpoint of the literalistic, common-sense empiricist mind, it's a question of returning to the worms and diffuse atomic energy. If, however, one poses it from Grof's figural, multireference perspective, you find yourself wrestling with the tensions between East and West, the larger plot of time and history, and the possible reconciliation of cultures organized around different central myths: God-the-Mother and God-the-Father. This latter formulation of the question, with its tensions, ironic double entendres, and implicit search for an answer, I think, lies at the heart of the consciousness movement. It's a specifically liminal, existential question, which only liminal states of consciousness can answer. What is the meaning of time?

RAIDING THE UNSPEAKABLE

From what we have just seen, it ought to come as no surprise that when LSD was officially proscribed in 1965, Robert Masters's and Jean Houston's next book was *Mind Games: The Guide to Inner Space* (1972). Not to be read so much as to be *done*, the book belongs to the genre of Ignatius of Loyola's *Spiritual Exercises* and Patanjali's yoga aphorisms. Wildly eclectic, it is a ritual manual and an encyclopedia of spiritual disciplines, much as if Mircea Eliade's *Patterns of Comparative Religion* were translated into a "how to" book. In four cycles of approximately fifteen separate rites arranged to explore the world at progressively deeper levels of psyche (as in the scheme above), this exercise book is intended to teach certain "inner space" skills to a group of not less than five and not more than eleven people working intensively, with a "guide" chosen from their number, over a period of roughly a year. The skills include enhanced sensory awareness, facility at self-initiated trance-induction (in the style of hypnologist Milton K. Erickson), tracking and interpreting dreams, deepened kinesthetic awareness and the capacity to think in images. The exercises also call for the use of music, chant, art, fasting, and solitary retreat. After several centuries of hostility toward monkish asceticism, Masters and Houston proposed to reintroduce Americans to the "methods and tools" George Leonard had gnomically referred to as opening a new frontier for human potential. It was a new kind of game they were asking people to play (Masters and Houston, 1972: 229):

> Those who play these games should become more imaginative, more creative, more fully able to gain access to their capacities and to use their capacities more productively.
>
> The players should achieve a new image of man as a creature of enormous and unfolding potentials. . . .
>
> The players should emerge from these games convinced that man is not something we know has to be surpassed; rather, man is still something to be realized — and is realizable.

Conspicuously, the promises (if not the hype) are easily confused with the logic of the hungry-ego, self-improving consumer mode of "human potential" identified with Dale Carnegie. On the other hand, an examination of the exercises themselves reveals a clear, transpersonal orientation to transform the self into an open channel—to let in the transmissions of a many-named God.

Meanwhile, at about the same time in the early seventies, Stanislav Grof moved into residence at Esalen—with a similar arsenal of modern and ancient nondrug methods for raiding the unspeakable. Jungian analysis, gentler forms of encounter, sensory isolation and overload, neo-Reichian approaches, gestalt, psychosynthesis, marathon sessions, shamanic rites, and various forms of meditation—all provided passports into old and new outer spaces. And, as might be expected, Grof introduced a range of techniques to facilitate working through and reconfiguring birth-death struggles. In this regard, his vision was, and is, specifically political in scope. For the third perinatal matrix, in his view, is the seed-bed of war and implacable social conflict. Was it mere coincidence that by the mid- and late seventies, people like cybernetics wizard Hans von Foerster, Daniel Ellsberg, Andrew Young, and California Assemblyman John Vasconcellos were passing through Esalen regularly? I do not know.

What I do know is that Esalen and what might be called the depth element of the consciousness revolution changed. Will Schutz, teaching what he most needed to learn himself, composed psychodramatic tests which dismantled the heroic self, either provoking an outbreak of bitter resistance or succeeding, leaving broken, often bloody human flesh hungry for healing which he did not readily supply. When Grof, partisan of the Great Mother of the Hindus, moved into residence, he brought some theoretical light which, among other things, suggested that brutal encounter methods were frequently playing into the hands of a one-upmanship macho hero. For some who needed assertiveness training (a problem particularly for those stuck in the second matrix configuration), that was entirely appropriate. For others it meant only reinforcing an all-American individualist pathology. All the while, from the outset, Esalen exhibited a tension at its core, between the nurturing Mother of Eden and brutal encounter methods. By the mid-seventies Mother had won out. How consciously, I don't know, but somehow it was decided that what the majority of guests required at that moment was a style more in keeping with the natural ambience of the place, the majestic but very feminine mountains undulating up behind, the sweeping calm Pacific on the horizon.

I think it began to dawn that for the most part those who came this way were already unhinged enough and did not need further assault. They were already too much like Joan Didion in her breakdown, perhaps too much the narcissists lamented by Christopher Lasch, who need a good dose of psychosomatic nurturance if they are ever to requisition the basic trust, the ego strength, which is deficient in them. What face God wears, manifests, at a specific historical moment—the Yin-Great Goddess or the Yang-One who summons out from Ur—may be a question of timing. What the hour, the *kairos*, called for, I am willing to believe, was the biocosmic unity of the womb-state, a ritual reenactment of the marriage of heaven and earth. Back, as it were, to ground zero, square one—where the bliss of a unified field could again be felt, experienced, taken in—for a new start. This does not require naively apotheosizing the "primitive" any more than it requires a literalistic redoing of biological birth. But it does require honoring the primitive and embryonic life as figures, as multiref-erence archetypes of primordial interconnection which human beings cannot do without. Our totemistic ancestors possessed a certain wisdom: whatever is "out there"—the life-in-death, death-in-life struggles of the animal world, the plant and microscopic systems that undergird human life—our ancient progenitors knew they were part of it, it party to them. The cosmic-womb experience retrieves such a sense of things, puts us profoundly at home in an astonishing world.

A LIMINAL QUESTION

The key liminal question: What is the myth which gets to the core of the human drama? Or is there one way of putting it? Either/or questions, I am still learning, are usually a mistake. But for the sake of creative tension in this book, if not to illustrate that tension in the consciousness movement as a whole, let me put such a question. The dominant mythos of the East, let me say, is that of eternal return, a pilgrim's regress to the time out of mind of primordial beginnings—union and synergy with the Mother. The dominant mythos of the West, on the othr hand, is that of a call from Ur, separation from the Mother, and the dying-rising god, a pilgrim's progress involving dismemberment. Both, as Northrop Frye would put it, represent central "myths of concern" around which whole cultures constellate—and they appear to pull in opposite directions. The one, as it were, is concerned with origins, inward-bound starts, the other with eschatons, outward-bound finishes, which gets to the core of planet earth, of our mattering? Must we choose—either/or fashion? Or can it be both/and? Grof's work raises such fundamental, and I have to say playful, questions.

It's time, then, to follow the movement, to head East, to eternal-return country—and enlarge the scope of the narrative line. It will show us the soul-archeology of Masters and Houston, and of Stanislav Grof outdoors, in fresh air.

PART II

Thickening the Plot:
India's Time Machine

Pilgrim's Regress:
The Eternal Return of
The Oral World

To come to know the mental universe of homo religiosus, *we must take into account . . . primitive societies. . . . But there is no other way of understanding a foreign mental universe than to place oneself* inside *it, at its very center, in order to progress from there to all the values that it possesses.*

Mircea Eliade

Events or processes transmitted through oral traditions tend to be recounted neither in terms of time past or time future in a lineal sense. Indeed most native languages have no such tenses to express this. They speak rather of a perennial reality of the now.

Joseph Epes Brown

> *The force that through the green fuse drives the flower*
> *Drives my green age; that blasts the roots of trees*
> *Is my destroyer.*
> . . . .
> *The force that drives the water through the rocks*
> *Drives my red blood; that drives the mouthing streams*
> *Turns mine to wax.*
> *And I am dumb to mouth unto my veins*
> *How at the mountain spring the same mouth sucks.*

Dylan Thomas

Psychedelic travel could spell problems. In the early sixties Allen Ginsberg found himself plagued by nightmarish flashbacks. He traveled to India to consult gurus. Telling a Tibetan lama of his troubles, the holy man told him simply, "If you see anything terrible, don't cling to it; if you see anything beautiful, don't cling to it." End of sermon. John of the Cross couldn't have said it better. Fascination with one's own toxicity is no help; but its opposite, "spiritual gluttony," may be even worse. Drugs were no substitute for the detachment that comes through patient spiritual discipline, an ideal not unlike the dispassionate scientific attitude.

So the consciousness movement headed East to learn. We were the other, penitential side of the missionary Peace Corps. We went, not to instruct and help out, but to find soul country, a way of life that still stood unbroken, intact. To the questing American, the pilgrimage to India, like Percival's initial encounter with the mysteriously materializing grail castle, was supposed to offer reentry into paradise. "Suppose," says the hero to himself in Walker Percy's *Love in the Ruins*, "man could reenter paradise, and live there both as man and spirit, whole and intact man-spirit, as solid flesh as a speckled trout, a dappled thing, yet aware of itself as a self." Not an easy task. For one thing because of what India herself is. Going there amounts to an extended exercise in Freudian anamnesis. It meant stepping back behind parental conflicts and the bourgeois mind's guilt over the exploited body of Newtonian nature—to a primitive world. In the Western imagination at least, India stood for the recollection of the "uncarved block" out of which both modern self and its world had been sculpted. It was a time machine. As such, it promised the discovery of a more fluid, dynamic world—not so much a settled world as a primeval chaos in process of formation, where "what is believed to be true is true or becomes true," where John Lilly's boundless "province of the mind" still grows and branches out, rooting like a vast banyan tree—the original tree of life sprung from the waters of life. In a sense, the journey there proposed to lift the ban on wishful thinking, to recover its legitimacy by rerooting it in the mother lode of earth's still vocal meanings, meanings which had become desiccated in the liberal West. In India, those meanings pulse with the force of a hierophany. The trip East, then, was to be a new kind of popular ethnography for the purpose of remembering one's own "original face before birth."

It was full of ironies, full of disappointments. The retention of self-awareness such as Walker Percy recommends for returns to paradise did not inhibit flower children; many travelers left their postcritical suspicions behind. Such self-awareness amounted to a privilege which the overwhelming mass of India's native inhabitants could only dream about. Moreover, for elite Hindus of the Advaita Vedanta sort, the irony was that phenomenal existence felt more like entry into hell rather than paradise. They are right. India had spiritual depth without action—hence great misery. Westerners, on the other hand, had plenty of action without depth—hence a different kind of misery. Visitors like myself found Hinduism's mystic castle occupied by one seriously maimed fisher-king, or rather by hordes of them. It was, perhaps, the most disillusioning trip of my life.

When Erik Erikson was living in India doing research for his book on Gandhi, he remarked that the "moving sea" of street life there affected him with "sensory and emotional seasickness." Precisely. I wonder now, if I were truly looking for that uncarved block, why I didn't go to the Outback of Australia, or to the Tasaday in the Philippines. India was a strange, misbegotten choice if you wanted primitive simplicity. For by no stretch of the imagination is India less complex than any Western industrialized nation. Like many an aristocratic society, it often does better than our egalitarian society at including diversity, both cultural and economic, within a shared moral order of mutual duties and claims. By comparison, U.S. culture looks straight-edged simple, like a graph in plane geometry. Whereas India's geometry is Riemannian, noneuclidean, nothing if not multidimensional. Parallel lines meet there—and I can understand why Hindus make good Einsteinian physicists. They've grown up on the principle of relativity, in a culture which rejoices in different space-time frames, and where almost every metamorphosis human consciousness has passed through in time—from Stone Age to present—has its living, breathing witnesses.

Yet, just because the concentric energies of the Great Chain of Being are always dancing, branching, splitting, dissolving, and metamorphizing before your eyes, India—where this tradition breathes from more than the pages of a book—reverses judgments, ends, even misbegotten choices. As I say, India is a time machine; time there is not linear, stretched out in causal sequence, but synchronic, the past spiraling about you like the winds of a cyclone. Is India timeless? No, on the contrary, what is so fulsome and bewildering about it is that all times are there, not merely in ruins but *alive*, breathing, and blowing you away from the narrow time-band of modernity. History is somehow cross-sectioned there. It has been ten years since I made the trip, and I am still absorbing, digesting all the conflicting impressions, feelings, images, and ideas it spawned. Which made it, after all, a wise choice, especially if you were educated, as I was, to imagine the human mind as "potentially all things."

HONEY ON A BLADE OF GRASS

In one of the more famous Hindu puranic fables, there's a parable made to order for the Westerner's first impression of India: a man is being chased by a tiger. He climbs out on the branch of a tree. The branch bends dangerously over a dried-out well. A pair of mice gnaw the branch on which he hangs. Below, he sees a mass of writhing snakes at the well bottom. But growing on the wall of the well is a blade of grass, on its tip a drop of honey. As the man falls to his death, he licks the honey.

And so it goes. The honey is easy to miss. In 1975, after finishing my Ph.D., academically armed but with an overlay of Alan Watts's mystification of the place in mind — and travel grant in hand — I took off to spend a summer in the Orient, mainly in India. I arrived in New Delhi just in time for the monsoon season, and for a constitutional crisis during which Mrs. Gandhi, convicted of election violations, declared a national emergency and suspended civil rights. I was also in time to witness a Jesuit friend's expulsion from the country for being an "outside agitator."

At home, I was a professor of religious studies; underneath, a seeker of something like a new start. I had come to India to examine its great religious tradition *in situ*, and of course it should be spoken of in the plural — for Hinduism is not one thing. But I wanted to see it outside the pages of a book, in its polymorphous flesh. My assumption was that every theology implies a sociology, and vice versa. This was not to be one of those blissful tours of the ashram circuit. What grabbed me was popular Hinduism, not the oracles of gurus but the extraordinary vitality of ordinary street vendors, waifs, village people — who cast me back to Western antiquity. Here antiquity was alive, still breathing a world I had only read of in books.

The national state of emergency, I learned, is permanent, and has been going on for millennia. In socioeconomic terms, the received Hindu wisdom insists that very little can be done about it. The "little" is of course significant. Though adjacent states frequently share no common linguistic roots (except for the colonial legacy of English), something like a nation, and at that a constitutional democracy, totters but survives. The year I was there, smallpox had been all but eliminated — against fierce resistance from local devotion to the god of smallpox. And Basil Mitchell, the World Health Organization official with whom I toured villages outside Allahabad, was full of praise for public health workers. In the interim, India has become self-sufficient in food production, even an exporter of grains — the only (chronic) problem being that masses of the land's destitute cannot afford the price. Is the position of women intolerable? Yes, the still revered *Law of Manu* demands that a "husband [and the mother-in-law] must be revered like a god," regardless of how faithless and cruel. But there is movement. The film that was packing crowds the summer I was there depicted a timid wife who hacked her dissolute husband and tyrannical mother-in-law to pieces.

Fissionable India resists generalizations. Aristotelian logic, at least outside the cities, need not apply for work; the principles of noncontradiction and identity gain no purchase there. One quickly learns that things teem with alter egos, both are and are not themselves at the same time.

As soon as you pass through the customs inspection, Indian thermodynamics hits you in the stomach. I mean turbulence, volcanic energy, *and* inertia, the entropic dissipation of energy. In the West, through literacy and the transfer of monastic discipline to the secular order (as Max Weber described it), we've learned to contain and harness this dual phenomenon, but in India energy and entropy seem to cancel each other out. Energy is diffused and dispersed, so uncontained and formless that like funny putty it offers no leverage, no Archimedean fulcrum, by which to move dream mountains into reality. Hence the dream quality of Indian life, its fearful lack of symmetry. At the same time, the ambient sense of pending, latent potency throbbing in the atmosphere, always about to let loose, to create or destroy no one knows for sure. One is thrown back, with the shock of recognition, to classical Greece, to Aristotle's negative feeling for the *apeiron*, the formless "infinite." But not just to that. For the agitated atmosphere of Indian space and teeming population carried another quality, a sense of urgent suspense, of pending heaviness. At the time I could not name it, but now this loaded atmosphere strikes me as closer to an ancient Hebrew sense of hidden boundlessness quite different from the Greek sensibility. It could as well be cast in Saint Paul's amplification, of a pregnant earth's groaning. In India, you palpably detect resonances of both Greek and Hebrew feelings for the world, somehow intermingled, the latter an undertone for the former.

"The great entirety," observed Heinrich Zimmer of India (in Lannoy, 1971: 327), "jolts from crisis to crisis: that is the precarious, hair-raising manner of self-transport by which it moves." From antiquity down to the present, however much the outward forms of the state have altered, very little, one begins to find, has changed out in the country where 70 percent of the population, still illiterate, lives on a subsistence economy. Plagued by power plays, riddled with conspiracy and intrigue, the government and its top-heavy bureaucracy stand remote, a thing apart. Caste is officially outlawed of course, but remains a virulent feature of the dog-eat-dog world of tribal competition for status and the diminishing returns of an economy built on scarcity. So newspaper reports in 1975 of unscrupulous moneylenders and a parasitic feudal rural ruling class expropriating the surplus wealth of the peasantry take on the aspect of *déjà vu*. In the fourth century B.C., the chancellor of the Indian King Chandragupt could write in the Machiavellian *Arthashastra*, "As for settling a land with the four varna [castes], the one where the lowest varna predominates is better because it will permit all sorts of exploitation." And so, as in the past, profiteers squander wealth in extravagant urban living and to a lesser extent in temple benefactions rather than invest in craft production or trade. Efforts to limit population growth, then, run hard against the peasant cunning for survival. For the majority, it's clear, the only available social security consists of bearing children who will work the fields and care for their elders in their old age.

My Jesuit friend, Rob Currie, had been counseling university students who were opposing the depredations of moneylenders on peasants in the northeast. His crime had been that he refused to accept the common culture of fatalism and cynicism, and that he was impatient and gave the appearance of taking the lid off Pandora's box. For that, the state government, with the collaboration of his religious superiors, issued him a quick exit visa.

GUILT AND EXPIATION

What I could see at the time, at one level at least, was that the honey of that prolifically diverse thing we call Hinduism smelled of opium in the Marxist sense. Hinduism was both: in the cities enervating, in the country-side empowering. On the positive side which I shall focus on in this chapter, Hinduism has innoculated generations of the poor against the dissipative, run-on catastrophes of feudal agrarian life; its staying power is anchored in its capacity to generate grandeur and an attitude of equanimity in the face of all the odds stacked against prosperity or what we would think of as opportunity. For peasant India's devotional *bhakti* religion raises food we know not of.

"What will come of my whole life?" asked Tolstoy in his *Confessions*. "Is there any meaning in my life that the inevitable death awaiting me does not destroy?" The central human fear, Ernest Becker reminded us shortly before his own death, is not so much death but *"extinction with insignificance."* Now this fear translates into the deadening weight, in great variety, of guilt, of that dumb, diffuse feeling of being blocked, limited, transcended, without knowing precisely why. The common lot: to feel thrown into an infinitely mysterious world that so exceeds our comprehension that we are either ahead of ourselves or behind, sticking out too much or in hiding — in either case, somehow in the wrong. The consequence is that much of our energy is spent making amends or justifying ourselves — according to Martin Luther's insight, a futile doing that undoes us. We never have sufficient space or enough time. We work against an undertow of deficiency and a suspicion that the universe which so transcends us expects much, but is either indifferent or hostile. Man, says Sartre, is a "futile passion."

Well then, if this is the problem, Hinduism, at least for the simple-hearted, redeems the time. Its failure to salvage much in the socioeconomic sphere is compensated for by its success in addressing the dread of meaninglessness. Could it be that the consciousness movement, which would later constitute the "me generation," moved East with a great burden of guilt? Underneath all the hoopla of self-realization, I suspect it is so. It was probably with that specific dread that most American grail questers went to India — curiously enough, in search of a rite of expiation that would grant a new start. That is, we needed to atone, make amends, and thus break the blockage so that the stream of creative energy could flow again. India was the country of mythic eternal return to such fresh beginnings; above all, in its radial way of thinking, in its monism, the land which had elaborated the complex variations of the first perinatal matrix.

Could unself-conscious India provide relief? That was doubtful. Most Westerners who traveled there had come too far from an orally structured consciousness, too far along the road of selfhood to turn back. If you were unself-conscious, however, capable of a "second naïevté," India might help. In addition, if you were Roman Catholic, raised on ritual Transubstantiation, that was a distinct advantage. "Beyond the desert of criticism," says philosopher Paul Ricoeur, "we wish to be called again" (1969: 349).

PENDING BACKGROUND

Let me pursue this theme with a few figures, memories. I spent several days walking about country villages. To do this is to feel your speedy, production-line, goal-oriented time palpably slow down, begin to creep, maybe even grind to a halt. So far as these people are concerned, you are a visitor from outer space, from another time. Conversely, from your perspective, theirs is another space and time, and they feel utterly strange to you. The moody texture of these villages is hard to name. But you feel as if you were inside an Einsteinian time-lapse film, your own reference system suddenly exposed for the collective fiction it is—and the villagers' too. And the shock of it quietly softens your focus, dissolves your hard edges, quickens and moves some part of you—in the stomach, I think—that had been asleep. These people, you say to yourself, don't stand out from the ground. One could not imagine Praxiteles sculpting them, free-standing figures of taut, articulated musculature. No, they're somehow occluded, masked, secreted, and (you hardly know what to make of it) *surrounded* by an atmosphere that is at once vast and confining. It includes, encloses even you, the alien visitor. It should be a pending summer thunderstorm, but it's nothing quite like that. It has a dream quality which desubstantiates what you can see with the eye. This voluminous storm, you think, has been waiting since time immemorial. You do not so much see it as hear it, smell it, sense it kinesthetically, like some kind of music in unfamiliar rhythms and harmony. Does it contain grief, despair, the sigh of the oppressed in a heartless world? Or some sort of quiet exuberance and play, a big-throated joke? Or is it endurance, of a people in exile? Or the patience of a woman listening to the heartbeat of her child in the womb? Do I hear the air weeping, a chorus out of Sophocles? It seemed all these things and more, a beating of birds' wings—inside a skin, inside a womb. The bigger, better part of things here, you begin to suspect, is hidden. There's an almost unbearable sense of latent suspense. But I do not wait with these people; I have my tourist's schedule to keep.

Some days later, I am standing outside a government guest house in Khajuraho, in the state of Madhya Pradesh in central India. I have come there to see the famous erotic temples commissioned by the Chandella kings of the ninth to eleventh centuries A.D. Ghostly beacons of an exuberant, expressive Hinduism scarcely evident in India today, every square foot of temple facade displays a sculpted jungle growth of smooth-skinned, sinuous bodies engaged in a great tantric dance. Tantra: the word means "to weave"—and what a weaving is here! The sensible world, these temples proclaim, emanates from the creative power of the triune Brahman-Vishnu-Shiva/Shakti. The figures of gods, animals, and humans exfoliate from a single divine seed hidden within each temple sanctuary. Simultaneously images of God, world, and the human body, the temples surge up, soaring weightlessly from their platforms, blooming at their pinnacles into lotus flowers. Atop the lotus, touching heaven in the image of the Himalaya, stands the *kalash*, the pot containing the nectar of immortality. This eroticism has nothing to do with Freud's release of libido, much less with stereotypical Hindu monism; nor is the vision at all reminiscent of Plato's transcendence of materiality. Earthly life, transformed by something like a Jacob's ladder over which there is constant coming and going between heaven and earth, is fully affirmed in all its polyphony and abundance. Earlier in the day, strolling through these temples, I had tried to take in the revelation. I had the feeling that here, once upon a time, the subcontinent's voice, caught for centuries in the throat, had burst into choral song—something out of Palestrina.

But now, standing on the porch of the guesthouse, I am looking across to a furrowed field where a farmer, hitched to bullock and plow, is hard at work. The plow is very primitive, a single blade; it was the same kind of instrument his forebears had used a thousand or more years before. Suddenly, I am hurled back to the middle ages, and very likely back even farther. I stand in the presence of a man without clocks, without books; he would not have understood my linear spatialization of time, my references to "back" and "forward." His world is synthesized orally and kinesthetically, not visually as mine is. His life is yoked to body rhythms, the pacing of heartbeat, pulse, and respiration—and to the rhythms of daylight and nighttime, monsoon and dry season, and to the corresponding religious rituals of planting and harvest and solstice. I have encountered others like him at close range, and have been touched by their *gravitas*. It is not sadness; no, the original Latin, the Roman sense of "gravity" takes its measure. Do not consider him simply a hapless victim of fate or malign overlords. Rather, understand him as someone whose personality is organized in the distinctive mode of an oral world. He is a ritualist, and thus a beneficiary—in spite of overlords and fickle weather—of a bounty of meaningfulness such as we might envy. The nearby temples may declare a renaissance which this peasant has never known. But they do not mock him.

The peasant's secret, I have come to think, consists of the residue—attenuated surely, but still accessible—of that primitive communalism which for us is all but shrouded in prehistory. The secret lies in the myth of eternal return.* The Indian peasant's time is only minimally sequen-

---

* When I use the term "myth," I am not using it in the popular sense, contrasting "myth" with "reality." I mean the expression in image-language and narrative form of some portion of the wisdom of the race which is at once psychological, sociological, and metaphysical. As I will employ the term, myth is not to be explained away as an expression of unconscious desire or fear (Freud), or of social solidarity (Durkheim); nor is it a mistaken description of nature (Max Müller).

tial; more fundamentally it is Parmenidean—it does not pass, remains inexhaustibly itself, inviting him to spiral inward to the time of aboriginal beginnings. That is, his world is rhythmed by the wisdom of primitive ritual and the enactment of mythic time—the perpetually fresh, "strong" time, as Eliade would put it, of great Vishnu the Preserver, who undergirds and replenishes existential, this-worldly time and makes it something more than drudgery or "watching the clock." This synchronic sense of God's time, penetrating human earth time and establishing an immediate communion where social roles and stratification no longer count, actually harkens back to a time before the earliest Hindu scripture, the Vedas. It is the legacy of a rich oral culture, in which the peasant still lives. Part of the genius of the peasant Hindu's charismatic *bhakti* faith, intensively developed in the middle ages (by seers like Ramanuja, d. 1137), is that it recovers for him this most ancient spiritual egalitarianism—from a "once and only time."

ETERNAL RETURN

There are two great periods of history, Ernest Becker thought, the first being the age of ritual, where each person possessed an intimate creative role as a priestly transformer of the powers of life. To a degree, the enactment of ancient ritual made each performer the prime distributor of power and the collaborative master of his or her own destiny. The second period, the machine age, dates from the time of the Renaissance and scientific revolution. And it has often meant the average person's despoliation, a transformation of an active being into a passive consumer—whose ritual functions have been preempted by the official mediators of church and state who redistribute power. There are problems with this rendition of things, surely. The primitive or peasant ritualist is hardly so inward or free, as we shall see, as this reading supposes. Yet there is some sobering truth to it.

Primitive agricultural societies have an acute awareness that they prosper on the freely given bounty of Mother Earth. As Marcel Mauss showed in *The Gift* ([1925] 1967), their life is immersed in debt and obligation to invisible cosmic powers. In order to maintain a balance for what they have received, and to keep the flow going, a return gift had to be made. Hence the rise of surplus economies; one had to have something extra to give to the gods. Primitive life, then, is embedded in a larger economy, a momentous commerce consisting of the exchange of gifts between the clan and its gods. The exchange relieves existential guilt. The sense of being trapped, blocked, unable to move without regard to an awesome vast totality can be freely acknowledged. The peasant who shares the primitive outlook moves daily into the oppressive hell made by feudal overlords, but unlike many a Western existentialist, he or she has an exit. The point of the sacrificial gift ritual, in this regard, is that it does not allow impoverished Hindus to wallow in helpless victimhood or self-hate, much less numb themselves with busy-ness to avoid these feelings. For the beginning time of the Vedic gods, paradigmatically "real" time, is accessible, and enormously life affirming. (Unlike the rather different attitude of some of the later Upanishads.) Ritual allows Hindus to offer their lives as gifts to something greater than landlords and bureaucracies. It constantly reminds even the most outwardly negligible that they stand at the center of things—from which all beginnings issue.

And daily, at the domestic hearth, these peasants invoke and perform this positioning of themselves. Take the simplest ritual act, the house-holder's construction of a Vedic altar to the fire god Agni—an image simultaneously of cosmos, home, and the worshiper's own psychophysical system. In performing this duty, he communes with the source of all being and thereby raises himself from the status of nonentity, moves from periphery on the wheel of life to the center. On the microcosmic scale of body and domestic hearth, he reproduces the aboriginal differentiation of homogeneous chaos into a qualitatively meaningful cosmos. Hence his body and his home are transubstantiated into orienting points of transit between heaven and earth, into temple mandalas. For as the peasant mixes his bricks, the water he uses is homologized with the primordial waters; the clay symbolizes earth; the lateral walls become the atmosphere; and the multiples of 360 bricks inside and out constitute the nights and days of the year.

At the same time, the domestic altar serves as image of the world, the macrocosm—not a passive spectator's image, please note, but a participant's image which unlooses energy. The rite is a microcosm of Prajapiti, the body of God veined in the elements. God's nervous system in earth extends itself, becomes manifest, in the worshiper's own body. The devotee's own backbone becomes *axis mundi*, his navel and heart the center of the world, his eyes sun and moon, his belly the earth womb, and his breathing continuous with exemplary cosmic weaving. In short, in his every nerve, fiber, and trivial action from sex down to eating and evacuation, the devotee knows himself as unlocking primordial flows of power. This applies equally to men and women. Both know themselves as active hierophanies of inaccessible Brahman in the energetic form of Shiva-Shakti. The utterly hidden God pulses as close as the artery in the throat—which by and large is what monism practically means among poor Hindus. "He who dwells in man and the sun is the same," says the *Taittiriya* Upanishad, "Wonder! Wonder! Wonder! I am food, I am food . . . I the food, devour the eater of food." The metaphorical kernel of this insight is not the act of the neonate's delivery, but dreamless, blissful sleep in a mother's spontaneously feeding womb. Yes, the remarkable thing is that Hinduism even in its most sophisticated forms, instills the consubstantiality with God-the-Mother that its peasant forms do. Epic heroes, then, like those of the *Mahabharata*, who provide models of "vital spirit" (or virtue) for the peasant, spin out into his struggles, and maintain his poise and equanimity in the midst of them, just because his identity is rooted in this primordial sense of cosmic connection.

As the great theoretician of sacred kingship, A. M. Hocart, put it, the identifications of ritual action constitute a preindustrial technique of manufacture, a way by which each individual retained the authority to transfer life and renovate the forms of nature without machinery—and without bureaucratic interference (see Becker, 1975: 6–25). However limited the opportunities for upward social mobility might be, when it came to essentials, each primitive had "the goods." Ritual is the physics, chemistry, medicine, and mechanics of a primitive society—and the peasant Hindu retains a piece of that action. The cycle of seasonal public festival and private *puja* devotions sets up a psychodramatic stage in which to humanize the fearsomely vast cosmos and, in turn, to spiritualize the earth.

External appearances notwithstanding, the real current of Hindu peasant life is hidden, a mystagogy in the everyday. The peasant does not live, as we tend to, in a homogeneous empty space; his roots lie elsewhere, in a realm untouched by moth and rust. He does not have to view himself as a victim of blind chance or the inexorable forces of history. He need not beg our pity. The honor of his life is not exclusively bound to feudal landlord, party, church, or state. In India as in medieval Europe, the lowly retain a participant's role in a cosmic liturgy of creation and regeneration. Life remains rooted in those streams of transpersonal energy we know of as the archetypal world. This means that the commonest episodes and actions of life—birth, puberty, marriage, tilling a field—are assimilated to the paradigmatic real, the activity of God in shaping, sustaining, and renewing the world. No passive spectator, the poorest

Hindu cooperates in the biggest event. The divine bloodline still flows in his veins.

If it's existential meaning you want, rooted not merely in will power or positive law but in the numinosity of earth and stars, popular Hinduism provides it. The secret of its staying power against a succession of foreign invasions over the centuries—Persian, Moslem, and British—one might say, is that though Hindu society presents the mask of being one of the most hierarchically organized in history, its inner core is precisely the opposite of a monolithic, hierarchical command structure. The truth is that inwardly, spiritually, the genius of this culture—and what so fiercely resists centralizing modernization in it—is that its ontological power, the power of being rather than having, is so remarkably *decentralized*.

How can we be at once astonished by the world, G. K. Chesterton asked, and at home in it? The Hindu peasant has an answer. The feudal aristocracy may have its pound of flesh, but deep down the peasant's life is hidden in God. Agreed, so hidden in God that the peasant's capacity to participate actively in what we call the modern world is virtually nil. It's unsettling. I do not know the name of the peasant I remember so vividly; he is anonymous. Surely part of what is so pending and suspenseful in an Indian village is just this: that as these nonliterate peasants ask entry and active voice in a well-lit technological society, the passage is tediously slow, like a dreamer who cannot wake up. Meanwhile the momentum of untapped energy heaves up, explodes at times of ethnic conflict, and diffuses, is dissipated into the heavy atmosphere. The land breathes deeply, but it's a sleep of prisoners.

ORALITY VERSUS LITERACY

Ernest Becker drew a sharp dichotomy between ritual consciousness and disenchanted modern consciousness that tends to feed on technology and an accumulation of material possessions. That is fine as far as it goes. But if we want to understand the East and its appeal to Western grail questers, another distinction, more fundamental still, is between an oral and a literate sensibility. The contrast is often misidentified as one between an oriental and a Western outlook. I will contend in what follows that this supposedly oriental approach to reality was the dominant mind-set of the West up until the Renaissance and the invention of linear type—precisely because the West too was largely an oral culture until then. In reaching to the East, the consciousness movement implicitly sought to recover a mentality that had once been Western as well. Modern consciousness is no more Western than Eastern; rather, it is more accurately characterized as the typographic mind.

The "primitive" Hindu identifies, not with *things*, but with essences behind them, the invisible animating forces, the insides of nature. The modern, literate individual has trouble following suit; in contrast, he or she typically feels distanced from nature, and may well doubt whether nature has any insides. The difference is cultural, a question of the dominant media in use in an oral society as opposed to those in use in a literate one. In a sense, the medium *is* the message. A typographic culture has its attention focused very differently from that of a culture paying primary attention to sound. Of course for thousands of years the two modes of perception have overlapped. Nonetheless, a world primarily synthesized by sound and a world primarily synthesized by type and sight will each appear distinct, if not utterly incongruous. Superficially, it will often seem that the oral world is uniquely sacred, religious; whereas the literate world is incorrigibly secular and hostile to religion. Though understandable, this is the mistake Mircea Eliade seems to promote. And I want to avoid it.

Literacy is by now so ingrained in the Western psyche that we take for granted its effect on the way we perceive the world. Yet by any criteria, when pictographic script and eventually the Semitic and Greek phonetic alphabets were first introduced (from ca. 3500 to 700 B.C.), they turned the world inside out. Before writing and reading, there was no such thing as a historical consciousness or, for that matter, anything approaching the modern sense of an objective world. More, before Gutenberg invented movable type in the fifteenth century A.D., what we call the observable world lacked the stability needed for the systematic study we associate with modern science. It was mainly type and the typographic mind that brought this fixative quality to the run-on contingencies of the temporal world. Aristotle (384–322 B.C.), couldn't imagine it; still dwelling in the fluid, chancy world of an oral sensibility, he was sure no strict science of nature was conceivable. Around 500 B.C., both Heraclitus in the West and the Buddha in the East stress the impermanence and transitoriness of the sensible world. You can't step into the same river twice, says the one; let go, there's nothing solid to cling to, says the other. The sovereignty of irreversible flux and rampant unpredictability are precisely what we should expect, for acute awareness of the fleeting present is one of the marks of a dominantly oral culture. Sound any word of more than one syllable, any sentence, and almost before you've begun the vocalization, the initial sound vanishes. Unlike a textual or typographic world, a world synthesized by sound doesn't linger long. Oral cultures are consequently tradition bound and tight knit, precisely in order to defend against the evident mutability of all things.

What's at stake in understanding the revolution of literacy? The answer is that these two technological innovations, writing and print, transposed sound into visual representation, either a pictogram or a letter. And this metamorphosis radically altered our habits of feeling and thinking about the world, indeed, changed our personality structures and the quality of our anxieties (Parry, 1971; Havelock, 1963, 1982; Ong, 1977, 1981, 1982). Before these technological revolutions, the world and its people were very different. But why do I say "before"? Nearly one quarter of the planet's current population (including 27 percent of the U.S. population) is still oral. More, all the classics of Western literature up until the Renaissance, most notably the religious ones, reflect to one degree or another an oral sensibility, and are nearly incomprehensible without understanding that sensibility in its own right. Understanding an oral approach to reality, then, represents a link to the so-called underdeveloped world and to our own historical roots and narrative line. To put it another way: to understand an oral culture in its own right—and the roots of our own culture there—represents a crucial step in remembering ourselves in the Augustinian sense. In this light, the consciousness movement's "primitivism" takes on a deeper meaning, begins to seem less romantic, even wise—or will be wise provided that a proper respect for oral intelligence doesn't turn into a mindless admiration that forgets the point of literate intelligence.

BREAKING THE MAGIC CIRCLE / FIXING THE WORLD

The script culture generated by the alphabet enabled our ancestors to arrest the visual field, to tame and stop the temporal flux, thereby fixing objects for inspection and analysis independent of movement. Where an oral sensorium highlights temporal evanescence (sound doesn't stay but moves), the emerging script culture highlighted space and sight, even converted time itself into the spatial categories of "lengths" and "distances." Unlike oral peoples, writers and readers can psychologically get off the molten, dissolving flood of time and sound. Script provided a

102 • THICKENING THE PLOT

means of quieting things down, enabled people to decathect from the
immediately symphonic and multidimensional flux from which, in a
sound economy, there is no escape. A "dry" soul, remarked Heraclitus in
the sixth century B.C., is preferable to a "wet" one. What did he mean?

A strictly oral personality tends to have very permeable boundaries, to
be diffuse, more corporate than individual; intense personal loyalties,
communal obligations, and the formulas of proverbial tribal wisdom
hold things together as members of one another. The mind is essentially
collective and at the same time exhibits a random looseness, a kind of
patchwork, free-associating quality that will pick up anything. There's
almost no concept of an individual human mind mediating and storing
the experience of a self. Aspects we would attribute to the self are diffused
atmospherically, attributed to the cosmic powers. From the little we can
reconstruct of Stone Age culture, still evident in an early manuscript era,
what we call subjectivity is virtually monopolized, under stress, by a
superindividual field of force—what the Greeks called *moira* or "fate,"
the Hindus *prana* or "spirit-breath," the Melanesians *mana*, and the Hebrews *ruach*, again meaning "spirit-breath." This magical flow, the seminal stuff of later cosmic Logos doctrines in the Mediterranean world,
stopped over indifferently in all beings, gods, the tribe, words—linking
them all in a common energy. It is anthropologist Lucien Lévy-Bruhl's
"participation mystique"; everything participates in everything else.

The modern reader of ancient epic segments of the Old Testament is
likely to be troubled by it. Yahweh dominates the action. Even when it
comes to the *herem*, the merciless command to King Saul to annihilate
noncombatant women and children. But the heroic Arjuna of the *Bhagavad Gita* stands in a similar fix. So do Achilles and Hector in the *Iliad*.
Like modern street gang members, all these epic heroes raise vituperative
verbal abuse of their enemies to an art form; and slogans, alliteration,
and parallelisms rather than cool analysis dominate speech patterns. But
these young and ancient heroes are captives of their enthusiasms and
rages, mere puppet automotons caught in the throes of starkly opposed
virtue and vice. The battle is typically rehearsed in rituals which divide
the tribe into partisans of light against those of darkness. As such, this
oral world is essentially polemical, fiercely combative, and violent. Lacking ego defenses and having little internal order in his imaginal life, the
oral person is often overwhelmed by an unpredictable world and goes
beserk, runs amok. Instead of withdrawing into a dreamworld as the
overanxious literate person does, the externalized oral person takes his
terrors into the marketplace. As Walter J. Ong (1981: 134) sums it up,

the individual here "is psychologically faced outward . . . and, under
duress, he directs his anxieties and hostilities outward toward the material
world around him and chiefly . . . to his fellow man." The strictly oral
personality tends to oscillate uncontrollably between moments of manic
excitement and moments of depressive inertia.

Comparatively speaking, a literate world is far more pacific, cool, and
dry—indeed perhaps so dry as to appear, say, to a D. H. Lawrence, as
emasculated (Ong, 1981: 192–262). Reading and writing drew people
inward. Reading focused attention on detail: rather than holistic gestalt;
writing required agonizing, solitary circumspection, demanded precision,
the ability to supply context, inflexion, tone, and a place for the reader in
the text. In effect, the writer had to take in the world, find interior space
for it as the oral person had not. In this way literacy carved out an interior
volume, a genuine subjectivity, and provided a way to order the high
incidence of confused excitement that is both the glory and affliction of
an oral consciousness. In short, literacy occasioned the development of
individual soul. That is, it disengaged collective personalities from the
tribe and from that unfree sympathetic continuum they enjoyed (and
suffered) with nature. At the same time, this withdrawal inward distanced
them psychologically from the surrounding world and tribal tradition,
both of which could finally, in the age of classic Greece, be taken neutral-
ly, objectively, reflectively—on the model of some kind of spatial dia-
gram.

What happened was a revolution in central cultural image, the kind of
metaphorical shift that always marks major historical turning points. The
central image of an oral world is an encompassing circle, a round table,
or a *mandala* symbol. Literacy froze the world "in front" of our forebears
as if it were a text. For the first time the immobility of a text (as it were, a
still shot) got them psychologically "above" the flux so that the aggregate,
holistic meanings and slogans of an oral culture could be taken apart,
piece by piece. That is, Socratic analysis became possible. Instead of the
synchronic, simultaneous invasion of events from all sides that an oral
sensibility has to contend with, the early scribes and accountants could
"go back over" (reflect) things and seemingly reverse time, which you can
do if you have a fixed text in hand rather than tumultuous and processive
immediacy all around. Yet even when the cool Aristotle begins to philoso-
phize about the world, it is largely the oral world of Homer's common
sense that he thinks *about*. Thus he does not think of his own mind as
separate but rather as participating in a single cosmic mind (the *nous
poiētikos*) which penetrates all things (Cornford, 1957). Initially, that is,

though the subject is polarized with an objective world, it is understood as being an integral part of that world, and as such a prime receiver of and responder to all the action of a cosmos understood as animate and minded.

THE DEATH OF THE MUSE AND THE GENESIS OF THE OUTSIDER

The textualization of the cosmos progressively devitalized it. A text is artificial; it provides a pretense, actually distorts a fluid, energetic, constantly perishing erotic world. But by means of the illusion texts created, our ancestors learned to take things diachronically, sequentially, that is, causally—like the lineally spaced words on a page. Linear nature as we know it, in contrast to nature experienced synchronically, began to appear. (Etymologically, the terms "subject" and "object"—lying under and lying over-against, respectively—betray this visual, spatial bias.) Gradually, as reading and writing turned the psyche outside in, and as printing turned disengagement into a mass movement, the holistic universe was broken up, metamorphosed; its tune and tone were changed from personal to impersonal. Over two millennia, an erotic, vocal objective world was silenced and deadened; it became something primarily to be sighted and captured in an abstract idea by a solitary thinker. Alone in his study, this solitary thinker (Descartes, 1596–1650, is a good example) will often be tempted to ignore social context (as the oral thinker cannot). Further, when the cognitive enterprise is conceived visually, it tends to be conceived as a one-way process rather than the reciprocal interaction understood by an oral culture. This one-way process produces the active, insular modern self, facing a natural world that is essentially inert and ready to be acted upon. That is, progressively pacified, the natural world invited dissection and active control. Eventually, by the seventeenth century, the world assumed that illusory permanence of words cast in lead—a passive world fit for Isaac Newton's (1642–1727) laws of motion; and shortly, fit for the industrial revolution.

Where the subject had once been conceived primarily as a receiver of action by the whole, it was now converted into the sole agent. We could compose and recompose our worlds in the way a printer can, thus reshaping consciousness which gets its self-understanding from its relation to its objects. This was the great Enlightenment idea. The catch, as the nineteenth-century romantic movement recognized, was that a leaden natural world is no longer very inspiring. Over the long term, literacy dried things out to excess; it led to a great divorce in sensibility that divided mind from matter, and nature from spirit. How so?

The relevant epistemological principle is that habits of thought are inseparable from the structure of experience—that the way we think controls the data which appear. I have said that literacy highlights space, but space conceived visually and therefore at a distance. That is, the sight dominance fostered by literacy puts us *outside* of things, working with light diffused over surfaces. Even depth perception, from an eye's viewpoint, will be a matter of relationships among light and shadow on surfaces. Carried to extremes, as sight dominance was by the eighteenth century, you get Imannuel Kant's classic disjunction between surface "phenomena," which the natural sciences investigate, and "noumena," the sphere of traditional metaphysics and religious insight. Having disengaged words from the nonverbal activity which they always have in an oral world, Kant saw that empirical science was confined to the surfaces of things. His conclusion, therefore, is a tautology. By definition the interior natures of things and the metaphysical order of the whole cannot possibly be known. And the inevitable tendency of this habit of thinking is that gradually the universe, which the oral sensibility acknowledges as qualitatively differentiated and mysterious, is reduced to one dimension and thus to neat, trim, and univocal meanings. And since human beings take their own measure from the kind of objective world they situate themselves within, the outcome is that you get something like Herbert Marcuse's (1964) spiritually hollow "one-dimensional man." (Carried to absurdity in the nineteenth and our own century, the logic of impenetrable surfaces brings you to disputes over whether the external world exists or arguments about how one knows other minds.)

As I've noted above, the oral person has deficits, but such people are in less danger than we are of losing connection with their biological roots. The oral thinker is a speaker, invariably something of a rhetorician whose meanings include vocal inflection, facial expression, and the entire situational context. Thinking is done in a voluble, vital social context, for instance, citing proverb and parable to the assembly if a tribal elder, or walking about the noisy agora if an Aristotle, or involved in a public disputation if a Thomas Aquinas. These people can hardly ever forget that in speaking a living language which they did not make up themselves, they enter a larger social tradition, a history. In such a context, moreover, one naturally lives close to the unconscious, that is, close to one's biological roots in nature which constitute a wellspring of spontaneous response to the unexpected. It's often a scandal to the modern reader of the New Testament to learn that the Evangelists put words into Jesus' mouth; but despite an oral person's reverence for the formulaic spoken word over what may be seen with one's own eyes, such a person has no difficulty revising his or her oracles to fit the immediate and perhaps novel situation. An oral person tends to live in the eternal now, and within the leeway of proverb and holistic parable will spontaneously readjust and go with the flow. Does this sound like an Esalen workshop?

Kant, on the other hand, exhibits the temper of his time in wanting to settle things definitively by the driest, putatively universal reason. He does his thinking in private and alone, where it is easy to forget social and historical context. His original model, the first individual, is the hermit monk meditating in his cell; more proximately, however, the model is Descartes who already by the seventeenth century shares the assumption of a then small elite that the material world is a machine void of any interior. But before that machine metaphor captivated the age's habit of thought, the massive impact of the printed-book metaphor had prepared the way. The universe, said the medieval Scholastics, was like a text with many levels of meaning, surface (or literal), moral, and mystical. The point is that a text and a fortiori a textualized material world are essentially silent and depersonalized. Exit the Muse; she faded as a vital force in Western culture in the seventeenth century, as John Donne and others lamented at the time.

With the exit of the Muse from popular consciousness, the ontological weight once attributed to the exercises of poets, and subsequently to the exercises of contemplative monks, began to erode from popular consciousness as well. Here lies a crucial difference between the modern, relatively prosaic literate world and that of a still oral culture. For in the latter, the most striking thing is that the natural world is not silent but vocal. The Muse of the poet and storyteller form the teaching heart of such cultures. Down to the late fifth century B.C., Eric Havelock (1982: 27–28, 184–207) points out, the education of the Greek leisured class consisted of poetic performance wedded to dance, playing instruments, and melody. The practice was known as *mousikē*. That's right, the "glory that was Greece" derived from a highly sophisticated but nonliterate musical education. Writing and reading at the time were confined to craftsmen and traders. An oral-audial culture's encyclopedia of information, its proverbial wisdom and even its technology, is stored in the epic memories of its poets and bards.

Beginning as a creative polarization of subject and object, then, disengagement from flux led to thorough disjuncture, fragmentation, and that dissociation of mind and body, soul and nature, nature and God which have been the plague of industrialized societies. For besides the evident gains for human agency in this evolution (also called secularization), there were severe losses, conspicuously a remoteness from actuality and a consequent loss of intensity, which help one to understand that implicitly the consciousness movement was seeking to reinform dead letters with the energy, the holism, and inspiration of primal oral cultures.

ACOUSTIC SPACE

How was it, one might ask, that Saint Paul insisted that the letter kills and that "faith comes through hearing" (Rom. 10:7)? Or that it is in the unknown God "that we live, and move, and exist" (Acts 17:28)? Again, how was it that Aristotle and Aquinas were so sure, and we are not, that they could discern an animate, moral, intelligible order immanent in the cosmos and its manifold creatures? The answer to these questions, I think, is that Aristotle, Paul, and Aquinas, though literate and obviously capable of thinking analytically and for themselves, were still open, in however diminished a way, to the kind of sensorium which my Hindu peasant exhibits. Though separated chronologically, these people dwell in an acoustic universe modeled on the paradigmatic experience of hearing sounds which declare and manifest intelligible, communicating presences behind the scenes. The issue is crucial for a correct apprehension of divine otherness and nonintrusive intimacy in both Western and Eastern traditions.

Acoustic space is the key. It explains how it is that in a predominatly oral culture, people naturally find themselves standing in the middle of the action, surrounded, enclosed in a vast, unfathomable sphere that is more mental than physical, more like a nurturing embryo than like the stage upon which Shakespearean actors stride about. Subject and object are not starkly opposed, as they tend to be in late literate culture, but readily interpenetrate. For in an oral world, speakers do not understand themselves as spectators but as participants in wind, water, fire, and earth. Hence their curious epistemology: "For it is with earth that we see earth," proclaimed Empedocles, "and water with water; by air we see bright air, by fire destroying fire." Over time, at least in the West, this fifth-century B.C. axiom gets attenuated by the psychologically distancing impact of Greek conceptual thinking and Jewish iconoclasm toward pantheistic paganism. Yet Aquinas, for instance, still presupposes a continuity, that what informs external nature is of the same nature as himself. In different ways, human beings and the natural world represent the same thing.

Again the contrast: literacy situates a person frontally before a visual field, thus in only one direction and outside the object. When from this perspective we think of contacting the interior of another, the tendency is to invade the other's space, to cut it open. No such intrusion is required in the case of sound. It communicates inner structure through barriers, and penetrates the hearer without interference. Sounds, as in knocking on hollow wood, tell what's happening *within* what is other. Or they inform the way voices do, or the way in which music tells of the structure of the instrument on which it is played. And it is precisely this resonance with the interior meanings of the sources of sound that makes an oral world at least vaguely animist. The cosmos communicates and registers with that peculiar depth quality that we associate with the symbolic. There is always more in such a world than meets the eye because sight (and the other senses) are attached to a world fundamentally interpreted by hearing. "The heavens *declare* the glory of God" (Ps. 18:19). The language itself shows that seeing here is subordinate to a hearer's way of synthesizing things. But this oral synthesis, I maintain, is the key to the Hebrew's sense of the presence of God—as it is in the Orient. When it comes to imagining the divine action, these qualities of sound are crucial. The point is that when oral cultures thought of communion with the divine, they used the metaphor of sound and speech to convey the subtlety and swiftness of the thing. But there was more to it, namely, the participatory element.

It has to do with the involving, implicating character of acoustic space. Sound registers simultaneously from many directions at once. It is not spread out in front of us, as visual space is, but diffused around us, enveloping and simultaneously establishing us at a core of sensation and action. Auditory space is centripetal, automatically centering, and thus a stabilizer against flux. Hearing is the primary unifying sense. Sound joins auditors and simultaneously positions them at the center of a circumambient, mysterious field of force. Taking account of this sense of location, one can understand, perhaps, how the Hindu peasant and indeed all oral cultures have much less difficulty than we do in imagining themselves unfolding from the center of the world, the navel of the universe. As Walter J. Ong (1981: 164) expresses it,

> Being in the midst of reality is curiously personalizing in implication, since
> acoustic space is in a way a vast interior in the center of which the listener

finds himself together with his interlocutors. The oral-aural individual thus does not find himself simply situated somewhere in neutral, visual-tactile, Copernican space. Rather, he finds himself in a kind of vast interiority.

Now insofar as an economy of sound both centers and registers interiority, it is the natural vehicle of the sacred, of mystery made manifest. The sense of divine transcendence and immediate intimacy or immanence, which to a visual sensorium often appear incompatible, fit together. The thing is no different in principle from how presences are felt in a busy household or at the village market. Simultaneously, one is both inside and outside such sounds, incorporated as a participant in the distinctive energy of their sources. Unless, of course, the sound is tuned out. But if it is not, one's foot or hand may be set beating, tapping in unison with the rhythm. The other senses, taste, smell, touch, and kinesthesia are annexed to the primacy of sound—and set moving.

THE KINETICS OF SOUND

Oral culture is "verbomotor." Exclusively oral peoples are utterly unaware of anything like a neutral world. Primeval chaos is never far distant, nor is death. Everything they are familiar with is committed, noisy, and passionate for good or ill. There is little time-out for speculation or for interest in classification or definition for their own sake. The primary concern is existential, situational, and practical rather than abstract. Lacking reference works to "look things up in" or reading and writing skills to freeze events, people live close to the lived experience of other actors, human and nonhuman. The latent powers of other beings, their good or bad vibrations, their *energeia* as the Greeks would call it—all of it registers. For there's no possibility that sound space can be impersonal like Newtonian space. Every sound will carry its own force and resonance, its distinctive texture, rhythm, volume, and tone. When you hear the sound of stampeding elephants, the rush of water, or the war cry of an enemy on the attack, you know something is occurring. Understandably, the relics of oral tradition come down to us in lively narrative, epic form whose larger-than-life, typecast heroes and heroines call a loosely organized, easily distracted oral mind to attention.

None of this is to say that oral peoples are not acute visual observers; only that dynamic sound dominates their apprehension of things. This is why such a world is primarily experienced as event and movement rather than as static things "out there." And why sounds in general and words in particular are felt as powerful and dynamic actions to which a practical, canny response of action is required in return. In our modern literate context, substantive nouns dominate precisely because the permanence of movable type has been transferred to the world it inscribes. And of course because our typographic minds enabled a technological revolution which creates the illusion of stability. With an oral culture it is otherwise. Verbs, words of action, multiply over nouns.

But given the essential dynamism of a sound world as it issues reports of the spirit world—in thunder, flood, wind, and voice—one can understand why the word of God, or its analogues in the religions of the world, is a word of power. The Hebrew sense is paradigmatic. "My word, is it not like fire, a hammer that shatters the rocks?" (Jer. 23:29) Or again, "The sea saw it and fled: Jordan was driven back. The mountains skipped like rams" (Ps. 114: 3–4). "For behold, the Lord is coming forth . . . . And the mountains shall melt under him, and the valleys will be cleft like wax before fire" (Mic. 1:3–4). Literacy would refocus attention, as it were, on God as noun or permanent substance, but the oral sense echoes strongly in these texts, of God as energetic action, as verb—as it does in the Hindu Vedas which date from the second millennium B.C.

A SYMBOLIC UNIVERSE, A PRIVILEGED MOMENT

It is not, as Max Müller in the nineteenth century (and other linguists since) have thought, that our oral ancestors were deliberately making metaphors, seeing the same neutral nature we do and then personifying it. Homer spoke Greek with minimal aid from static substantives. Where we would use nouns, he used verbs: Speaking of a bearded elder, he says that the man "foamed"; of a youth, that he "blossoms." In both cases, he links human appearance to the action of seas and plants—to *processes*. This is not conscious metaphor. That is, it is not a deliberate invention by which a poet expands consciousness by joining two different levels of being, taking a dead "thing" and turning it into a living image or figure. Strictly speaking, metaphor in this sense, indeed nonfigurative meaning as such, comes very late, only after common sense, influenced by the scientific revolution, began to view the material world as all surface, with no interior. In contrast, Homer was talking straight, spontaneously, expressing what it was like to live in a psychically charged material world where there can be no outer meaning that is not at the same time an

expression of an invisible, inward, and immaterial meaning that surrounds one (acoustically). He knows nothing of the psychological distance which allows us to draw distinctions between word and thing,
subject and object, mind and matter. He is simply inspired. The unities,
the organic relations he finds between sea, plant, and human purposes
are directly perceived, given; the reverberating, moving echo of living
nature in his anything but individual being. To imagine Homer's universe
as he experienced it, we might well think of the ordinary mode of perception as being what we would call extrasensory.

Our habits of thought expose us to an entirely different sense of the
"literal." For us, physical meaning tends to come first, a bedrock from
which symbolic meaning may thereafter be conjured with some effort.
Not so for Homer's mentality. What we would call symbolic or figural
talk was his bedrock; it expressed the first note of togetherness which
struck the ancients about the sensed world. To put it in visualist terms,
the physical was translucent, full of omens, signatures, and kinetic presences which *showed through* the physical and often overwhelmed the
perceiver. To sense things in this way was to feel (and think) oneself
informed by the energies of one's environment, and this sense of participation and organic kinship did not require, as it does with us, any artifice
or effort to imagine. The poet's art at this stage of human development is
manic, literally an enthusiasm or a state of possession by the gods or
Muses. The mind, insofar as one could call it one's own at all, was felt to
be the precipitate of cosmic mind, like rain condensing from air.

It is out of this atmosphere of enveloping vitality, remarkably oriental
in its texture, rather than any kind of depersonalized space, that we can
see the far more sophisticated Heraclitus, Socrates, Plato, and Aristotle
doing their thinking. The bright Greek sky, the divine *aither*, energizes
them, sparks their thinking; is that *with* which they think. Again, as if
they were freshly awakened from sleep in the bosom of Brahman, they
attempt to do self-consciously what the purely oral personality did randomly, spontaneously and compulsively: to attune their minds to a vast,
pending background, a cosmic interior out of which their minds, indeed
all things, unfold or materialize. From Saint Augustine on, through Giordano Bruno in the Renaissance, this sense of finite mind as somehow a
contraction of infinite, cosmic mind is the dominant one. And I would
say that despite its retirement from modern mind and brain theory, it still
makes a good deal more sense than imagining mind to have originated
from dead matter.

"It is *we*," writes Owen Barfield ([1944] 1966: 54), "who are trying to get back, *via* poetic metaphor, into the kind of consciousness which the Greek had and could express quite naturally and straightforwardly." This is to say that, normally, the first step in a dissociated Western mind's recovery of the plot line—the *mysterium tremendum* ingredient in our story—requires an aesthetic turn, an awakening to the many-leveled, symbolic nature of any and all events. This doesn't come naturally to us any longer, as it once did to our manic and mantic peasant ancestors. We have noses and eyes for prosaic detail, fine points, and particularity: the legacy of the precise descriptions of seventeenth century naturalists, Dutch painters, and later scrutinizers of subjectivity like Stendhal and Proust— all made possible by Gutenberg's revolution and unthinkable without it. The precision and discrimination are invaluable, indispensable for the kind of world we live in. But with such habits of mind and in such a precision-instrument world, the tendency is to lose the larger narrative, and one's conscious participation in the bigger story.

Oddly enough in a chapter on India, the latter absence of mind may bring us back to Thomas Aquinas—who was no less coolly objective than we are, and no less a master of distinctions, exact and exacting. With one big difference—he stood at the threshold between an oral and literate culture, at a kind of privileged moment in history not unlike the first millennium B.C. Accordingly, he still dwelt in a wrap-around psychophysical space similar to the synchronic eternal now in which a Hindu peasant is immersed. No longer spontaneously, but with the aid of his contemplative disciplines—meditative reading (*lectio divina*), the celebration of the sacred "hours" and liturgy, and prayer—Aquinas situates himself in the middle of the action, as the receiver of an absconded, anonymous Presence that informs all things as the soul informs the body. Like the Hindus, he finds the great Anonymous polynomous, veined and many-named in the complex events of earth—which are therefore full of messages and portents. Every event is to be probed and plumbed, as a scriptural text is, for its exact letter (what precisely happened) and more deeply, for the moral of the story and what it may foretell, its prefigural (or mystical) bearings for the ultimate end of human existence, reunion with God. For this kind of mind, this kind of world, the decisive question is the investigative reporter's and editorialist's call to penetrating judgment, "What lies at the bottom of this mystery story?" "What is the point, the forward thrust of the unfinished tale?"

Since he was writing in a highly abstract code, decipherable for the most part only to fellow academicians, it's easy to forget that Aquinas was the disciple of Albert the Great, a fellow Dominican friar and an alchemist; both men would have been used to imagining their spiritual disciplines as a way of transforming base physical energies into spirited gold. Letting go of preconceptions, learning to dwell nakedly in the no-thing of a virgin soul, earth's frustration, madness, and inertia are to be contained, raised like bread and wine at Mass, to be quickened, transfigured by the breath of immanent Spirit and a "word of the heart" (see Barfield, 1965: 84–91). In the Aristotelian code of the time, physical nature is incomplete, sheer potency, until united with a human being's act of imagination, naming, and judgment. No longer perceived in the animist mode, the physical world can mean anything or nothing, and now waits to be ensouled by us, made over, and finally inspirited insofar as we, its receivers, are flushed with Spirit. This is the big, overarching drama within which medieval Christian Aristotelianism implicated the meaning of a human lifetime.

In Aquinas's view, then, the fate of nature cannot be isolated from the destiny of the problematic individual. The two issues, nature's inertia, frustration, and madness and the parallel phenomena among the proto-middle class, are continuous events, parts of a single narrative line. "Everything is received according to the mode of the receiver," went the Scholastic axiom, and the corollary was that if we, the receivers of nature's potencies, are full of ourselves, dull-witted or asleep, nature loses her bid to be transfigured. Hence the big stakes involved in Europe's burgeoning new secular cities of the thirteenth century. Somewhat obliquely it has to be admitted, Aquinas and his confreres are addressing veterans of the Crusades and the new breed of independent women left at home to manage the estate. The audience on the university benches, in other words, was composed of the *homo faber* prototypes of bourgeois civilization and a feminism to come—and already their bad humors, excesses of choleric bile, phlegmatic inertia, sanguinary utopianism, and melancholy were making the streets of Paris and Bologna unsafe. (Does it sound familiar?)

For a medieval investigative reporter like Aquinas, this grim news-event would have been seen as symptomatic of a collective blood crisis. Those restless urbanites lacked soul food, palpable *arterial* blood, the carrier of "vital spirit." Medieval common sense sharply distinguished (but did not separate) the latter from *venous* blood which only nourishes the body (Barfield, 1965: 79–83). Glossing this anatomy lesson a bit, we might say that as soon as literate selves ceased to experience nature animistically, to that extent nature would stop feeding them with vital spirit. By carving out a self from the uncarved block—and distancing the self from nature—

inevitably literacy and the technology it made possible severed our umbilical connection to Mother Nature and, correlatively, her main artery through us to spirit. The freeloading phase of the story was over—and hence the bad blood, the ill humor, and distemper. If you felt driven to respond in kind to sterile, milkless Mother Nature, you resorted to exploitation and rape of the environment. Lacking technological wonders, the medievals couldn't do that so effectively as modern industrialists would. Instead they had Crusades, Guelph-Ghibelline feuds, and mass banditry. Either way, the prototypes of modern carelessness, the fall-out of an abandonment complex, riddle medieval society.

If you did not wish to respond in kind or tell that heedless story, however, you would have to discover something like the contemplative monk or anchoress in you, an Aquinas, better perhaps a Meister Eckhart or a Julian of Norwich. The tradition they represented spoke of the human cognition-action process as not only an exact replica of how the Creator-Father breathes forth his creative Word of Love, but as an active participation in that inner divine economy. The contemplative's intuitive, essentially poetic intelligence becomes all things and is to transfigure them, thus assimilating itself to the ongoing creation *ex nihilo*. The idea was to experience oneself in rapport with the Creator's movement toward the eschaton, the "new heaven and earth" of Saint John's Apocalypse. The thrust of the story was to get with the movement and give it voice.

Could it be that consciousness-raisers were reappropriating from Eastern gurus what had once been a commonplace, at least in certain circles, in the West as well? I think so. Speaking for myself, I had no conscious intention of rediscovering in India what Aquinas had meant by participation or natural law. But when I walked around those Hindu villages and felt the momentous suspense there, something a good deal more like silent music than law, I encountered something awesome, a place to return to and depart from with reverence. Was it the uncarved block or simply the earth heaving like a pregnant woman? Whatever it was, it bound me to those occluded villagers who did not have the freedom of movement that I did. They symbolized frustrated nature herself, still rich but fallen into the grasping hands of an alien, less-than-human world; despite my mobility, I could recognize myself as nursed by that soil and part of her unfinished story. Aquinas must have felt this too, and something more. He stood poised at a threshold, a new kind of liminality, between an oral world still immersed in peasant fatalism and an exploding literate, urban economy filled with landless people wanting an active role in a great project. If what I have suggested in the above survey of the differences between an oral and literate culture is true, then we should expect, I think, that this in-between time is a particularly privileged moment in history.

FIVE

Pilgrim's Egress:
A Genesis of Consciousness Story

The whole structure of heroism is, and always was, a damned lie.

James Joyce

For nothing can be sole or whole
That has not been rent.

W. B. Yeats

You should not find the boundaries of soul, even by traveling along every path: so deep a measure does it have.

Heraclitus

Can the history of Hinduism reveal something of the course of Western religious history, and vice versa? Can we see these two historical trajectories in parallel, the better to observe where they join and diverge? The central myth of Hinduism, if not exactly of the East, is synchronic, an eternal return to Ur-conditions. Its strength, if you will, is feminine. In contrast, the Western mythos rises from Abraham's summons from Ur (and Odysseus's wandering far from home); the fundamental orientation is therefore diachronic (or temporal), directed forward toward a messianic age, a new dawn. Its strength is masculine. Do these great myths really pull in opposite directions, as I suggested at the end of chapter 3, or can they be understood as complementary and mutually enriching? To some extent, I think a marriage can be arranged. In this chapter I want to weave the broken trajectory of us grail-questing Westerners into a privileged moment, the storied rise of the great religions of the first millennium B.C.

PROGRESS?

Philologists like Owen Barfield tend to notice something that Social Darwinists with their one-way myth of progress often miss. History, conspicuously Western history, tells the story of a progressive detachment of individuals from the majestic solidarities of nonliterate culture which are alive with a pervasive sense of the sacred. It is a tale of growing self-consciousness and freedom. Other combining factors than literacy were involved—developments in agriculture, trade, political organization, transportation, and family organization—but the spread of writing and reading has probably been the principal factor that shook us loose from immersion in the participatory oral world. This liberation has had its dark side. For it has been won at the cost of uprooting us from nature and that plenum of meaning manifest in primitive myth. With detachment from a numinous nature, *pari passu*, goes an impoverishment of language. That is, the further back you go in time the more richly figural or poetic does language become. Conversely, over the course of time, with the notable exceptions of a Dante, Shakespeare, or James Joyce, language has grown more abstract, precise, and prosaic. In this sense, history recapitulates the shrinking, partializing process that Ernest Becker saw taking place in the ontogeny of the individual self. To avoid the too muchness of the *mysterium tremendum* of the universe, whole cultures have contracted, shrunk, and atomized into prison-egos. This is one pole of modernization, its fragmentation into a polyverse; the other pole being the "global village" consciousness brought on by electronic communication. At this point the critical issue is whether we can discover, as an alternative to the unfree, primitive mode of being, a free mode of participation in a *uni*verse.

Young or old, Westerners are torn. The modern, literate mind distances itself, abstracts, dissects, tends to flatten the earth into one-dimensional, univocal meanings. As Carl Jung (1965: 245) said,

> The predominately rationalistic European finds much that is human alien to him, and he prides himself on this without realizing that his rationality is won at the expense of his vitality, and that the primitive part of his personality is consequently condemned to a more or less underground existence.

Example: I traveled through India with one American university student who had been greatly attracted—intellectually—by his Hindu studies at home. But when confronted by Hindus devoutly engaged in public devotions, he found himself a visibly saddened bystander unable to join in.

Early on in his life, he had been taught an old-fashioned American contempt for ritual, and for any sign of loss of control. Habituated to distancing himself, he was an outsider looking "at" things—as if they were inert words on a page. In a way, the young man had been put "out of it" by the long term effects of the Semitic invention of the alphabet around 1500 B.C. The great trouble lay in a disproportion (one I could easily identify with), his exaggerated sense of *separation*.

THE CLOSED WESTERN BOOK

There were reasons, varied and complex, why the consciousness movement could not turn to its own Western tradition. The route had to be indirect, by way of detour East. People were coming from different places. Some of the consciousness movers, disillusioned by one-dimensional secularism, sought to recover a sense of the sacred. Others were fleeing the moralism and biblical literalism of Christian fundamentalism. Still others, more like myself perhaps, were seeking an experiential path that would liberate them from a more sophisticated form of the letter that kills. Any way you cut it, however, the biblical tradition stood in a bad way in our culture in the sixties and seventies. But that hadn't happened yesterday. The danger of a sensorium based on script and, even more, typography has been to forget the artifice involved in letters, and thus to homologize the fluent world with a fixed text. The long-term effect of this amnesia has been that the reader's soul fossilizes. To put it in Heraclitus's terms, the fiery, transforming divine ether freezes; it had been thought to fill the bright sky, to surround and penetrate the world. The soul breathed it in, and accordingly was felt to be a boundless abyss, as measureless as the sky. But what has happened by the time of the Western Renaissance and Gutenberg's printing revolution? As the Rhineland mystics and John of the Cross testify, the *mysterium tremendum* was no longer to be found above, in bright heaven, but in a "dark night of the soul"—as if Plato's parable of the cave, in the course of fifteen hundred years, had to be reversed. Or, as if the sages of the Upanishads, in their search for the *atman*, already had the secret cure for literate minds.

"Print," observes Walter Ong (1982: 132), "encourages a sense of closure, a sense that what is found in a text has been finalized, has reached a state of completion." In particular, Ong has in mind the tradition of the perfect textbook promoted by people like Peter Ramus (1515–72). The idea was to exhaustively define each and every subject matter as a self-contained unit dichotomized from everything else. From the sixteenth century on, this became an educational ideal, infiltrating both the sciences (as "settled fact" rather than pursuit of the unknown) and the humanities, including theology. And it meant the establishment of a centralizing, fixed point of view graven, as it were, in stone. As such, it served as a prescription for various forms of lethal orthodoxy or thought control.

To make a textbook of the Bible in this way virtually closes it. To be sure, even by medieval times the Bible's stories had already been diluted by allegorizing interpretation, so that their dense, essentially metaphorical meanings were subordinated to a putatively higher conceptual language of doctrine and moral maxim. Commentary and theoretical interpretation, both necessary, had begun to supplant rather than elucidate the action reports of the thing itself. Thus the Bible's closeness to the performance world of a spoken language, its narratives of event and theophany, its flood of genealogies, prescriptions, parables, fictions, proverbs, psalms, liturgical texts, and quickening pericopes (i.e., brief encounters with a spirit-filled person who exceeds normal categorization) increasingly come to stand as proof texts for the abstract propositions of a legalistic mind. The Bible had originally been heard as a recital of God's deeds in time, or of various wrestling matches between the Jews and God. It had to be sung in a liturgical context, that is, in a performative context, wherein a living community remembers itself as a living body of believers in whom the God of its ancestors is present and active *now*. Made a textbook, the Bible was desiccated. It came to signify dogma, and dogma itself, once understood as a concatenation of great symbols signifying the ever-present possibility of joining heaven and earth, degenerated into dogmatism.

There was a further problem, however, which applied in particular to those reared in a secularist environment but which also affected those coming from conventional church and synagogue backgrounds. The fact seemed to be, so far as I could tell, that for the most part, whenever grail questers heard the name of the Judeo-Christian God invoked, they imagined Isaac Newton's remote cosmic clockmaker—who stands apart from the world he has made, wound up, and left with a rule book rather than a presence. The problem is the *otherness* of this kind of deity, the implication that, in Karl Barth's metaphor, he intersects with this world only in the most tangential way. My impression is that this conception of deity had all but preempted the orthodox Judeo-Christian notion, which, as I pointed out in the last chapter, had originally employed the metaphor of

nonintrusive sound as fundamental. In any case, the Newtonian conception combines with the idea of vacuous matter, incapable of mediating
anything more than itself, to situate human beings as alien incongruities
between machinelike nature and its "totally other," divine legislator. The
consciousness movement had no stomach for this arrangement—which
was bound to aggravate any lingering pathology of a tyrannically punish-
ing superego. Revolting against a persistent deism, which it mistakenly
took as representing Judaism and Christianity, movement tracts continued throughout the sixties and seventies to betray hostility toward the
Western religious tradition. And even into the eighties. Writes movement
theoretician Ken Wilber (1981: 3):

> Jehovah—God of Abraham and Father of Jesus—is an ontological Other,
> separated from us by nature, forever. In this view, there is not just a tempo-
> rary line between man and God, but an immovable boundary and barrier.
> God and man are forever divorced. . . . Thus the only contact between God
> and man is by airmail. . . . Across this gaping abyss God and man touch by
> rumor, not by absolute union (samadhi).

But an orally oriented culture would have understood the meaning of the
"Word became flesh" in a corporate, inclusive sense (as Saint Paul's "one
body" image indicates). Wilber apparently never read, at least never understood, my old catechism text which defined sanctifying grace as a
direct participation in the nature of God.

Instead, Wilber caricatures the Western God-world relation by assimilating it to mechanistic notions of contact interactions between sighted
objects (like billiard balls) in space. What happens when things are imagined this way? Well, the whole notion of God's otherness is coarsened, in
effect conceived materialistically. At sharp odds with even a residually
oral culture's sense of a uterinelike circulatory system, the contact image
sets up an unbridgeable gulf which will inevitably make the language,
say, of the Gospel of John, look like a series of category mistakes, mixing
apples with oranges (how can God be man or the human partake of
God?). It's as if God's existence runs parallel to our own like another
solar system. In which case, in order to inhabit our space, such a God will
have to interfere from outside, feloniously breaking and entering into our
world. Understandably, absentee landlords of this type are unwelcome.
As Enlightenment thinkers like Immanuel Kant and Ludwig Feuerbach
well saw, admitting this meddling deity spells heteronomy, self-alienation.

But it does little good to protest that an intrusive, absentee landlord notion misconceives Judeo-Christian orthodoxy. It may well be that seventeenth-century notions of causality are neither exhaustive nor particularly applicable when imagining how beings and Being are internally related. But the issue of understanding how we live, breathe, and move in God is more than a conceptual one. So far as the consciousness movement was concerned, about the only Western theological voice they could hear that seemed to weave God back into earth's elements after his Newtonian estrangement in outer space, was that of Teilhard de Chardin. Alone among spokespeople of Christian orthodoxy, Teilhard's earthy spirituality attracted New Age types. Which is not insignificant, for the theological tradition Teilhard represents reanimated both medieval Celtic nature-mysticism (of the ninth-century John Scotus Erigena, for one) and the outlook of Gregory of Nyssa (A.D. 330–79), which departed from the Platonic tradition in giving time and history spiritual significance.

FORETIME PRESENT

On the surface, the rubric "I feel, therefore I am," and its attendant quest for rhapsodic intensity, looked like another bout of American antiintellectualism. Underneath that appearance lay a search for wisdom, for another kind of intelligence to inform the neutered calculations of utilitarian reason. The project, as I said before in relation to Esalen, was to put Apollonian fact and Dionysian value, reason and "reasons of the heart," together. It was not farfetched to imagine that an oral culture like India's might hold the secret to a richer soulfulness. For in many ways the time frame of its esoteric guru circuit remains that of the fifth or fourth century B.C. That is, the living masters of the classic tradition of the Upanishads, Vedantic schools, and the great religious epics are virtual contemporaries of Socrates and Second Isaiah. At their best, India's contemporary gurus still live at that privileged moment, at the cutting edge of creative tension between the horizon of orality and the reflexivity of the literate mind which once generated the West's golden, axial period of philosophy and religion. To sit at a guru's feet, then, might mean a transfusion of vital spirit. Surprisingly, it might recover memory of our own plot line by giving access to the common bloodline of the old oral cosmology.

What you have to understand is that if you had possibly lost the thread of the Western narrative line, and went to the springs of Western culture, say, to Athens or Jerusalem, to regain the pulse of our odyssey, you'd find only the archeological ruins of our beginnings. In contemporary Greece and Israel you would not taste the sensibility, the felt imaginal world, of Plato or Aristotle, Moses or Jesus. Only the geography remains as mute testimony, a vacant lot for their words in a book; otherwise you meet only mirror reflections, with slight variations, of your own modern mind. But the original context, the real background of the speakers and enactors of our mythos, where would you find them? My suggestion is India. In India's very strangeness the sensorium, the worlds of our cultural progenitors are alive, if not exactly well. India presents a cross section of the tree of life, of the history of consciousness, all there, present and unaccounted for, at once. The very strangeness defamiliarizes the familiar, wakes you to the heart of your own culture and to what is going on still in our unconscious life.

MULTIPLE TIME

Intergenerational continuity and a larger sense of historical genealogy do not come easy to the individualistic habit of thought. Modern Western culture typically locates itself as standing, eyes open, *before* the future; whereas the past is perceived as *behind* us and out of sight. To that extent the past is hidden and our relation to it problematic. Søren Kierkegaard is representative in this respect. The main preoccupation of his authorship, you might say, was how to become contemporaneous with Christ, to experience firsthand the Logos becoming flesh in the here and now. Had Kierkegaard shared the mentality of an ancient Hebrew, the problem would not have been so severe. The Hebrew mind-set virtually reverses the modern stance. The past was "foretime," represented *in the present* by the emblematic deeds of one's forebears—their cultivated fields, works of art, cultural and political constructions. For those who come *after* to speak of what these precursors did, lived, or suffered was equivalently to enter empathetically into a shared journey, a common project to join and carry on. What was therefore hidden from the Hebrew is not the past but the future, the "aftertime" of one's descendents who may or may not remember who they are. I am not at all sure, but this perspective on time may account for one of the prime meanings attributed by scholars to the ancient Hebrew term for "word" (*dabhar*) as "to be behind and drive forward" or "to drive forward that which is behind" (Boman, 1960: 65).

To visit India retrieves this Hebrew sense of what is open and hidden in time. It is not a matter of an H. G. Wells time machine, taking yourself out of the present by rolling back the clock. No, India is foretime *in the present*. The past is not shelved in a library but is represented all about you in the flesh. The whole thing calls you to attention, oddly enough in a country so timeless, to the mystery of time. All our time frames, all our multiple ontologies are alive there. Historically, an outline (Zaehner, 1962) of the development of Hinduism, with a rough indication of the Western parallels, might go something like this:

I. Formation of Classic Hinduism:

1. *Rig Veda Period* (2000–500 B.C.): The Rig Veda *samhita* hymns, sacrificial texts, and "forest treatises" out of which develop the largely panentheistic (God-in-world) Upanishads, which interiorize the sacrificial ritual of the Vedas, emphasize the eternal moral law (*sanatana dharma*), reincarnation (the law of *karma*), and spiritual rebirth (*moksha*) from cyclic reincarnation. The Upanishadic era parallels Plato and Second Isaiah in the West.

2. *Sutra Period* (500–200 B.C.): Confrontation with Buddhism's moderate and Jainism's severe asceticism and both their challenges to caste, sacrifice, and the classic Hindu stages of life (student, householder, recluse, and renunciant of the world [*sanyasin*]). The extreme inwardness and other-worldliness of the Upanishads, a religion for the elite, assumes a trinitarian form (Brahman-creator, incarnate Vishnu, immanent Shiva-Shakti). In some respects parallel to the era of postexilic Jewish monotheism and wisdom literature.

3. *Epic period* (200 B.C.–A.D. 300): Minor Upanishads, earliest purana legends, philosophical sutras such as Patanjali's *Yoga Sutras* (150 B.C.), and final rescensions of the great incarnational epics of popular Hinduism, the *Ramayana* and the *Mahabharata* (of which the *Bhagavad Gita* is a part), and the *Law of Manu* regarding mutual caste duties. The parallels here are with Philo of Alexandria's (20 B.C.–A.D. 42) synthesis of Platonism and Stoicism with Mosaic religion, and the rise of the Jewish sect that came to be Christianity,

4. *Puranic age* (A.D. 300–750): Continued development of puranic saga (of Krishna and Rama, avatars of Vishnu), the development of tantric Shakti (Great Mother) worship, and the elaboration of the six schools of Vedanta, only one of which holds the world to be an illusion, another of which (Samkhya yoga) espouses an atheistic pluralism in which the individual attains liberation by isolation. Each of these schools in its own way illustrates the tension between liberation from the world

(*moksha*) and the obligation to do right in the world (*dharma*). Similar tensions to be found in rabbinic Judaism, and in the catechesis of the fathers of the Christian church (e.g., Gregory of Nyssa's sermons, Saint Augustine's *City of God*).

5. *Late Darsana period* (A.D. 750–1000): The *Bhagavad Puranas*, possibly the most popular romances of Krishna (playing with cow herding girls, etc.); the rise of the Alvars (mystical poets of Vishnu), intense Shaivite devotion, and, in the ninth century, Shankara's definitive exposition of Advaita Vedanta, the most extreme understanding of the *Mandukya* Upanishad's monism. The parallels are complex: with the Christian cult of icons and saints; with Shankara, the fifth-century Neo-Platonic mysticism of Pseudo-Dionysius the Areopagite and the ninth-century Celtic nature mysticism of John Scotus Erigena.

II. *Medieval Hinduism* (A.D. 1000–1800):

With the Islamic destruction of its monasteries, Buddhism is virtually wiped out in India. In south India, Ramanuja's universalist consolidation of devotional, *bhakti* Hinduism; Madhva's synthetic Shaiva Siddhanta system, which bears strong resemblances to Christianity. In north India, Tulsi Das's devotion to Rama; the Muslim mystic poet Kabir, and Nanak, founder of the Sikhs, both of whom devise accommodations between Islam and Hinduism. The parallels here are to be found in Jewish Kabbalism, Franciscan piety, and in the efforts of Albert the Great and Aquinas to assimilate Aristotle and Islamic Sufism into the Christian tradition. In a sense Hinduism had experienced its version of a Protestant revolution with the Buddha (500 B.C.); and though Ramanuja's redemptive vision encompassed all social classes, that inclusive vision was not accompanied by a Gutenberg revolution in literacy that would erode the master-serf relation as it did in the West.

III. *Modern Hinduism* (1800–):

This period, led by figures as diverse as Ram Mohen Roy, Devendranath Tagore, Keshub Chander Sen, Swami Dayananda, Sri Ramakrishna, and Mohandas Gandhi, is marked by efforts at accommodation with Christianity and Western rationalism; at the same time, Christian theology in the nineteenth century sought to assimilate the Enlightenment and historical consciousness.

Each of Hinduism's branchings—from ancient Vedas to the Upanishads, from the Upanishads to the great popular epics and *bhakti*—embody a liminal anti-structure in relation to its predecessor. The process can be seen, in a highly simplified form, as a sequence of time frames, again roughly parallel to developments in the West. If the visible universe is understood in emanationist terms, as issuing forth by a process of involution from higher orders of reality—as it was in the West as well, until the seventeenth century—then the following fourfold sequence represents an evolutionary return home.

First, there's the mythic time of eternal return, what Jung called the "paradise of childhood" and which could also be called the time frame of the round table. The literary remains of this time frame (2000–1500 B.C.) are contained in the enormously life-affirming, polytheistic Rig Veda hymns, the sacrificial texts (*Brahmanas*), and "forest treatises"(*Aranyakas*). It is that virtually timeless, pantheistic Eden of collective consciousness, of shamanism, of primitive republicanism where, for the Hindus, the blessed hunter-gatherer people of Uttaraburu dwelt. In the Western tradition, it is no less romanticized; God walks with creatures "in the cool of the evening." It corresponds to Stanislav Grof's first perinatal matrix; nature is experienced as a "good" or "bad" womb. With the rise of agriculture, Mother religion predominates. A visit to a backcountry Hindu village recalls such a unified field. But its real contemporary representatives are the *sudra* class, the outcast "tribals."

Second is the time in which the epic hero is called forth, an essentially adolescent era. The old oral cosmology falls apart, and society is coercively reintegrated, in the polemical atmosphere of an oral culture, around solar kings. It is a time of henotheistic patriarchal religion, of tribes on the march, and the beginnings of empire. The record is contained in classic, oral epic, the Sumerian *Gilgamesh*, stories of judges and early kings of Israel, the *Iliad*, Norse saga, and *Beowulf*. To a large degree (though this is not the whole story), it is the tale told in the Hindu epics, the *Mahabharata* and the *Ramayana*. The old primordial unities shatter, are felt to be too confining—as in Grof's second perinatal matrix. Synergistically linked to the mother-archetype, the hero proceeds to divide, conquer, and centralize—from Ramases II and Alexander the Great up to Louis XIV, Napoleon, and Josef Stalin; from Brahman priest elites up to the Chandella kings and Muslim maharajas. The masses are proletarianized. A sense of the common divine bloodline being lost, the master-slave dialectic reigns supreme.

Heroic priest-kings, prototypes of the modern self, hurled themselves into a sado-masochistic struggle to win immunity from death by vanquishing their enemies—a feature of the third perinatal matrix. They stand out from their environment, bestride the stage of history. Gradually, under the impact of literacy and other technological inventions, an original polarization with nature turns into disjunction, a great divorce. The modern self envisions itself outside the world picture, able to redraw its lines and thus reshape its own psyche. Wearied by the antagonistic fanaticisms of the oral mentality (i.e., wars of religion in nationalistic form), the unheard of virtue of tolerance becomes exigent in the West. There's a new drive for international law. At the same time, detachment from the world generates problems of its own. *In extremis*, the self is surrounded by artificial light and feels alien to nature viewed as a complex of iron-bound laws. It follows that the self, an anarchic cosmic anomaly in such a context, is a passion story full of *Sturm und Drang*, an interminable subject of saga, novel, and biography, and in recent times the supply side of psychiatric exchequers and litigation. For the last two hundred years, this self's institutions provide the nemesis targeted by the "masters of suspicion"—Marx, Nietzsche, Kierkegaard, and their successors.

Third, the pilgrim time frame of the grail quest transposes the hero's sado-masochistic struggle into another key—of self-sacrifice and the religious seeker. This is a time of individual ascetic seclusion, rebirth, and reincorporation (the old rite of passage at a new level). In India, the Upanishads show literate, introspective minds internalizing the external rites of the Vedas, and discovering in the process a vastly expanded human identity and possibility rooted in a transcendent horizon. That horizon surpasses a sense of identity founded either on the old tribal culture or the power arrangements of a heroic society, both of which, in comparison, begin to appear as worlds of darkness and imprisonment. Still oriented by an acoustic sensibility, the ecstatic visions of this new religious elite pour into Hindu oral epic (e.g., *Mahabharata*, etc.) and the sagas of incarnate gods such as Krishna and Rama in subsequent purana literature—even as Greek dramatists and postexilic Hebrew editors of tribal epic begin in the West to complicate and civilize their polemical oral traditions.

Despite their wide differences, this is the new time initiated around the globe by first-millennium religions of the following time frame: classic Hinduism, Buddhism, Taoism, Judaism, Christianity, and Islam. They are all marked by a new sense of freedom established by an experience of transcendent liminality, and accordingly of moral conflict between the old order and the new. To one degree or another, they all propose a new ideal of the human—sage, saint, the just one—which is not to be confused with an antiheroic denial of the world. And a new ethic (Mosaic law, *Law of Manu*, code of chivalry) to discipline heroic arrogance. If the hero is Prometheus, the person of foresight and on-the-make, this is the season of Epimetheus, the afterthought which critically assesses the damage of "progress," knows remorse, and repentance. (Pandora, wife of Epimetheus, symbolizes the unforeseen consequences of heroic imagination.) The adventure continues but the essential struggle is internalized, becomes a purgative trial in search of a new calling forth, beyond critical damage control. "Beyond the desert of criticism," observes Paul Ricoeur, "we wish to be called again." The call means reconnecting with a wisdom that spells death to the self-justifying deeds of the heroic ideal, and spiritual rebirth, a "new creature."

Finally, apocalyptic time, Grof's fourth perinatal matrix, the grail's discovery—and you are it. I am simplifying, for the moment ignoring differences, but this is the time of those breakthrough sages—Zoroaster, Buddha, Second Isaiah, Lao Tzu, Socrates, Jesus, Mohammed, Shankara, Ramanuja—who reverse the normal subjugation of people to society and state, whose example bids society form itself in their individual image. To one degree or another, for them, "the kingdom is come," nirvana equivalent to samsara (eternity joined with time). With a twist, these figures attempt to restore the aboriginal sense of participation in a common divine bloodline. That is, they recapitulate the unified field cosmos of primitive culture, but now extended beyond the tribe to exclude no one. Their language is often iconoclastic, full of riddling paradox, parable, and koan designed to subvert the old in order to release imagination for the new. They stand "beyond the law," at once in unparalleled freedom and communion with all sentient beings, and as such they constitute a lure for the wayfarers of the previous time frame. Immeasurably, they are ahead of their time, prefigurements of the end-time.

These time frames are present, pending, and overlap in contemporary India. It is one reason one speaks of its time as *synchronic*, not sequential. Of course if it's obvious that my scheme crudely oversimplifies Western history, it is even more true, as my outline of Hindu religious development attempted to indicate, that Hindu culture is vastly more complicated. Nonetheless, if you're looking for the human narrative line, even crude typologies may help.

THE PARADISE OF CHILDHOOD

The richness of primitive myth makes visible, as it were, a subterranean stratum of psyche-and-world that is typically subconscious for the modern Western mind. The intensity of this level of being was enormously magnetic for us grail questers. But the trick was to tap the wellspring of primitive culture without some of its well-known and less attractive features: authoritarian social structure, an easily scattered mind, proneness to violence, and lack of individual freedom. One could not afford to forget that the Western tradition had insisted that education in the liberal arts (which included mathematics and the sciences), though not enough in itself, prepared the way for an assimilation of one's spiritual tradition—in a free, not driven mode. Literalistic primitivism, as some of Esalen's early experiments demonstrated, hardly offered a cure for what afflicted us.

Australian aborigine culture is probably our best surviving example of the primitive mode of participation at intense pitch. For these hunter-gatherers, the world is of a piece; as their monistic symbolism tells it, the world is panpsychic and single. Sacred and profane, religion and politics intermingle without clear distinctions—and each tribal member functions as his own religious specialist in a society whose political form is basically republican. Death as an individual event is a shadowy affair; so little is the structure of selfhood developed that its loss is not felt or avoided to the anxious degree that is usual with the literate person. Formal cult is minimal, choice and will hardly present. Aborigines live almost wholly in the eternal now, a grammatically untensed "everywhen." Consequently they experience little gap between what is and what might be. Mythic powers (not strictly gods) hover closely, densely compact with every rock, tree, person, and utensil. Whatever disharmonies occur in tribal life are resolved by totemistic rituals of identification with mythic ancestors who have archetypally prefigured correct action for every occasion. Like the child (even a modern child), primal peoples shift easily into becoming what they behold; they are the original founders of Actors Studio methods. The rites reestablish an interspecies kinship, and enable these people, as anthropologist Godfrey Lienhardt attests in regard to African parallels, to "assent to life, as it is, without morbidity." Evocatively, the aborigine calls this life "the Dreaming." It's a telling name, for one has the impression that they feel themselves dream figures, more dreamt than dreaming. E. H. Stanner, the closest student of aboriginal culture, remarks that their philosophy of life offers them little flexibility; it is but a "one possibility thing."

Psychologist Erich Neumann evocatively called this condition a "cosmic anonymous" state, often symbolized by a snake swallowing its own tale, a uroborus. Neumann (1976: 33) says,

> In this primitive magical state, there was no clear dividing line between man and the animals, man and man, man and the world. Everything participated in everything else, lived the same undivided and overlapping state in the world of the unconscious as in the world of dreams. Indeed, in the fabric of images and symbolic processes woven by dreams, *a reflection of this early situation still lives on in us*, pointing to the original promiscuity of human life.

Presumably the modern, deracinated self does not want this uroboric mode of participation in its original, dreaming state. The oral sensorium is commanded by externals and scarcely knows what individual agency means. Asked what kind of person he was, one of A. R. Luria's illiterate Russian peasant respondents of this century remarked, "What can I say about my own heart? How can I talk about my character? Ask others, they can tell you about me. I myself can't say anything." The modern self may want the primitive's connection and polysemic meaning, but not at the price of that conscious freedom it has won through heroic trial.

OUT OF UR AND THE POLITICS OF INEQUALITY

The legendary heroes and heroines of ancient oral epic testify to the release of the self, called forth by the rise of agricultural technology by at least 10,000 B.C. Nomadic hunting cultures could live on instinct, in the present, from moment to moment nesting in Mother Earth. Large-scale agricultural societies required a sharper distinction of past and future in language and thought; demanded elites who could detach themselves from immediacy, who could plan ahead for planting, harvesting, and marketing the crop. In short, these cultures demanded Prometheuses, new, liminoid beings of calculating foresight. Fortunately the demand coincided with a supply of just such individuals, freshly awakened from their untensed "everywhen" state by the first scripts. Sumerian cuneiform appears around 3500 B.C.; Egyptian hieroglyphics around 3000 B.C.;

Indus valley script from 3000 to 2400 B.C.; Chinese pictographs and the Semitic alphabet in approximately 1500 B.C. The Greek alphabet, in whose phonetic letters any language could be transcribed, came into use between 720 and 700 B.C.; it was at once democratizing and internationalizing, the perfect instrument for global trade and empire. The coincidence is no accident; for the first time, script enabled the world to be inspected, surveyed from a distance and in relative detail. With that, the order of one-possibility "dreaming" explodes into multiple-possibility choice. Without the managerial "new class" of scribes, the new "solar kings" of the period would have been impossible. Together, they were the stealers of heaven's fire, bottlers of animal and vegetable energy, and prototypes of the modern self-made entrepreneur, artist, and captain of industry.

Before it was integrating, the new Promethean consciousness was sociologically and spiritually shattering. First of all, the old, purely oral cosmology of hunter-gatherers lost its unity. An essentially monistic cosmos was sectored, differentiated, named by tutelary deities—like the estate of a large farmer or the divisions within a bureaucracy. This polytheistic reorganization of the cosmos into fields under the supervision of willful, controlling powers with definite intentions required more intentionality on the part of more individualized humans who simultaneously experienced the passage of time and the threat of death more acutely than their ancestors had. To cope with the heightened anxiety, an organized cult began to appear. Names changed—Abram to Abraham, Jacob to Israel. Abraham in *Genesis* does not simply submit to fate; he negotiates with Yahweh, strikes bargains and compromises. Jacob wrestles with the angel, will not let go until he extracts a name and a blessing. So also with the princes Arjuna and Yudhisthira in the Hindu *Mahabharata* epic; they argue with deity, ask for explanations, demand justice. In the old, purely oral cosmological dispensation, the spirit-world could hardly be said to have a relationship of mutuality with its creatures; the action, as I have noted, was virtually one-way. But with the appearance of the hero, you have the embryo of a creature with a will of its own. There can be genuine interaction, purpose on both sides, and obviously, heightened tension, conflict, and opening to sharp dualisms which may be extended (as in the case of Persian Zoroastrianism) to the cosmos itself. Incipiently, the distinction between natural and supernatural begins to appear, paralleling that of subject and object.

Expanded commerce and exposure to the trading partner's myths brought on the world's first major conflict of interpretations. It would eventually prove an immense stimulant to thought, but before that it meant war. Trade brought the heroes of tribal epic, each claiming that his set formulas infallibly represented the whole, into conflict with other equally assertive claimants. For these people were heirs of the hard-set personal loyalties and polemic texture of oral cultures. Bloody heroic epics accurately reflect the resulting social upheaval. As once exclusively collective personalities protested against suffocating enclosure and broke away from the tribe, the intimate family circle, the round table of the old tribal culture, dissolved into something like an adolescent gang war. The ruins of Troy, Jericho, Persepolis, and Mohenjo Daro are there to tell us of the social devastation. But if Ernest Becker is right, the most serious catastrophe for future generations lay in the *centralization of ritual* in a now divided but still pervasively sacral universe.

It made sense, at least initially, that people would trade their independent ritual functions in the old cosmology for the manifest capacity of the new solar kings and their technocrats to deliver expanded life, health, and prosperity. The diffuse, collective psyche of an oral society would have had little difficulty making the transition to this new mode of totemic identification with the world's first experts. Identifying with the new technology, the new social organization and its organizers, provided an evidently superior immortality mechanism, the preferred way of avoiding death. The new trading boundaries virtually required politico-religious innovation and new moral unities that spanned old tribal borders and hostilities. Hence the rise of large city-states and a new class of big bosses, both religious and secular, and minor bosses, whose claim to esteem-as-a-person came to be based, not as in the old cosmology on communal lands but on "individual" property holding. In the case of Alexander's empire, Asoka's Buddhist state in India, or the *Pax Romana*, the arrangement paid off—for a while. There is no question but that such vast unifications of territory created a new kind of cosmopolitan citizen who is presupposed in the emerging world religions of the first millennium B.C.

Yet Hebrew ambivalence regarding the appointment of a king (1 Sam. 8: 5–22) seems eminently justified in terms of the sequel. For the long-term cost of centralization, as Ernest Becker insists, proved excessive. And that excess, moreover, is the key to understanding the *moral* force behind Israel's campaign against pagan pantheism (and the aboriginal mode of divine participation). In order to save God, the earth, and the human, the order of creation had to be distinguished from God, in effect, secularized. Sacred kings concentrated power and possession in themselves, even as their priests ratified the move by reimagining the old pantheon consolidated under a supreme deity. Invariably, the "shepherd of the people" sought to set up an immutable, eternal order as vehicle of his personal immortality project. The consequence was an immobile hierarchical society; everything in its place and station, time and process were artificially made to stop cold. The underground story of ancient kingdoms—Babylonian, Persian, Greek, Roman, and Aryan—is a record of petrification and the four horsemen of the Apocalypse. The four-caste system enshrined in the Hindu *Law of Manu*—a governing military elite, cultural-religious specialists, lower status merchants and craftsmen, and a yet more inferior peasant class—shifts during this heroic era from a system of reciprocal obligation (analogous to the members of one body) to a sacrosanct, immutable command structure in which biology becomes destiny. Was man made for the Sabbath, for the sacralized institutional set-up? Yes, indeed. Viewed as divinely sanctioned, this hierarchical system—only recently vanished in Europe it is well to remember—excommunicated a *sudra* class who represents the tribe and the old oral, communal cosmology. Forgetting an earlier wisdom, indeed repudiating it insofar as heroic religion legitimated exclusion, the solons of a heroic society expropriated the once universal divine bloodline. Divine descent, magic *mana, prana,* or *ruach*—call it what you will—had once been widely distributed; hereafter, it was restricted to select "blue bloods."

Proletarianization of the masses followed. Above all, the immortality-bound hero must displace any reminders of decay and death. The outcasts became the scapegoat object of projection for all the solar ego's feelings of inferiority, guilt, dirt, and mortality. The "shadow" side was thereby institutionalized, and continued in various forms, in Hindu attitudes toward "tribals," in Christian anti-Semitism, and in racism. Inequality cloaked itself in the mantle of the sacred. The group that held the means of symbolic production developed a theology that justified, reinforced, and socialized its power by attributing divine origin to its historical exercise of that power. In short, the centralization of ritual, as Ernest Becker argued, serves as the prototype for all subsequent rationalizations of oligarchical and totalitarian control of passive, proletarized masses. In this process, as Becker says (1975: 61–62), "man has changed from a privileged sharer of goods to someone who [is] dependent on the redistribution of goods; and second, . . . he [is] gradually dispossessed of the most intimate creative role he had ever invented, that of the practitioner of ritual." It is precisely this characteristic maneuver of heroic societies—buying power for the few at the expense of impotence for the many—that persuades me that the Jewish desacralization of nature and culture was a wise, indeed indispensable religious move. Which is not to say that pious Jews could not sense nature and the civil order as a medium of divine glory.

PILGRIM TIME

Pan, symbol of the old oral cosmology and its unities, died resisting. The hero emerges as archetypally a self-assertive male of divided loyalties. Standing out from the world and relatively responsible for its course, he is guilt-ridden. On the one hand, he is called out by a patriarchal sky god from the Ur of mother religion — to prove himself no mere appendage but an active center shaping his own destiny. On the other hand, having scorned the old cosmology's erotic unities (Innun-Ishtar, Astarte, Circe), there is resentment, a sense of abandonment and paranoia. The Hebrew Bible is full of this conflict, relentless trial, and ambivalence. Will failure to uphold the covenant call down Yahweh's wrath, destine Israel to the same fate as her idolatrous enemies? Caught between violent rage at the constriction of Mother-Right and dread of death-threatening trials in unfamiliar territory to which Father Right calls him, the hero experiences the world's first genuine identity crisis. "Who am I?" "What are my limits?" The hero's exploits at the bidding of his implacable *daimon* (only note, it is not at this stage an "inner" spirit like Socrates') seem always in danger of exceeding bounds: Ariadne is abandoned, Cassandra ravaged, the altar of Athena defiled, the feminine reviled. The repressed returns, driving the hero to suicide (Ajax), immobilizing him (Ixion), condemning him to futility (Sisyphus), making a one-eyed monster (Cyclops), provoking dismembering revenge (Pentheus). Greek myth offers an encyclopedia of heroic delusion and punishment.

Classic Greek drama, an up-date of ancient Dionysian rites, re-fashioned typecast heroic saga. Homer's heroes and heroines had been only too clearly outlined, uniformly illuminated, wholly expressed, orderly even in their feelings and thoughts. All is foreground (Auerbach [1946] 1968: 3–23). Sophocles, Aeschylus, and Euripedes poured some of India's pending background, and therewith subtlety, complexity, and soul into overbearing Ajax, Clytemnestra, Oedipus, and Orestes. The various postexilic editors of Hebrew scripture did likewise with tribal Jewish lore. Abram, Isaac, Jacob, and Moses become subtle and wise. By common scholarly consent, the initiation of classic, postexilic Judaism in the fourth century B.C. begins with a text and a public reading (probably the Deuteronomic account of exodus from oppression in Egypt). "They asked Ezra the scribe to bring the Book of the Law of Moses . . . [and] in the presence of the men and women, and children old enough to understand, he read from the book from early morning till noon" (Neh. 8: 1–3).

Early fourth-millennium cuneiform and hieroglyphic scripts started it, but internalizing the Semitic and Greek alphabets created the alchemical vessel and channel for all that energy that in places like India, to this day, disperses, drains away. As Walter J. Ong (1982: 105) puts it,

> By separating the knower from the known, writing makes possible increasingly articulate introspectivity, opening the psyche as never before not only to the external objective world quite distinct from itself but also to the interior self against whom the objective world is set. Writing makes possible the great introspective religious traditions such as Buddhism, Judaism, Christianity, and Islam.

Let me elaborate. To stay within bounds, to avoid self-destructive guilt, the heroic epics seem to say, the hero requires a strict code of "thou shalt nots"—such as the *Torah's* commandments, the Hindu *Law of Manu*, Plato's new paideia, or the codes of ethics propounded for samurai and in Western medieval chivalry. Having once been expelled from the unified field of the old oral cosmology, only a few—the clever Jacob, the wise old Gilgamesh, wily Odysseus, or the good knight Galahad—recover the grail. Self-limitation, duty, and stringent rules, however, are not enough. Such moralism doesn't get to the overmasculinization of the hero, his loss of psychophysical gravity. Much of this era's ascetic withdrawal, furthermore, is simply reaction. It is heroism reversed, an antiheroism which too often turns austerity against the self and the body, which lays waste internally no less than the outward-bound hero lays waste to the environment. Classic Hinduism, Buddhism's "middle way," classic Judaism, Taoism, and Christianity—all go further, recovering feminine eros, empathy, and coinherence reminiscent of the unified field of primitive orality. The pathologies of the outward-oriented hero, the tension between fight or flight, nemesis and hubris, and the fear of death form the base metal, the leaden stuff, which the spiritual disciplines of the world religions attempt to transform into gold.

RUNNING ON TIME

Once Judaism and Christianity are seen against the backdrop of sacred kingship's centralization of ritual, their message begins to stand out as a liberating *decentralization* which attempts to recover primitive communalism extended beyond the tribe. For the prophets, the critical test of "knowing" God rather than some idolatrous displacement is whether one remembers the stranger and the lowly; for they compose the crucial link to the God of the exodus from oppressive Egypt. To forget the forgotten is, for the Jew, to have forgotten oneself. "The most important single fact about the Old Testament," writes Northrop Frye (1982: 83), "is that the people who produced it were never lucky at empire. Temporal power was in heathen hands; consequently, history became reshaped into a future-directed history." For the most part, the Bible is a figuration of time interpreted by losers "from below." Right away, this single fact sets Hebrew literature off from the classic Greek which is written from "the top," and where the common man appears only for comic relief. For the low-born, Greek writers assumed, there can be no tragedy; nothing really momentous happens to them or because of them. They are mere chorus.

The forward prospect of Hebrew thinking also represents the antithesis of Platonic recollection which attempts to fit the present into the archetypal patterns of the past. Greek thinking works backward, from effect to cause, in this respect echoing Hindu eternal-return thinking. Like all still dominantly oral cultures, Hebrew thought works with typologies too. But again, as Frye puts it (1982: 84), the repeatability of myth for the Jew—of genesis, exodus, Sinai, the promised land, and so on—"carries on the primitive perspective but reverses its significance." The present is not known by its identification with the old, but discerned as *prefiguration* of what is coming—the promised Messiah, the restoration of Israel, and so forth. That is, the type adumbrates, foreshadows, always refers to its future antitype—as the recitation of the exodus story (type) would serve for Ezra's hearers as a clue to what was happening then in the return from exile (antitype) under Cyrus the Persian. The understanding of current events, therefore, does not look backward to a golden age but hinges on anticipation, a prophetic vision which interprets the present in terms of what is on the way, *becoming*. The God of the Jews doesn't repeat; the Jew cannot go home again.

> *Now I am revealing new things to you,*
> *things hidden and unknown to you,*
> *created just now, this very moment.*
> *Of these things you have heard nothing until now,*
> *so that you cannot say, "Oh yes, I know all this."*
> *You had never heard,*
> *you did not know,*
> *I had not opened your ear beforehand.*

[Isa. 48: 6–9]

The Hebrew's sense of gravity, consequently, is sunk in the movement deep below visible surfaces, below the imperial arrangements of the big bosses — where the God of exodus moves. This open-endedness startlingly negates the ancient world's agricultural and solar myths of integration which reduced the individual to a passive subject. The Hebrew myth is essentially an iconoclastic, revolutionary mode of thought set against closure and geared to faith, hope, and vision.

Where the Greeks had a genius for necessity and fate, the Jewish imagination is keyed, then, to intelligible contingencies, time's concrete opportunities, its slim chances. What does the Bible look like, Northrop Frye (1982: 76) asks, "when we try to see it statically, as a single and simultaneous metaphor cluster"?

> Ordinarily, if we "freeze" an entire mythology, it turns into a cosmology. . . . But what the Bible gives us is not so much a cosmology as a vision of upward metamorphosis, of the alienated relation of man to nature transformed into a spontaneous and effortless life — not effortless in the sense of being lazy or passive, but in the sense of being energy without alienation.

The same Hebrew spirit pervades the New Testament. Why does the pericope of Peter's denial elicit the most serious attention and sympathy, Erich Auerbach asked in the second chapter of his classic *Mimesis* ([1946] 1968: 43)? Because, he wrote,

> it portrays something which neither the poets nor the historians of antiquity ever set out to portray: the birth of a spiritual movement in the depths of the common people, from within the everyday occurrences of contemporary life. . . . What we witness is the awakening of a "new heart and a new spirit." . . . It sets man's whole world astir. . . . Peter and the other characters in the New Testament are caught in a universal movement of the depths which at first remains almost entirely below the surface and only very gradually . . . emerges into the foreground of history.

The minimalist narrative style of the Bible, so short on foreground detail, so long on background suggestion (think of Abraham's sacrifice of Isaac), draws the imagination in, concentrating it Zen-style on all the emptiness between the lines. From start to its open-ended finish this is a world in suspense, a world *pending* and in process. The Christian Bible ends, in the Book of Apocalypse, with a beginning: "Behold, I make everything new" (Rev. 21: 5).

This was the point of the doctrine of the trinitarian nature of God enunciated at the Council of Nicaea in A.D. 325 (Cochrane [1940] 1968: 234–38). Classical Greek philosophy conceived God as immutable, the principle of order over against volatility and change. One is tempted to say that it is a model of divinity built on the heroic delusion, where any sign of passivity and change is equivalent to imperfection. Like the sacred king and hero, God was assumed to stand above the messy flux of this world like a nonparticipant spectator. Plato's deity, for instance, cannot suffer and therefore has no business in our transient world. The corollary is that the material world is only the dramatic imitation or image of the eternal God; consequently, we virtually have to shed our bodies to make contact with divine ideas. The Jewish experience had been different. In fourth- and fifth-century Christological disputes, mainline Christians were still close enough to their Hebraic roots to understand that any dualism which put God exclusively outside time was abhorrent. Above all, the God of Abraham, Isaac, and Jacob had been experienced as one who broke time open, who made things happen, whose preeminent gift and expression was time itself. The Christian experience of the Christ only reinforced that conviction; Jesus fulfilled prophecy, broke open a new age of the end-time. For the council fathers of Nicaea, this latest advent of God in history was no mere association of a human individual with God but the fullness of God in the flesh—from whose "fullness we have all received" (John 1: 16). As Alfred North Whitehead (1933: 214–16) realized, in commenting on the theology of Alexandria and Antioch, this doctrine of immanence was, for its time, an extraordinary improvement over Plato.

> These Christian theologians [of Alexandria and Antioch] have the distinction of being the only thinkers who in a fundamental metaphysical doctrine have improved upon Plato. . . .
>
> [They] rejected the doctrine of an association of the human individual with the divine individual. . . .
>
> They decided for the direct immanence of God in the one person of Christ. They also decided for the direct immanence of God in the world generally. This was their doctrine of the third person of the Trinity. . . .
>
> [I]n place of Plato's solution of secondary images and imitation, they demanded a direct doctrine of immanence. It is in this respect that they made a metaphysical discovery. They pointed the way . . . to give a rational account of the role of the persuasive agency of God.

To be sure, the agency of the Creator remains absconded for these theologians; it is not an object of experience so much as the basis of all experience, behind the mind rather than in front of it. That's essential to affirm; but the other part, equally essential and "persuasive" to affirm, was that what had been hidden from eternity, the very destiny of the whole human race as they thought of it, had finally broken through earth's crust. Nicaea's insistence on the consubstantiality of the Son with the Father forthrightly denied that there existed any such hiatus as the pagans supposed between being and becoming, between God and nature. Against all pretensions of irreformable, "eternal Rome" dear to the heart of the classic mind, orthodox Christians at the time represented the party of process. G. K. Chesterton understood the kinetic energy of the classic symbolic creeds of the church in just this way. The natural font of revolution and reform, he maintained ([1908] 1959: 137), is the old orthodoxy.

> that God could have his back to the wall is a boast for all insurgents for ever. Christianity . . . has felt that omnipotence made God incomplete. Christianity has felt that God, to be wholly God, must have been a rebel as well as a king.

It is true, of course, that the royal metaphor—the identification of people and king in glory and defeat—pervades the New Testament. But it's turned inside out. The Gospel's mock-king identifies with "the least" (Matt. 25: 40). Why? To break the whole master-slave dialectic upon which nightmare history hinges, to bring that horror show to an end. For when master and servant become the same person and represent the same thing, we have passed over from serving time under the closed, integrating myth of the hero. For the hero would achieve a spurious victory over death by identifying with a God wholly outside of time, a God who somehow withholds himself from the perpetual perishing which marks nature. But the Christian God knows no such limit; he gives himself even unto death.

Now "upward metamorphosis" is not simply a key to the Bible; it is also a key to the apocalyptic time frame being ushered in around the globe. It opens the seal on oriental myth as well.

APOCALYPTIC TIME

It is probable that in the second and first millennia B.C. ecological disaster and calamity were already destroying the credibility of accessible vegetation gods who were supposed to guarantee prosperity. The usual blood sacrifices ("the king must die") to such underground deities proved unavailing. In the emergency, disillusioned heroes began turning as a last resort, as if they needed air and another kind of water, to the usually otiose creator deity modeled on the infinity of sky. The distinctive feature, however, of this period is that, thanks to literacy, for the first time there were humans who possessed an inner sanctum of their own, a "soul." The shining *div* (Sanskrit for "God") might now find its Himalayan cave dwelling in the heart. Consequently, the direction of numinous energy was felt to have reversed itself. In an exclusively oral culture, the *anima mundi* had been felt to invade from without; hereafter, for the literate mind, it could be felt arising from within, as from a bottomless well. The sages of the period—be it Lao Tzu, Second Isaiah, Plato, or the Hindu "forest dwellers" who wrote the Upanishads—feel themselves moving out of a cave, flooded with new light, and able to swallow, to take in as never before the outer world and its energizing cosmic source, the original Poet, the *nous poiētikos*. Crossing the frontier between oral and literate religiosity, then, signaled a new experience of liminal anti-structure and a major *ontological revolution*. It released the aboriginal divine bloodline in a new, freely chosen mode.

For the first time, all across the emerging literate world, the *mysterium* by which the oral world had felt itself fielded was truly experienced as "tremendous and fascinating," beyond words or images—that is, radically other-worldly, transcendent. The resonances, the tones and overtones in the following examples are distinctive, but reveal something similar. In China:

> *The way is forever nameless.*
> . . . .
> *The way is to the world as the River and the Sea are to rivulets and streams.*
>
> *The way is broad, reaching left as well as right.*
> *The myriad creatures depend on it for life yet it claims*
>   *no authority.*
> *It accomplishes its task yet claims no merit.*
> *It clothes and feeds the myriad creatures yet lays no*
>   *claim to being their master.*
>
>   [*Tao Te Ching*, xxxii, xxxiv]

In India:

> The Spirit, without moving, is swifter than the mind; the senses cannot reach him: He is ever beyond them. Standing still, he overtakes those who run. To the ocean of his being, the spirit of life leads the streams of action.

He moves, and moves not. He is far, and he is near. He is within all, and he is outside all.

Who sees all beings in his own Self, and his own Self in all beings loses all fear.

[*Isa* Upanishad]

In the case of the Buddha the thing could not even be expressed in customary God-talk, and in Hebrew case, the Name could hardly be spoken.

> *To whom could you liken God?*
> *What image could you contrive of him?*
> . . . .
> *For my thoughts are not your thoughts,*
> *my ways not your ways — it is Yahweh who speaks.*

[Isa. 40: 18; 55:8]

To understand what is happening globally, I think it helps to use Judaism as heuristic. There are two premises to the incomparable critical power of Jewish thought, writes Olivier Revault D'Allonnes in *Musical Variations of Jewish Thought* (1984: 50–65). The first is the vertical dimension: its rootedness in an absolute beyond history, the unconditional divine will and promise of a world of justice in the certain but indefinite future. And the second, put in place by the first, applies to the horizontal: that any empirical order whatsoever is consequently seen as relative, nonobligatory, and inconclusive. The world, particularly the structures of culture, is no longer automatically sacred; it is envisioned as a neutral medium which may or may not manifest the sacred. In this regard, the prophets are normative; their spirit is nomadic, they will not be taken in, sedentarized, or assimilated by the settled, theocratic, eternal-return empires which surround them. The mystical object of contemplation is not an empyrean Eternal above and beyond earthly affairs. One could contemplate the movement of that Eternal Spirit in ordinary affairs, the marketplace, and in political forums of power. The Eternal is not *of* the world but surely *in* it, even in the mean and unclean. While this leaves room for mountain-top experiences of the Sinaitic type, such events do not claim disproportionate attention over the more pedestrian. The Bible reflects this: consistently it probes the *problematic*, concrete historical situation, its politics and everyday events. By long discipline, the faithful Jew instinctively has what C. Wright Mills called a "sociological imagination." In part, of course, this comes of viewing secular power arrangements from the bottom up. For history's losers, the imaginal takes precedence over the sheerly factual. As Olivier Revault D'Allonnes writes (1984: 67),

> To affirm the City of God, to write and describe the reign of justice, is certainly a falsehood, because that reign and city are illusory, because the world is full of injustice and impiety. But this is done essentially in order to oppose to this unjust world a radical, absolute, unconditional refusal, a refusal which appears in its most pathetic form in Job and Amos: if the world cannot be just, let it vanish.

Spinoza, Marx, Freud, Schönberg, Kafka, and Einstein are the prophets' natural heirs. For Jewish thought gives priority to *what must be* over *what is*, to the imagination of the promise over sealed fates, closed books, and deadly *realpolitik*. Hence the genius for negation, for refusal.

Decisively, the nay-saying hinges on the vertical dimension of soul and spirit. The authentic Jew feels loosed, sent out; there was nothing in the temple sanctuary except the nomad's traveling equipment, a portable ark of covenant. As we observed before, in the original setting of oral, acoustic space which the Hebrew shared with the so-called oriental mind, the *mysterium tremendum* is felt as the surrounding atmosphere out of which individual mind precipitates—as a kind of dim emanation from outside in. With the shift to inwardness brought on by literacy, however, there's a change in direction. It's as if the universe had been turned outside in, as if the whole movement of the cosmos were now blooming outwardly *through* the human organism.

Wherever the wandering Jew goes, then, God is there in the sanctuary symbolized by the empty temple sanctum: the human heart. At this point, however, let me reverse interpretive frames. The inwardness of the third chapter of the *Katha* Upanishad, I think, illuminates the inwardness of the moral law for the Jewish ethos.

> When he knows the Atman, the Self, the inner life, who enjoys like a bee the sweetness of the flowers of the senses, the Lord of what was and of what will be, then he goes beyond fear.
> This is in truth That (*tat tvam asi*).

There are grounds for the cross-reference. Etymological derivations are tricky, but sometimes, if not pushed too far, they are instructive. The divine Name YHWH of Exodus 3:14 derives from the Hebrew verb *to be*, which also signifies "to breathe." But the word for "Jew" derives from the same verb. So as Owen Barfield (1965: 113) once noted,

> A devout Jew could not name his race without recalling, nor affirm his own existence without tending to utter, the Tetragrammaton. Written, as all Hebrew words were, without vowels, when any true child of Israel perused the unspoken Name, YHWH must have seemed to come whispering up, as it were, from the depths of his own being.

The Jewish campaign against pagan idolatry, against pantheism, against the old oral cosmology, must be seen in this light. It is to be understood as a defascination of the *numen* in nature, which charges images *from without*. It is a move to decathect, for the sake of interiorizing God's freedom. No less than the sages of the Upanishads, the Jews cultivated the *inwardness* of what was represented through speech. In this way, the negation and suppression of primitive participation moved to preserve its essence. Through concentration or centripetal deepening of participation, the idea was that the *vox dei* might speak through a human throat. So just as the voice of Brahman speaks through authors of the Upanishads, at bottom the word that speaks through the Jewish story is the great I AM of the Exodus, spoken by the time of the great prophets and the wisdom literature *from within*. Ezekiel eats the divine scroll (Ezek. 2:8–3:3). And Jeremiah promises wide distribution of this kind of digestion.

> See, the days are coming . . . when I will make a new covenant. . . . Deep within them I will plant my law, writing it on their hearts. . . . There will be no further need for neighbors to try to teach neighbor. . . . They will all know me, the least no less than the greatest. [Jer. 11: 31–34]

For Christians of course, God's writing on the heart is what is secretly working its way into time's weave, the exemplary "type" being Jesus of Nazareth, the "antitype" being ourselves. As I tried to indicate, this is what Aquinas's medieval epistemology is all about. My claim is that if one uses the Upanishads (and also the stories of Krishna) heuristically to understand the whole thrust of Jewish thought, it's easier to see Christianity as a graft on Judaism's tree. As Barfield (1965: 155) says of the Jews, "it was the logic of their whole development that the cosmos of wisdom should henceforth have its perennial source, not without, and behind the appearances, but within the consciousness of [a human being]; not in front of his sense and his figuration, but behind them." Another way to put it is to say that the Jewish path opened a way to become a cocreator with the prime Mover and Shaker. No one who calls his God I AM can be naming a wholly other and external being.

On the whole, then, I don't find the Upanishads foreign to the orientation of Jewish thinking. But turnabout is fair play. If spiritual depth, the vertical axis, of Jewish vision fired prophetic social criticism, why should we not expect some of the same social impact from Eastern transcendentalism of this period? The germ is there, I think, though there are special reasons why it was neither as effective or as volatile as in the West (of which more in the next chapter). What is clear, however, is that the transformation of human identity was no less profound during this period in the East than in the West. And one might expect what we actually find, that the development of Upanishadic contemplation leads to a triadic formulation of the nature of God, and consequently to stories of divine incarnation.

HOLY DISCONTENT AND THE NEW CREATURE

Rather than being typecast like Homer's heroes and heroines, the characters of the Bible extend into depths of time, fate, and many-layered, often contradictory consciousness. Figures like Abraham, Saul, and David are only partly manifest at any one time; unlike the static figures of heroic saga whose destiny is clear from the outset, the Hebrew figures only gradually and errantly develop into their destinies. Why? Because they are no less hidden and laden with mystery than the Name Apart which informs them, which they seek to obey. Hereafter, the individual "I" is no less, and no more, knowable than the *mysterium tremendum*.

But something analogous must have been occurring around the world. The transformation of human identity is fairly clear. As long as people remained enthralled by a numinous nature, they could neither think nor act without compulsion or outside the juggernaut cycles of nature. Nor, as long as they were bound by the *numen* of tribal solidarity and the spellbinding power of the priest-king, could they ever escape the shame and fear-ridden dialectic of master-slave. In this context, it is not remarkable, then, that both the Hebrew Psalms, the Chinese *Tao te Ching*, Buddhist texts, and the Upanishads speak so often of going "beyond fear" and bitter resentment. Once literacy began to concentrate minds, the constrictions of tribal society and the ravages of competing heroic societies became self-conscious, gained voice. If literacy made the examined life possible, literate seers and saints intensified guilt in direct proportion to their new sense of human responsibility and possibility. The thing often went too far, collapsed into self-hate, escapism, or got stuck in a merely reactive antiheroics like some of the U.S. drop-outs of the sixties. In the Judeo-Christian case in particular, the danger of internalizing the unlocalizable, commanding presence of the God of Sinai was that, when combined with a still tribal mentality, it produced an ideological zealot.

Such aberrations do not invalidate the real thing. "World rejection," as sociologist Robert N. Bellah remarks (1970: 45) of the period we have been discussing, "marks the beginning of a clear objectification of the social order and a sharp criticism of it." The point is that other-worldliness sets up a creative tension with things as they are — and that tension gets the world moving. As Bellah writes (1970: 35–36),

> Whether the confrontation was between Israelite prophet and the king, Islamic ulama and sultan, Christian pope and emperor, or even between Confucian scholar-official and his ruler, it implied that political acts could be judged in terms of standards that the political authorities could not finally control. The degree to which these confrontations had serious social consequences of course depended on the degree to which the religious group was structurally independent and could exert real pressure. . . . Religion, then, provided the ideology and social cohesion for many rebellions and reform movements in the historic civilizations and consequently played a more dynamic and especially more purposive role in social change than had previously been possible.

Across the globe, then, the first-millennium sages were uniformly negative about the state of the world. Looking about at what hubris had wrought, they reckon the human flaw deeper and more serious than anything earlier religion had conceived possible. The whole structure of self is a burning house, cries the Buddha; an illusion, claim the Upanishads; a soulless forgetfulness of God, jibe the Hebrew prophets. These critics find virtue newly problematic and the old religious regimes of Homer, tribal Hebraism, Brahman priests, and other state functionaries insufficient. "I hate your feasts, and take no pleasure in your solemn assemblies," rages the eighth-century Hebrew prophet Amos. More softly, Hindu forest dwellers and the Buddha rebuked contemporary Brahmanism in the same way. The point was that religious acts whose main function had been to reinforce social cohesion under the ruling status quo were no longer acceptable, and perhaps more to the point, were inadequate to civilize the imperious, heroic "I am." The crisis called forth the invention of contemplative disciplines: ascetic ways of dismantling false consciousness and of remembering a core self, a true self, by means of identifying with embodiments of the new ideal: the Buddha, the yogi Pantangali, the mystic warrior Arjuna of the *Bhagavad Gita*, the Gods-incarnate Krishna and Christ. In short, the crisis elicited a novel battery of interior disciplines to amplify what literacy had started: yogas, paideias, and therapies of meditation and dialogical reflection whereby totemistic worship and sacrifice were interiorized, and by which the quality of inner movements could be discriminated. Hereafter, at least for self-conscious elites, the cake of custom and external rite would not suffice. Ritual observance would have to be supplemented, vigilantly and critically, by voluntary inner discipline.

These new inner disciplines opened the way to the new hierophanies of first-millennium religion and, in turn, to their relatively universalistic reconceptions of human identity. The key words of this period are detachment and attention. Whether it be in the form of Plato's Good, the Buddha's plenum-void, or the inaugural visions of Ezekiel and Isaiah, this experience shattered the set of highly charged transference relations, the customary heteronomy, that in the old oral cosmology bound the psyche to the tribe or to the priest-king. "Only by withdrawing cathexis from the myriad objects of empirical reality," observes Robert N. Bellah in this connection (1970: 45; see also 32–34), "could consciousness of a centered self in relation to an encompassing reality emerge." No longer defined exclusively as the king's property, much less by membership in tribe or clan, in principle and for the first time it becomes possible to conceive of a truly common human nature that cuts across cultural boundaries, that is independent of biological descent, social lineage and rank. Henceforth, these world religions define a human being by the capacity for enlightenment or salvation; that is, the ability of a responsible self, deeper than the flux of ordinary experience, to apprehend and participate actively in the fundamental structure of reality. And when that sense of active participation dawns, it typically unleashes a new joy in manifold existence, the kind of jubilation one finds in the erotic Khajuraho temples or the total round of Indian life and culture celebrated and affirmed in the Buddhist cave paintings of Ajanta in northwest India. The earth is renewed, after all, "very, very good."

"Who are my mother and my brothers?" Jesus asks when his mother, blood brothers, and sisters come to visit (Matt. 12: 48–50). Gesturing to those who have ears to hear, he answers, "Anyone who does the will of

God, that person is my brother and sister and mother." It's a reply both aristocratic and democratic at one and the same time. Ernest Becker (1975: 69) stresses the democratic aspect:

> The son was now completely independent; he could freely choose his own spiritual father and was no longer bound to the fatalities of heredity. The individual could fashion his own salvation, independent of any earthly authority. Christianity was a great democratization that put spiritual power right back into the hands of the single individual and in one blow wiped away the inequalities of the dispossessed and the slaves that had gradually and inexorably developed since the breakup of the primitive world and that had assumed such grotesque proportions in the mad drivenness of the Mediterranean world. . . . Christianity in this sense dipped back into paganism, into primitive communalism, and extended it beyond the tribe.

If Becker had not coupled his "independent" with "primitive communalism," his "single individual" here might smell of a disembodied, Cartesian individualist bereft of social relations and history, inventing himself *ab ovo*. But as he does make that connection, his point carries — even though he is well aware that subsequent Christianity lost much of this democratic thrust.

Only that thrust is not restricted to Christianity. To one degree or another, all these emergent transcendental faiths "dipped back into paganism" and overreached tribalism. The Buddha or a Hindu sage might have replied as Jesus did. In almost every case, it is true, heroic patriarchalism overtakes the breakthrough. It is compromised and coopted by the state and the tyranny of cultural fathers. But in its charismatic origins, the breakthrough generates religions of fraternity based on the fundamental spiritual unity of the race — what Victor Turner called a sense of *communitas*. The Buddhist *tathagata* or enlightened one is a "man of no title" and rejects caste; the Hindu equivalent, the *sanyasin*, and the Taoist stand beyond caste as well. This is what happens when identity rests on the *Torah*, the eternal *dharma*, the *Tao*. In a way that the Vedic sages, Hebrew patriarchs, and the company of Hammurabi and Solon had not been able, these newly made religious people of the book could stand free, erect, and move in the world with enhanced leverage. They were *in* the world but not *of* it.

Then what happened to the leverage of universalists in India? If the Western historical record serves as a clue, whether a world-shaking religious vision actually catalyzes social change hinges on whether those gathered around that vision form themselves into a structurally independent organization that is recognizeably distinct from the organon of the state and secular life. Without such institutionalization and a hiatus between institutions, the necessary creative tension is not likely to develop. The vision will wither or remain in a state of latency, its social impact severely reduced. To a degree this is what I think happened to visionary, classical Hinduism. There is a lesson here for the consciousness movement which headed East well supplied with an all-American brand of liberal individualism and romantic antiinstitutionalism. The movement's great weakness to this day, it seems to me, has been sociological, its limited ability to go public with its vision. Privatism consumes it. As with India, the social promise is there but it tends to dissipate.

SIX

India's Leaky Grail

In all stages of civilization the popular gods represent the more primitive brutalities of the tribal life. The progress of religion is defined by the denunciation of the gods. The keynote of idolatry is contentment with the prevalent gods.

Alfred North Whitehead

The Indian saint may reasonably shut his eyes because he is looking at that which is I and Thou and We and They and It. It is a rational occupation: but it not true . . . that it helps the Indian to keep an eye on Lord Curzon.

G. K. Chesterton

It is the dimension of time wherein man meets God, wherein man becomes aware that every instant is an act of creation, a Beginning. . . . Time is the presence of God in the world of space, and it is within time that we are able to sense the unity of all beings.

Abraham Joshua Heschel

India is nothing if not conundrum. How could something as austere and self-denying as Buddhism produce the psychedelically colorful cave paintings of Ajanta, whose panoramas of contemporary Indian life bless planting and harvest, village market and civil life no less than the rounds of religious pilgrimage? These huge cathedral caves are excavated out of solid cliffs of granite, carved from the proverbial "uncarved block," and their synesthetic murals declare that all the pulsing rhythms of the sensory world are to be found and transfigured within the heart of our Buddha-nature. The Ajanta caves replenish the wasteland worlds of the hero,

148

make them one in many, many in one—and give that hero a new anatomy. In the chamber of Buddhist inwardness, the visible world's many wells up from the *bindu*, the primordial point, source, germ, and seed—a new creation. From the perspective of that "ontological revolution" I spoke of in the last chapter, it's a vision comparable to the second genesis Christians celebrate at the Easter Vigil liturgy.

Or how do you explain the Khajuraho temples? When you stand before them, you find yourself thinking that the anonymous artisans who breathed life into their stone were weaving Hindu history in hieroglyph. What animates, streams through all, what flowers in time, makes time bloom in multiple forms, say these temples, is the River of Life, the play of Brahman in the erotic, tantric dance of Shiva-Shakti. The vitality of the Vedas are here but transformed, without their strenuous heroics. The Upanishads' unity and yogic mindfulness are here, but without anesthetic withdrawal, class stratification, or the rejection of time. Mother-religion is here, affirming the goodness of earth, but without apotheosizing impulse. The friezes display and celebrate the metamorphosis as well as the excess, the sheer abundance of the sidereal Ganges's flow chart, one breath, one differentiated body. To achieve this full-throated vision of one in many, you imagine, the sculptors must have passed through energetic Vedic polytheism, through the Upanishads' inwardness, through the dry detachment of Buddhists and Jains, and back out the other side to the earthy fruitfulness of Great Mother devotion and *bhakti*. And as they absorbed each in turn, you think, they must have negated the limits of each, reclaiming its core, the essence of each, in a broader context.

To this day, I think, Khajuraho's renascence, its affirmation of what was, is, and will be forms the core of what the "twice born" Hindu is called to wake up to. And in the sixties and seventies, American pilgrims went in search of this promise. Some found that promise alive, and staying with it, were radically changed. Many did not; the journey amounted to no more than another detour. As for Hindus themselves today, Ajanta's meanings had all but vanished into thin air until the caves were accidentally rediscovered in the late nineteenth century by an Englishman. Until that time, the memory of this great ritual center had been erased by Islam's destruction of Buddhist monastic foundations during the medieval era. And the Khajuraho temples, as my guide remarked, are "dead." They have had only mausoleum status since the Moslems destroyed the fiercely resisting Chandellas in the twelfth century. In many ways, for India herself, the promise of medieval Hinduism and an earlier Buddhism is a failed, broken one.

In this chapter I want to understand two contradictory outcomes. How could sophisticated Hindu disciplines be so regenerative for at least some Westerners, and yet so ineffective for the vast majority of native Hindus? The previous two chapters should provide the background necessary to comprehend these divergent results. Literacy makes all the difference.

BROKEN PROMISES

Let me put it provocatively. High-status Hindus are right; the masses are soulless in the sense in which I use the term. The Great Mother has devoured them. Unfortunately, the high Hinduism of the Upanishads, which broke through into oneness in God and naturally issued into sagas of divine avatars, remained dammed up, because its yogic disciplines were designed to reyoke a separate self to a greater center—whose center is nowhere, whose circumference everywhere. But the presumption is that the self has sprung loose from its uterine condition, which for about 70 percent of India's nonliterate population is contrary to fact. Pouring into the modern city, these people are lost.

To a Christian raised on the celestial Jerusalem, or on Saint Augustine's two cities, the absence of the city motif in Hindu iconography is notable. When it does appear in sacred texts and art, the city stands for a massive delusion system. The wonderful, energetic Bombay that appears in the pages of Salmon Rushdie's recent novel, *Midnight's Children*, may suggest a radical departure from this tradition, but till lately Hindus have taken the city as the demonic creation of benighted selves who have lost their cosmic connection. In part, this negative attitude toward the self and its creation, the city, accounts for the harsh things V. S. Naipaul had to say about Hinduism in the *New York Review of Books* about a year after my visit there. I could understand Naipaul's [1978: 50] sentiment.

> Hinduism hasn't been good enough for the millions. It has exposed us to a thousand years of defeat and stagnation. It has enslaved one quarter of the population and always left the whole fragmented and vulnerable. Its philosophy of withdrawal has diminished men intellectually and not equipped them to respond to challenge; it has stifled growth. So that again and again in India history has repeated itself: vulnerability, defeat, withdrawal.

Naipaul observed that the European Renaissance gained headway to the extent that people put distance between themselves and the past in order to understand and profit from the past. "The past has to be seen to be dead; or the past will kill." That's hard, penultimate wisdom. In order to escape the dead hand of the past, the woof of time, which in a feudal society knits the generations of patron and serf closely together, must be broken.

In those accelerators of time, cities like Bombay and Calcutta, Hinduism's strength seemed perverse. There, it had destroyed as much as in the countryside it saved. There, for me, Alan Watts's romanticization of the great tradition of the Upanishads seemed blatant fraud. It was more than the caste system that affronted me. There were features of the mainstream culture—the sense of time, an attitude toward the self, a purism in its yogas, a law-and-order rigidity in its classic texts—that I found repugnant. Like most travelers to a foreign culture, I had taken for granted the legacy I brought with me—an instinct for process, opportunity, evolution, an open society, the recurrent Western theme of a new age dawning. I discovered I had the soul of a Jew.

COSMIC PESSIMISM AND TRANSCENDENTAL DENIAL

Historically, the yogic ashram circuit worked well only for a miniscule privileged elite who had attained literacy, and who therefore were possessed of a pressure chamber for burning away the bad karma of their former heroic egos—a purgative rite that is the precondition for discovering *atman*. Something stopped this process from spreading effectively to the masses, an accident of history as it were. In the first millennium B.C. India had an *excess quantification of time*. The tradition of the great renouncers, of yogic homeopathy, and mystic flights of the "alone to the Alone" were built on the immense periods of Brahman's cyclic time. Only with modern astronomy has the West come upon anything like it. A single cosmic epoch of creation-destruction-recreation, according to ancient Brahmanic astronomy, lasted 4,320,000 years. Such accuracy penalized elite Hinduism, indeed severely crippled it, for against this mind-boggling time expanse, almost no sense of finality was possible. This is especially true if, as was the case, the wise men of the time calculated that a cycle of decline, the *kali yuga* (black age) had begun in approximately 3,000 B.C., when affluent agricultural economies began to construct cities like Mohenjo Daro and Harrapah in northwest India. Now while one may claim with justice that the *kali yuga* notion is a secondary gloss on the Upanishads and a distortion of their essential thrust, the fact is that the influence of this idea has been powerful. And debilitating.

In the first place, the awesome temporal sense undercut the timefulness which I am convinced the seers of the Upanishads must have let loose. It conveyed the sense that nothing different is really happening, that time is a waste, a repetition *ad nauseam*. Under this specter, the nerve of human agency is cut. The performance principle inevitably appears the merest vanity. Round and round, there's nothing new under the sun, and nothing significant to be done about altering a decadent age which will proceed, willy-nilly, to its destitute end. As Mircea Eliade has noted, the consequence can be — and often was — a refusal of history.

A refusal of history contaminates the ascetical impulse. It turns the traditional Hindu pilgrim stage of life, a quest for deeper wisdom after one's householder duties are discharged, into a self-deceiving escape from evil. In quest of purity and perfection, the aspirant misguidedly seals off vulnerability and limits, leaving the devil to the hindmost — which in the concrete means the lower orders of society. Such angelism, really a strategy to avoid dirt and mess, arises from the socially ingrained mental habit of projecting the shadow side of self upon vulnerable nobodies, and intensifies that very habit. Socially, such ascesis too often represents the ego's effort to deliver itself from prolonged suffering in, and slavery to, the jaws of corruptible matter and time — such as the miserable poor must endure. In the West, spiritualities of ascent motivated by such taboos of the earthy have been indicted as "gnostic" heresy.

The tactic has a theological dimension. Underneath the withdrawal from social and material corruption lies a conception of deity too much like the pure Good of Neo-Platonism. This God is implicated in only one end of the spectrum of traditional opposites, the tidy side of order, immutability, unity, centrality, and so forth. Such a God, unlike the one embodied by the Krishna and Rama epics and legends of incarnational Hinduism, cannot get his hands dirty or raise hell. To postulate this frozen God, in whom there is no movement, and the *kali yuga* are indeed two sides of the same gasp of despair. James Hillman (1975b: 64–67) has the accurate name for this kind of spurious theology and its high-toned spiritual practice. He labels it "transcendental denial." In various Neo-Platonic shapes, it has been popular in Western Christian circles since the early Greek fathers of the church — who had a difficult time distinguishing themselves from Stoics, Pythagoreans, and Platonists for whom time wore the mask of terror. Once time wears that mask, the universal tendency has been to grasp for a mode of transcendence that short-circuits the tumult of social connection and history.

It seemed to me that much of the talk of *sat-chit-ananda* (being, aware-ness, bliss) which I heard in India represented little more than a way of callousing oneself against suffering and appalling living conditions. High Hinduism of this type began to smell of survivalist mentality which glosses over the alienation of others and one's own wounded psyche. When joined with doctrines of reincarnation and karma (in the form of what sounded like rugged individualism), the thing seemed a primary instance of bad faith. Transparently, I thought, this is the pathology of an obsessively anal personality rationalizing its social inertia. I required an eschatological myth *for this world*, an apocalyptic opening to the future. It seemed too true: elite Hinduism, when isolated from the ethical con-cerns of the Krishna and Rama myths, did not have enough room for the prayer, "Thy kingdom come."

THE SOCIOLOGY OF DEPENDENCY

Hinduism is a culture of the antipodes (Lannoy, 1971: 168–76). The most advanced Indian civilization nurses its most primitive substratum, the underground folk culture of remote tribal peoples, pariah gypsies who crowd the sides of highways, derelict beggars who populate the slums. The Brahmin priest cannot remain ritually pure without the un-touchable's labors, and neither priest not yogi can function without the civil order, craft products, and agricultural surplus, respectively, ensured by warrior-ruler, merchant, and peasant—and vice versa. Ideally, the various *varna* (castes) of Indian society intimately depend on each other, and taken together signify the diverse members of a single moral person cooperating in a common spiritual project. There is wisdom here, the wisdom of a necessary hierarchy built on a society's choice of ends, and hence standards of importance and value against which human acts can be ranked and judged (Dumont, 1970: 1–20). No society, even one like ours with an egalitarian ideal, can avoid hierarchy (or an aristocratic sense of virtue) in this sense, except at the steep price of a corrosive leveling tendency, the outcome of refusing to make collective decisions about what constitutes the good life for all. Americans tend to miss the point ("it's up to individual taste or feeling"), and I did too when I went to India. The issue is quite distinct from questions that concern inequalities in the distribution of power. The latter question is so insistent in India that it almost makes a spiritual seeker forget that the flatland he came from gives little basis for feeling superior.

Besides, at her roots, India shares the Western ideal of universal equality. "All this universe is in the glory of God, of Siva the god of love," says the *Svetasvatra* Upanishad, "The heads and faces of people are his own and he is in the hearts of all." Then why does this universalism make so little headway? From a psychoanalytic angle, the people who have nowhere to lay their heads and who symbolize for the upper classes the intractable irredeemability of earth represent the negative identity upon which the dominant classes rest their sense of superiority. Secretly, the upper classes know something they're not telling themselves: that tribal life knows nothing of the climate of psychological dependence in which higher caste children grow up.

This dependency begins to explain why the upper classes stall in the face of massive social and economic problems. "Thou art that," says the classic Upanishadic aphorism. In the West, the problem lies with the "that," the realm of spirit. We have difficulty imagining that at base the objective material world could be spirited. In India, the problem runs in reverse. It is the "thou" which is problematic—the weakness of "I am."

In the *Law of Manu* the "joint family" is translated as "inseparateness." Unfortunately, such symbiosis often entails a fear of letting go lest one lose oneself in experience or relationships. To this day in India, two adhesive factors, extended family and caste, inhibit the individual in the task of differentiating itself from the rest of the world. The typical situation, mirrored in many of the popular amplifications of the Krishna-Rama epics (puranas, developed from A.D. 300–700) is that one never leaves home. Unlike the case of Abraham, any call to abandon a sedentary life is taken as a temptation to be avoided. In fact if you imagined the grail legend in an Indian version, the rustic Percival would probably never have left his weeping mother in the lurch. Brahman, one begins to suspect, has too many images before him. One of them, the Great Mother, will not release her children to grow up and, in the form of a bloody goddess Kali, devours men alive.

Studies show that child rearing emphasizes passivity and punishment, and gives little stress to self-reliance, personal integrity, or the necessity of sustained discipline to achieve distant goals (Lannoy, 1971: 85–101). As admirable as it is in many ways, popular *bhakti* religion conditions people to regard the whole sphere of personality, of ego, as a shadowy affair, poorly defined, and very likely displeasing to God. The ambiguity of the weaning process means that identity and autonomy in India are always fragile and in doubt. In clinical terms, borderline and narcissistic personality disorders abound. Somehow, the culture has not absorbed the paradox that you have to differentiate in order to unite in freedom. So far as I could see, a tradition of courtly love, of an inspiring woman who is also best friend, never sprang up in India. And in a way that has meant that real affection between sexually active adults has been dissociated from procreation and generativity in the larger sense. Mother-son affective bonding, as we might expect, is intense. But it comes as no surprise that in a 1961 study in Bangalore, affective relations between husband and wife were shown to be minimal, barely on the scale.

In adult relationships what counts is impersonal, the prosperity of family and caste. Wider community interest must constantly fight an often losing battle against the tide of virtually numberless interest groups whose sense of obligation stops at the blood and caste line. Within such confines, loyalty is intense, but its range tends to be narrow and suffocating for the individual and the country at large. The American writer Gloria Naylor observes a similar phenomenon among "losers" in our culture: they tell their stories without broad cultural reference, exclusively in terms of family. Public service under these circumstances becomes elusive.

REBELS NEED NOT APPLY

No revolutionary tradition lures on the destitute Hindu. So far as I am aware, the encyclopedia of Hindu myths contains no stories, as in the Judeo-Christian mythos, of being expelled from Eden and, most importantly, of the expulsion as a "happy fall." Nor are there accounts of heroes or antiheroes of rebellion on a par with David and Jonathan against Saul, or Ezekiel, Jeremiah, or Jesus against the authorities—much less, a Martin Luther or Giordano Bruno.

The great epics of popular, incarnational Hinduism, the *Mahabharata* and the *Ramayana*, are ambivalent. In the former, Arjuna is uncomfortable with his caste duty to slaughter his family's enemies; and Yudhisthira, the great archetype of *dharma*, refuses the god's command to enter paradise without his faithful dog. Decidedly, the *Mahabharata* does recognize the tension between striving to obtain liberation from the world (*moksha*) and *dharma*, the obligation to do right *in* the world. It also articulates the tension, and often the confusion, between *sanatana dharma*, the absolute moral law (never precisely defined), and the *dharma* of caste duties laid down in law books. Nineteenth-century Hindu reform movements, Ram Mohen Roy's *Brahmo Samaj* and Swami Dayananda's *Arya Samaj*, made much of such distinctions. As in this century have Rabindranath Tagore and Mahatma Gandhi.

In the classic epics, then, the temptation to rebel against the letter of caste rules occurs, particularly it would seem, among women. But usually the proverbial patriarchal wisdom of submission to the hierarchical order of things, however unjust or ludicrous, triumphs. The Durkheimian distinction between sacred and profane, one may well think, is drawn too sharply in the West; but in India the impertinence of this distinction often means that "fate" or the governing social order is confused with the will of God. Thus in the *Ramayana*, the heroic Rama and his wife Lakshmana are burdened with a father's apparently careless commitment to an irascible stepmother. "Whatever be the reason," Rama advises his wife, "a king must keep his word and a son must obey his father. You [to Lakshmana] should show that you too are free from any sense of injury." To which the less compliant Lakshmana, albeit in vain, replies:

> Very well, then. This is the work of fate. Fate, I grant, is the cause of our stepmother's sudden folly. And I am not angry with her. But are we, on that account, to sit still and do nothing? It is *Kshatriya dharma* [warrior's duty] to overcome evil and establish justice. A hero does not bow down before fate. . . . Is it manly to call this fate and obey it meekly?

Despite what Gandhi made of their spirit, extrapolating as an oral bard would do, the letter of popular incarnational classics like the above enjoin strict obedience to caste duties — in a way that invariably strikes one reared in the Hebrew tradition (and maybe a little Erich Fromm) as servile and oppressive.

Penultimate dualisms have their purposes, and India could have used some — like an energizing gap between religion and politics. Until very recently, however, the state remained theocratically conceived. Yudhisthira, the perfect *dharma* king of the *Mahabharata*, and Rama of the *Ramayana* epic are both of the ruler-warrior class. Their very stature endows the state and its laws with unchallengeable sacrality. But note the *kind* of sacrality. It is not the dynamic shake-up of a world religion; rather, it is the enveloping kind associated either with traditional oral societies or with heroic, patriarchal religion which created theocratic empires designed to remain forever. In such a system, tensions that might keep both church and state honest are automatically illegitimate. To this day, India's omniverous, all-encompassing spiritualism constitutes a liability here. The strong monistic element tends to blur and diffuse the tension — and to harmonize, often falsely, the real felt-conflicts in the society.

THE MISSING VESSEL

I do not know the history well enough to be categorical, but my impression is that Upanishadic Hinduism never succeeded well in organizing a congregation which could have a significant transformative effect on society. Made to order, as classic Judaism and Christianity were, for literate, urban elites, it never gathered these groups together either for yogic inner discipline or for concerted social action. It remained singlemindedly aristocratic and esoterically other-wordly — and noninstitutional, acting as if the primary relationships of primitive republicanism, long after their eclipse, were still the norm and effective.

Evidently and sadly, until the British came along, the elite were never able to draw from their subtle psychological *raja* yoga, or their intellectual's *jnana* yoga, the impulse for a literacy campaign such as "peoples of the Book" did. I have said enough already to indicate how important that is in occasioning a genuine subjectivity, and thus a basis for critical reflection and resistance to the status quo. By itself, evidently, oppression did not stimulate the Hindu literary imagination, as it did with Jews, to jeer at the mighty with eschatological and apocalyptic visions of their inevitable fall. Nonliteracy in effect meant that India at large never had a chance to develop a "hermeneutics of suspicion" toward its own social institutions.

But the lack of widespread literacy also explains why high Hinduism had trouble getting a congregation together. For without the dream-ridden hero in whom literacy has carved an interior, containing vessel for psychic contents and messy conflict, there's nobody for yogic disciplines to work their magic reform upon. A congregation released from family and caste ties is simply missing. Thus the Upanishads speak into a vacuum and remain a marginal phenomenon. To make use of them you have to first be a self, some kind of aspirant-hero out to slay dragons, as Buddhists seem to know.

Against this happening, *bhakti*'s antiintellectualism sets up obstacles. It so stresses the heart that it effectively ignores that the revered Upanishads were created by readers and writers, by scribes, who but for these new skills would not have imagined an *atman*. In short, it forgets that these literary capacities, though subject to grave abuse, are spiritual disciplines no less than hatha yoga. Nor is it any help, frankly, that popular Hinduism, like late medieval Catholicism, has supersaturated the landscape with religious symbolism. In this regard India resembles the "waning Middle Ages" described by J. Huizinga ([1924] 1954). The very merger of sacred and profane at the popular level, the endless growth of religious images, observances, and interpretations has virtually — for the peasant — annexed the secular order. And one suspects, as Huizinga argued in the case of fifteenth-century Europe, that this oversacramentalization has had the inverse effect of trivializing the sacred, making it so commonplace that it can no longer be felt deeply as an energizing contrast or tension.

ROLE MODELS

A big part of the problem here consists of the character models offered by oral epic scripture. In chapter 4, I adverted to the issue, the flat, typecast characterizations found in oral epics. Historically, these epics and their offshoot purana legends, which form the daily meat and bread of the poor Hindu's imagination, purged Hinduism of world-denying ascetical extremes, its tendencies to something like dualistic Western Manicheanism. In effect, they represent a move to bring the too vertical spirituality of at least some of the Upanishads down to earth, and warm it up with a more urgent ethical appeal. Yet incarnate gods tend to dominate the action as much as they do in the *Iliad*. The stories feature outsize aristocratic heroes and heroines exemplifying static virtues and vices. Their lives run smoothly to type against the backdrop of a socially stable world. They are not complex human individuals, multilayered, conflicted, and refractory people in a socially turbulent situation — such as we meet in the psychologically developing careers of Jacob, Saul, David, and Joseph in the Bible. In contrast, the mythic time of Hindu epic does not open a space in which personality develops. Events do not prefigure anything new; rather, they reinforce social solidarity and the ruling aristocratic ethic.

The atmosphere of Hindu epics is rarefied, as if meant to remove their hearers from problematic contingencies; consequently, their dream quality. One senses that, like Arthurian legend, much of this serves as a mystification, a rousing story to disguise what the ruling class is actually doing to make life miserable. One has the impression that the sublime does not so much enter as hover over the everyday domestic and political scene. And real tragedy doesn't enter at all. Furthermore, as in Greek literature in general, this is legend "from above," upper-class adventure story, in which aristocratic ethical categories stand immutable and the lower classes figure only for comic relief. In a way, these stories show almost nothing moving under the surface of heroic Indian society; they portray a static world. They do not probe problematic social, economic, or political contexts—again, such as the Hebrew scriptures do.

And thus, especially for their hearers today, the tales are not about the common people's lives. Novelists like Salmon Rushdie and Anita Desai, film directors like Satyajit Ray, are only beginning to correct the deficiencies here. A powerful dream, yes, but theophany and *incarnation* do not have the salt of history to it. The manifestations of the sacred ground themselves in a time-out-of-time, not in concrete historical events, an exodus, a fall of Jericho, the disputes over foreign policy Jewish prophets engaged in with their rulers. And you can see the difference. Saturated with such story lines from infancy, even highly educated Hindus—not to mention the masses—lack sociological imagination. Whereas in the Bible, the subsurface movement and release of historical forces virtually beg for dynamic, pliable concepts like "industrial capitalism" or "absenteeism," and synthetic terms which apply to the data-in-motion of specific periods like Renaissance or Enlightenment.

So the great energy of India goes uncontained, gets dispersed—and repeatedly breaks out into pandemonium. For without the more or less successful negotiation of separation from the mothering family, there's no alchemical vessel for the chemistry of Gandhi's "soul-force." The question, "Whom does the grail serve?" cannot be asked of the lower classes because they have no awareness of an inner cup or bowl to hold the nectar of the gods. Instead of Khajuraho's *kalash*, the pot that holds the nectar of the gods, the oral personality's structure is, as we saw, diffused, a leaky seive. The enormous, pent-up energy which is so evident in the peasant's hearth-fire altar requires an emissary, a self both gentle as a dove and cunning as a snake.

It got to you. I spent a lot of time in India with idealist professors who sounded like Bishop Berkeley. It got to be that whenever I heard them calling for a "return to traditional values and discipline," I winced. Too typically—and professionals and business people were often worse—the Indians I met seemed all but incapable of that sociological imagination I referred to. If they did not suffer our walls of separation between value and fact, sacred and profane, science and the humanities—though the Western educated frequently did—they seemed to suffer from something worse: an inability to see through the social order of things as a human, not a cosmological, convention. I began to long for austere Calvinist churches bare of images. A bit of Voltairean throttling of maharajas with the guts of Brahmin priests and pontificating gurus might do some good here, I thought. In desperate moments, I even toyed with the idea that

Mao Zedong's "cultural revolution" ought to be invited over to put Marxism's mythic "must," its irresistible dialectic of history, behind peasant fatalists as they bid to reclaim their rightful place on the stage of history. Where capitalistic consumerism offered only the invisible hand of the market, mythic Marxism, I conjectured, offered newly literate peasants and outcasts a tenuous link to the old cosmic powers who had once prospered their labors and battles.

SWALLOWING GOD

But that was the frustrated reaction of the moment. And I retract it. Many-splendored Hinduism, even in its Great Mother form, offers the despirited literate self much to feed on — as any number of pilgrim Americans found in the sixties and seventies. The ostensibly timeless, apolitical Upanishads, despite what I have said above, are subject to another interpretation. "We have revolutionary thought," writes Northrop Frye (1982: 83), "whenever the feeling 'life is a dream' becomes geared to an impulse to awaken from it." The caves of Ajanta and Khajuraho temples draw you back to an earlier, apocalyptic promise. One Aurobindo, one Mahatma Gandhi are enough to remind you that some great current of soul-force still runs in Hindu culture. It's not usually to be found at the top of the social pyramid, I think, but at the bottom.

Historically the oral-audial folk culture is a great underground stream of creativity in India. The ascetic style of early forest dwellers and monastic sects, for instance, betrays its ancestry in a tribal institution known as the *ghotul*, a self-governing youth dormitory for audio-tactile education which condemned possessiveness, opposed private property and individual accumulation of wealth. As for modern times, whether it be Ghose, Tagore, Aurobindo, or Gandhi, the *mahatmas*, the "great-souled ones," identify with the *harijans* (people of Hari, God). This is not romanticism but fighting talk. As Richard Lannoy (1971: 183–84) writes,

> When the Great Tradition was on the verge of sterility, when asceticism and dry scholasticism threatened the general health of Hindu society, waves of fresh energy seem to have coursed from the Antipodes, inspired by culture heroes nurtured among pastoral folk.

The ballad of the *Bhagavad Gita* is one such antipodean product. The story occurs as an intermission, a moment of self-doubt, in the midst of a folk-epic, dynastic battle, and thus clearly falls within the time frame of a fairly well-formed self. But it dramatizes a *kairos*, a moment of opportunity, when the hero, Prince Arjuna, passes over from heroic zealotry and terrorism to a new mode of being in the world. What rearms the prince for the oncoming struggle is not blood-lust or prestige-hunger but his charioteer, the Lord Krishna in the flesh. Abraham and Moses, Jesus and Saint Paul, Mohammed and Martin Luther, each in their own way, found their backing, their wheels turning in a similar way. The real battle, the moral equivalent of warfare, says the *Gita*, lies in a person's own heart, in going "against nature" only in the sense of nonviolent resistance to one's program of heroic self-justification. As Gandhi so well understood. But who is this warrior of the heart that the *Gita* addresses? Certainly not the illiterate peasant, for the *Gita's* heroics are likely only to reinforce his submission to external fate, or worse, hand him over to grandiose but impotent fantasies. No, the moral of the story is primarily directed to a literate self whose caste duties have begun to seem oppressive and self-defeating. Arjuna, the hero of the tale, is a man caught in the throes of mid-life crisis; on the threshold of a new passage in the life cycle. In order to cross over, he requires a set of inner weapons, precisely the yogas in which the Lord Krishna instructs him—just as Americans in the sixties and seventies were instructed by Hindu gurus.

In other words, if the promised land of selfhood is established, thereafter another sort of revolution, in the first instance psychological, must occur. The trick is learning to wake up, to deliberately swallow the wisdom already secreted in the veins of earth. Again, Hindu folk wisdom knows how we resist taking it in. There is a famous puranic legend (cited in O'Flaherty, 1980: 96) according to which the mother of Krishna, Yashodha, discovers that the young Krishna (whom she does not recognize as an avatar) has eaten dirt while playing with other children.

> Yashodha took Krishna by the hand and scolded him and said, "You naughty boy, why have you eaten dirt?" "I haven't," said Krishna. "All the boys are lying. If you believe them instead of me, look at my mouth yourself." "Then open up," she said to the god . . . and he opened his mouth.
> Then she saw in his mouth the whole universe, with the far corners of the sky, and the wind, and lightning, and the orb of the earth with its mountains and oceans, and the moon and stars, and space itself; and she saw her own village and herself. She became frightened and confused. . . . Instantly Yashodha lost her memory of what had occurred. She took her son on her lap and was as she was before.

Yashodha's perspective represents, I think, something beyond the old oral cosmology wherein she would have recognized the world's and her own participation in God's acoustic presence. She obviously stands out enough from her environment to objectivize it, and thus to separate the quintessentially good God in whom she piously believes from the evil world her shrewd peasant's eyes see around her. Her downfall consists in the separation, a form of transcendental denial which turns the physical world into a spiritual wasteland. Given this imaginative construction, she is overwhelmed, terrified, and represses the vision which so contradicts her assumptions. She falls back asleep. The momentary vision (for a mere woman, the text seems to imply) is too much; she can't stand the intensity, the magnitude of the thing which, the text goes on to say, a true (male) yogin can absorb. More to the point, she can't tolerate the horror that Krishna eats all that to her represents the mean and the unclean, that signifies *death*.

So she settles back to loving her incognito son more intensely, the text proceeds to say, without realizing that in being drawn to him she is being drawn to the death which he swallows. But this is more than a story of resistance and repression. The perspective of the God-man Krishna anticipates, as the Christ figure does in the West, the fullness of time, and thus signals the process taking place "between the times" of beginning and end. Born "out of time," and ahead of Yashodha's implicitly heroic time frame, we might say that Krishna stands for the future—for a new mode of participation in cosmic wisdom which requires a new kind of death-rebirth struggle beyond the range of a heroine's bid for relative independence and self-esteem. That struggle for independent credit, one might say, applies to the third perinatal matrix, and the route is familiar and well traveled. Yashodha's son lures her into the birth throes of a fourth perinatal matrix whose territory is for her uncharted. He lures her into a thickened narrative plot, that "ontological revolution" we referred to in the last chapter. But the Krishna stories articulate the implications of that revisioned passover more precisely: that in time the Creator is gradually taking on human flesh. By totemistically identifying with Krishna, the incarnation of God, the teeming millions of India are literally being seduced into making the myriad world as Brahman, their lover, does. The scenario begins to sound like the Hebrew *Song of Songs*—and curiously, that foreign love song brings us closer to the eroticism of the Khajuraho temples.

The puranic story brings it down to earth, but it is what the seers of the

Upanishads had been proclaiming for centuries. After describing creation, the *Svetasvatara* Upanishad, part six, declares,

> God ended his work and he rested, and he made a bond of love between his soul and the soul of all things. And the One became one with the one, and the two, and the three and the eight, and with time and with the subtle mystery of the human soul. . . .
> May God who is hidden in nature, even as the silkworm is hidden in the web of silk he made, lead us to union with his own Spirit, with Brahman.

For an exclusively orally structured person, hearing these words in the context of customary ritual action might well lead to a diffusion into an undifferentiated unity—probably stated in monistic terms, if articulated. It might be that oceanic regression Freud so feared. But if the subject were literate and possessed genuine interiority—as some Americans in the sixties did—the result could be quite different. Then India's spiritual disciplines could offer entry into the secret of her own sacred texts and architecture, and entry as well into some Western texts and figures. They could open a way out of the desert of criticism to what philosopher Hans-Georg Gadamer calls a "hermeneutics of restoration."

But let me stay with the root Hindu image for this process, which is based on the rhythm of breath—in-out, up-down, expansion-contraction, filling-emptying, taking-receiving, holding on-letting go, opening-closure, entry and exit. When you think of it, there is nothing more basic in life than this diastole-systole pattern. Analogously, it joins all the opposites one can think of: work and play, hard and soft, same and different, light and dark, gain and loss, birth and death, structure and antistructure, heaven and earth. The secret of Khajuraho and Ajanta, and of the East in general I would say, lies in deepening the breath. Like a woman in childbirth. Which brings us back to the Great Mother.

SOUNDS OF MOTHER EARTH

The Western Abrahamic myth celebrates leaving home, the call from Ur to find a promised land. Looking back over the shoulder spells death. India's homeostasis allows you to understand the advantages of repression and amnesia, and how well both have permitted the West to lighten its load while getting ahead in a certain way. "The great boon of repression," said Ernest Becker, "is that it makes it possible to live decisively in an overwhelmingly miraculous and incomprehensible world." At the same time, following the Western mythic path exposes us to deracination, a loss of animal vitality, and to complexes of abandonment and severe Oedipal terrors. On top or out there in front, it often seems, nothing is there, in the nature of things, to back us up. The voice that calls us out from a maternal matrix leaves us, without a father's blessing, in the cold. In his excoriation of Hinduism, V. S. Naipaul was blind to what it could open up to a chilled, wandering Ishmael or Esau. Or to a crafty Odysseus who returns home after his wandering, only to be bored stiff.

Great permissive, mothering India did not forget, as the West has been inclined to do, the old vegetation gods of the underworld. Consequently, she has a message for the uprooted, outward-bound, overworked Western hero and heroine. Her acoustic space is moon to our sun. It hits you, as I said, in the stomach, in your instinctual mother wit. Hindus call this psychophysical center of gravity (about one inch below the navel and two inches in) the *kath* chakra, and Zen Buddhism calls it *hara*, the center of life. It's as if, though the biological and tribal umbilici have been cut and you stand out from nature and ethnicity, the wisdom of the Great Mother remains intact in your belly: on the one hand, a reminder of the chaos still in you, the bloody mess, the multiple pressures in the gut from which the work of your life began to form; on the other, a reminder of primal unity and the values of sedentary living, of cultivating a centering sense of place, home, vital warmth, and hospitality.

Let me cite a personal example of what the *kath* center means. When I meditate, often on a subway to work, I descend below the street noise, put my bloodless, professional mind on hold, retreat into my body center, temporarily shut out the external world. Once settled there, I've often found myself spontaneously hearing (and imitating) a circumambient murmuring sound, as if a mothering universe were humming with contentment and pleasure that she gave me birth and that I'm here. Or is it a father's sound of good pleasure? (For it sounds at times as if I were surrounded by a group of guttural Tibetan monks, chanting from the navel of the universe.) Kinesthetically, it's as if your innards were getting a rubdown, and you could now breathe expansively, with your whole body. The sound is at once outside and inside; it massages nerves, the marrow of bones, warms the digestive track, expands the lungs, quickens the heart and intelligence from the bottom up. It's an unfamiliar you that nests in the sound, attends it, attunes to it, pleasures it; and, identifying with it from the belly, a stranger that echoes the humming — as if you were lalling an infant's "It's good to be here." Certain people and places seem to evoke a similar phenomenon, of touching base as it were. Esalen often did. And as I say, India did. Their mothering spaces gave an undertone of trust to carry away with you, one which sets the blood running again, and creates volume inside you that holds the real and imaginal worlds taken in over a lifetime. It also offers an anodyne for all those false starts built on cold reason and a sense of inferiority or superiority. It's a lunar place from which to hear a call, without fear, to come out of the dark; a subterranean space where you feel grounded, and hence a place to depart from and return to. Normally, when I do come out of this dark, the tone of my voice is several registers deeper. And I feel a little more ready to father a world—and mother it, nurture its growth.

THE PRIMAL SCENE OF WIT

The first thing one might say about this kind of meditative experience is that it recalls, more accurately, reworks, a primal scene. How, one might ask, did that "big, blooming, buzzing confusion" of my infantile sensorium get transformed into meaningful experience? How did I open to language and thereby to hundreds of thousands of years of human experience encoded in language? Developmental and cognitive psychologists may still be very puzzled as to the exact whys and hows, but they seem more or less agreed that the awakening of human intelligence is tied into that intense, reciprocal interaction between child and mother. Linguistic ability, and therefore operative intelligence, is somehow quickened in us by the wrap-around, somatic presence of a mother or mother substitute who, at this fragile, preverbal stage, symbolizes the whole universe to us. Her nervous or caring touch, the glad or pinched expression on her face and in her eyes; above all, the tone of her voice told us whether the world was trustworthy or not, a reliable or dangerous place to come forth in. This initial psychic symbiosis, at once tactile, kinesthetic, and vocal, is apparently indispensable in order to activate the distinctive human potential for meaning and language (Montague, 1971: 1–37, 183–219).

The tactile sensations establish boundaries, acknowledge mutual otherness; at the same time, the mother's voice manifests an interior with which we may commune. In some way that still eludes comprehension, the whole transaction evokes and nurtures the lalling stage of infancy whereby we surround ourselves with a buzz of experimental vowels which we gradually begin to cut with consonants and pauses, imitating and thereby assimilating meanings "mama" has first conveyed somatically. At this initial stage, she is the *anima mundi*, the world-soul speaking, and as such the carrier of that basal ontology, of either blessing or curse, that we carry with us throughout life and frequently appeal to—from a foxhole, at the moment of death. The whole process is perhaps the exemplary case of unity in diversity, of a union which need not repress but actually may inspire difference. It is also the exemplary case of ensouled nature giving birth to meaning—and thus midwifing soul and voice in another.

ANIMAL SPIRITS

My meditation, so far as I can discern, is not a literal memory of my relation to my biological mother. Nor does it evoke the regressive, cthonic Great Mother who swallows and destroys her children through their desire to return to her undifferentiated womb. On the contrary, I have a sense of the inspiriting breath of *both* mother and father on a vast, archetypal scale. The fundamental sensation is one of being breathed into at my core, and thereby released from enclosure; particularly released from constrictive conventions of that leviathan, the secular world which hems me in, contracts my free breathing in daily life. What is going on here, if I can figure it, is a marital rite between paternal sky God and maternal earth Goddess, an act of heavenly coitus (echoed in my biological parents, I think), which gives me a second lease on life, a momentary second birth. As I said, I come away from this kind of regenerative experience, having taken it into my bones and nerves, a little more able to generate myself—for one thing, because I come away expanded inwardly, as if I have a great, secret cavern inside that flows with currents which make the ocean's seem small in comparison.

This brings me to a second effect, which I alluded to, the fact that the cavern inside is more like a womb, ready now to bear a new world. After the downstroke to the bottom of that womb-cavern, there's a rush. Suddenly, I return to my ordinary world and face it with virgin eyes and ears, quickened senses all around—precisely as if I had recovered an animal's quick instincts and senses. If I'm outside the city, I begin to hear nature's voices, her groans and shouts, her cries and whispers; I can feel the same currents of her growing and dying and giving birth in my flesh. If in the city, newspaper headlines of public events, buildings, faces on the subway, acts of nature, and odd bits of conversation that drift my way—all seem to penetrate to a different level in me, strike chords that they hadn't before, and unveil themselves as if I were catching puns, punch lines, and portents that only minutes before I was dumb to, that had merely bounced off my shut-down receivers and passed me by.

Things that only a short time ago seemed opaque, even heavy and depressing, now appear ironic or even comical. Odd reversals. Matters that appeared weighty, as if I were believing what CBS and the *New York Times* said, now appear obviously trivial. Whereas otherwise trivial exchanges between a panhandler and a passer-by, a mother and child, two old people on a park bench take on significance. I can see through them. Can see through myself. Everything has become metaphor. It's as if things had suddenly turned inside-out, and therefore translucently symbolic— because down deep, in my belly, I am connected to everything "out there" by underground streams. The poetic inspiration here can be a little overwhelming and out of control; it takes some getting used to. Symbols are thick with implication and ramify, begetting metaphoric conjunctions, which in turn stimulate further imaginative conjecture and speculation. Such plenty provides more than enough work for the prosaic mind's stores of exact information and analytic skill. If you are going to create real toads in imaginary gardens, you'd better know something, the more exact the better, about toads.

In other words, a virgin mind's metaphoric blitz opens the door into the unknown and is the starting point of creative science. To speak of one's mind becoming virgin, however, is not mere figure of speech but straightforward description of what is going on. My mind becomes virgin when it contacts the animal spirits of soul space, traditionally conceived as feminine and receptive. Rightly so. When the hard lines of my heroic project yield and soften, my inner senses open and I sense with new eyes, ears, taste, smell, and touch. I am more willing to take in what is sensed because I have that vast cavern inside to hold and reimagine the world's flood of images. My hero's diagrams of things, actually a highly subjective world in that its images are largely projections of my craze for esteem and will to power, fall apart. No longer so rigid, sensory apertures now open, I can be more attentive, objective.

Like a mother with infant, or more, like the Virgin Goddess out of whom (in ancient myth) the whole material world unfolds, I welcome the raw world into my fertile womb-soul and brood over it, muse upon it, reimagine it. I do not distance myself from what floods in by pinning it to the wall with conventional, abstract concepts and categories. Rather, I put my analytic, categorizing mind in suspense, and yield to the highly charged images arising spontaneously. The images often come in mineral, vegetable, animal form; if in human form, the shape is grotesque, somehow implicitly mocking or caricaturing one's public persona. I've found that when I speak in such imagistic language, it possesses electric current which seems to be amazingly transformable. The images are enigmas which do not stay put. They offer an underground commentary on life's movement; dwelt on, meditated, they amplify and ramify, opening doors and passageways into the unexplored complex of life that you'd never imagined before. The symbols provide rich food for thought and new starts. But not just for yourself. Remarkably, I've found that imagistic language has an extraordinary power to welcome others to enter its stream of associations, as if it were their very own. Am I a stone, a fog, garbage dump or stuck record, a cold reptile or a dumb ape, a ground hog, leopard, or clockwork machine? Or a whole medley of mythic heroes caught in the devices of their tragic flaws? You name it and others will recognize their affinity, their participation in the figuration. In a way that conceptual discourse is not, imagistic language is erotic and coupling; it not only sticks to the ribs but ribs others to you and you to them.

THE PRIMAL BOND

This news is not only important for the top-down, typographically educated individualist in a functionally specialized world. It is also a clue to what is afoot in the Ajanta caves and the Khajuraho temples. Let me explain. A positive mother-infant bond is psychologically and socially so important for the career of the outward-bound self precisely because, at the preverbal level of our organism, it opens us up to a life lived under the archetype of the Great Goddess (or the feminine aspect of God) who nurtures while she lets go. With that established as the undertone of existence, the whole process of developing object-relations takes on a different quality—of unity in diversity, of a world that mothers you as you mother-father it. There's parity and intercommunion here. Rather than feeling isolated or cut off, the objective other need never appear utterly disjunct or separate. Your boundaries, you sense, are permeable, a medium of communication; you extend into the not-self; the not-self penetrates you. As an adult, the people and materials you work with, impress yourself upon, are part of you, you of them, each activating the other as in the original primal scene. Whatever proper distancing you achieve within this archetypal matrix, whatever proper defensive measures a situation may call for, in principle you can remain, as a child, open and empathetic and basically erotic. You can both acknowledge otherness, the freedom of things and people to be themselves, and simultaneously sense their connection, the mutual claim of attention and affection you and they have on each other. As Martin Buber would have put it, the primary relationship to the world, the context for knowledge and action, can remain one of I-Thou.

I do not mean to suggest that my meditation example by any means contains the whole of what Ajanta and Khajuraho, much less the Upanishads, figure. Only that it gives a prefigural taste of the thing, and an indication of how the soul or *atman*, alive once more to her animal spirits, discovers a deeper intentionality that transfigures the world. Being soulful is a *sine qua non* for penetrating the temple enigmas, and for reaching the point where one begins to suspect that in their view, staring back at you from their temple sanctums, as it were, all of what we imagine as phylogenetic prehistory and the ages of human history are but the story of one lifetime—call him or her what you will, the Buddha, Rama and Sita, Krishna, the Christ. For these figures have a way of telescoping the homogeneous linearity of time and its delaying action. If not now, they seem to declare, when? On the face of it, given the usual inertia, reincarnation through a countless succession of lifetimes seems entirely plausible; getting the point of existence in one lifetime extremely unlikely. But slowly now, how might one condense all history into a single lifetime? For the literate, the trick lies in making the transit, via soul, from nightmare heroic time to apocalyptic time.

SOUL SPACE

What do I mean by soul? Strictly oral cultures offer a clue—through their sense of what "loss of soul" means. It is neither insanity nor physical sickness. Rather, you are not there, out of yourself as if you'd forgotten your name, disconnected from others; hence unable to take part in your society, its rituals, and traditions; in short, out of communion with self, others, and the gods. An analogous sense of excommunication and of being a spiritual nonentity, I'm saying, afflicted us grail questers. Denizens of the city that we mostly were, at the very least all our lateral involvements had been wearing us thin—and ironically, *down* to soul space where big breath becomes possible again.

In an oral culture, the magic was to discern and control the spirits in wood, vale, stream, and mountain. With the death of Pan, magic did not perish but merely changed its venue. For the literate person, magic involves discerning and discriminating among interior movements—calls of the wild, of siren, of hearth, of fear and flight, calls to work, to battle, to dance. Soul is not to be confused with an insulated ego shut off from the outdoors; it is essentially a crossroads where the labyrinthine winds of the great outer world meet in private, behind closed doors. With cultivation, especially when linked (as it typically is in our culture, by reading good fiction) to the "higher" centers of mind and imagination, this imaginal space is a place for stewing, brooding, judging and deciding. It offers a *middle ground*, a mediator between you and events, between the doer and the deed, to be differentiated from the physical and the strictly spiritual but partaking of both. It is the nowhere in you in which reflection and discernment can occur. It is your vertical axis or interior pivot of stillness, coolness, darkness, and connection that can bear the strain of all the outer, lateral involvements of your city life. Maybe.

Depth psychologist James Hillman (1967: 42) refers to soul as that unknown, finally indefinable human factor of depth and fantasy which "makes meaning possible, turns events into experience, is communicated in love—*and has religious concern*." Hillman adds elsewhere (1975: x), "the significance soul makes possible, whether in love or in religious concern, derives from its special *relation with death*."

In the first instance, Eastern spiritual disciplines were simply humanizing; they awakened you to the refuge of soul. From this angle, soul is a sunken city of Ur in which all the old cosmological connections remain intact. As such, it is not the end but the starting point, the loamy soil to which spirit gives blood, which spirit enlivens; in turn, however, soulfulness gives gravity or body to flights of spirit which otherwise have no weight in heaven, I am inclined to think, or in the empirical world. Soul rather than self-promoting ego is the container, the potential vessel of the grail.

To the Buddha, that vessel was provisional. The teaching regarding the causes of the soul's suffering (basically, clinging to people or things) was the raft by which one passed to the "other shore," a vehicle to be dispensed with, along with the concept of soul itself, once you got there. Naturally then, very much like Meister Eckhart and Saint John of the Cross in the West, the Buddha stresses the downstroke of breath, emptying and letting go. That's how you carve an Ajanta cave out of solid rock, how you build a Khajuraho temple.

TANTRIC YOGA AND THE PURE CONDUCTOR

Enlightenment involves transformation not just of what we call mind but the whole body sensorium. In Hindu anatomy, the chakra system corresponds to what Western medieval theology spoke of as the "inner senses."

The lower chakras which I have globally called the visceral *kath* center refer to the sensorimotor drives for food, security, emotional or erotic exchange, and the will-to-power—what Freud loosely called libido. These in turn connect with higher, more subtle chakras, verbal capacity (in the throat), reflective capacity and the psychic "third eye" chakra (in the neocortex), the heart chakra in the chest, and the crown chakra (at the crown of the skull and above), signifying one's spiritual aura. Moving up the spine, each psychophysical center relates to progressively more subtle realms of transpersonal energy and consciousness. The early pyrotechnics of the consciousness movement were associated with openings of the lower chakras. As the movement matured, people began to notice the more subtle energies of the higher chakras.

Before one can move on to release the flows of subtle eros (which Christians call *charis* and *caritas*, grace and charity), say the yogic disciplines, the heroic self must contain itself and symbolically die, just as the tribal persona had to die before the heroic ego could be born. The hero's desperate fear of death prevents transformation, keeps him fixated in his neurotic pattern. But ironically, death wish and suicidal impulses, if not literalized, open passage to self-transcendence, provide the energy by which old heroic virtues, loyalty to flag and courage in the face of death, can be redirected to a deeper, wider service that surpasses tribal nationalism. The process requires self-renunciation: first, the withdrawal of scapegoating projections; second, introversion, in effect, an internalization of the sacrificial process. The task is to contain and reintegrate those dissociated nether regions, the soulless outcast and raw natural energies in ourselves—which yogic Tantrism envisions as the sleeping, serpent of Shakti power, containing all the earth's fecundity, coiled in the "root" chakra at the base of the spine. The hero must somehow descend into that chaos, that hell, and die in order to be reborn (Wilber, 1981: 21–36, 128–29, 134–50, 240–52). This is the real death-rebirth struggle, and as such, the key to the ancient Mediterranean myth of the dying-rising god.

According to the tantric system, our deepest ontological hunger is buried in the alimentary system and the cold passion of our most primitive, reptilian brain, for whom everything is food. Even God. It's as if all the energies of the physical world are pent up in our viscera and base parts, precisely the parts that evoke shame from the hero pretending to be a god without an anus and feces. It's just when we learn to contain all this erotic energy's hunger for union with the *mysterium tremendum*, and release it inwardly, up the spinal column, that it blows open the crown chakra and lights a great fire upon the earth. Western medieval alchemy's "subtle body" may be the best clue to what goes on in this left-hand

Hindu and Buddhist path of descent *ad inferos*. To find the "philosopher's stone" of great price, according to this path, the light must enter into the darkness, the commonest, most overlooked and rejected elements of life. The stone of stumbling, the things which take our breath away are key. Before the heart can stand being fired and its dross turned into gold by the sun of true wisdom, the axiom went, the full gamut and pain of ordinary emotional experience, instead of being avoided, had to be held in the alembic of soul and alloyed by silver. Silver represented steady mindfulness, distracted by neither likes nor dislikes, boring down to the unconscious roots of everyday occurrence. Just the opposite of cathartic therapy, the first rule was not to leak energy (by projecting, blaming, or taking anger out on others) but to concentrate impartially upon the elements of a situation, separating out the truth and returning the excessive subjective component to one's own vessel without repressing any affect of fear, disdain, love or hate. The idea was to play the uroboric snake consuming its own tail; in effect, to circle about and eat into the unconscious roots of one's past. Our vegetative inertias, the most deadened and fixed elements of our being, constitute the prime matter, the rotting mulch pile, the fossil fuel, which produce heat, pulverization, and liquefaction, all to be held in the hermetic vase (Harding, 1963: 435–68).

The alchemical *opus* or "work," as it was called, was to mine and refine your own base metal; that is, to attend and befriend its salty tears and sweat, its sulfuric bitterness, its dull, leaden states and hot, mercurial fluids with the cool, bright, and silvery, subtle air of the moon—the exemplar at once of hard stability and fluent receptivity. The moon, it was thought, was the recipient of all planetary influences, a pure conductor which resonates perfectly when struck. Unlike the sun, it does not burn or destroy other things which come into its orbit, but is a noninterfering mediator or mirror. Purged of its attachments to the things of the world, to body and the contents of mind, the soul is to become moonlike and thus superconductive. For apophatic (or negative, mystical) Christian theology from Pseudo-Dionysius through Meister Eckhart and Jacob Boehme, the aim was similar but put in terms of the soul becoming nothing, an image of the nameless Ur-Ground and End.

Standing within the ambience of a more intensely oral culture than Western medieval theology did, tantric Hinduism and Buddhism had the advantage of describing the physiology of the process in concrete, imagistic language. From long practice of minding leaden states, both traditions recognized that the flow of libido could be reversed, sleeping instincts awakened, and the *kundalini* serpent coiled about our roots in the

Ground of Being released. Then the giant anaconda would shed its skin, transform. Within the anatomy of the Hindu chakra system and "burning bad karma," the process involved moving down and up with the breath, "up" the spinal column from the relatively gross energies of the lower chakras to the "subtle body" of the brain—and then "down" again—thus minding compulsive desire and helpless affliction with grains of silver, flashes of insight into the genesis of suffering, all those holding actions and strategies of defense and compensation that we initial with our names in the course of adjusting to a world of equally contracted selves. "Aha, so that's it!" Releases from fixations, tears, and intimations of a human face do come. Yet flashy insight (or "peak experience") cannot be allowed to turn into flighty verticality, something which has happened often in the history of religion. To keep to the alchemical analogy, without the alloy of lead—depressions, messy symptoms, conflict, and suffering—shiny mind loses its luster, tarnishes in open air. Hiding away on mountain tops, the mind either burns away or becomes disembodied and prey to hapless melancholy—the plague of the thinker who simply stews and goes nowhere. Dimitri and Ivan Karamazov in Dostoyevsky's *Brothers Karamazov* brood about the heart's darkness a great deal, but only Alyosha, with his monk's purity of mind, has the capacity to move in and out of the dark, and to kiss the earth.

BREAKTHROUGH

Acting as moon, then, the contemplative, tantric mind mediates between sun and earth. It channels the groans of Mother Earth so she can rise up, through us, to greet the sun. Let go, and when you get to the bottom of that exhalation, in a kind of black hole which admits no light, let heaven inhale you—and you may find raw nuclear energy blooming glorious, right through the top of your skull! Khajuraho temples figure alchemy like that, as do the Ajanta caves—a marital rite of heaven and earth. The image in Buddhist texts is of breaking the roof open and flight. The Arhats, enlightened ones passing from one mode of being to another, "fly through the air and break the roof of the palace."

A big breath indeed. Apocalypse, revelation. But the breakthrough here, as I suggested in the last chapter, begins to look like a joint enterprise of East and West. In the Western narrative line, the heroic ego must suffer dismemberment and die to its neat and orderly "upper world," its pretensions to superiority and permanency, its self-legitimating images of

God. All these idols are to be surrendered in order to awake from nightmare history, to release that fullness which replenishes the earth's emptiness. If I understand it, the Buddha took a similar path: the godlike hero not clinging to godhood, emptying himself—as in the hymn Saint Paul cites in Philippians 2:6: "His state was divine yet he did not cling to his equality with God but emptied himself, to assume the condition of a slave, becoming as men are . . . even accepting death." The stumbling block for Christian participation in the ensuing exaltation, as for the gnostic and pseudoangel in everyone, is that you can't take God whole without swallowing what God stomachs—the gritty mineral and vegetable world explored by the natural sciences, the dirty, underground worlds exposed to view by social historians, by Balzacs, Dickenses, Zolas, Steinbecks, Dreisers. This earth groans to give birth, says Paul in Romans 8, to be replenished with Spirit. Nature having fallen with our fall, in effect we are Mother Nature's big opportunity to become spirited, her chance at second birth.

Can it be that East and West converge, that the Buddha's "diamond body" is not different from the body of Christ which knew "no more distinction between Jew and Greek, slave and free, male and female?" I wonder, and as usual it's figure in stone that offers a glimmer. I think of that seeker of the Great Sower's seed, the ever-restless Trappist monk, Thomas Merton on his Asian journey in 1968. There he is, barefoot, standing wide-eyed before the giant Polonnaruwa Buddha statues of Sri Lanka, discovering what he had been "obscurely looking for" on his trip.

> The great smiles. Huge and yet subtle. . . . Filled with every possibility, questioning nothing, knowing everything, rejecting nothing, the peace not of emotional resignation but . . . of sunyata [the emptiness of all form], that has seen through every question without trying to discredit anyone or anything—*without refutation*—without establishing some other argument. . . .
>
> Looking at these figures I was suddenly, almost forcibly, jerked clean out of the habitual, half-tied vision of things, and an inner clearness, clarity, as if exploding from the rocks themselves, became evident and obvious. The queer *evidence* . . . no puzzle, no problem, and really no "mystery." . . . simply because what matters is clear. The rock, all matter, all life, is charged with dharmakaya [buddha-nature]. . . . Everything is emptiness and everything is compassion. [Merton, 1973: 233–35]

The wordless expression of the Buddha, caught by the sculptor at the moment of death, spoke to Merton, who was about to die himself, from rock. Somehow it was a primal recognition scene—of the cross-connection between two itinerant preachers, the one of the Sermon on the Mount and the other of Sarnath's Deer Park outside Benares (where that ex-prince gave his first sermon). Is it conceivable that those two spoke a common tongue, a language of egoless love whose communication outlasts the language of argument and refutation? Short of standing where Jesus and the Buddha did, perhaps the question is unanswerable.

So let me turn now to a more modest question. How is it that stones speak? Only slightly facetious, this question brings us the consciousness movement's search for ideas which disclose a deeper order underlying Newtonian gravity and atomic theory. Just a few decades ago, the notion that unargumentative compassion could speak from the dead, from cold stone, appeared ridiculous. This is no longer the case.

PART III

Recovering a Genesis Story

SEVEN

Waking Mother Nature

The Element of fire is quite put out,
The Sun is lost, and th'earth, and no man's wit
Can well direct him where to look for it.
And freely men confess that this world's spent.

John Donne

The order of reason is repetitive, and the train of thought that
comes from it, infinitely iterative, is but a science of death.
. . . The order of reason is martial. . . . The laws are the
same everywhere; they are thanatocratic. There is nothing to
be learned, to be discovered, to be invented, in this repetitive
world.

Michel Serres

A clash of doctrines is not a disaster—it is an opportunity.

Alfred North Whitehead

How does silent stone speak? How did Michelangelo warm up Carrara marble and draw out a Moses, a Virgin Mary mourning her son, and at the last an unfinished, living slave? That's a Western riddle to match the Zen Buddhist's koan about freeing a goose from a sealed jar without breaking it. If India's problem lies in the weakness of the "I am," since the seventeenth century the West's consists in resistance to the idea that matter can be spirited. But are we so sure any longer that we know what we're made of, what matter is? Or that the classic Cartesian separation of immeasurable mind and measurable matter, *res cogitans* and *res extensa*, holds up? Is the mind a computer or the computer like a mind? Which is it? In a nuclear age of high energy physics, what sense does it make to view atoms as inert, stable constellations running in neat, military file within homogeneous euclidean space? In a Big Bang age, the metaphor of a machine won't do for us what it once did for Galileo, Descartes, and Newton. Do linear trajectories, the immutable, reversible stuff of Newtonian law, continue to write straight in an Einsteinean world? Are we and this condensed star gas upon which we stand, in fact the whole Milky Way galaxy, cosmic errors drifting inevitably toward an icy heat death? What are we to make of evolution, of irreversible processes working against the tide of entropy? Do we know that matter is dead, that the physical universe doesn't pulse and breathe, doesn't heat up and cool down, communicate, circulate, and break with the past like a human being does?

These are some of the questions we shall be dealing with in the three chapters of this section. The chapters will explore the possibility, opened up by the new physics, that far from being dead, the cosmos is fundamentally erotic, a balancing act of knottings (matter) and information in a sea of noisy energy. If this is the larger environment, our evolved planet is chancy but not a strange accident; we belong here, have a home, and simultaneously provide a home, a voice for nature's roar. In short, these chapters will offer another way of penetrating and amplifying the theme sounded in discussing psychedelics and India: that our larger narrative line involves the conscious recapitulation and transfiguration of cosmogenesis and the human genesis story. A glorious project, an obligation—that we neglect at the price of steep guilt. The stones, the subatomic world, are to rise up through us, if we are willing, and greet the sun. Against the backdrop of the modern world's image of dead nature, obviously, this story, if we choose to tell it, would be one of resurrection and the rebirth of nature.

At this very moment, 1987, we are still at a very preliminary stage of telling the above tale. Questions are fortunately plentiful; answers still in a state of flux. What is the nature of matter? So far as answers are concerned, what we do know for certain, with a kind of Cartesian clarity, is largely negative, that the classic mechanistic schemes proposed by godlike observers are seriously wanting. But what schemes of participant observers, what new paradigms, will now replace the old models? At this fluid juncture, any new proposal ought to be met with a healthy sense of Socratic ignorance. What is clear is that the mystery of elemental matter, specifically of the unstable quantum world, grows daily curiouser and curiouser. As particle physicists get closer to the blooming confusion at the bottom of things, projected back some 15 billion years, the mystery of this story deepens and empties out into a vacuum, sheer nothingness — from which null-point come the galaxies and our strange planet earth.

THE TWO CULTURES

When the American pilgrim-yogi of the sixties and seventies returned home from the East, readjustment was often difficult. It meant, among other things, returning to C. P. Snow's "two cultures" — to life in the "fact" world of empirical-analytic science and the "hermeneutic" world of the humanities and social sciences. If you were a college teacher as I was, you lived daily with the split, because the university institutionalizes it. The departmentalization of natural science and the arts implies living with the double truth of Apollo and Dionysius, the one modeled on correspondence (or crudely, copying), aligning a structure of words with external phenomena; and the other deriving from poetic incantation and mystic rhapsody. Mediating between the two paths are the strange arts of the god Hermes. In the ancient world, an image of Hermes typically stood at a crossroads signifying the passage between different structures of order; the god was thought to provide inspiration, a second sight, a thread through the labyrinth of diverse spaces and conspiratorial plots. The task of hermeneutics involves interpreting the bewildering complexity of human communication and the myths or social visions through which we understand our past, present, and future — our destinies. In this chapter, I will play Hermes examining the entrails of contemporary science, but a Hermes who has acquired some of the tastes of a yogi or monk. From that vantage point, we pick up our story at a wake, with sacerdotal scientists watching at the bier of patient nature, informing the mourning survivors of the deceased that they can no longer have any part with their mother. She has breathed her last.

Until lately, the West's two-culture split has left us survivors two equally deficient paths, neither of which the consciousness movement was willing to accept. On the one side was the way of rationalists seeking to impose order on the natural and social environment with nothing but their reason; on the other stood the modernist mystic seeking to find order within a self divorced from the larger environment. Rejecting this dissociated sensibility, the madness of the one and the hollowness of the other (was not such mysticism always psychologized away?), the movement sought to recover a larger ecology for the mind, beyond individualistic humanism and reaching to a deeper order underlying Newtonian mechanics and modern atomic theory. It wanted, in other words, to reclaim its rights as a relative, a living relationship with deceased Mother Nature. Kinship with fellow human beings, humanism in the narrow sense, would not suffice. We must have kinship with quantum particles, molten and condensed star gases, diligent mitochondria, rain forests, grasshoppers, the animal kingdom—at least two of every kind for this ark, this ship of fools. That was the word—and it meant a variation on the theme of tantric descent, begun perhaps in India, into the nether world of quantum physics. At this juncture, our story begins to take on the aura of a Christian ceremony, a wake which celebrates the ultimate rite of passage through death to new life. The dead rise.

BREATHING SPACE

Why did the movement enthuse over the new physics? Why didn't it follow the well-beaten track of its romantic forebears in the nineteenth century who drew back from technology's mindless nature and inward to "creative genius" or a lazy pantheism? (Or why didn't it retreat into some existentialist's Black Forest and cling to dismissable vatic utterance?) The short answer, I think, is that Eastern spiritual practice had induced experience that made premodern cosmologies seem plausible. But that only intensified the two culture split within us all—and made the task of reconciliation suddenly urgent. These neo-theosophists did not care for soul experience locked inside Kantian psyches and running on totally separate current from that which makes the atoms spin. They wanted soul breathing outdoors, and soul's language speaking not simply from the heart, but from the heart of the physical cosmos where Dante's Light moved the stars and planets. They wanted inwardness referring, as it did for someone like Pierre Teilhard de Chardin, to the world of the hardest sciences. For that, they were impatient for a new scientific paradigm.

To rationalist critics whose religion, if any, was art, the movement's raid on the new physics was nearly inexplicable—or outright thievery. Not to worry, Hermes is the god of thieves and of reconciliations between strangers, in this case between matter and mind. Unwittingly, the movement had Copernicus's piety, and Newton's and Einstein's, on its side. It was rationalism and scientific positivism that constituted the exceptional aberration within the long tradition of physics. That the movement sought a blessing through physics was as old as the inception of science in

Greek literature's love of lucidity and its skill at representing foreground detail with eminent dispassion and precision; and as old as the romance Western culture had long had with the earth, since the Presocratic Ionian philosophers and Pythagoras's transformation of qualitative sound into mathematical ratios (acoustics) around 500 B.C. Pythagoras had been a guru, the mainstay of a cult of sacred numerology.

The founder of atomic theory may be even more to the point. For when Democritus, "the laughing philospher," arrived around 460 B.C. preaching his atoms and an imperturbable mind (*ataraxia*) to bloodthirsty Greeks, he was promoting a radical religious reformation. His atoms were conceived as erotic vortices in the flux, knottings of the goddess of love rather than the fixed ranks of the god of war. His physics was salvific, a way out of a cyclic politics of merciless reaction. Like the Buddha's physics, Democritus (and later, around 60 B.C., the Roman Lucretius) proposed a new morality which directed one to carry the tumult of soul back before the initial deviation in the flow, to an undisturbed center of being. Resting in that nonviolent center, there was a chance, these atomists believed, to neutralize an obsessive heroic religion's blood sacrifice and enter into an erotically playful relation to nature and one's fellows (Serres, 1982: 120–24). Instinctively, the consciousness movement seemed to have intuited something like this direction in the new physics.

The ancient Hebrew contribution to this romance with earth is often slighted. Instructed by the *Whole Earth Catalog*, the consciousness movement was oblivious of it. But it was the Jews who knew, as Greeks of Aristotle's sort apparently did not, that irrational contingencies conceal a rational order; and until this presumption captured the Western mind in the high Middle Ages, modern science (and probability theory) would not have developed. (You might have a strict science of the immutable, crystalline spheres, Aristotle thought, but no such exactitude was conceivable for sublunar affairs.) It was their builder-artist's story of genesis that made the Jewish difference. The Jews believed that the great Beginner, *Aleph*, not only created but perpetually broods and moves over the dark void, the formless *tehom* or primeval waters which preceded creation— informing, quickening, projecting, breathing itself fully into the chaos. Like some kind of metaphysical X-ray, the temple of Jerusalem inscribed this anatomy lesson of an open cosmic system—the insides of materiality as a theogony or God-process unfolding in a cosmogony or world-process. The temple not only symbolized the gate of heaven, but below, reached down into the mouth of the *tehom*, death itself. The temple reiterated the great deeds of Genesis, telling a story of unnameable energy every instant starting, sustaining, incorporating itself into the limited frames of time and materiality — and transforming them. To a later, medieval Jewish Kabbalism, it meant that every particle of the universe was encoded within a magical divine numerology and a mystic alphabet. Light emanated in the darkness, even penetrating blank contingency. Moses de Leon, a Spanish Kabbalist of the thirteenth century, drew out the source (in Scholem [1941] 1961: 223):

> Everything is linked with everything else down to the lowest ring in the chain, and the true essence of God is above as well as below, in the heavens and on the earth, and nothing exists outside Him. . . . When God gave the Torah to Israel, He opened the seven heavens to them, and they saw nothing but His Glory; He opened the seven worlds to them and they saw nothing but His Glory; He opened the seven abysses before their eyes, and they saw nothing was there but His Glory.

This was a perfect invitation for any budding physicist or chemist who would come along to draw the consequence — small or large, evanescent or stable, there was nothing that was not good, nothing that was not implicitly intelligible. That message whispers through the history of Western science — and into contemporary physics's equivalent of watery *tehom*, the indeterminate world of quantum energy.

THE FIRE GOES OUT

But let's not get ahead of ourselves. By the seventeenth century, as least in northern Europe, the whisper of that message, ingrained in earth, was barely audible — except in figures like the Protestant shoemaker mystic, Jacob Boehme (1575–1624). The hidden God (of Catholic and Jewish mysticism) infusing the elements, who makes the elements somehow translucent, had been supplanted by the intensely interpersonal dyad of "me and God" promoted by Protestant Reformers. In its Calvinist form, this came to mean a "totally other" God, one who touched earth only tangentially, in the human heart, but who had otherwise fled for the high heavens — with the effect that the material world became utterly opaque. The point of the triadic God, wholly hidden but moving in the earth and the human heart, fell into eclipse. Monopolar Unitarianism was in the air. Significantly, the seventeenth-century scientific revolution flourished, for the most part, in highly literate Calvinist Europe, where a God-of-the-earth's eclipse meant nature's eclipse as well. So while Calvinist divines persecuted witches, feminine custodians of an underground God, secular Calvinist scientists felt the urgency to compensate by penetrating the mysteries of opaque and impenetrable nature.

The tension and drivenness are clear in the split personality of Isaac Newton (1642–1727). The daylight side of him made nature perfectly geometrical and legal; it conducted his investigations under the auspices of the predestinarian, Calvinist deity whom Newton himself so resembled. The shadowy nighttime side experimented in alchemy under the auspices of a God of the underworld who disturbs an idealist's perfect order with fire. The daylight Newton achieved something John Calvin had never accomplished in Geneva; he transformed a messy sublunar world into a lucid, adamantine order which permitted no deviation. The latter, the shadow side, worked for a restoration, a reconciliation of order and chaos, a meeting eventually arranged by nonequilibrium thermodynamics in our day (the 1960s).

But I wonder if Mr. Newton would ever have been so creative or launched such a movement had he been polarized only by his starchy Calvinist God and not also by the mercurial God of the alchemical elements. For it is clear that he had more than a dyad going for him; vestiges of a triad remained—and the long-term sequel, evident in our century, has been that Newton's solid objects dissolve under our feet, appear more like gas or rainbow clouds than rigid apples or billiard balls. As the industrial revolution discovered by heating metal and oil deposits, you could do more with matter in gaseous form to change the face of the earth than was possible with sharp-edged, hard objects. If the prophets and sages of first-millennium B.C. religion had had this kind of science and technology at their disposal, my guess is that they would have been delighted to move mountains.

What is even clearer, however, is that by the late eighteenth century Calvinist predestinationism was unconsciously in full command of physics. Early on in the story of modern science, the study of fire and transformation was all but relinquished to chemists. The obsessive dream of modern physics has been Pierre Simon's, Marquis de Laplace, who at the close of the eighteenth century proposed (before Napoleon) that if he could ascertain the initial positions and velocities of the "corpuscles" of the cosmos, he could deduce with absolute certainty their entire history, backward and forward. In such a changeless world, Laplace continued, the hypothesis of God (i.e., of the Judeo-Christian God of time) isn't needed. The man was absolutely right about that. A single vision and one-eyed sleep, William Blake called it.

Until recently, that is to say, classical modern physics practiced its own version of transcendental denial, attending to only one pole—the godlike, unimplicated spectator observing inert objects only externally related and fixed immutably in perfectly symmetrical, linear cycles of repetition that allow precise, complete descriptions invulnerable to time, decay, and change. So while most fields of scientific inquiry from 1750 forward were revising a static outlook with process concepts, physics was the stubborn holdout. The laws of a Laplacean dream machine disclosed a macroscopic universe of unforgiving fate utterly independent of mind; they provided Darwin's evolutionary century with the curiosity of hollow "building blocks" from which nothing could evolve. According to the most exact science, the nineteenth-century verdict was that our asymmetrical planet must be a cosmic anomaly. Thermodynamics, a nineteenth-century invention and a subdivision of physics, could easily dispose of such anomalies; volatile matter, whose future might deviate from its past, was thought to be the result of exceptional conditions on our statistically negligible planet. As for titanic and demonic disturbances, for much the same reason, they were relegated to geologists, biologists, and to inexact humanists: Balzac, Marx, Nietzsche, Freud, and their successors. Few recognized that in exploring the social underworld and reinventing the unconscious, the latter were picking up where Newton left off, studying our subterranean links with unstable subatomic particles—and therewith, perhaps, with the medium of an unsettling God.

Briefly, then, if you weave the above tale into the story of rising literacy which I have treated previously, you have a medical examiner's report of the causes of Mother Nature's demise. Now for the autopsy in greater detail.

INTO THE FOUNDERING DARK

What does it feel like to be one of the relatives surviving in a cosmic anomoly? It can be like staring into an icy, Dantean hell—or into the face of a Medusa that turns us to stone. Let me spell that out with a showing, taken, you might say, from the ranks of the lower clergy of science, a true mourner with the bereaved family. I think of a scientist and a humanist who poured soul's quick wit into the domains of natural science and culture, bridging both—and it was not enough. I mean Loren Eiseley. He wrote evocatively, tellingly of the puzzles, the riddles of nature; and yet Eiseley himself graphically illustrates the modern problem of human alienation from nature. In his autobiographical *All the Strange Hours: The Excavations of a Life* (1975), he is searching, like Saint Augustine, into the dark of his origins, trying to remember—even as in his professional career he searched back into the "immense journey" of evolutionary time. Implicitly, tacitly, it is a quest for a fresh beginning in the face of death. The quest apparently fails: nature blocks the way—no new lease. The book gives more than one parabolic episode to sum up the message all his years of studying nature had delivered.

In one of these episodes, Eiseley tells of being on a Caribbean vacation in Barbados; he is recounting to some fellow travelers the story of a retarded man in his thirties who momentarily seemed to wake up from a blissful incomprehension in which time held no terrors. The sudden awakening, Eiseley says, reminded the boy-man of his abandonment by childhood playmates. It sank him into a "haunted cavern to which he returns inwardly for a sound that never comes." Eiseley, the naturalist, lives in that cavern too, and the sound doesn't reach his ear either. After telling this story to his vacationing companions, Eiseley then goes for a long walk on the tidal flats of the beach—as the tide comes in, effacing his footsteps in the sand. It is nature, he says, "busy washing away or burying memories. It would continue until nothing was left." This is one parable among many in the book which discloses nature—to which this great naturalist has devoted his life—as finally a prison, an antagonist, a devouring mother wearing the mask of death. In nature Eiseley sought to find a clue to the meaning of the human epic; but she is finally silent, a formless, primeval soup swallowing up her offspring, containing no succor for the heart's cry to be known, remembered, loved. No, says the naturalist (Eiseley, 1975: 245, 249),

> I have come to believe that in the world there is nothing to explain the world. . . . Nothing to explain the necessity of life, nothing to explain the hunger of the elements to become life, nothing to explain why the solid realm of rock and soil and mineral should diversify itself into beauty, terror, and uncertainty. . . . It is as if matter dreamed and muttered in its sleep. But why, and for what reason it dreams, there is no evidence.

Not quite struck dumb, nature mutters, dreams, wanders.

What then remains except our place in human, social time? The bold face culture wears for Eiseley is that of a riddle; human striving, all that we call civilization, is mocked by encompassing nature. He tells of being deep in the bowels of a great private library one night, ruminating over the meaning of human history in the midst of so many volumes encasing, as it were, the "brain" of the race. "I wished I knew the destiny of this brain," he asks, "in which I was but a momentary, ephemeral visitant." And he hears, in all those shelves of books, myriad voices, including fragments of his own, murmuring in vast dialogue. "The Brain was talking to itself, carrying on some vast dialogue I was incapable of deciphering. . . . The Brain was oblivious of its ending in the foundering dark." Once again death rules, vanquishing history and all the mind's pretensions to know its own course. Eiseley ascends from the stacks and, as he leaves, the night watchman echoes a parting epitaph on the scholar's life: "Doesn't pay to see or hear too much now, does it?" "I had sought in my own small way," says Eiseley (1975: 29), to preserve the memory of what always in the end perishes: life and great deeds."

THE CLASSICAL PARADIGM: A SCIENCE OF DEATH

The objective correlate of Eiseley's stoicism is the abstract world, first, of classic Newtonian mechanics and second, of nineteenth-century thermo-dynamics—both of which conform to what consciousness movers like to refer to as the "old scientific paradigm." If we are to understand where modern science is coming from, and what the consciousness movement would like to see displaced or included in a larger scheme, these two fields represent a good place to start and deserve some explication.

Newtonian dynamical motion, as Alexander Kóyre once dryly observed, is "a motion unrelated to time or, more strangely, a motion which proceeds in an atemporal time—a notion as paradoxical as that of change without change." The approach supposed a godlike observer, really an angel, whose size and instrumentation would not disturb the data. The chosen data consisted of "integral systems," stable, closed systems whose every instant, like that of an automaton or pendulum, is the integral repetition of the preceding instant. Such systems did not interact or exchange energy with their environment or undergo abrupt shocks and turbulence. The procedure posited a body in isolation, endowed with rectilinear and uniform motion (the so-called initial conditions); it then calculated the modifications of this movement from place to place (the trajectory) as determined by external forces—wind, waterpower, horse-power, gravity, muscle, whatever. The point was to deduce the whole truth concerning all possible other states of a system—the distribution of masses in space and their velocities, for instance—from the instantaneous state of the system, whatever positions it might take up on a time axis. The time variable is irrelevant; in principle, the motion of integral systems is perfectly symmetrical and therefore reversible. The film of gravitational order could be run backward without disturbing the geometry of immutable, deterministic law. Big nature is stuck, neurotically repeating itself.

Obviously, the ensuing story of Newton's selective approach to nature is a scene in the drama of letting nature's dependable regularity work for us, if not exactly speak through us. The method has been staggeringly successful in extracting nature's wealth and transforming it for human benefit. For at least two centuries, until the environmental costs began to be assessed and until the psychological price of having roots in a machine-nature dawned on us, it seemed like the perfect arrangement. Nature didn't talk back. On the deficit side from the strictly scientific perspective, however, the method eliminated (or is the word repressed?) contingency, randomness, and ambiguity—and therewith the chance of making sense of the evolution of a planet such as ours. In a Newtonian universe earth is a cosmic anomaly. Now the remarkable thing (to the layperson) is that Einsteinean relativity and even quantum mechanics largely adhere to this static dynamics of a passive, inert material world. But it is no wonder that such a steady-state picture jars an evolutionist like Eiseley, as earlier in this century it had repelled the French philosopher Henri Bergson. If believed, it closes off genesis. Thus the epigraph to this chapter from the French philosopher of science Michel Serres: "The order of reason is repetitive . . . a science of death." Serres (1982: 100) goes on:

> A science of dead things and a strategy of the kill. . . . The world is in order, according to this mathematical physics in which the Stoics are met by Plato up the line and by Descartes further down, and where order reigns supreme over piles of cadavers. The laws are the same everywhere. . . . There is nothing to be learned, to be discovered, to be invented, in this repetitive world, which falls in the parallel lines of identity. Nothing new under the sun of identity. It is information-free, complete redundance. . . . You might very well think that the bloodied rulers were thrilled to find this world and to seize upon its laws of determination—their own in fact—the very same ones they had. . . . Nothing new and nothing born, there is no nature. There is death forever. Nature is put to death or it is not allowed to be born. And the science of all this is nothing, can be summed up as nothing. Stable, unchanging, redundant, it recopies the same writing in the same atom-letters.

We have encountered this apotheosis of redundancy before in the cosmic pessimism of India's eternal return. Its ancient Western antecedent is cyclic nature fastening us with Medusa's snaky stare. At the outset of this first act of converting nature to our purposes, the Greeks shouted a warning.

Could that warning possibly be heard by the study of the movement of heat, what is called thermodynamics? Thermodynamics marked the shift in the nineteenth century from the laminar flows and geometrical trajectories of Newton's machines to the fiery physics of the industrial revolution's motors. Does our changeling planet appear less of a cosmic error in this perspective? The fire of Fulton's steam engines and Bessemer's smelters freed matter imprisoned in geometrical Newtonian diagrams of fixed form. Fire melted all the straight edges, made matter vibrate, oscillate, and explode into clouds. And fiery matter opened the door to the discovery of atomic and nuclear dissemination. Here, for the first time in classical physics, unpredictable contingency and irreversible time began to count. Physics looked forward, had to weigh not the certain, but the probable outcome. Thermal phenomena tend to forget their initial conditions; their yesterday is not equivalent to their tomorrow. Initially, before it was clear that its time arrow ran the other way, thermodynamics seemed the perfect match for Darwin's century.

The era began officially in the 1820s with Nicholas Leonard Sadi Carnot's theory of how an engine converts heat into the mechanical work of driving a piston. Carnot's concepts became mythic for the century. The notions of a reservoir of fuel, circulation of hot and cold, differentials of pressure, and the dissipation of energy were quickly extended to electricity, magnetism, light, work itself, and analogously to capital, labor, gene pools, and the unconscious. The world turned into a dynamo, and painters like J. M. L. Turner captured this dramatically on canvas. In 1847 Heinrich von Helmholz enunciated the first law of thermodynamics, the law of conservation, that though energy can be converted from one form to another its "potential" or "rest energy" remained constant, the equivalent of its capacity to work ("kinetic" or bound energy).

At this point, the problem was to understand the erosion and loss of usable energy, which in 1850 Rudolph Clausius labeled "entropy." In his second law of thermodynamics, Clausius enunciated the principle that any flow of energy involves an inevitable heat loss, so that though the quantity of energy remains the same, over time the quality of that energy degrades. In time, the kinetic energy available for mechanical work, whatever its form—electrical, chemical, or heat—had to be paid for in waste, irretrievable structural dissipation, decay, and aging. As Clausius put it in his famous second law of thermodynamics, "the entropy of the world endeavors to increase." Yes, irreversible time mattered in thermodynamic systems such as the sun and planet earth, but the direction of that time arrow fated our small meanings to dissolution. From this time forward, entropy began to wear the mask of death.

About this same time, however, Ludwig Boltzmann, experimenting with contained gases (like Newton's closed systems, free of turbulence, friction, and explosive flows of energy), found that the microscopic meaning of entropy translated into randomized molecular activity—the so-called Brownian motion such as dancing sunbeams have in the air when they are doing no work. In this respect, entropy wore the mask of eros. But not quite. Boltzmann was a master of the new mathematics of probability, and he found that all the odds are stacked in favor of disorganization or that return to chaos which physicists refer to as thermic "equilibrium." That is, a lot of disconnected buzzing but no heat and no work, a big chill. In our century Erwin Schrödinger and others related entropy to the indeterminate behavior of the subatomic, quantum world. There too, highly charged particles are awash in Brownian instability. Suddenly it was clear: macroscopic Newtonian mechanics was an exercise in statistics, a lawfulness of large numbers riding on a wildly chancy underworld both manic and depressive.

The chancy underworld might have been turned to the advantage of understanding how our improbable planet reversed the direction of entropic time and moved uphill. In fact, Boltzmann sought to fathom the evolutionary properties of matter. He saw that chaos is somehow the key to breaking the symmetrical slide downhill, and the key as well to increasing complexity. Only a system that behaves in a sufficiently randomized way will break symmetry and show a difference between past and future. But finally, overwhelming quantity and the rule of large numbers prevailed; Boltzmann opted to see the physical universe as a whole in terms of the first law of thermodynamics, the physicist's law of karma (with a vengeance): the overall energy of a (closed) system doesn't change. In the big picture, then, energy exists in a symmetrical state of thermic equilibrium, all gains in heat and complexity offset by equivalent losses. In a homeostatic, closed system, as the cosmos was presumed to be, that's simply the way it is. Again, India's vision of the black age had been way ahead of us. The opportunity to see the unruly mob, the unsettled element at the bottom of a structured world, as a complementary antistructure and vast reservoir of energy that would make a difference and thus change the entropic direction of time—all this had to wait. In short, so far as physics was concerned, the elusive key to Darwin's chance variation and increasing complexity was lost—for a time.

To this day, most physicists follow Boltzmann's judgment. The temporal arrow introduced by entropy is regarded as characterizing only a small sample in our corner of the galaxy, which from the statistical vantage point can be disregarded or deemed to derive wholly from the observer's ignorance of hidden variables at the microscopic level. The great universe, it is commonly supposed, resembles a gas in an insulated container whose macroscopic (and reversible) properties do not change over time. The article on entropy in the latest edition of the *Encyclopedia Britannica* sums it up, "In the evolutionary cosmologies, the present dark and relatively empty universe is doomed to greater darkness and emptiness. . . . An eternal future lies gripped in a frozen state of meaningless death."

Where Newton had announced an unambiguous universe timelessly maintaining itself by running in circles, never getting anywhere, at least his mechanics had given anomalous but enterprising human beings a stable world to manipulate with levers and pulleys. Ironically, thermodynamics, a science of the chances involved when water meets fire, wrote the finale to such industry—death without a whimper. The science of the very smelting and refining that turned matter molten so it could make such a difference to the face of our planet, once again removed ambiguity. It proposed that ultimately there's no riddle to our environment; from the physical angle, we are traveling down a dead-end street. One way to react to this prophecy is the classic either/or of Henry Adams at the close of the last century, to choose either the dynamo or the Virgin of Chartres. The other way is to recognize that the riddle of human industry and civilization simply intensifies in the face of death, especially if you recognize the double irony that despite our best efforts to be impersonal, an entropic universe is the spitting image of a human being who accepts that it must die.

A CODA OR INTERLUDE?

The stars, our principal reservoir of energy and our major manufacturing system, are slowly but at a tremendous rate running out of gas. The lights will go out; night will swallow up all human endeavor. This is the irreversible reality, over against which Loren Eiseley gains his truth-seeker's self-consciousness. Alternately, he conceives his life as an escape from a burning chicken coop, a prison break into the cold, or a game of dice played with personified death. We have encountered this vision of nature before in John Lilly's mechanical hell. It's as if the last word on our ultimate environment were set by Stanislav Grof's second perinatal matrix. There's no exit, breathing space for stoicism perhaps but none for erotic spirit or a *Song of Songs*. Stoicism, in fact, is what is usually recommended, for instance, by Jacques Monod (1972: 172–173):

> Man must at last finally awake from his millenary dream; and in doing so, awake to his total solitude, his fundamental isolation. Now does he at last realize that, like a gypsy, he lives on the boundary of an alien world. A world that is deaf to his music, just as indifferent to his hopes as it is to his suffering or his crimes.

But Eiseley's response is not limited to the stoical — because he is always trying to weave together the two cultures in himself, the scientist and the poet. His vision is double. He respects the integrity of both personas, the austerity of the one and the latter's continual effort to break the boundaries of the former. It's what is known as living honestly, consciously with dualism, a potentially creative split. The rules of Eiseley's discipline forbade him to acknowledge nature as a grail container, a carrier of spirit. Perversely, those rules virtually command the scientist to mix himself up in his materials — and to disidentify from them. Eiseley broke the last rule in a particularly dramatic way. Apparently suffering from genetic damage, he and his wife refrained from bearing children. Mother Nature is barren, impoverished, perhaps dead; but willingly and consciously, as his writing so often shows, Eiseley identifies with the living and the dead of nature. And despite the rules, despite being confined to the solitude of his own heart, Eiseley dialogues with nature, lets her chaos enter him and hymns her, gives her darkness voice, makes her agony his own, conducts a wake. An aesthetic turn, we said, is the preliminary to becoming a mystic, to finding the big mystery ingredient in our sound and fury.

"I who profess no religion," Eiseley confesses, "find the whole of my life a religious pilgrimage." That much is transparent. Did the journey end, as his final autobiographical essays suggest, in Sisyphean absurdity? Not likely; Eiseley is no hero escaping evil or death. His motto for the beginning, middle, and end of his story — "Behind nothing, before nothing, worship it the zero" — sounds a Buddhist chord. I suppose the question, an impersonal one, is whether the tight squeeze of nature's death, of which ours is an incident, is the last word or the signal for something more than the death of the hero.

The meaning of death, nature's and ours, reduces to the same issue. Our riddle is hers, hers ours. That was the thrust of my excursus on Aquinas at the close of chapter 4, and equally of my rendition of tantric descent in the last chapter. There is no such thing as a private death. I think I have said enough in my chapters on India to explain why consciousness-raisers might well return to America with a passionate interest in earth science, most especially when it was in an unsteady state, on the verge of breaking old paradigms and launching into time as it had not previously done. But the amplified meaning of this interest ought now to be clear. It has to do with a death-rebirth passage, nature's and ours. So before I move directly to the question of paradigm shifts, I want to put a question. Is there a lesson in a God who contains polarities of order and chaos, death and life, which science, the arts, and religion have always to relearn—that creative movement off dead center comes of fraternizing with unruly folk and with the chaotic *tehom*?

PARADIGM SHIFTS AND BROKEN TRAJECTORIES

The idea of paradigm shifts in the natural sciences derives from the work of Thomas S. Kuhn on "scientific revolutions," and to a lesser degree from philosopher Paul Feyerabend. The progress of science has hardly been a smooth, cumulative affair of increasingly accurate theories, Kuhn (1962) informed us. Nor has the history of science been governed by a system of firm, unchanging, and absolute principles, argues Feyerabend (1978). Contrary to the impression often given in textbooks, science has proceeded by violating basic epistemological rules and established canons of inquiry. More like the history of constitutional or biblical interpretation, science has remained vital and has survived by breaking deductive symmetries and through overruling what, to previous generations, seemed like "reason." As Feyerabend phrases it, development has been anarchic, marked by a succession of unpredictable quantum leaps.

Thomas Kuhn put some order into the chaos; he showed that the process follows definite stages. At every period, there exists a relatively stable body of orthodox, "normal science" governed by something like a grammatical paradigm—a set of rules, declensions, ways of parsing the material (as complex as you like), which generate theories and models (e.g., genetic coding and the double-helix DNA molecule). Then there are the "anomalies" which don't quite fit the dominant theorems; if they multiply intolerably, they generate a philosophic "crisis," and call for radical revision—a "scientific revolution" that produces new paradigms until a new consensus is established. At which point, the cycle begins again.

Every era in this broken trajectory exhibits a dominant paradigm, which in the broadest sense can be defined as a constellation of beliefs, values, and techniques shared by members of a given scientific community. Data do not arrive with labels attached; a *tabula rasa* mind, an empty slate advancing no leading hypotheses about what might be expected, would not be a scientific mind. Some sort of a priori equipment—in effect a paradigm—functions as an absolute requirement for scientific investigation. Most scientific research is not exploratory except within the syllogistic logic of its governing assumptions; within those self-set limits, it clarifies obscurities, and, through useful tautologies, draws out entailments already contained in the premises. Kuhn calls it "textbook" or "normal science," and if important increments in knowledge do occur within such defined boundaries, major breakthroughs do not. The limits of this situation have to be recognized.

The map is not the territory; facts are typically inconvenient, and the best theories will not only leave certain anomalies unexplained but will prescind from whole areas which might logically elicit their attention. Which is to say that all science is abstractive, the product of selective attention; if only for the sake of efficiency and careful penetration, science has to operate this way. A controlling paradigm such as Aristotle's psycho-biologistic conception focused attention on certain aspects of the world, but almost by definition precluded the kind of mathematical precision Newton obtained by attending to the spectrum of light refracted through a prism. Similarly, the mechanistic paradigm of the universe sets the kind of problem to be worked at, prescribes the rules of research, specifies the criteria for valid theory, and precludes the methods behind global reports like those of the Khajuraho temples, the sculpture of Praxiteles, and St. Peter's Basilica in Rome, all of which entertain different guiding assumptions about reality. The Copernican revolution did not displace geocentric astronomy by adhering to Ptolemaic assumptions, even though one of the keys to the acceptance of a new view is that it must incorporate the old. Paradigm shifts occur when observed anomalies begin to mount up, or when issues previously considered trivial suddenly appear major, casting doubt on business as usual, generating a crisis of definition, and demanding a leap of imagination which typically involves cross-fertilization from disparate fields.

A paradigm shift implies more than an increment in existing knowledge; it means a change in basic assumptions and key concepts which bend consensual reality out of shape, sparking a reevaluation of existing facts and observations. In such cases, the rise of the new interpretation ("extraordinary science") generates a period of chaos in which the old criteria loosen up, and a variety of competing formulations proliferate.

STRANGE SOUNDS

Take the case of Rupert Sheldrake, a young Cambridge University trained plant physiologist, now working in India, who has drawn much interest from the consciousness movement for his new hypothesis of morphogenesis (i.e., the becoming of structural form and patterned motor action). Sheldrake's problem stemmed from his dissatisfaction with his trade's current habit of throwing so many problems into the computerlike programming of the double-helix deoxyribonucleic acid (DNA) molecule. Embryonic growth, self-regulation, regeneration, reproduction, characteristic patterns of motion, and identifying traits — all these complex phenomena are supposedly explained by Francis Crick's and James Watson's (1953) model of how chromosomes duplicate themselves. But Sheldrake wondered whether this wasn't too much. Cut out a newt's eye and it will generate another, not from its skin as in embryonic growth but from the edge of its iris. The trees of a rain forest orient their leaves toward or away from the sun — and disconcertingly change the performance in the course of a day or a lifetime. In only a few generations, the peppered moth modified its color to adjust to heavy pollution. Or how do you explain that when new organic compounds are once successfully crystallized (very difficult in the first instance), subsequent crystallizations become easier all around the world? To Sheldrake, there seemed to be more flexibility built into the formal wholeness of these systems than mechanical determinism could account for.

So in *A New Science of Life* (1981), which he wrote at Father Bede Griffith's Catholic-Hindu ashram in south India, Sheldrake hypothesized that material things do not function exclusively by immutable law; rather, patterns reinforced over time generate invisible organizing fields, "morphogenetic fields" he called them, which channel form and govern motor behavior. Whether it be a proton bonding with an electron to form a hydrogen atom, crystal formation, or something as canny as a sheep trematode "body snatching" an ant's brain in order to wait for a passing sheep on the ant's blade of grass, Sheldrake argues that whenever one member of a species learns a new behavior pattern it sets up a subtle, energyless field or "morphic resonance" which affects the behavior of all the other members of the same type. Strictly local causality (or actual contact across time and space) need not be a barrier to communication. The analogy is that the form of a species is tuned as a violin string is to other strings of its family. When one string is plucked, others of exactly the same tension, mass, length, and vibrational frequency will vibrate without being touched.

The idea is that if repeated often enough and by sufficient numbers, an innovative, epigenetic path cuts its way into a species which subtly alters, as the case may be, atomic bonding or genetic coding. Atomic structure, chemical coding, and genetic apparatus are thus understood to be the physical mechanism *through* which morphogenetic fields translate their information—rather as in the mechanism of a TV set its wiring, condensers, and transistors serve as the requisite circuitry for electromagnetic signals. Morphogenetic fields, though undetectable by standard measuring devices, do imply testable predictions—for instance, about the learning behavior of mice or the global chain reaction when a new chemical compound is first crystallized. The tests are currently in progress. But the theory serves as a good example of a new theory doing its duty to incorporate the old. Sheldrake's morphic resonance does not mean to displace mechanistic accounts so much as to complement them.

When Sheldrake's proposal was editorially reviewed in the British journal *Nature*, it was anathematized as "the best candidate for burning there has been for a long time." On the other hand, *New Scientist* (in *Brain/ Mind Bulletin* 8 no. 3 [1981]: 1) lauded Sheldrake as a "good scientist" with a testable idea, noting,

> No one who has worked with particles within particles, or at distances and temperatures that are so out of scale with what humans can comprehend could doubt that the modest "morphogenetic" fields that Sheldrake proposes could indeed exist.

Conflicting reactions are what we should expect. During transitional, liminoid periods of a paradigm shift, scientists—or a significant portion of them—must revert to a discussion of fundamental philosophical assumptions, legitimate methods, and problems in an atmosphere of growing professional insecurity. In this in-between time, sociological flux reflects the conceptual suspense, and disputants typically cannot agree on what the important problems are, their nature, or what would conceivably amount to a solution. In a moment of major redefinition, communication across the conceptual divide—between new and old paradigms—will be partial, bewildering, and extremely discomforting. Einstein opened the door to quantum physics, which radically recast the dominant images of matter, space, and time, but could scarcely pass through that door himself; the new quantum world upset his prior commitments to a deterministic world in which God does not play dice. Consequently, his relations with the Berlin Academy of Science, with Niels Bohr and the Copenhagen school, were strained, anguished. The central problem was indeterminancy, the apparent chaos within and below all cathedrals of nature and man. To Einstein, it spelled the death of science and his Spinozist God.

DEAD END SCIENCE?

"Physics is finished, young man," Max Planck's teacher told him in the 1890s. "It's a dead-end street." That was all before the turn of the century's great plunge below into the microscopic world, an event which, as I say, eventually brought something like rainbow volatility and a new kind of opacity to the underworld, turning massive atoms into electromagnetic fields and radiant fields back into discontinuous quantums of energy. That is to say, it was before Planck's discrete packets of energy which violated Newton's perfectly continuous motion and ostensibly broke the taboo against moving faster than the speed of light; before Einstein shattered the tablets of Newton's absolute space and time with the curvature of space-time and mass = energy; and before Werner Heisenberg's indeterminancy principle (which do you want, position or velocity?) and Niels Bohr's rule of complementarity (which is it, field or atom?). The plot thickened and borders grew fuzzy. By 1925 physics presented an image of matter that was increasingly difficult to separate from mind. The discovery of unstable subparticles came much later; as did the detection (in 1963) of the 3° Kelvin background radiation of the Big Bang echoing in our atmosphere—evidence of a universe still expanding in all directions like a vast exhalation. Up until then steady-state cosmologies had dominated the field; no longer.

Determinism in some form, to be certain, remains in place, but matter at the microscopic level resembles something very different from New-ton's rank and file bodies (or atoms) only externally related in absolute space and time, and proceeding reversibly along linear trajectories—all for the edification of a godlike observer. The evolving, asymmetrical structures of galaxies, stars, planets, life, and culture have no purchase in that description. What is emerging in our time, according to the late University of California systems analyst Erich Jantsch (1980: 8), is a new paradigm of physical reality that has room for the multiple, the temporal, and the complex. It goes something like this:

- a view of matter, not as passive object or automaton, but as active, self-determining, self-organizing, self-renewing.
- a recognition of a systematic interconnection over space and time of all natural dynamics.
- the logical supremacy of processes over spatial structures.
- the central role of fluctuations which render the law of large numbers invalid and give a chance to the individual and its crea-tive imagination as a factor in natural process.
- an open evolution which is not predetermined in its emerging and decaying structures or in its end result.

"Those who are not shocked when they first come across quantum physics," observed Niels Bohr at the dawn of the nuclear age, "cannot possibly have understood it." It all began when physicists started playing in new ways with light. Up until 1905 light had been supposed to come only in wave form rather than particle form. The first paper Einstein published in 1905, which really started the quantum revolution, was on the photoelectric effect, that is, on the then puzzling question of why it is that when metals are struck by light, electrons are emitted as if kicked out of their atoms. Using Max Planck's novel idea that energy only traveled in certain "quantized" packets rather than continuously as classical mechan-ics had supposed, Einstein argued that vibratory photoelectric fields, which everyone "knew" were different from particlelike matter, came in particle form (photons) as well. He thus breached the wall of separation, the dogma of the time, between matter and fields. Up until then Planck's now heralded paper (1900) on why a heated black block of metal (e.g., iron) glows red at 1300 degrees had attracted little attention—for the simple reason that its assumptions ran against the dominant either/or logic. Planck's paper, concerned with the interaction of radiation and matter, had restricted particles to energies that are certain multiples of their vibration frequency—as if energy only came, like money, in certain denominations. Einstein's first paper lifted Planck's so-called quantum of action from obscurity and inaugurated the new physics—which among other things does away with Newton's perfectly continuous world.

Then came the second paper (1905), announcing the "special theory of relativity," which set the stage for the later development of information physics and cybernetics. What would it be like, Einstein asked, to ride around on a beam of light? The short answer is that with increases in velocity approaching the speed of light (186,464 miles per second in a vacuum), strange things happen. Matter contracts, increases in mass, and slows the pace of time—so that, if another planet exactly earth's size were to shoot past at 163,000 miles per second, it would appear foreshortened by 50 percent, ellipsoid in shape, and twice the mass of earth. The deformation has to do with the fact that communication (or local causality) between spatial entities is a matter of signals which cannot exceed the speed of light and hence require time to happen. Indeed, every material entity is a communication system composed of such signals, each with its own complex set of clocks involved in becoming itself. As Whitehead observed in this connection, "there is no nature at an instant." Nature is not a static thing but *process*. The result, so far as measuring observers are concerned, is that an absolute point of reference is impossible. We have to choose; and any reference system will be valid, but not necessarily more "true" than another. A person on a passing planet would find ours equally bent out of shape.

Special relativity eradicated Newton's homogeneous, absolute space and time; it made space multiform, order plural. Time and space were no longer separable; Newton's rigid bodies became the elastic, wormy process-events of four-dimensional space-time (a fusion of length, breadth, height, and time). Einstein's famous formula, $E = mc^2$, meant that mass is convertible with energy. Distributed haphazardly, stochastically in an entropic sea of Brownian movement, structured bodies, be they subatomic particles or stars, literally impound and bind radiant energy in free flight. And what energy! To calculate what thermodynamics speaks of as the conserved rest or potential energy, mass must be multiplied by a huge constant, the velocity of light squared. (One gram of mass energy produces 900 billion ergs, enough to keep a 1,000 watt electric bulb lit for 2,850 years.) What had Einstein done? Well, for one thing he had resuscitated low-level nature's extraordinary *potency*.

But he had not done as much as is sometimes supposed. It took a while for Einstein's colleagues to assimilate the loss of fixed frames of reference for measurement, and later, with general relativity (1915), it took time to digest that gravity was not a force but a curvature of space generated by massive bodies like the sun and earth. (Again, contrary to the Newtonian belief, the physical cosmos bent back on itself, and was therefore finite.) But with a little juggling and some expanded geometrical concepts both special and general relativity could be fit into the classic mechanistic viewpoint. Grainy atoms could still be conceived as separate objects signaling each other at less than the speed of light. It was still Newton's world of external relation, everything outside the other. Yet our view of the physical world had altered. Max Planck's teacher had been wrong; physics wasn't finished but barely begun. For Planck and Einstein breathed new life into their field, made it pregnant with unanswered questions. They took its dead-end world of fixed, impenetrable objects, negated them and subsumed them under the figuration of event and process. Matter of fact began to change its face.

"It is a magnificent feeling," Einstein once remarked in a letter, "to recognize the unity of a complex of phenomena which to direct observation appear to be quite separate things." What Einstein did serves as a good example of the power of metaphoric thinking to trigger a major paradigm shift (see Gerhart and Russell, 1984). But this is not metaphor as we usually think it: as decoration or a way of explaining some unfamiliar doctrine of ours to the simple-minded by way of familiar analogy. It is rather metaphor as the indispensible vehicle of a "Eureka!" experience which conjoins what had been separate—without losing differences and their tensions. Philip Wheelwright spoke of metaphor in this sense as a "diaphor," a movement through particulars of experience (or bodies of knowledge which have become stereotyped) which generates new meaning by juxtaposition alone. Einstein's procedure here was fundamentally aesthetic, an act of imagination. Using Planck's discrete quantum of action, Einstein took electromagnetic fields traveling smear-fashion at or near the speed of light and converted them into Planck's energy packets, the grainy stuff of matter. That is, he took two subject matters, previously disparate, that of electromagnetism (wave families, frequency) and particle physics (energy, charge, mass, gravity), and without collapsing the one undifferentially into the other (monism) he asserted that light carried both features. Putting the two together, asserting that wave acted like particle, incidentally explained why the Michelson Morley experiment (1887) had been unable to detect any "ether" wind through which light had been supposed to travel. With particlelike transmissions, the stationary ether medium was no longer needed. But more important in the long run was that Einstein's metaphoric act deliberately distorted, bent the world of classic physics out of position and reshaped the great exploration of the potent underworld.

Nothing has been the same since. The borders between the inorganic and organic were once sharply drawn; they no longer can be. In 1913 Niels Bohr devised a planetary model of the atom whereby he was able to explain a good many of the spectra phenomena associated with the elements of the periodic table (hydrogen to hahnium) by the behavior of planetlike electrons absorbing and losing energy as they jumped from inner and outer orbits around a sunlike nucleus. But by 1926 the planetary model was already in trouble. Reversing Einstein's major point that waves behave like particles, Louis de Broglie showed that all particles act like waves. Weird. It seemed that particles were wrapped up in each other's fields ("phase entanglement"), interconnected in some systematic way as the macroscopic world is not. That same year the German physicist Erwin Schrödinger proposed that electrons did not circle around the nucleus but constituted a wave that curved all around at once. Working out the mathematical formalism, it began to appear that at least on paper, quantum systems possessed an unlocalizable character. Through their wave features, they seemed to spread out all over the universe and to be indefinable in isolation. What defined them was the whole cosmic state in which they were implicated.

Hereafter, matter and fields were neither one nor the other but both/ and: cloudlike, chance-ridden quantumstuff (Herbert, 1985). After three centuries of analytic disconnecting, it began to appear that relationship is no accident supervening upon static, indivisible substance, as both Aristotle and Newton thought; no, relationship is internally constitutive of what, after the quantum revolution, had to be understood as process-reality. The atomized substrate of our familiar world, the very paradigm of separate reality, had turned suddenly and radically *social*. But in being so, quantum reality appears virtually amorphous, indeterminate when it comes to specifying particulate properties independent of the observer.

This was the golden age of quantum physics, when it took on consistent theoretical shape in various forms: Werner Heisenberg's matrix mechanics, Erwin Schrödinger's wave-form quantum laws of motion, and Paul Dirac's representation in vector (or arrow) form, which is largely concerned with how you make the transformations from one description to another. The mathematical accounts have multiplied since—and include, among others, John A. Wheeler's "hyperspace" concept, according to which the elements of the world are immediately linked without the limit of the speed of light. Weirder yet is Hugh Everett's recent "many worlds" hypothesis regarding spread-out Schrödinger wave functions: but for the limits of the human observer, we might see that those ubiquitous waves are actually realized at one and the same time in other worlds than our own. As the plural formalisms suggest, it meant—or should have meant—the end of the Newton-Laplacean dream of universality, of a single scheme common to all levels of description. It probably should also have meant the end of the whole notion of the elementary particle as something with attributes independent of its significant others. But the theorists, well enough agreed on the phenomenal facts, could not agree on how to interpret quantum reality—or if it deserved title to "real." For there was this irascible measurement problem having to do with the underworld's manic, spread-out quality. Who or what determines that a wave "collapses" into a particle, becomes one not many?

REENTER THE PARTICIPANT OBSERVER

Quantum reality was like looking into a mirror (Briggs and Peat, 1984). You seemed to get what you set out to find, wave or particle, depending on the instruments in use. But it's worse than that. The problem is that we are so massive in comparison to the small world of the quantum. If we want to locate the position of some entity at this level, a single photon of light that we shine into this spectral gloom will alter that entity's position. Where electrons or the whole family of new subparticles are concerned, our measuring devices decisively determine the object measured. In the 1920s the German physicist Werner Heisenberg expressed the problem in his principle of uncertainty: the more you try to determine the position of a quantum system the less you know about momentum; conversely, the more you know about momentum the less you can be certain of position. Unwittingly, the ruthlessly objective Einstein had opened an epistemological nightmare. Heisenberg's uncertainty principle threw scientists of the crude empirical realist school into near despair. "Atoms are not things," Heisenberg said; those old innate, fixed properties independent of the observer will have to go. But what would happen to the traditional legal system? At the quantum level, nature seemed to be rejecting it.

Niels Bohr's principle of complementarity, which rested on the wave-particle duality, made matters worse, for all intents and purposes fatally blurring the meaning of locality. According to the Copenhagen interpretation (of Bohr and Heisenberg), the underground quantum world is as far away from Newton's world as can be imagined; it is an unstable maze, downright jumpy, a throbbing mass of "tendencies to happen" rather like Aristotle's formless, pure potency or the watery *tehom* of the Bible— somewhere between being and nonbeing. More like a rainbow than a bushel of falling apples, in this reading the quantum world possesses definite attributes only under observer-defined measurement conditions. Thus all the standard mechanical and field attributes (mass, charge, spin magnitude, position, momentum, spin orientation, and their correlative wave-form families) turn out to be *contextual*. We are bound to disturb as we put our questions and take our reckonings. The observer whom the distancing illusions of literacy had put outside the "facts" is thus compelled back into them as a participant in their construction. The medieval Scholastic principle, that everything is received according to the mode of the receiver, was sneaking its way into the holy precincts of physics! "There is no quantum world," said Bohr. "There is only an abstract quantum description." Retorted Einstein, "I cannot imagine that a mouse could drastically change the universe by merely looking at it."

Physicists, so far as I can tell, are still deeply puzzled. What started out as a rite of mourning turns into a wake out of James Joyce, with the high priests polarized and arguing over the identity of the supposed corpse. It sounds like a rabbinic dispute and it is. But let me suspend the story at this point and leave it as prelude to the next chapter on physicist David Bohm's "hidden variable" solution to the riddle, one which Einstein found disagreeable but which the children of the sixties jumped for as exhibit A of the new paradigm. However much the earth shook under his feet, Einstein remained loyal to the old paradigm of innate properties and universal law, even if such laws had to be statistical. Formless, manic potency was just unacceptable. (Most physicists today would agree.) In any event, while it wasn't at all clear in the 1920s and 1930s whether the physical cosmos exists in an unsteady state or not (nor is it exactly agreed today), in retrospect it needs little argument that, within limits, an unsteady state in physics is very good for science. Polarized though physicists were, they had a third pole to keep them poised and creative—the riddle of nature itself. Secretly, it was mother devotion on their part, nor was her Muse dead.

I shall come to the principle behind the value of unsteady states and fluctuation in chapter 9, which will consider Nobel prizewinner Ilya Prigogine's theory of nonequilibrium thermodynamics. That theory convinced me, if I needed any convincing, that my revered Saint Augustine was quite wrong when he argued that what theorists say about the natural world has no bearing on religious faith. I know what he meant. Scientific theories come and go, and certainly over the centuries theologians have been reluctant, having been burnt so often, to pin theological propositions to any assumption borrowed from natural science. But so do theological formulations come and go, and it seems to me only another example of the heroic delusion of trying to live above time (as in transcendental denial) to imagine that religious theorizing can be exempt from contingency. To avoid the risk of connecting theology to science equivalently abandons earth for the sake of an otiose religiosity. A bad deal. Conversely, to avoid connecting science to theology equivalently insists that science remain inane, irrelevant to the deeper questions that haunt the human spirit. Besides being untrue, that's no way to recover a genesis story.

EIGHT

Holonomic Mind Fields

That one body may act upon another at a distance through a vacuum without the mediation of anything else . . . is to me so great an absurdity, that I believe no man, who has in philosophical matters a competent faculty of thinking, can ever fall into.

Isaac Newton

I think it is safe to say that no one understands quantum mechanics. Do not keep saying to yourself, if you can avoid it, "but how can it be like that?" . . . Nobody knows how it can be like that.

Richard Feynman

The essential point of science is not a complicated mathematical formalism or a ritualized experimentation. Rather the heart of science is a kind of shrewd honesty that springs from really wanting to know what the hell is going on.

Saul-Paul Sirag

There is probably no axiom in the reigning paradigm of modern science more absolute and agreed upon than the one which holds that if A is to effect B, then A must touch B or something else that touches B. Either there must be direct contact or a mediated interaction. Basically, this is what the doctrine of local causality means. If a single gear in a gear chain is removed, motion stalls. The gap is uncrossable. Newton's law of gravity, which seemed to imply such uncrossable action at a distance, therefore constituted something of an embarrassment. How does the sun's gravity cross all those millions of miles of empty space to hold earth in its orbit? "I frame no hypotheses," Newton replied.

His successors came to his aid. According to them, there really is no empty space between. The sun's mass disseminates a gravity *field*, diminishing with distance, which pulls the earth, and vice versa. That is, what solves Newton's contact-puzzle is not a mechanistic bumper-car game but the surrounding medium, the field of relationship in the space between. In addition to gravity fields and radio waves, the gaps are largely composed of virtually massless light containing enormous energy. Einstein spent his whole career seeking a unified field theory, one which would put electromagnetism and gravity (and any other fields) together—that would show in effect that massive, heavy objects are condensers, impounders of radiant-free energy and, conversely, dispersers of the same. He was sure, but unable to devise the formula, that finally everything in the cosmos absorbed and emitted an identical energy. Still, any way you figure it in the Einsteinian scheme, interaction is local.

Today, physicists usually postulate four fundamental force fields or patterns of information extending in space, all empirically detectable, at least indirectly, which hold the universe together in a locally connective way: (1) gravitational, (2) electromagnetic, (3) the strong field which holds atomic nuclei together, and (4) the weak field which breaks the nucleus apart in certain kinds of radioactive decay. (If grand unificationists, Einstein's successors, have their way, they will succeed in reducing these four to aspects of a single field.) From the quantum perspective, of course, fields are convertible with particles. Thus one can speak of all local interactions being mediated by clouds of discontinuous particles—in the case of gravity, by gravitons. In all such wave-particle interaction, however, the toughest limit is that imposed by the universal constant of the speed of light. According to Einstein's special relativity, no deforming influence of one thing upon another (or within anything as large as a star or small as an atom) can propagate faster than the velocity of light. The overwhelming scientific consensus, then, is that superluminal communication (which comes down to simultaneity) is taboo. Or used to be.

A subatomic quantum system does not appear to pass through a continuous series of intermediate steps in shifting from one quantum state to another, as would be mandatory if it were limited to the velocity of light signals. The transitions are discontinuous "jumps." Compelled by the logic of Planck's quantum of action, physicists like Henry Stapp of Berkeley argue for communication without signals—in effect, for superluminal messages. As we shall see shortly, there is an even stronger case to be made on the basis of other quantum weirdness.

A RENAISSANCE STREET FAIR

In the fall of 1979, my conventioneering obsession brought me to the Fifth International Conference of Transpersonal Psychology, which turned out to be largely concerned with quantum physics and, in particular, with David Bohm's startling interpretation of what is going on underneath all our feet and behind the facades of all the stars in all the galaxies. It was only then that in earnest I began to read Fritjof Capra (1975) and Gary Zukav (1979). That the new physics too easily conspires with wishful thinking is of course a danger for one of my background—a Catholic who never got far in entering the modern world. In a way, it told me about a world I had never left.

Transpersonalists believe in biting off a big chew. The theme of the conference was "The Nature of Reality: Dawning of a New Paradigm." The speakers would address the issue of integrating the new physics, psychology, and spirituality. The Cartesian-Newtonian paradigm which could only relate things *externally* to each other, which had in addition canonized the schism between mind and matter, was to come in for a thorough drubbing. The charge was that the dominant mechanistic paradigm was failing to provide insight into, much less solutions for, the urgent individual and social problems of the time. "Normal science," the argument ran, had not been meeting the challenge of observed anomalies which did not fit into mechanistic assumptions. The physical and social sciences were in a state of crisis. And so on.

The convention was also a birthday party to mark the tenth anniversary of Anthony Sutich's National Association of Transpersonal Psychology with, as it were, a more strictly intellectual debut. The period of inarticulate "good vibes" was past history. Articulate polymaths like Ken Wilber had begun to emerge into print in the mid-seventies. The time was ripe for some synthetic theoretic consolidations that would map the boundaries crossed in the previous two decades. No doubt in acknowledgment of the growing sobriety of the movement, the American Psychological Association (APA) had the year before designated transpersonal psychology an official area of inquiry alongside social, industrial, and behavioral psychology. The prestigious APA had also decided to recognize the transpersonal as a distinct mode of therapy. The "lunatic fringe" was being brought into the establishment.

What distinguished the 1979 transpersonal gathering from other professional conferences that I attend was its cross-disciplinary and popular character. It brought together psychologists, neurophysiologists, physicists, parapsychologists, comparative religionists, management consultants, assorted gurus and shamans, and a diverse group of nonprofessionals. The presence of the latter, hordes of ordinary enthusiasts alerted by the movement's networks and proliferating mailing lists, give these meetings the quality of a nonsectarian church—something like the audiences I imagine Ralph Waldo Emerson must have once addressed. More than any gathering of academics that I know of, meetings of consciousness-raisers—of whatever sort—approach something like a Renaissance street fair held on a holy day. The circus atmosphere provided every kind of soul food and saving device with its own booth, showcase, and sales pitch. What was all this psychic healing, physical therapy, and meditation jazz doing mixed up with subatomic particles?

HIGHER VIBES

The big excitement of the convention was the holonomic (lit., law of the whole) paradigm of mind and matter, a conception designed to do the impossible in multiform, subliminal Einsteinian space-time. According to theoretical physicist David Bohm of London University's Birbeck College, the seemingly unsystematizable pluralism of the visible cosmos constitutes the merest "ripple" upon an encompassing, yet hidden ocean of energy transcending space-time. A superluminal field several torques beyond the unified field Einstein had in mind, Bohm calls it the "holomovement." His thesis is that this ultimately immeasurable field is the "common ground" of both matter and mind.

Born in Pennsylvania, a student of J. Robert Oppenheimer's at Berkeley, and later a colleague of Einstein's at Princeton, Bohm is the author of two standard texts interpreting quantum facts and theory (1951; 1957). Already implicit in these works is a focus on the larger implications of "phase entanglement" as the key element of the microscopic quantum cosmos. For Bohm, quantum formalisms were not simply ideal fictions convenient for calculation. Contrary to the dominant positivist school of thought, he joins Geoffrey Chew's current "bootstrap" interpretation of quantum physics in arguing that the formalisms disclose something deep about reality, its essential interconnectedness and "undivided wholeness." (Rather than starting with elementary particles, the bootstrap theory approaches nature as a fabric of interrelated events, the attributes of each deriving from the characteristics of all others.) In the 1920s Prince Louis de Broglie had maintained that space-time issues forth from a single cosmic "pilot wave." Bohm plays variations on this notion, applying it not only to the order of physics but extending it metaphorically to every level of manifest being. The things of this world, he claims, display, are holograms of, the movement of a "whole" which finally lies beyond all figuring. For Bohm (1980), quantum action becomes the clue to something like William Blake's metaphysics. Bohm takes on the role of "natural philosopher," cosmologer in its original sense. He extrapolates upon his model of the physical universe, and develops a full-blown ontology, a panentheistic vision into the nature of things. After writing *Principia Mathematica* with Bertrand Russell, Alfred North Whitehead had traveled a similar route.

As Bohm acknowledges, the original proposal of a superluminal pilot wave in his 1951 work did not "catch on" among physicists, principally he thinks, because its nonlocal connective features "did not appeal to Einstein." That's probably putting it mildly. But there were also other reasons for its dismissal. Contemporary quantum physicists as a group are probably more positivist than were any of the founding fathers. Any interpretation which accounts for the same data as standard quantum theory does without proposing new, predictable element-traces on accelerator screens is destined for the wastebasket. Bohm did not propose any different observable data; he simply tried to give a more adequate account of what had already been discovered. Moreover, until very recently when Bell's Theorem of interconnectedness was laboratory tested, a critical test for a holonomic order had been absent.

I was to meet Bohm later at a Kettering Foundation meeting. A modest, reticent man more at home with his mathematics than at the lecture forum, Bohm was not present at the 1979 transpersonal conference. His case was ably presented by neurophysiologist Karl Pribram of Stanford University, who had his own applications of the holonomic paradigm to the solution of the puzzle of nonlocal memory distribution in the brain. Taken together, Bohm and Pribram represent a formidable attack on the mechanistic paradigm. Obviously this was a conspiracy designed to convince skeptical New Yorkers that we too ought to be interested in higher vibrations. The new paradigm had arrived, some of the proponents declared; at last we had an epistemological handle that would give a unified account of the diverse phenomena of quantum physics, ordinary perception of densely meaningful wholes (the person in the face, neighborhoods, cities, forests, nations, cultures), parapsychological events (telepathy, clairvoyance, psychokinesis, psychic healing), and transcendental experience. The fallout implications for education and learning theory, for health care and psychotherapy, for understanding music and aesthetics generally, advocates claimed, would be rich. Pantheistic-minded transpersonalists at the conference, misunderstanding the subtlety of Bohm's position, gobbled up all this promising millennialist talk with a glib "all is one." What might be called the evolutionist, incarnational wing of those present (probably the majority) stressed what might be knocking at our door to let itself into space-time. For the latter the crucial issue was our responsibility to let new sounds into our public works.

Though a minority report when it comes to interpreting (or extrapolating from) quantum physics, a holonomic order is anything but farfetched. Einstein and many of the original pioneers, Planck, Schrödinger, and de Broglie among others, shared a realist assumption that the quantum world, like our world of separate objects, possessed innate attributes whether measured or not—and to an extent David Bohm belongs to their number. For these classicists, quantum formalism referred to reality, unveiled reality in some way. Till his dying day, Einstein insisted that quantum theory was probably incomplete, that it was missing "hidden variables" independent of the observer, perhaps empirically inaccessible but nonetheless inferrable. Bohm's "holomovement" is precisely such a hidden variable.

EPR AND BELL'S THEOREM

A nonlocalizable quality seemed to constitute the principle characteristic of quantum systems. Through their wave feature they appeared to spread out all over the universe—like one of Leibniz's "monads" defined by the whole cosmic state in which it is implicated. This is bad news for closed, integral systems assumed in classical mechanics. Still under the spell of the Laplacean dream, in the late nineteenth century James Clerk Maxwell hypothesized a "demon" who could ascertain exactly the microstate of a gas in his laboratory. But in addition to the severe limits imposed upon the observer, what Heisenberg's indeterminacy implies is that the microstate of a containerized gas in a lab will be significantly altered in a millisecond if a single gram of matter in Sirius, the dog star, light years away, moves only one centimeter. By quantum accounts, then, regardless of how much technological advances improve the measuring apparatus, Maxwell's "demon" is *impossible*. Is this impossibility merely a fiction of the mathematical formalism, useful for making calculations of probability (as many physicists today believe), or does the formalism reflect reality?

In 1935 Einstein and two Princeton colleagues, Boris Podolsky and Nathan Rosen (hence the acronym EPR), devised a thought experiment—later tested—to show that there indeed were situations in which the determinate attributes (e.g., spin and direction) of a quantum system could be determined, and hence the theory of Heisenberg and others must be incomplete. The EPR experiment involves a source producing pairs of electrons (today usually photons; let me call the photons Red and Blue) in a so-called twin state traveling in opposite directions toward detectors (X and Y) which can measure their correlation. If there is something to this indivisible business, the twin state means that each partner photon knows what the other is doing and behaves accordingly—goes up when the other goes down or vice versa. Einstein's trick consisted of trying to trap Blue into suddenly altering its course with a polarizer at the Y detector—without Red being the wiser. Unless there's something like telepathy going on, Red's behavior, the reasoning went, will not be affected by what happens at the Blue detector. Keep in mind that theoretically this experiment can be performed within the confines of a laboratory or set up with one detector on earth and the other on the giant red star Betelgense (on the shoulder of Orion located 540 light years away from earth), the source of light being a spaceship-lighthouse emitting the twin photons, parked halfway between.

Commenting on this experiment in his autobiography, Einstein wrote, "On one supposition we should, in my opinion, absolutely hold fast; the real factual situation of the system [Red] is independent of what is done with the system [Blue] which is spatially separated from the former." But his Copenhagen friends remained unpersuaded by the master's ingenuity, and Princeton's John von Neumann convinced most that the quantum formalism born out in experiment excluded the innate-attribute/ordinary-object interpretation.

There is nothing like death when it comes to loosening up an old paradigm. The EPR experiment gathered dust until 1964, when most of the pioneer quantumizers were in their graves. At which point John Stewart Bell, an Irish physicist working at CERN, the European Center for

Nuclear Research in Geneva, Switzerland, resurrected the argument—or did he settle it? Bell advanced a startlingly simple logical "proof," thereafter known as "Bell's Theorem," that *no local model of reality can explain the experimental results at either the quantum or macroscopic levels.* The steps were those of a *reductio ad absurdum.* (1) Assume the principle of locality. (2) Show that it is contradicted by the facts. (3) Conclude the assumption is false, and therefore reality is nonlocal. Setting up the EPR thought experiment again, Bell started with Einstein's locality assumption; namely, that what happens at Red's detector X will not affect what happens at Blue's Y, and vice versa. With that single theoretical assumption, Bell then marched to the quantum predictions of the polarization results at X and Y, which told another story contradicting the assumption. The logic was thus compelling that Red and Blue are instantly interconnected at rates exceeding the speed of light!

Is the principle generalizable beyond the quantum level where most physicists had wanted to confine it? The answer seems to be yes. In the quantum formalism what accounts for the strong correlation in the twin state is what is known as "phase entanglement." When quantum Red meets quantum Blue, their phases intermingle; part of Red's wave goes off with Blue's and vice versa. Bell's argument is that since there is nothing that is not a quantum system, this phase entanglement applies alike across the board, linking up all systems that have once interacted in the past in a single waveform whose remotest parts are joined in an unmediated, unmitigated, and immediate way. Given the massive tangle during the first instants of the Big Bang, the picture is of an exceedingly sociable cosmos: a bit of everything is seamlessly webbed in the being of everything else. As I mentioned above, phase entanglement lies at the heart of Bohm's reasoning too.

But as was the case with Bohm, since Bell's logic (1) did not actually discover a nonlocal interaction that had been directly observed, (2) did not propose a new experiment, and (3) predicted no new phenomena-relevant mathematics, the general reaction of his positivist peers in 1964 was: "mere philosophy." Since that time, however, physicists have been forced to take Bell's Theorem of interconnectedness more seriously. In 1972 John Clausner and Stuart Freedman of Berkeley devised an experimental test to show that either the world is local and quantum theory wrong; or the world is nonlocal and quantum theory right. (The experiment, by the way, does not involve actually observing faster-than-light communication.) Clausner and Freedman anticipated that the first alternative would be the case, that quantum theory is mistaken; the result showed the opposite. Objections which found loopholes in this test then led to a more refined test, conducted in Paris in 1982 by Alain Aspect, which by all accounts confirmed Bell's Theorem as definitively as these things can be.

One should note, of course, that technically Bell's argument does not depend on the validity of quantum theory. If quantum theory should someday go the way of Newton's mechanics, its successor will still have to incorporate Bell. Second, if you are thinking of opening up a superluminal channel with your distant terrestrial or extraterrestrial lover, the curious or consoling fact seems to be that though you are already superluminally linked, communication over the channel is blocked by quantum randomness. Nature may be able to use information in this form, but humans don't know the code—not yet anyway. According to special relativity, of course, if you could communicate faster than light, time would stop. You would open up a channel into the past—which would allow you to undo yesterdays. Would that be an advantage or just a nuisance?

CAUTION: HOLONOMY SLIPPERY WHEN WET

After apprehending a bit of what phase entanglement and Bell's Theorem imply, David Bohm's new natural philosophy may still seem strange but it is definitely a part of a larger conversation in which holonomic order is scarcely the wildest notion around. People at the 1979 transpersonal conference imagined that Bohm's cosmology might heal the West's division between mind and heart and body, between science and religion.

What in particular caused the excitement, I think, was the remythologization of the atomic world. Bohm's hidden variable interpretation gives the vast Mobius strip populations of space-time an inside, and turns the perceptual world into its emanation. For several centuries now the atom, more recently its profusion of elementary particles, has stood metaphorically for the triumph of the analytic mind and its ability to reduce composites to isolated parts—to incommunicative "windowless monads" 10^{-10} meters in diameter. The atom has also stood surrogate for the reduction of the material world, standard of the literal real, to virtual emptiness. Xenophanes (ca. 570–540 B.C.) was sure if horses could draw, they would "draw the forms of the gods like horses"; after Heisenberg, it's anything but clear we haven't done the same thing with atoms—imputing to them our own bourgeois individualism. But between noneuclidean quantum logic, "hyperspace," bootstrap theory, "many worlds," and Bell and

Bohm, the metaphoric power of the atom is being turned around—to stand for vast implication in all other things. The atom is joint and joiner; its putative emptiness, almost Buddhist fashion, begins to look full, a reminder of primitive, internal interrelationship. Well maybe. Not everyone at the 1979 transpersonal conference saw the dawn of the new paradigm.

David Bohm's understanding of things is subject to criticism on two fronts: (1) from scientists who accuse him of "mysticizing" the pedestrian data of physics; (2) from the religiously oriented who object, as Ken Wilber does, to collapsing the Great Chain of Being, and thus reducing mysticism to physics. Thus on the one side, from science writer Jeremy Bernstein to physicist John A. Wheeler who is often cited in connection with the new paradigm, the confusion of physics with mysticism has been anathematized as "superficial and profoundly misleading," "moonshine," "pathological science," and "charlatanism." From the consciousness-movement side itself and a strong belief in a "spectrum" of consciousness on the other hand, Ken Wilber ridicules the "shotgun wedding" of physics and mysticism, objecting to a more subtle form of reductionistic "melt down." Unless carefully discerned, he fears Bohm's paradigm involves "subscendence" rather than transcendence; and he lashes out at the pantheistic way some enthusiasts have taken Bohm. "Pantheism," Wilber retorts, "is a way to think about 'godhead' without having to actually transform yourself." Quantum oneness represents something more modest: discovering only "the *one dimensional* interpenetration of the material plane . . . that all hadrons, leptons, etc. are mutually interpenetrating and interdependent." This is not to be confused with the "infinite ground of mysticism." For reality, Wilber insists, is more complex, involving a spectrum of degrees corresponding to a spectrum of consciousness. As he says (Wilber, 1982: 160):

> The various levels . . . are interpenetrating and interconnecting. *But not in an equivalent fashion.* The higher transcends but includes the lower—*not* vice versa. That is, all of the lower is "in" the higher, but not all the higher is in the lower. As a simple example, there is a sense in which all of the reptile is in the man, but not all the man is in the reptile; all of the mineral world is in a plant, but not vice versa, and so on.

In sum, and rightly I think, Wilber denies that a "cosmic plasma" does much to explain ego goals, sociology, or mysticism. Nor, of course, would Bohm claim that it does.

What leads to such confusions about Bohm's standpoint is the isomorphism, the structural affinities, between various levels or subtotalities of the cosmos he contemplates. This does not entail reducing differences to homogeneity. As we shall observe in the next chapter, a mechanistic universe of iron law would do precisely that. No, structural convergence between physics and mysticism does not spell equivalence. Bohm does not have in mind blending all differences in some kind of subatomic cosmic soup, much less turning hadrons into God. Bohm reads the book of nature with a musical ear. He has tuned into an orchestral universe, where every grain of sand, every level of being, possesses a harmonic valency, is some kind of metaphoric sound—and not merely as a figure of speech. The figure of speech comes second, follows on the metaphoric structure of reality. Finally, this means that his universe is linked together by more than isomorphism, more than a set of abstract patterns of resemblance. His universe is an analogy of being like Aquinas's.

In order to understand this, there are at least three levels of cognition in Bohm's talk—all of which involve figuring out what is going on in the cosmos (or how to overcome being lost). The first, and in a sense most basic, lies at the level of fundamental concrete world-image or basic figuration—full of the primitive's multidimensional, holistic meanings (e.g., fire, river, thicket, nausea, wasteland, potter's clay, etc.). If you will, this is the level of myth, a point of departure and return for thinking. ("Symbol gives rise to thought," says Paul Ricoeur.) Bohm's figure here is elusively simple, the *in/out* rhythm of a breathing organism (rather than up/down hierarchy of Ken Wilber). At the second level of cognition, the conceptual, this figure translates into the categories of "implicate-explicate."

The second level involves the task of systematically exploring and relating the things of experience-as-a-whole ingredient in a working world-image. For the purposes of developing an insight into some aspect of the whole we break this operation down into the various sciences, physics, biology, physiology, psychology, and so on. Bohm speaks here as a hard-working theoretical physicist, but a physicist acutely aware that conceptualization and theory shape the "facts" that appear. Provisionally accepting the specialized attention of physicists, at this level Bohm proposes to make sense of what quantum formalisms refer to and imply within a restricted focus (pilot wave, etc.). In this regard, Bohm is quite clear: "It would be just as foolish for mystics to try to prove their case from physics as it would be for physicists to prove their case from mysticism." On the other hand, not being merely a cookbook physicist experimenting in recipes, Bohm does not forget the artificiality and selectivity of the physicist's way of looking at the whole; it is partial, an abstract slice—whereas, he implies, the natural mystic in us all is apt to have the whole in the concrete.

Accordingly, there are times when the provisional self-restriction of the physicist is lifted, and the whole Bohm speaks for the omissions in the scientific accounts. This brings us to the third level—of seeing the structure of the physical world as an icon through which to understand what's going on in a broader context. The third level involves reflection or thinking about thinking, questioning assumptions, assessing basic images and derivative conceptualities, and drawing forth wider implications. Reflection of this kind is normally associated with philosophy: the love of wisdom. After analytically parsing the whole into its parts, as it were, one tries to put things together (the Greek verb *symbolein* means "to draw together" or "unite"). At this level, Bohm addresses us as a "natural philosopher" or cosmologist, as these roles were understood before 1600. This occupation has all but passed out of existence, but it involves extrapolating from physical theory and putting together an integrated understanding—what the Stoics called a *cosmopolis* that had room for physics, political theory, and metaphysics. In the latter capacity, Bohm is performing one of those mind-bending metaphoric juxtapositions I referred to in the case of Einstein. Only in this case, Bohm (a student and friend of the late Krishnamurti) addresses us as poetic ontologist. Without reducing tensed realities to each other (pilot wave = God), Bohm-the-ontologist senses not only isomorphic resonances but the metaphoric capacity of the quantum world to mediate a richer sense of reality, maybe even an awakening. If you know what you are doing at the reflective level, "quantum action" can stand for the polynomial God who transcends all names, who resists all systematizing closure.

As we shall see, two voices, that of theoretical physicist and poet-ontologist, join forces in Bohm, and the images of the new physics in the former are such that the borders blur between these supposedly separate subject matters. Given our culture's besetting dualism of mind and matter, and materialistic literalism, someone who blurs walls and walks through them is probably a very useful kind of person to have around. But for certain purposes, it is useful to keep in mind a soft distinction between the two voices.

THE HOLONOMIC CIRCULATORY SYSTEM

The quantum physicist who focuses attention on the bizarre behavior and disappearing acts of *single* elementary particles (a fiction?) can more easily remain within the frame of the classical mechanistic paradigm. But as we have seen, the one who attends to two or more interacting particle systems runs into anomalies. This is where, to the dismay of any classical scientist, phase entanglement or Bohm's "undivided wholeness" enters the picture. The puzzle is that subatomic wave-particles, at least under certain conditions, do not appear to be governed by the laws of objects separate in space-time. The so-called disjoined particles in the EPR case act as if they knew instantaneously what was going on in the whole cosmic system, as if causality as we think of it in the discrete-object world of familiar four-dimensional space-time did not apply to their multidimensional order. Such implications illustrate one of the key questions in recent quantum inquiry: *How does information get around so quickly*, seemingly in defiance of the speed of light? For the exclusive hold of the mechanistic paradigm over the minds of scientists, that question opens up a mine field. Or is it mind field?

You can of course take refuge in the supposition of many mathematical physicists that though their formalism works with amazing success in predicting the apparition of new elementary particles, actually the mathematics refers to nothing in the real world. Instantaneous phase entanglement then exists only on paper. On the other hand, if there is some connection between mathematical theory and fact, then the physicist must go back to the drawing board for a new notion of order, measure, and structure. Which is what Bohm did. His first effort consisted of trying to make sense of quantum interconnection among electrons. Defying the von Neumann "proof" that it couldn't be done, in the 1950s he constructed a model for the electron as a particle which at all times has a definite position and momentum. In addition, it was connected to a new kind of field — an invisible pilot wave observable only through its effects — which guides the electron's movement by laws of motion which are highly contextual. Whenever a change occurs anywhere in the universe the pilot wave registers it, changes its shape as it were, and instantly communicates that information to the electron, which accordingly changes its position and momentum. Some of the changes the pilot wave incorporates consist of the measurements (not to mention nuclear explosions) physicists make — which through the mediating guide wave of course disturb the electron.

Following this line of thought, in the early 1970s Bohm suggested that what quantum equations were really formulating might best be understood as a hidden variable — a "superquantum potential" to account for the outgoing wave emitted by subatomic particles. Otherwise, he reasoned, it was difficult to explain the relatively independent interference patterns, the particlelike structure, of microphysical elements *and* their phasal entanglement properties. The superquantum potential not only organizes the whole cosmic field of plural space-times, but determines which subwholes, if any, will exist within the whole. Conversely, insofar as quantum events are held within this inferred field, they will contain information from the whole of space-time—in every so-called part. As Bohm (1985: 120) expressed it:

> Out of this emerges a picture of a wave which spreads out and converges, again and again, to show a kind of average particle-like behavior, while the interference and diffraction properties, of course, are still maintained. All this flows out of the activity of the super-quantum potential, which depends in principle on the state of the whole universe . . . .So now, we see that the whole universe not only determines and organizes its subwholes; it also gives form to what have until now been called the elementary particles out of which everything is supposed to be constituted. What we have here is a kind of universal process of constant creation and annihilation arranged into a world of form and structure, in which all manifest features are only relatively constant, recurrent, and stable aspects of the whole.

In Bohm's scheme, the electromagnetic field studied in the dominant quantum field theory is secondary and not self-contained; it depends on the superquantum potential, a kind of cosmic version of Rupert Sheldrake's morphogenetic fields. "With the superquantum potential," Bohm claimed, "the whole may be said to organize the parts. In a certain sense, quantum wholeness is thus closer to the organized unity of a living being than it is to that obtained by putting together the parts of a machine." Exit classical mechanics; enter a cosmic organism that sounds like the Renaissance conception of the cosmic human being. Resemblance, however, does not mean identity. The thrust of Bohm's "living being" analogy is directed to controvert the a priori assumptions of his professional colleagues.

At a minimum, Bohm (1973: 164–65) the physicist is asserting that at a very subtle physical level:

> "All implicates all," even to the extent that "we ourselves" are implicated together with "all that we see and think about." So we are present everywhere and at all times, though only implicately (that is implicitly).

Such implication (or participation) in the world we objectivize, one might think, has much bearing on our capacity to "know" it—as an insider. And yes, of course Einstein's speed of light applies to the explicate order; Bohm (1973: 165) does not deny it, but goes on:

> [Coimplication] is true of every "object." It is only in certain special orders of description that such objects appear explicate. But the general law [is that] all objects and all times are "folded together." . . . In a context [in which] explicate order ceases to be relevant, the notion of a signal will also cease to be relevant (e.g., if an order is "enfolded" throughout all of space and time, it cannot coherently be regarded as constituting a signal that would propagate information from one place to another over a period of time). This means that where implicate order is involved, the descriptive language of special relativity will, in general, no longer be relevant.

And this is the kind of thing that is being said out loud in prestigious journals of physics!

THE HOLOGRAM MODEL

The classical paradigm's focus on analytic parts had been closely tied to the technology of the lens, where the image cast bore a one-to-one correspondence to a *part* of an object. Bohm's principle model for the implication of whole in every atom and grain of sand is a bit of contemporary high tech — the *hologram*. But what is holography? Described mathematically by Dennis Gabor in the 1940s (one of the pioneers of information physics and Nobel prizewinner in 1964), holography is a method of lenseless photography that was realized in laser hardware in the 1960s. It is based on the curiosity that light waves scattered by an object can be recorded on a photographic plate as a swirling interference pattern — the so-called hologram. It is so named because of its striking difference from an ordinary photographic plate, where each point on the surface corresponds, one for one, to an object's image. Should the plate be damaged, that part of the image will be lost. With a holographic plate, the case is otherwise. Phase relationships between waves and their interference patterns — be the source sound, optical shapes and movement, waves of water or radio waves from distant quasars — carry enormous amounts of information about the whole distributed state of the object. Under the coherent light of a laser beam, information from the object-as-a-whole can be transferred to a holographic plate, and as such will be distributed *over the whole plate*, and in every part of the plate. The result is that when any single piece of the blur on the plate is again placed within a laser beam, the total original pattern is regenerated to "materialize" a three-dimensional image in space—which you could walk around and observe from any perspective. In Bohm's view, the analogy is that the physical world and everything in it, to one degree or another (the resolution may be weak or strong), are holograms implicitly enfolding the whole. And most quantum experiments, he thinks, reflect this: not an antithesis between part and whole but their interpenetration.

But if the hologram model applies to every particle in the manifest world, then it invites the close student of anything, including vanishingly miniscule quantum activity, to find the nature of the whole inscribed in his or her particulars. In an Einsteinian world, matter had been shown to be a vortex process-structure, inseparable from others, in a flowing stream. Heisenberg had shown that it was no longer possible to separate out the observer from the observed. Adopting his second "symbolizing" voice, Bohm (1980: 149) the physicist moved on to name the immeasurable stream:

> There is the germ of a new order here. This order is not to be understood solely in terms of a regular arrangement of *objects* (e.g., in rows) or as a regular arrangement of *events* (e.g., in a series). Rather, a *total order* is contained, in some *implicit* sense, in each region of space and time . . . . So we may be led to explore the notion that in some sense each region contains a total structure "enfolded" within it.

For Bohm, the new order is not a mirage. He calls it the "implicate order"—and yes, here begins his extrapolation from strictly physical theory. Instead of starting with the assumption of separate particle-fields which scientists abstract from the *implicit* whole (electromagnetism, radio waves, sound, life, libido, consciousness), Bohm begins by assuming a comprehensive "carrier" of the holistic implicate realm. The carrier, please note, is something a good deal more than his own postulated "superquantum potential" field (another abstracted aspect). Not limited to any specific form or measure, though manifest in all, he terms this encompassing kinetic energy the undivided "holomovement."

We've been getting pieces of it—as in a jigsaw puzzle—for millennia. The Greeks thought of it as an organism, or a geometrical earth surrounded by crystalline spheres carrying living stars and planets. Saint Augustine thought of it as the providential unfolding of God's time, a tension between two cities. Hindus and Kabbalists imagine it as the unfolding of an interior divine anatomy, *Prajapiti* in the one case, the glory-laden *Adam Kadmon* in the other. Newton's version was a clockwork universe. Every world-image and every scientific theory exploring such an image, whatever the subdivision, Bohm thinks, focuses attention on a certain aspect within a certain limited context, and catches a piece of the holomovement. But of the whole itself, history would seem to instruct us that there can be no fundamental theory because it is *undefinable and immeasurable.*" Yet the visible world, Bohm thinks, is telltale, revealer, and thus worthy of respectful attention and observation. For finite materiality and mind "enfold" this incomprehensible formative movement, and "unfold" jointly out of it. The unfolding is the vast "implicate" order becoming "explicate."

In a new idiom, in a new context of understanding, Bohm returns us to the Hebrew genesis story which is never simply eternal return but always "more to come." Which is to say that the holomovement, a resuscitation of the Judeo-Christian cosmic Logos symbol or the Hindu vision embodied in Krishna legends, expresses itself in different ways depending on and limited by formal explicate structure — which, however, is understood as fundamentally elastic and transformable. Bohm speaks of a new kind of measure different from that of the arrangement of separate things. He talks of an "implication parameter," by which he means different degrees of implication that could be arranged in a certain order. What aspects of the holomovement are explicit when we speak of electrons, gravity, unnucleated cells, carbon molecules, amino acids, generation by division, sexual generation, brain functions, psyche, the Renaissance, the rise of scientific mentality, and so on? Is it possibly the case that the more differentiated the complex and its constitutive relations, the more the hidden implicate realm comes out into the open? Is a human being so baffling precisely because its implications reach to the nth degree? It follows that Bohm (1980: 147) is also speaking of a new kind of physical law, the possibility

> that physical law should refer primarily to an order of undivided wholeness . . . similar to that indicated by a hologram rather than to an order of analysis of such content into separate parts indicated by a lens.

On the other hand, Bohm is at pains to argue that holonomic description is perfectly compatible with analytic description of things externally related — or what he appropriately calls "heteronomy." Like particle/wave alternatives, whole-part descriptions go together. Analysis is a *lysis*, a dissolution or loosening of the whole from the standpoint of attentive distance or height (*ana*), an abstraction within the whole.

UNCOMMON COMMON GROUND

For those familiar with pre-Renaissance conceptions of reality such as Aquinas's analogy of being, or with modern thinkers such as Hegel, Samuel Alexander, Jan Smuts, William Ernest Hocking, or Whitehead, the idea of an implicate holomovement is certainly not new. It resonates with the Hindu's sidereal Ganges and Aquinas's "unfolding" which we spoke of in the last section—a wrap-around or radial sense deriving from an oral sensibility wherein manifest, empirical reality is the outer, diminished edge of a process of involution from more intense orders of being. Presumably on the basis of experience outside the cloud chamber, yet inspired by what he found there, Bohm's notion of a superquantum potential ramified, expanding beyond its original reference in physics, and transposed into a multiproportioned analogy of being-in-process. Quantum acts turned into metaphorical clue, and their attribute of "every-when" crossed into social psychology and beyond. If coimplication functions at every level of complexity, it becomes understandable and natural that Stanislav Grof's psychedelic subjects remembered the Big Bang and phylogenesis. If Bohm is right, all prehistory and history ought to be ingrained in our tissue. And yes, as Ken Wilber put it, "not *all* the higher is in the lower"—but like Aquinas and Dante, Bohm would stress the whole that moves at every level. But he is not advancing a doctrinal claim to final truth. Rather, as he says, a holonomic order represents a tender offer, a "plausible or reasonable avenue to pursue" (in Wilber, 1982: 198).

It is an avenue that goes against modernist, but perhaps not postmodernist, cultural traffic. Bohm would counter the spirit of fragmentation. Physics is physics, theology is theology. As conventionally practiced, Bohm knows the distinctions well enough—if some of his enthusiasts do not. Yet if Hindus can use jewels as meditation objects and Buddhists lotuses blooming out of a drainage ditch, there is no reason in principle why the data of science are any less or more opaquely numinous. At the very least, Bohm's analogously expressive holomovement bids to offer a linguistic "common ground" for communication among various fields of human inquiry. He wants physicists to be able to talk across borders, across the fragmentation of specialties, to mystics. But I think he would also like all scientists to acknowledge that they have no privileged access, when it comes to the truth of nature, over the most ordinary citizen's communion with mountains, sea, and sky. It is these not extraordinary experiences of nature-as-a-whole out of which the scientist carves an abstract domain of concentration. Buried in them are the scientist's point of departure, if you will, the incentive and lure for research into what is implicit there. Bohm is no detractor of the gains of such specialization, but he encourages one to credit the unspecialized experience of explicate nature as a richer manifestation of the holomovement in nature than the abstractions of physicists and chemists—abstractions which, properly considered, may contribute to the richness of perceptions of mountains, sea, and sky.

In this regard, Bohm is suspicious of those who, like Ken Wilber, so stress the hierarchical differentiation between various so-called levels of reality that the physical world ends up degraded and the sacred is confined exclusively to places like churches. I would add that when people "transcend" and detach themselves from their social and natural environments in innumerable self-serving, self-destructive ways, one wonders whether hierarchical images don't pull in the wrong direction—among other things reinforcing solitary elitism and its unacknowledged dependency on our updated form of those patriarchal orders of heroic societies from which, after all, the Great Chain of Being borrows heavily. One wonders if some earthy "subscendence," as Alexander Lowen has been showing for years, isn't what a contemporary faith-healer should order (see Lowen, 1969, 1973).

Moreover, in a modern context, a grades-of-being approach stands in danger of taking uncritically science's claim to give us "the facts." "What we learn about," observed a chastened Heisenberg, "is not nature itself, but nature exposed to our method of questioning." After Heisenberg, selective, abstractive attention following limited kinds of questioning should be seen for what it is—what it isn't is an exhaustive index of all reports from the material world. On the other hand, in taking the physicist's world as necessarily one-dimensional, Wilber unwittingly buys stock in the seventeenth-century dualism between overvalued self-consciousness and undervalued matter which matters not. In this regard, the whole notion of "mere" materiality represents, I think, an idol of the study. By no means all, but some scientists are like people looking through the wrong end of a telescope and wondering why the world looks so small.

As a philosophically minded physicist, Bohm is acutely aware of just how selective and confined the normal scientist's attention is when speaking of materiality, and correspondingly, how confined the humanist often is when speaking of psyche or spirit. Bohm (in Wilber: 1982: 190–91) writes:

I am not trying to deduce life and consciousness from physics, but rather to see matter as a part of a relatively independent sub-totality which includes life. Leaving out life, we get inanimate matter; leaving out consciousness, we get life; leaving out something unspecified which lies beyond, we get ordinary consciousness and so on. I don't call this a hierarchy, but rather a series of levels of abstraction.

To Bohm, the "higher" and "lower" grades of being beloved by Great Chain of Being thinkers like Wilber miss the point that the various subtotalities of the universe implicitly contain and unfold the whole—whatever that whole is. From this perspective, the things of this world are not simply mementoes, extrinsic symbolic mediators, a set of "this" whose function it is to point to an external "that." Following his quantum clue, the things of this world are *embodiments* of "that"—the all, whatever it may be, implicated in whatever exists. When it comes to conscious beings, of course, awareness may be another thing; doubtless Wilber's spectrum of consciousness is illuminating on this score.

Of course, Bohm concedes, "there is an asymmetry" involved "in that the form enfolds the whole only in a limited and not completely defined way." Presumably, then, quarks are incapable of unfolding (or revealing) what more complex organisms like banyan trees, whooping cranes, and human beings at the top of their form can. But radically, in Bohm's view (as for Aquinas) every material thing functions as a concrete metaphor in the root meaning of the term; it is a "carrier-across," a manifestation of the numinous. "All matter," says Bohm, "is in some way holy." "When I see the immense order of the universe (and especially the brain of man)," writes Bohm (1985: 124) the contemplative ontologist, "I cannot escape the feeling that this *ground* enfolds a supreme intelligence. Although it is not quite so evident, I would say also that this intelligence is permeated with compassion and love" (italics mine). The "ground" here is no ethereal "Ground of Being" but rough earth under foot, the stuff Dostoyevsky's Alyosha Karamazov knelt to kiss.

HOLONOMIC MIND

"I had long felt," says Bohm, "that the quantum theory describes processes that are, in certain key ways, analogous to those arising in our experience of consciousness." For instance, the uncertainty principle: as with the position and momentum of electrons, to fix a train of thought is to lose its development. Thought unfolds weighted with implication enfolded into it, in a series of particlelike manifestations—like a quantum mechanical field. Or like a photon it emerges from a larger, implicit whole—at this level, that of an enfolded, active *intention* to which the meanings of its expression are internally related. Both mind and matter, Bohm theorizes, unfold from a common dynamic structure, an implicate order which is the basis of their relationship. Through intentionality, "we directly experience the implicate order." Intention is not concocted whole, out of the willfulness of human subjects; it is no less natural, no less given by the cosmos, than the behavior of leptons and bacteria. Bohm (Wilber, 1982: 194) states:

> In the old physics, matter (which was the only reality) was completely mechanical, leaving no room for mind. But if, according to the new physics, everything is enfolded in everything else, then there is no separation of domains. Mind grows out of matter. And matter contains the essence of mind. These two are really abstractions from the whole, relatively invariant subtotalities created by our thought. Therefore, if we probe matter deeply enough, we will find a reflection of the same qualities which are revealed when mind is similarly probed.

Again, this is Bohm the cosmologist in Aristotle's style—where thinking is a sign of intense participation in the *nous poiētikos*.

Enter neurophysiologist Karl Pribram. Pribram's problem ran parallel to the nonlocal quantum phenomenon; his project had been to understand the nonlocal distribution of memory throughout brain tissue. Near his wit's end in trying to make sense of this, his son, a physicist, had directed him to Bohm's holonomic theory. Pribram's mentor had been the famous neurophysiologist Karl Lashley, whose major research had sought for the "engram," some sort of physical imprint in the brain corresponding to a memory trace. More recently, researchers like Wilder Penfield had been showing specific sites in the brain for hearing, vision, emotions, motor control, and to some extent memory. But in the case of long-term memory in particular, surgery had shown the portions of the brain associated with memory—indeed even 20 percent of the brain—could be removed without leaving a hole in memory. In some sense memory appeared "delocalized." In 1929 Lashley proposed the "principle of mass action," the notion that certain sorts of learning involve the whole cerebral cortex. Similarly, he came up with the "principle of equipotentiality," the proposal that when one part of a sensory system is damaged its function can be assumed by another part. (This has proved to be the case for the so-called split brain; the normally intuitive, artistic right hemisphere can acquire analytic skill, and conversely, the rational left hemisphere can acquire symbolic dexterity.) In any case, Pribram was following Lashley's track, trying to fathom the nonlocality of memory. As things worked out, his theory represents an extrapolation of the whole-in-part theorem of atomic physics to neurophysiology.

As with Bohm, holography serves Pribram as a model or analogy for understanding the brain. Other models in current use, which also try to sift and constellate the evidence, are the telephone relay exchange or that of a computer processing, programming, and storing information—but neither of these is particularly apt for comprehending the nonlocal distribution of memory. In brief, the idea is that our minds mathematically construct three-dimensional reality by interpreting wave frequencies from another order of reality of infinite dimensions. This other realm is an order of meaningful, patterned reality transcending time and space—at least linear space and time (frequency still has to do with cycles per second or space per time). The brain, asserts Pribram, functions like a hologram. But of what is the brain a hologram? Inspired by the symbolics of quantum physics, he answers that brain neurons holographically store an image of the entire universe. Does Pribram mean "universe" in Bohm's finally more mystical sense? My impression is that he stops a good deal short of that — at least in public.

For Pribram, however, the brain is like the laser beam, interpreting, not images across space, but the unextended frequency store, the vibrations of quantum events interfusing with and influenced by their whole environment, implanted subatomically in the synaptic endings of neurons—as holograms. Animal experiments suggest that these holograms are not in fact distributed equally over the entire cortex but occur in tattered patches. The pattern is strangely analogous to mathematical models of Einstein's space-time. In each region, space is represented by a patch which cannot be run smoothly into its neighbor. The result is a quilt or archipelago effect, regions of order amid a sea of thermodynamic "noise" which together make up the somewhat wild topography of the warped geometry of general relativity. The brain is one of those notoriously open systems exchanging information with its environment in code. Mathematically, Pribram and others have found, the multiple fields of space-time are converted into the form of Fourier sine and cosine wave functions, a kind of storage code. The brain-mind deciphers this frequency code enfolded into itself and then projects aspects of it, depending on the situation, into three-dimensional images—sounds, shapes, movements, traffic patterns, facial profiles—much as stereophonic speakers project sound. But for us and our mind's magic transformation, our familiar world "out there" would not be. Oh yes, of course, something would be happening, but it would not be the "things" we in particular perceive at all.

Sirius, the dog star, disturbs us, we it. The frequency interference patterns that intersect with our relatively autonomous systems contain vast quantities of information. Some of this energy-information is quantifiable; some registering in tonal, mood quality, and teleological terms. We are truly *informed*, receivers if Pribram and Bohm are right, on a gigantic scale. Differentiating ourselves from this influx—the formative, informing world—gives us our self-consciousness and freedom; but correlatively, that self-consciousness would have no content except in terms of that informing world. A sense of *telos* or intention is part of that reception, part of the holomovement.

If I understand what Bohm is getting at, intentionality represents our primary experience of the implicate order and its forward thrust or lure. We don't primarily apprehend such appetition through external sensory experience—say, in the traces of a cloud chamber. The method of questioning there rules it out. Relatively speaking, cloud chambers, accelerators, paramecia on a slide give us the surfaces of the explicate realm. Relative to what? As Whitehead claimed, we primarily apprehend what is most deeply implicit in the nature of things, if we do at all, by paying attention to influence from the body, and through the body, from the greater world. Though our cultural programming has taught us to prescind from a body teeming with messages in deference to external, sensory perception, this interior experience of the body, and not a high energy cyclotron, is our most fundamental experience of nature—and its implicate formative movement. Beyond any complete reckoning, most of it unconscious, our bodies synthesize a storm of information. They represent our depth probe into what is happening in nature, a coming-together of myriad events, of which there is only some telling.

NINE

Tantric Thermodynamics

In any attempt to bridge the domains of experience belonging to the spiritual and physical sides of our nature, time occupies the key position.

Arthur S. Eddington

For us who are convinced physicists, the distinction between past, present, and future is only an illusion, however persistent.

Albert Einstein

What is an organism? A sheaf of times. What is a living system? A bouquet of times.

Michel Serres

The physical cosmos resounds in strange ways. In 1965 radio astronomers detected a residual "black body" phenomenon, a 3° Kelvin background radiation from the Big Bang some 15 or 20 billion years ago. With that discovery, steady-state cosmologies, which until then had dominated the field, yielded their absolute hegemony. Physics had found its own arrow of time. From zero, it would appear, the universe is currently expanding in all directions like a great balloon in the process of inflation. What is the ultimate direction of this astronomical time? Does it conform to the law of entropy, running toward incoherence like the irreversible time of a self-consuming star? Or is it negentropic, running against the flow to disorder, analogous to the complexification of civilization? If so, how can this be? But before this last question, astronomers have to ask themselves the big question that is exactly analogous to the one we posed at the end of chapter 3 regarding the difference or indifference of time:

229

Are all the works of the cosmos predestined to return to oceanic oblivion or not? Is the process of expansion, as the predisposition of a physicist would prefer to believe, reversible or not?

The form of the question for a physicist is this: Is the physical universe a closed system, the kind of integral system which alone permits precise description in linear equations; or is it an open, essentially ambiguous system whose future escapes precise determination? Do things start out from an initial state of uniform energy, with entropy at a maximum, and ultimately return to that undifferentiated state? Or did the universe, even from the outset, exist in a nonequilibrium condition? In 1966 Andre Sakharov proposed a model which gave nonequilibrium and irreversible processes cosmological status. If Sakharov is right, it would mean that the expanding physical cosmos as a whole is a symmetry-breaker spiraling irreversibly into the unknown future. It is difficult otherwise to account for the present structure of things. For according to the law of mass action, if everything were perfectly symmetrical and reversible at the start, antimatter would have continued to annihilate matter as soon as it was created, producing lots of photons (or light) but not the asymmetrical dominance of matter that we actually have.

Others have argued that the initial conditions of the Big Bang were such that the current complex state of the cosmos (e.g., galaxies and solar systems hospitable to life) was built in from the outset—almost teleologically. According to the so-called anthropic principle (see Barrow and Tipler, 1986), if just one of the universal subatomic constants—proton charge, strong force, Planck's constant of quantum action, the speed of light, neutron mass, or weak force—had been off even an infinitesimal fraction from what they are, stars would not have decayed to produce the prebiotic stew of chemicals necessary for life on this planet. Given what these constants are, our improbable planet suddenly looks probable. Good news: the universal constants seem to have worked for our eventual emergence from the elements; but bad news for neoclassical (i.e., probabilistic) physics, because a symmetry-breaking cosmos would mean that macroscopic nature eludes the kind of timeless martial law which science has sought to establish.

In this connection, one has to remember the whole orientation of classical and neoclassical physics. "You have to accept the idea," Einstein admonished (in Prigogine, 1980: 203) his friend Michele Besso, "that subjective time with its emphasis on the now has no objective meaning." "For us who are convinced physicists, the distinction between past, present, and future is only an illusion, however persistent." Quantum physics didn't change that. Werner Heisenberg's uncertainty principle introduced probability into the micro world, but such indeterminacy is commonly thought to be confined to that micro world; at the macro level of stars, planets, biology and ourselves, the strict *law of large numbers* reimposes determinism. The focus being on linear trajectories, that is, on mere change of place or velocity, there is no need for a formalism to express phenomena like "greater than," "later than," or "one-way temporal direction." The famous Schrödinger equations, which characterize the wave amplitude that evolves in a quantum energy packet, are written in reversible, deterministic terms. If the wave function at a given instant is known, the equations allow it to be calculated for any previous or subsequent time.

Moreover, so far as thermodynamics is concerned, the statistical mechanics Ludwig Boltzmann developed to deal with fiery matter focused on the trend toward dissolution, and his linear equations for this trajectory are time-invariant. "In the universe as a whole," wrote Boltzmann (in Prigogine and Stengers, 1984: 254), "the two directions of time are indistinguishable, just as in space there is no up or down." To this day it is common for the majority of physicists to consider that irreversibility is the result of unusual initial conditions, not a fundamental fact intrinsic to nature. As I noted in chapter 7, the temporal arrow introduced by entropy is usually shunted aside as a statistically insignificant case of improbable initial conditions. The great universe, it is supposed, resembles a gas in an insulated system or water in a bottle; the macroscopic properties do not change over time. Just as Einstein implied, our phenomenological feeling for the irreversibility of time has no precise scientific meaning.

Consequently, when it comes to interpreting the expansion of the macroscopic universe, habits of thought tend to vote for expansion as only a first phase. The process may be oscillatory, an expansion from an initial density moment (which preoccupies grand unification theorists) to a turning point (perhaps 50 billion years ahead) when expansion will stop, reverse itself, and contraction will begin—whereupon long-term symmetry will reestablish its rule. To this day, the majority of particle physicists hold that the complex universe, a kind of disturbance in the field as it now stands, will return eventually to equilibrium—if that is where it began. The balloon will burst. Consequently, the past, present, and future we associate with the structural differentiation of most processes with which we are familiar, and which do not spontaneously run in reverse, are considered marginal. Stars consuming their own fuel don't recover their original state; chemical mixtures do not spontaneously separate out again; broken eggs do not reconstitute themselves—but so far as physics is concerned, there's no reason why not. Whatever asymmetries exist, we are told, apply only as supplementary approximations, to the disturbed interactions of "weak" nuclear forces. The big scheme, supposedly, can correct for all the errors of middle earth and the Milky Way. History has no purchase in the physicist's domain.

So where does that leave us? Most fundamentally, it leaves us with the stark antithesis of being and becoming. Our most exact science harbors an idealism which is indifferent to past and future. And what difference does that make? Philosopher of science Karl Popper (in Prigogine and Stengers, 1984: 255) could hardly contain his distress.

> It brands unidirectional change as an illusion. This makes the catastrophe of Hiroshima an illusion. Thus it makes the world an illusion, and with it all our attempts to find out more about our world. It is therefore self-defeating (like every idealism).

But this is a conflict within science's own house as well, between physics and all the other natural sciences. "Fire changes" (*Ignis mutat*) is the motto of chemistry. But at the base of a many-storied nature, textbook physics blows out a Heraclitean fire. Physicists' fundamental building blocks, the layman might think, ought to be describable in a way that accounts for a building process, but they seem to be warehoused in a perspective from which nothing can become. Conventional physics cannot explain the irreversible, complexity-building behavior of matter studied in the science of fire, chemistry, or in the science of life, biology. Biologists are talking about a different time *direction*: complex systems far from disorganized equilibrium whose movement is uphill, counter-entropic, and which create functional rather than linear space. Whereas, in the physicists' world, the cards are stacked in favor of sheer disorganization, a return to chaos. The *tehom* always has the odds. Time figures, but its direction is downhill, the exact opposite of evolution or morphogenesis. Scientists are therefore left with the problem of trying to reconcile the time-symmetrical, reversible process with three arrows of time:

- The arrow of cosmic expansion—away from the initial state of condensed and uniform energy (entropy at a maximum).
- The arrow of history—evolving structures of galaxies, stars, planets, life, and culture.
- The thermodynamic arrow—the spendthrift price of macrostructures, their unraveling decay.

One might well argue that the issue at stake in such a reconciliation, if it can be achieved, is probably as central to our culture as any that can be imagined. For as the Belgian physical chemist Ilya Prigogine writes (1980: xvii),

> It is probably not an exaggeration to say that Western civilization is time centered. Is this perhaps related to a basic characteristic of the point of view taken in both the Old and the New Testaments? It was inevitable that the "timeless" conception of classical physics would clash with the metaphysical conceptions of the Western world. It is not by accident that the entire history of philosophy from Kant through Whitehead was either an attempt to eliminate this difficulty through the introduction of another reality (e.g., the noumenal world of Kant) or a new mode of description in which time and freedom, rather than determinism, would play a fundamental role.

The problem is that so long as one-directional time, as biologists and humanists understand it, doesn't count, we are forced to keep our understandings of energy in a separate department from the sign-world of human culture. David Bohm's holomovement theory represents a bridge, a way to open communication between these separate accounts that is reminiscent of Aquinas's habit of seeing all creation as a proportionate participation in God's act of existence. Or reminiscent of a Kabbalist's habit of seeing cosmogenesis as the unfolding of a process within God. Ilya Prigogine's nonequilibrium thermodynamics, the main subject of this chapter, represents another passage through the wall of separation which may be even more Judeo-Christian in spirit. For just as the Judeo-Christian God stretches down into the *tehom* and identifies with the lowly of this earth, Prigogine's theory reaches for the lowest current, that most primitive subatomic ferment labeled entropy, as the spark for transformation and greater structural complexity. Order emerges from chaos.

Despite all the attention paid to a process world since 1750, physics had been the stubborn holdout. So much so that Lancelot Law Whyte was once provoked to declare ([1960] 1978: 53) that,

> *No clear fundamental idea of the essential character of transformation has yet been formulated in any branch of knowledge.* No general rule is known which tells us when and how new entities or arrangements appear or disappear. In this respect the world of transformation, after three and a half centuries of exact science, still lies beyond our rational understanding.

Is this statement still valid? I think not. A scientist like Whyte who did not consider Darwin's evolution by natural selection a "fundamental idea" sets a high standard for what may qualify. But in 1977 Ilya Prigogine won the Nobel Prize for elaborating an elegant mathematical formalism for the nonequilibrium thermodynamics of open systems, or what he called "dissipative structures." Such processes, which include everything from galaxies down to planets, organic compounds, and embryos, conform to thermodynamic laws, heightening the quality of energy internally even while they give off waste, degrading energy externally. But the circulatory process is nonlinear. Open systems break symmetry, forget their initial conditions. The beauty of Prigogine's theory is that it provides a place for both determinism and chance. (As with Sheldrake's morphogenesis, the two concepts are seen as complementary.) I suspect the work of Prigogine's Brussels school is fundamental.

Before explicating the theory of dissipative structures, however, I will make a detour through information physics, as an introduction to nonequilibrium thermodynamics and the new value ascribed to entropic *disorder*. Once again we will see that new scientific models back away from isolated systems and return to viewing nature as a circulatory communication system. Nature gives signs, not necessarily signs that an animist would appreciate but signs congenial to life.

ENTROPY AND INFORMATION

What energy was to the nineteenth century, information is to the twentieth. Cybernetic physics took hold of Heisenberg's uncertainty principle and turned the ratio of the frequency to infrequency of events into a powerful organ of understanding relative stabilities in an unreliable, chancy universe. Implicitly the move brought the physical world closer to the medieval communication-system cosmos; matter-energy, it now began to appear, is actively, inwardly informed, coded, a set of signs. Nature, the realm of *physis*, is not merely matter-energy, but a triad of matter-energy-*information* (see Campbell, 1982).

As defined in physics, information is the nonrandom element which exploits the quantum uncertainty discovered by Bohr and Heisenberg. The correlation of entropy with what appears its opposite, organization swimming against a degenerative tidal flow, offered a new insight into the nature of organization. As the twentieth century dawned, it was quickly demonstrated that a connection existed between the thermodynamics of Rudolph Clausius and Ludwig Boltzmann, and concepts like information, noise, and redundancy—notions of a burgeoning information physics. Information (emitted, transmitted, or received) amounted to a form of negative entropy (or negentropy). What is the difference, asked the early pioneers of cybernetics trying to "govern" telecommunications, between the "noise" of randomly dispersed energy (Brownian motion) and intelligible "messages" which have a certain complex order? The wormy space-time smears into which Einstein had translated Newton's rigid bodies are constituted by signals limited by the speed of light. Bohm's implicate order which issues the superquantum potential is not limited to the speed of light, but also signals and orders the explicate realm. Both viewpoints invite us to think of nature as semiotic, a sign-system. In any case, how are such organizing messages translated into measurable units reducible to mathematical symbolism?

The answer to these questions put together statistical mechanics (Boltzmann), quantum mechanics (Planck's calculation of how uncertain we are—or how much information is missing—when we try to determine what the infinitely spread-out wave function will actually be), and communication theory. To a communications statistician taking the viewpoint of a receiver, a message is a time series, a discrete or continuous sequence of measurable events distributed in time which represents a set of alternatives. If only one alternative is available (say a monotone over the phone), there is no uncertainty but no real information. If there are too many alternatives, utter randomness in the distribution of signals, the result is incomprehensible static or "noise." A message that communicates, that makes a difference, falls somewhere between these two extremes.

The answer to the question of what the mathematical equivalent of a "bit" of information is, then, turned on translating the improbabilities of organized energy into the inverse of random disorganization—or maximum entropy. In this manner, a precise statistical technique was found for discriminating the ratio of information/organization by *contrasting* it with the backdrop trend toward entropic incoherence. If heat death is in the long term the most probable state of things (metal rusts, wood rots, coffee grows cold), then order—and by implication the order involved in anything from the message of quasar radiation to that of a DNA molecule—can be probabilistically measured as the negative of its entropy, and the negative logarithm of its probability. In more accessible terms, DNA, the telegraph, telephone, and TV transmissions can function only by continually varying their signals according to some sort of statistical regularity—in effect, a standard code, an alphabet, or set of grammatical rules that generate, within their limits, a wide variety of programs, messages, and images.

In these terms, the new information theory could span any kind of communication—electrical, chemical, biological, social, and economic. It could explain why the improbable rhetoric of James Joyce communicates more information than the more conventional Jane Austen; or why a Jackson Pollock painting (at least in 1950) contained more than a painting by Frederick Church of the Hudson River School. As information theory saw it, the utterly expected, the cliché or platitude, gives only one alternative—and thus, for the receiver, represents little or no information. In my example, Joyce and Pollock offer many alternatives, a rich feast of ambiguity—and thus the information content is dense. But as these two figures may suggest—by their seemingly random, symmetry-breaking styles (like Brownian motion?)—in this context entropy (provided it does not go too far) begins to look positive.

During and after the Second World War, engineers like Claude Shannon of Bell Labs and Norbert Wiener of MIT worked out the details. Communicable structure or information falls between two extremes, two idealized parameters of total constraint on one side and total freedom or variability on the other. On one end of the spectrum stood maximum information, but in the unabsorbable form of complete, random variability, the alternative possibilities so great that the receiver (be it DNA molecule or scientist concerned for some kind of predictability) can make no sense of the torrent (entropy value 1). If you translate this into phone terms, the message would be garbled "noise," as if you were hearing at once all the voices of a great city or the teeming sound of everything in the cosmos. This is what neoclassical physicists speak of as maximum entropy production, because the slide toward incoherence is presumed to be greatly accelerated. David Bohm may be correct in asserting that it is mislabeled "disorder"; rather, he thinks, the order is too subtle and complex for us—though for our chemical systems, it may not be noise at all but convertible into information. Obviously, molecules got to the quantum rules of the periodic table before we did. The point is important: what is noise or waste for one system (e.g., the sun) can be sustenance for another system (e.g., the bacteria of plants).

On the other side of the spectrum stands another null-point of information: complete determinism of one alternative or utter redundancy (entropy value 0). In this rigid, steady-state "order" of timeless repeat, past, present, and future have no meaning. The order at this end is that of the perfectly repeated pattern of wallpaper, a perfectly static crystal, or a mere monotone over the phone. Obviously, the order of complex chemical and living processes is not of this static kind. Rather, such processes are comparatively unstable, what you might call balancing acts (thus nonequilibrium structures) somewhere between "noise" and sheer redundancy. Such redundancy, of course, had in effect been the ideal of Newtonian "law." As the telephone monotone illustration may suggest, the information such recurrence transmits is zero—and this, above all, is why Michel Serres accuses classical modern Newtonian science of communicating nothing, of being a "science of the dead." Not only is such a totalizing, frozen "order" not relevant to complex functional organization of nonequilibrium systems like *Gaia*—Mother Earth—but if the universe as a whole is basically overloaded with "too much" information (that is, high entropy production), then classic mechanism would appear to be the exception, applicable only to the rare case. One begins to have the suspicion that we've had our notions of "order" and "disorder" confused—and that what scientifically influenced common sense has regarded as chaos should be radically turned around. (Prigogine does precisely this.)

A compromise, rather than a reversal, is what is called for. Most of the processes of our familiar world—the diffusion of an aroma from a kitchen, ink mixing in a liquid, ice melting, a waterfall diffusing in spray and mist, mechanical gears heating, hot air rising, sugar fermenting, caterpillers mutating into butterflies, stars forming—are irreversible, nonequilibrium structures in which often radical difference exists between past and future. An example proposed by H. Atlan (in Peacocke, 1984b: 414) may help to bring out the balancing act feature. Think of a cultural system contained in a library. The culture exists as a kind of optimization between the above-mentioned parameters. On the one hand, you can imagine the unlikely case that each book in the library is utterly independent, with no references, allusions or relationships with any other. In short, the library is a case of utterly random variation, all its books behaving like molecules, ignoring each other, at perfect thermal equilibrium. (Prigogine calls the units behaving in this particlelike way "hypnons," sleepwalkers.) On the other hand, imagine a library in which every book exactly repeated the other—perfect redundancy—so that the culture was reduced to the sameness of one volume. At neither extreme would we have a cultural system; thus with all nonequilibrium systems which at various levels decode energy and convert it into organizing information: they exist relatively far from equilibrium, striking a precarious balance between perfect stability and total randomness. As Wiener and Shannon put it, for a communication system to operate, both turbulent "noise" and steadying redundancy must be incorporated. Contrary to the classical notion, which really goes back to Plato, contingent fluctuation and complex order are complementary. Chance and necessity fund each other, producing nonequilibrium that awakens hypnons—as we shall see, to self-organizing activity.

ORDER THROUGH FLUCTUATION

Ilya Prigogine is a professor of physical chemistry at the Free University of Brussels, Belgium, and the University of Texas at Austin. Like Ludwig Boltzmann, he has been concerned throughout his career with the apparent contradiction between classical physics and Darwinian evolution. Can both Boltzmann and Darwin be right, he asks? Can the timeless laws of classical dynamics be reconciled with evolutionary change? He thinks so, and basically his find, that nonequilibrium systems *cannot* run on reversible time, falls into line with all other advances in physics over the last century. For if one follows the history of physics—through thermodynamics, relativity, and quantum mechanics—in each case progress has come by discovering a limit, an *impossibility*—for example, of signals faster than the speed of light, or of getting by the indeterminacy of quantum phenomena, or of perpetual motion machines that don't wear down. The point is that Prigogine has discovered another impossibility, namely, that processes at a certain level of complexity can ever reverse time. Nature's show may run backward for isolated systems; it not only does not but cannot run backward for systems which interact with their environment. The Newtonian-Laplacean ambition to encompass the universe in a single law is doomed to failure.

Physicists had been seeking all-embracing, universal schemes; instead, they were finding time, unstable events, evolving particles. The suspicion grew that the great simplicities arose from the idealizations of macroscopic models built around the latest technological wonders. The true implications of relativity and quantum theory were finally being absorbed: that no single model or logic could encompass the thing. Reality was too rich, and required multiple languages.

Prigogine's contribution to this scientific revision lies in vastly widening the field of dynamics to include unstable or nonequilibrium systems. He has put together classical dynamics and thermodynamics in such a way that reversible time appears as the exception to the rule of irreversibility. In so doing, he gives us a vision of nature in which life and our feeling for time has a precise scientific meaning. Life is not opposed to the laws of physics but expresses the very conditions in which the biosphere is embedded—nonlinear chemical reactions and the far from equilibrium conditions of the sun's radiation. We are no longer out of place; we fit here.

Boltzmann's failure to reconcile Darwinian evolution with modern physics was principally due to the fact that he concentrated on gases in closed containers, thus on *closed systems* which did not exchange energy with their environment. For all practical purposes such systems permit no circulation of heat, light, or matter across their boundaries. From an information physics standpoint, the equilibrium order here approaches that of a pendulum, a dead log, a rock, or a perfect crystal—where the entropy value is 0. There is no question about it; near or at thermal equilibrium, matter does behave redundantly, leveling out any fluctuations which occur. It follows a symmetrical trajectory from its initial state, whatever that happens to be, and returns to that state, and the path can be precisely expressed in a linear equation. Near equilibrium, the significance of structural differentiation, complex correlations within the system, and relations to the environment are negligible. The elements of such a system are, as Prigogine phrases it, isolable "hypnons," ignoring each other and other cosmic company. Note the restriction which the choice of closed systems imposes. The first two laws of thermodynamics, the constant quantity of energy and yet its tendency to degenerate in usable form, apply *only* in cases of such closed systems. These laws deal with bottled-up processes, most of them artificially contrived in a laboratory, and assume that the universe is similarly closed.

But such systems aren't the only kind of dynamic system around; in fact, as I observed above, most systems in nature are not of this type. The galaxies which swarm the skies and the bacterial mitochondria which swarm in our cells constitute *open, nonequilibrium systems* whose very instability enables them to exchange matter and energy with their environment. The farther away you move from equilibrium, the more you move away from repetitive, universal behavior, and toward the specific and the unique. Given the barest circulation with the environment, the open system far from equilibrium eludes the linear equations of classical and statistical mechanics; it doesn't redundantly repeat the past. Such "dissipative structures," as Prigogine calls them, consume and waste energy in the very process of maintaining their structure. Within limits, they thrive on instability, on buzzing noise. This is the second and crucial factor which Boltzmann almost saw but could not get straight because, like so much else in contemporary physics, it runs against common sense—

that entropy is the key to real change. Open systems move off dead center, are full of surprises because they stay off balance by eating chaos.

All stars, for instance, are remarkably unstable nuclear reactors consuming themselves and spewing forth waste—which the unnucleated microcells of plants gobble up for photosynthesis, in turn exhaling the oxygen which animal life survives on. What is waste, sheer random noise produced by one unit or level in this galactic circulatory system, is converted into information-organization for another, more complex system. The exchange is not egalitarian. The receiver of energy in one form doesn't return it in exactly the same form. Think of the hierarchy of communication within your own body—how oxygen, water, and food are absorbed to become cellular enzyme production until eventually, after a succession of conversions in which noise is integrated at many levels, you return a good story at the dinner table for all that you have received! Nor can your body system, any more than any other open system, be isolated from the wider environment, from the light of the sun to the flow of matter (food, oxygen, heat, signals) which have their noise-signs changed as they pass through it. Just as water moves through a whirlpool and simultaneously creates it, energy—or the stream of random activity physicists call entropy—moves through and forms a dissipative structure at the same time. Since equilibrium literally spells death, such a process-structure will maintain itself relatively far from equilibrium, as an instability—or as a balancing act. That is, assuming a certain minimum complexity, these systems are self-organizing. They consume and transform noisy energy in order to sustain their form or structure. Consequently, their entropy production is not low but high, approaching a value of 1.

The paradox is that the more coherent and complex a system is, the more unstable it must be. Such systems must keep their taps open (as a star does when it consumes its own fuel), and this very flux of energy keeps the system unstable, critically sensitive to external conditions like the gravitation of earth or magnetic fields, and subject to internal fluctuation—and abrupt change. Even at the inorganic level, such systems have memories; like old villages periodically transformed by bridges, roads, and superhighways, they are carriers of internal time, a history of networks knotted in the great stream. Unlike the units of a system near equilibrium, the elements here are not blind sleepwalkers; they can properly be spoken of as "sensitive," as "taking into account." One can speak of prebiotic adaptation. These traits don't just apply to living systems. Disequilibrium runs the gamut—from the dog star Sirius to cells and cities.

EXAMPLES OF AN ANALOGOUS CONCEPT

One of Prigogine's favorite examples is the Belousov-Zhabotinsky reaction, the oxidation of malonic acid by bromate in the presence of cerium ions in sulfuric acid solution. It created a sensation among chemists in the 1960s because it seemed to indicate the self-organizing activity of inorganic matter, and more remarkably, of order emerging out of chaos. British biochemist Arthur Peacocke recently described it (1984b: 425) as follows:

> With the right combination of solution conditions and at a constant temperature, the original homogeneous reaction mixture changes into a series of pulsing waves of concentration of cerium ions, moving up and down the tube, until eventually a steady state is reached in which there are static, banded layers of alternating high and low concentrations of ceric ions. From an originally homogeneous system, a highly ordered structure has appeared through the fluctuations that are possible in a nonlinear system far removed from equilibrium.

Peacocke omits the aesthetic element, that in the oscillations the solution shifts at regular intervals from red to blue.

Superconductivity in metals also illustrates the phenomenon. In many metals at low temperatures, electrical resistance is understood as a sign that electrons are bouncing erratically off the nuclei of the metal lattice. Yet at critical temperatures all resistance vanishes as the electrons realign themselves in harmonic resonance. Or take the nonequilibrium behavior of chemical clocks. The reactions are such that all the colliding molecules change identity simultaneously, oscillating in a coherent, rhythmic pattern. The molecules communicate with each other and coordinate. Such phenomena are the rule in biological systems, but these correlations, chemical clocks show, already occur at the microscopic molecular level in inorganic systems. In contrast to the relatively rare case of an equilibrium structure, actual nature is replete with dissipative structures. They happen to include most of what is interesting in nature from quasars and stars on down to the biosphere, amino acids, cells, metabolic processes, and ourselves.

A biological example would be the way ants, bees, and termites create a nest, first zig-zagging around at fever pitch until finally the chaos subsides into remarkable order. Critical fluctuations in a society (a scientific paradigm shift being a good example) offer further illustrations which shed light on what transpires in the former examples. Technological and social revolutions initiated at the periphery of a social system can generate—as Prigogine puts it—"a dialectic between mass and minority." If the disturbing innovation reaches sufficient pitch, it can fashion "new average stage in a social system." As in the case of chemical and biological structures, the old average will attempt to damp down, suppress, and "integrate" the novelty. That is, it will attempt to remain a linear, integrable system at low entropy. But sometimes the law of large numbers is not successful. The creative, heterogeneous minority reaches a "critical mass," and establishes a "preferential direction" for the entire social system. In this case, the small group functions magnetically, reordering the complex in the way a newly synthesized crystal seeds a solution. All these illustrations are of *nonlinear* processes in which fluctuation compels the elements to interact more intensively—with the result that a new, more complex regime emerges out of the flux. Prigogine's formalism for dissipative structures provides insight into limited, productive anarchy in analogous shapes. Each type of transformation must be examined in its own terms. The law is not global, but essentially regional and pluralistic.

Order emerges out of chaos, out of random activity, and random variability prevents any would-be classical physicist from reversing the clock on these processes. This is the heart of Prigogine's theory, and it gives us a new image of inorganic matter as active or, as the Chilean biologists Humberto Maturana and Francisco Verela term it, as "autopoietic" or self-making (see Jantsch, 1980: 7, 29–41). The key concepts in Prigogine's theory are those of symmetry-breaking, bifurcation, and irreversibility. The thermodynamic description, which holds priority for the introduction of time and complexity, can be seen as compatible with a deterministic dynamic description which accents stability.

CHANCE AND NECESSITY

First, consider the evolution of structure in the examples just cited. In nonequilibrium systems, it is the intrinsic randomness or high entropy production that acts as the *selector* of which among several probable (future) initial conditions will actually occur. Contrary to the proposition in neoclassical physics which confines indeterminacy to the microscopic scale, probabilistic interpretation becomes a necessity on the macroscopic level as soon as you have time-creating symmetry-breaks. At the level of minimally complex, unstable systems, the disjunction betwen permanent macroscopic states and microscopic flux dissolves. Randomness occurs at both levels and is decisive for the essentially stochastic activity of non-equilibrium systems.

In such systems a local heterogeneity breaks ranks, starts to act as an autocatalytic agent; instead of being integrated into the reigning order, its flux radiates, warps space, and amplifies, charging the global system. It is not mere local motion of passive matter, but active, internal transformation. In the process, chemical organization moves from a stable state of low entropy ("information tight"), like that of a closed, equilibrium system, to the random activity associated with relatively high entropy production (thus a "dissipative" system), before choosing the new organizing pattern. It thus begins to escape the determinism of the prior regime, and therewith any *possibility* that a physicist could fit such a process within a strictly linear, reversible time scheme. In cases like these, it is not the ignorance of an observer (as in the quantum world) which makes for indeterminacy, but the actual *physical* situation. The high degree of noise or flux constitutes an "entropy barrier" (Prigogine and Stengers, 1984a: 272–86) that precludes the kind of precise information required for an exclusively deterministic description.

The next step in the process consists of reaching that "critical mass"— or the "bifurcation point." From the viewpoint of the physical chemist, the bifurcation point represents a crucial branching point, where one possible solution would follow the trajectory posited by traditional thermodynamic theory. Predictably, the structure of the system would proceed to degrade, to move toward incoherence. Whereas the other branch represents an unpredictable jump to higher organization and complexity. Either way, the radically stochastic nature of the process means that time here is irreversible. The second law of thermodynamics is implacable: if structural loss turns out to be the branch followed, even so, only initial conditions that proceed to equilibrium *in the future* are possible. But since far from equilibrium systems are intrinsically random and nonlinear, precarious balancing acts whose entropy value approaches 1, they enjoy the possibility of moving against the eroding tide of entropy. Curiously, a high degree of fluctuation or entropy production constitutes the undoing that is their doing, that enables a monotonous order approaching an entropy value of 0 to be broken, and suspends the clock of the second law of thermodynamics. This is to say that the process cannot be circumscribed in classic dynamical terms as a rectilinear trajectory.

In the examples cited above—and often enough in nonequilibrium systems which thrive on perturbation—the route taken is the latter. The appearance locally of the most probable state of chance-ridden flux opens up the opportunity for the improbable state of more complex organization. Local disorder releases the negentropic time arrow by reorganizing the global pattern of the system in a more differentiated way. The local *turba*, the unruly mob, has become a *turbo*, a reservoir of energy that makes a difference. The process violates the law of large numbers; it breaks Rudolph Clausius's thermodynamic law of erosion. The minority innovator counts, has repercussions throughout the whole system. Says Prigogine (Prigogine and Stengers, 1984: 177–78):

> Whenever we reach a bifurcation point, deterministic description breaks down. The type of fluctuation present in the system will lead to the choice of the branch it will follow. Crossing a bifurcation is a stochastic process, such as tossing a coin. Here we can no longer follow an individual chemical trajectory. We cannot predict the details of temporal evolution. . . . The existence of an instability may be viewed as the result of a fluctuation that is first localized in a small part of the system and then spreads and leads to a new macroscopic state.

The technical nature of Prigogine's mathematical formalism escapes me, but note what that formalism for this reorganizing random factor aims to provide. It gives a precise microscopic meaning to Darwinian chance variation, the mechanism of mutation on the macroscopic, evolutionary level. Biological systems, therefore, no longer represent exceptions to the laws of physics, but follow naturally once the requisite conditions of relative instability are in place.

The central role of flux, however, does not exclude the deterministic description of traditional dynamics. Once the new organizational script is in place, the system settles down to a low entropy stability (approaching the value of 0) which resists further change. The resistance and damping down of further change corresponds to the element of determinism which follows classic dynamics. But in nonequilibrium, open systems capable of sustaining intense perturbations, dynamic stability is seen as a procedure for propagating innovations—for holding them invariantly in place. In such systems, Prigogine observes (Prigogine and Stengers, 1984: 176) that

> the "overall" behavior cannot in general be taken as dominating in any way the elementary processes constituting it. Self-organizing processes in far-from-equilibrium conditions correspond to a delicate interplay between chance and necessity, between fluctuations and deterministic laws. . . . Near bifurcations, fluctuations or random elements would play an important role,

while between bifurcations, the deterministic aspects would become dominant.

There is therefore no contradiction between Boltzmann and Darwin; each refers to a different moment or period in the history of a nonequilibrium system. The mathematical formalism, then, must allow for both the linear equations of traditional determinism and the nonlinear equations which leave the future open. By placing the time arrow of random noise first, in the very definition of unstable systems, Prigogine converts the elementary howl of entropic chaos into information which sets going a new negentropic organization. Once in place—like oxygen and hydrogen atoms have been for some 15 billion years—such systems may have a stability approaching immutability. They are redundantly in place according to classical dynamic principles. Accordingly, Prigogine can speak of a "new form of complementarity"—one between dynamical and thermodynamical descriptions. He can also speak of an "evolutionary paradigm" grounded in physics. In such a world, predestination is not the last word; we have a chance.

TIME INTRINSIC, FUTURE OPEN

Turbulence breaks down old forms; it is a sign of death heralding new beginnings. In the pure, noiseless realm of mathematics, then, physicists may play as they like with the clear and distinct idea of time-symmetrical equations. It is an idealist's game, a dematerialization of reason that mistakenly eliminates the demon of noise in the effort to achieve perfect control and perfect communication. Could the effort succeed, we now know, nature's polyphony and our discourse about it would be reduced to the sound of a monotone saying nothing at all. Fortunately for the subatomic world and what's come of it, galaxies and the carnival of animals we live among, things are messy, riddled with a large ambiguity factor. Formless, buzzing chaos sneaks into the structured order and keeps formations open.

Physical nature itself imposes certain taboos on the physicist, and the irreversible direction of time in complex systems is one of them. For nonequilibrium systems, one-directional time, either branching to decay or to heightened organizational instability, lies at the heart of matter. Time is no extraneous factor, a mere numerical coordinate, but intrinsic to unstable systems—as the examples given would suggest. The upstart flux in the Belousov-Zhabotinsky reaction doesn't act *in* time; it *is* time in its own specific rhythm—moving from relatively settled past toward unsettled future. For such systems, even if the turbulence is eventually damped down, one-directional time must be expressed in the mathematical formalism as an *internal* operator governing functioning. "Out of the reversible, nearly cyclic noise level in which we live," writes Prigogine, "arises music that is both stochastic and time-oriented." Or, as he says elsewhere (1984: 443) in explicating the theory,

> Future is open from the point of view of internal time. . . . In other words, future is not contained in the present for systems satisfying the second law of thermodynamics. Therefore, according to this description, states have an orientation in time. Time is now intrinsic to objects; it is no more a container for static, passive matter.

The centrality of thermodynamic noise introduces the strong parallel, now on the macroscopic level, to indeterminacy on the quantum level. Is temporal *becoming*, then, built into the physical world at the subatomic level? Is the Heisenberg uncertainty rule therefore more than an observer's problem? Is that too buried in the physical situation? Prigogine's theory implies that thermodynamic irreversibility comes at all levels of physical reality or none at all. He writes (1980: 199),

> The classical order was: particles first, the second law later—being before becoming! It is possible that this is no longer so when we come to the level of elementary particles and that here we must *first* introduce the second law before being able to define the entities. Does this mean becoming before being? Certainly this would be a radical departure from the classical way of thought. But, after all, an elementary particle, contrary to its name, is not an object that is "given"; we must construct it, and in this construction it is not unlikely that *becoming*, the participation of the particles in the evolution of the physical world, may play an essential role.

The instability of elementary particles makes Prigogine's maybes highly likely. Does nonequilibrium unruliness amount to a cosmological principle? Prigogine cannot say. The evidence is still unclear. Tests are currently underway to verify a temporal orientation at the quantum level.

But a nonequilibrium order even in limited regions of space-time makes a new dialogue with nature possible. Our contract with nature need not be conceived as an appointment with immutable fate. Life itself is no longer an anomalous exception attributable to unusual initial conditions.

Those unusual conditions in which yesterday is different from tomorrow are those of nature herself. In Prigogine's scheme, irreversible processes are no longer supplementary approximations introduced into the laws of dynamics. The situation is reversed: the deterministic model appears as a special limit case, in fact an idealization, serving as a useful fiction, a reference point, against which to measure the imbalancing act through which nature gives birth to a proliferation of new forms. Empirically, so far as can be seen at this point, the repetition model of classical dynamics refers to very little found in nature, and of which we know almost nothing. As an imaginative construct, it fits within a larger matrix whose law is fundamentally that of disequilibrium. Nature, here returned to her more feminine manifestation, appears as a breaker of Newtonian law, a giver of multiple chances. She is illegal, only periodically at rest, an opener of multiform times. Our contract with her need not be adversarial; it can once again be what Democritus and Lucretius imagined, an alliance with eros.

DEATH AND EROS

I began Part III with two cultures, a static world set against the arrows of time. On one side stood martial law, a science of the dead; and on the other, the moveable feasts of erotic culture, expressions of desire, of the quest for health, healing, and wholeness. That dualism forced us to keep two separate accounts: one for the physicist's immutable dynamics of energy, and another for subtle information states of the life-world. Subject and object were not simply polarized but disjoined, with the result that for scientists energy was nearly everything and information negligible. A nonequilibrium and information theory world allows us to return our separate energy and information accounts to a single balance sheet. In this view of nature, information and energy are always on the same scale and proportionate. In principle this means that a science preoccupied with energy displacements can be reconciled with humanistic disciplines concerned with signs. Conversely, in every instance the transformations of energy that we have been discussing are equally transformations of signs. Let me backtrack and come at these conclusions more slowly.

Entropy need no longer be seen as a cosmic sink hole or a tide running against the experiment of life. Rather, chaos constitutes an aspect of that eros in nature which Bohm calls the holomovement. In the technical terms of our science, it is a differentiated field of radiant kinetic energy in free flight, wildly dispersed yet connective. Structured bodies literally weave themselves in and out of such radiation: intercept it, withhold, contain, disperse it (see Young, 1986: 117–37). Mass, twentieth-century science tells us, consists of nothing else than this free field energy stored rather than dissipated. In a contained, latent state, it's called "rest energy" or "potential energy." Since Einstein's $E = mc^2$, we know that in order to calculate that latent energy in a given object, its mass must be multiplied by a huge constant, the velocity of light squared. Is it any wonder then that chemical chains, microbes, algae, plants, animals, and human be-ings—given what they centripally build up inside themselves—have the energy, for a season, to overcome the dissipative drift of entropy? Were one to mythicize the thing, it cues an open-ended myth which both appreciates and relativizes all integrations and centralizations as tempo-rary pauses in a process which circles around but never settles back into the same position. The dancing Shiva, the quickening Holy Spirit belong in such a world.

Nature, Prigogine lets you see, is an act of coitus between death and eros, a coupling of chance-program, information-noise, entropy-negen-tropy in a third, dancing container of these polarities. Without the stream of radiant energy, there can be no coupler, no eddies, vortices, forma-tions—in short, no grainy particles, material complexes, stars, planets, organisms—to receive, store, exchange, and give off energy and informa-tion in all its forms. For it is the very randomizing current of the cosmic river which provides the disturbing reservoir both for deforming depar-tures from the law of repetition and for the subsequent reformations. Disturbance in the flow creates the difference—in temperature and pres-sure—which turns the universe into a heat engine that works, that makes a difference. Yet that irregularity which makes the difference between yesterday, today, and tomorrow—which in becoming a counter-entropic force changes the vector of time—is inconceivable without the main cur-rent. Background noise represents thermic disorder, irreversibly pushing systems toward death. But is is not just that; it also assumes an organizing function. Integrated into a system of minimal complexity, noise is trans-formed into potential organization—which reverses the arrow of time. Negentropy goes up stream. From this perspective, thanatos and eros, death and life, coincide and continually exchange roles as agents of meta-morphosis. As Arthur Peacocke has it (1984b: 430), "the apparently de-caying, randomizing tendency of the universe provide[s] the necessary matrix . . . for the birth of new forms—new life through death and decay of the old."

WOVEN INTO THE WOOF OF TIME

What Prigogine gives us, it would seem, is a tantric dance, a great weaving—with some ironies. A stochastic universe no longer possesses the transparent simplicities and certainties beloved by classical science. Does that make you pine for a return to nature? Well, according to a nonequilibrium perspective, the most accelerated course for nature's lesson might consist of living in London, New York, or Bombay—sites where order and chaos interpenetrate at high intensity and open spaces for novel chances. Nature is like a city, Prigogine implies, and equally opaque; neither provides a setting for blind confidence. Radical uncertainty and the threat of a return to nothingness haunt a nonequilibrium world more than it does a Newtonian world. Fittingly, Prigogine (1984a: 313) closes his recent popular explication of his theory by citing talmudic texts suggesting that twenty-six failed attempts preceded the present Genesis story, which in its turn arose out of the antecedent debris. Exclaimed God as he created this world, "Let's hope it works!"

Meanwhile, the weaving goes on. What is an organism within this perspective? Philosopher Michel Serres answers (1982: 74–75) as follows:

> Neither static nor homeostatic, it is homeorrhetic ["flow" of the "same"]. It is a river that flows and yet remains stable in the continual collapse of its banks and the irreversible erosion of the mountains around it. . . .
>
> This river, almost stable, although irreversible, this basin, poised on its own imbalance in a precarious state of quasi-equilibrium in its flow toward death, ferries energy and information, knowledge of entropy and negentropy, of order and disorder. Both a syrrhesis [flow together] (rather than a system) and a diarrhesis [flow through], the organism is hence defined from a global perspective. . . . Within the context of an even more general circulation which goes from the sun to the black depths of space, the organism is a barrier of braided links that leaks like a wicker basket but can still function as a dam.

Like the quantum particle which it resembles, an organism can only be defined within its global environment. In another form, this is David Bohm's appeal for a new approach to the conception of physical law based on complex wholes. The isolated entity, simply located in space, emerges as a nonentity, an idol of the study (Whitehead's "fallacy of simple location"). The more complex and relatively self-organizing an organism is, the more "braided" it is; the more it is made up, colonized by myriad atomic, chemical, cellular, and neuronal threads to a vast ecosystem.

In this sense, organisms recapitulate phylogeny; they knot together the plural time rhythms of the flow-through systems of which they are to some degree composed. Again, as Serres observes (1982: 75),

> All times converge in this temporary knot. . . . The living organism, ontogenesis and phylogenesis combined, is of all times. This does not mean that it is eternal, but rather that it is an original complex, woven out of all the different times that our intellect subjects to analysis. . . . Homeorrhetic means at least that: the rhesis flows, but similarity pushes upstream and resists. All the temporal vectors possessing a directional arrow are here, in this place, arranged in the shape of a star. What is an organism? A sheaf of times. What is a living system? A bouquet of times.

Any nonequilibrium system, we said, integrates noise, converts it into a sign-system, a message, and relies on a whole set of both internal and environmental converters that have been doing the same. The slightest twist in the flow—an elementary particle, a chemical reaction—hollows out a receiver, channel, and transmitter, that is, an apparatus that produces signals from noise and information. In a more complex way, an organism is woven of photons from the Big Bang, carbon manufactured by the stars, the prebiotic soup that spawned bacterial centrioles which swim in its cells, and an atmosphere originally dependent on blue-green algae—all diligent transformers of loose energy and changers of its sign from obstacle, sheer stochastic chaos at the bottom, to some kind of negentropic proto-language, perhaps instructions for cell nucleation or enzyme production. In short, repeatedly, these interlocking homeorrhetic vessels or feedback loops convert waste into information and thereby alter the direction of time. By the time background noise reaches an organism such as ourselves, the senseless din of random event feeding into our system from all over the cosmos has been successively repressed and displaced by countless rectifiers—whereupon the torrent is harbored in the black box of our unconscious, the last observer of chance, the last decoder.

What does it mean to be the final observer in this chain? The first thing to say is that the concept of the isolated observer flies in the face of all the evidence. By another route, that of science itself, we are rediscovering our participatory status in the cosmos. We are the most relational, recycled beings we know of. Nothing in our genes today was present a year ago. Even our protein DNA molecules have a lifespan of only a few months.

The skin is replaced monthly. Ninety-eight percent of our body's atoms are replaced annually. Each time we breathe, we take in a quadrillion atoms breathed by the rest of the human race within the past two weeks. So much for the strictly bounded, separate body; even while we live, we are constantly returning to earth, constantly engaged in a tremendous exchange, a cooperative partnership with, among other systems, the bacteria that hundreds of millions of years ago may have stored the carbon for our bones and created a breathable atmosphere from the sun's deadly carbon and nitrogen waste (see Lovelock, 1982).

Second, we are information and thermodynamic systems. "We are submerged up to our neck, to our eyes, to our hair," Michel Serres asserts (1982: 77), "in a furiously raging ocean, We are the voice of this hurricane, this thermal howl, and we do not even know it." In the early decades of this century, Alfred North Whitehead suggested that instead of modeling human society on Newton's static bodies in space, we ought to model the whole cosmos on the body-subject's internal experience of time and of being actively implicated in a huge stream of influence to which it was internally related. Every "actual entity," he claimed, represents a synthetic "concrescence" of the entire perishing universe in its immediate past and that "final surd" which he spoke of as the "primordial nature" of God. (The metaphorical kernel of the whole process derives from the experience of breathing; as such it is analogous to David Bohm's implicate order becoming explicate.) The object cannot be separated from the field; it is nothing else than a set of modifications of its multidimensional fields—constituting itself with every inhaling pulse, then contributing with every perishing exhale to other, subsequent syntheses of itself and the rest of the cosmic company. As active synthesizer-internalizer of its macroscopic field-connections in the present, every actual entity becoming itself is subject—poised at the brink of dying to become object for others. No less than a human being, Whitehead effectively argued, the universe breathes—takes in and lets go, lives and dies in every now.

Substitute dissipative structure or "sheaf of times" for actual entity, and the thrust of Prigogine's theory is not very different from Whitehead's or Bohm's. In these approaches, the standard subject-object division that keeps psychological and objective knowledge apart breaks down. This coincidence of opposites is perhaps easier to understand, however, within a nonequilibrium world. There is only one kind of knowledge, an observer who is structured exactly like what he or she observes—noise, disorder, and chaos on one side and complexity, order, and distribution on the other. Writes Michel Serres (1982: 83):

Nothing distinguishes me ontologically from a crystal, a plant, an animal, or the order of the universe, and our diverse complexions are flowing up the entropic stream, toward the solar origin, itself adrift. Knowledge is at most the reversal of drifting, that strange conversion of times, always paid for by additional drift; but this is complexity itself . . . virtually stable turbulence in the flow.

Objective nature, in other words, for better or worse is our other half—running on the same current, drifting as we are. There is no need to find material nature panpsychic as Whitehead did, much less to divinize atoms or mitochondria. The gains of psychological detachment from a hyper-charged nature are too clear. Without this neutrality, we would never have escaped from the bloody religiosity of narrow tribal and dynastic family interest. There's no turning back. Nature represents us, no less, no more. At this juncture in nature's story and ours, when developments within science itself make nature appear again as a potent "tendency to happen," we are nature's big happening, her main chance. For it ought to be clear that from an information and thermodynamic standpoint, nature is the medium of a message whose deciphering finally depends on us. But what's the message?

THE INITIAL/FINAL SURD

The big question: "I know who the final observer is," remarks Michel Serres (1982: 82), "the receiver at the chain's end: precisely he who utters language. But I do not know who the initial dispatcher is at the other end." This is the ultimate black box. We return, then, to the dark noth-ingness with which we began this chapter, and to Loren Eiseley's zero, and to the multireference question of the meaning and end of time I asked at the close of chapter 3: Are we and nature simply circling back to nothingness or to some oceanic condition with no change to show for the in-between time? Is the end identical with the beginning? An equilibrium logic would answer yes. Or, as Christians say, is this already the end-time, the beginning of nature's end through us, our endings being nature's chance for another kind of beginning? Inasmuch as death conceals boundary-breaking eros, nonequilibrium logic would suggest that the Christian proposal may be nearer the truth.

How do you go about answering questions like this? Do you fathom the ultimate black box, the final surd, as theologians are in the habit of recommending, by "transcending" your condition? I think the metaphorical kernel of the term transcendence is all wrong; it summons high altitude flight when in all likelihood we have crashed and the pertinent intelligence we want lies at the bottom of the sea. The way up is the way down. I prefer to stay with some tantric subscendence and with the unsettled body, the counterpart of soul, where I left things hanging at the end of the last chapter on holonomic theory. But at the close of this chapter, having recovered a Heraclitean world, it ought to be clearer what I meant by saying that the body teems with information. More importantly perhaps, the body is riddled with chaos. "The Lord whose oracle is at Delphi," Heraclitus aphorized, "neither speaks nor conceals, but gives signs." To decipher chaos as a sign of the final surd's purpose, the observer's viewpoint is not enough; you require a means, a receiver and channel, and my proposal is that the body's internal sensation is it.

The issue is how you go about receiving the message of the final surd streaming through the whole medium of restless nature. I would reverse Whitehead's procedure and go back to the subject-body's internal sense of implication in that huge stream of signals. If the final surd registers anywhere, it will be through proprioceptivity, kinesthesia, and coenesthesia—resonances of the vagosympathetic nervous system. The consciousness movement's preoccupation with "body work" sometimes had only the purpose of relieving stress, and at worst was diverted into hyping desire or beating the body into shape; but at bottom it was a means of diving for the message in the ultimate black box. At its best its listening to the body rediscovered the difference between mere "flesh," the counterpart of egotistic will and rationality, and "body" as the counterpart of soul. It was saying yea to physical life as a vessel of something transphysical and transpersonal, yes to the body as a dwelling full of grace.

PART IV

Resurrecting the Body

_____ TEN _____

Narcissists and Meditators

The greatest danger, that of losing one's own self, may pass off as quietly as if it were nothing; every other loss, that of an arm, a leg, five dollars, a wife, etc., is sure to be noticed.

Søren Kierkegaard

I said to my soul, be still, and wait without hope
For hope would be hope for the wrong thing; wait
without love
For love would be love of the wrong thing; there
is yet faith
But the faith and the love and the hope are all in
the waiting.

T. S. Eliot

The obstacle to incarnation is our horror of the void. Instead of vanity, emptiness. Being found in the shape of a human being, he emptied himself.
A pregnant emptiness . . . is the precondition for all creation. Creation is out of the void; ex nihilo.

Norman O. Brown

"Let's hope it works." The vessels of Ilya Prigogine's nonequilibrium thermodynamic world keep breaking, dissolving, perishing into nothingness. The Buddhists are right; there's nothing here to cling to, nothing to satisfy a desire for permanence. But the Hebrew tradition seems to have

257

gotten the other side of the truth about this unsteady-state, eroding world. The vessels keep reforming—as if to allow unfinished stories to unfold and be told. Does the "frozen misery of centuries" break, crack, begin to move? Does Shiva dance in the atoms, in our veins? Do Khajuraho's syrrhesis and diarrhesis or Thomas Aquinas's unnameable "pure act" throb in the stars, planets, whooping cranes, and us? Most transpersonalists would answer in the affirmative. The transpersonal world is essentially dramatic, a vast play unfolding. Atoms and molecules, organisms and individuals, institutions and cultures—none of these can be taken in isolation but must be considered in relationship, enacting roles in a process much greater than themselves. Nor, as physicist John A. Wheeler asserts, does the "universe . . . exist 'out there' independent of us. We are inescapably involved in bringing about that which appears to be happening."

Aristotle and Thomas Aquinas would have agreed; the physical world, they claimed, remains incomplete until it passes through human cognition, until it is taken up and named by us, endowed with meaning, transfigured. What have we made of the physical world—purgatory, hell, heaven? What shall we make of it? With what spirit shall we imbue it? What shall we have it represent, symbolize? The new physics does not dictate any definitive answer to such questions, but in a fresh way, it leads to them, sharply poses them anew, and suggests that the decisive limits may lie less in external physical nature than in ourselves and a failure of nerve. Or a failure of vision. In these final chapters, I want to refocus on the inner journey as a way of acquiring both vision and the energy to put vision into action.

When I ask myself where the momentum of the consciousness movement comes from, I have to think that it has something to do with the retrieval of contemplative *practice*. That is, the movement gradually acquired disciplines which aim to take big ideas out of the abstract and ingrain them in what de Tocqueville spoke of as "habits of the heart." Inwardness is the crucial third factor, the secret of a spirited life and *movement*. Individually, socially, politically, and pseudoreligiously, we get polarized between immovable forces—instinct and ego, male-female, friends and enemies, liberal-conservative, true believers and heretics, and so on. Stymied between all or nothing, chance or necessity, high entropy or none at all, eros and civilization, nothing moves. There's no space to breathe. Intercourse ceases, qualitative time stops cold. The point is that the key to movement lies in a third pole not on the same horizontal dimension as the immobilizing dualism. Diverse human individuals and groups do not couple to produce a common, four-dimensional world (where the fourth dimension is real time)—any more than matter-energy, chance-program, order-disorder in the strictly physical realm do—unless a third pole somehow informs the tension. Analogously, this triadic structure works across the board, notably at the human, social level where communication only occurs when two or more share a world woven by shared symbols or a common language. But it is preeminently a theological principle—the insight presaged in that ontological revolution of first-millennial B.C. religion that, I argued, got the world moving. God was not to be thought of as undifferentiated cosmic soup, as oral peoples had thought, nor as the top of a hierarchical pyramid as sacred kings had thought, but as One in three modes, a triadic polarity—the unknowable source, the hidden wind of the elements, and the voice from the pit of the stomach and heart that catches in our throat.

Many Americans in the sixties and seventies rediscovered this ontological revolution by learning, in a lotus posture, to breathe. By and large, whether the criticism came from mainline or fundamentalist Christianity, or from the political Left or Right, the phenomenon was put down as an un-American, oriental fad (never, I think, has there been a better example of our not-so-subtle racism). In the first instance, meditating was harmless enough. All that was being done by "just sitting" (as Zen speaks of meditation) was little more than clearing the mind and relaxing—good physiotherapy. Then it might happen that people remembered early childhood traumas—okay, it was becoming psychotherapy. But when people started encountering wrathful deities, *kundalini* serpents coiled at the base of the spine, or worse yet, a blissful void—well, they weren't talking (or thinking) officially prescribed biblical language. An enormous communications gap opened between the meditators and their fellow Americans, facilitated by a rash of cultic authoritarians, occult bookstores, and the general impression that sitting on a cushion is either self-indulgent, a waste of time, or a narcissistic effort to dissolve all tension in life by surrendering to instinct and merging with the atmosphere. Norman O. Brown's visionary *Love's Body* (1966) was generally misunderstood as an invitation to orgy. Not to worry, pollster Daniel Yankelovich (1981) assured us after the economic contractions of the late seventies, in an age of limits such behavior is "no longer adaptive."

Social critic Christopher Lasch (1984), on the other hand, finds the movement very much alive and conflates it with the "party of narcissus" in our culture. In his categories, it is to be distinguished from the "party of superego," mainly neoconservatives who appeal for a return to standards of excellence, duty, and tradition; and distinguished again from the "party of ego" that continues to champion the acquisitive, competitive ego and a kind of Lockean social contract. The trouble with Lasch's critique of the movement is that he makes little allowance for people in the movement who often started out desperately to save their own skin by self-manipulation only to find themselves, at a certain juncture, serving a cause far beyond the self-serving ego. But their orientalism leads to gross misunderstanding. The language of nonattachment and selflessness is confused with what, on the surface, looks like symptoms of inner emptiness and despair suffered by someone trying to survive in the extreme adversity of a prison camp. What may be contemplative equanimity and the ability to live fully in the present is taken for apathy, emotional disengagement, the determination to live unreflectively in sheer immediacy, and an irresponsible renunciation of history and politics.

Lasch's treatment of Doris Lessing is a good illustration of this confusion. Lessing, a student of the Sufi teacher Idries Shah, speaks of the value of detaching oneself from the sound and fury of emotionalism and false individualism which contaminate so much of our private and public life. Lasch proceeds to misconstrue the whole thrust of Lessing's jeremiad against false subjectivity (the point of her space fantasy novels) and identifies her with an egocentric *survivalist* mentality which, having abandoned any hope for collective, political solutions, advocates cutting social ties and looking out exclusively for Number One. This, I think, is a good case of not knowing who your friends are.

Yet Lasch's critique of the movement deserves and rewards attention. For one, the narcissist charge actually helps to clarify the difference between what the movement has come to identify as a *prepersonal* loss of selfhood from a *transpersonal* experience which carries the self beyond its former horizon. In turn, this ought to clarify what is meant by "self-transcendence," a term which is frequently very misleading. Viewed strictly from the psychoanalytic angle, transcending the self makes little sense, for it seems to imply a renunciation of everything that makes us human — thinking, planning, remembering, anticipating, organizing, self-reflecting, distinguishing reality from fantasy, exerting voluntary control over impulse, and loving. The rest of this chapter will try to clarify the misapprehensions associated with this term: first, by considering Lasch's critique of narcissistic culture; second, by taking up Buddhism's radical transcendence of selfhood in the context of different types of meditation.

THE MINIMAL SELF

Christopher Lasch's *The Minimal Self* (1984) clarifies the problem he was trying to lay out in *The Culture of Narcissism* (1978). In the American cultural scene at present the debate about narcissism has nothing to do with charges of hedonism or selfishness. It is rather a continuation of the controversy about the corrosive effects of mass consumer culture upon the American character—that we are turning passive, losing hold of our active participation in making our world. In this debate Lasch positions himself against any who would implicitly dissolve the critical distance or tension that the self must sustain in order to be creative. There are three ways of collapsing that tension: first (the party of superego), by surrendering conscience to a received body of authoritive law; second (the party of ego), by advocating total self-sufficiency and independence of nature; and third (the party of Narcissus), by denying the self's differentiation from nature. In reacting against the boundless confidence of the rational, Promethean self and promoting the ideal of a more Dionysian, androgynous self that is to enjoy an ecstatic union with nature, Lasch finds the consciousness movement going too far—even though he is sympathetic to the notion that a cultural revolution must precede any real political change.

Lasch points to the transformation effected over the last sixty years by mass production, mass communication, mass culture, and mass consumption. The production methods, marketing techniques, and one-way style of management introduced by General Motor's Alfred P. Sloan and Henry Ford changed an economy of handicraft and regional exchange into a complex network of large-scale technologies. These have undermined the institutions of local self-government, weakened the party system, and discouraged popular initiative. Skilled labor has been replaced by machines; education changed into "manpower selection" (which slots some for management, others for monotonous labor) and politics into administration. What Lasch calls the "intermediate world" of practical activity which binds a person to nature as caretaker and cultivator has all but vanished, swallowed up by bigness.

The democratizing effects of the new industrial state, argues Lasch, are largely an illusion. People have more, admittedly, but participate as agents less. The trade-off, supposedly, is enhanced prosperity and freedom of choice—the pluralism, multiple options, and protean self so often celebrated by the consciousness movers. But widened consumer choice can be an illusion, falsely assuming that all choices are matters of lifestyle, and that none involves commitments which limit or rule out other options. John Naisbitt (in *Tarrytown Letter*, 1982: 3), however, is euphoric:

> We are expressing our individuality and pluralistic nature to a greater degree than ever before. Fashion, entertainment of all kinds, eating habits, religion, all show developments that are contradictory, with plenty of options.

To hear futurologists Naisbitt and Alvin Toffler is to enter the mind of the supermarket. What is offered as diversity of choice is often nothing of the kind. Rather, everything is flattened to a uniform logical status where no choice is momentous enough to exclude another. Religions, marriage partners, neighborhoods, cigarettes, fashions, and diets—all are readily exchangeable, matters of style not substance. Neoconservative free-marketeers understandably object to the erosion of moral discrimination, conveniently forgetting that the productive system they celebrate is fueled by consumer hedonism which undermines the Protestant work ethic. That's the basic contradiction of late capitalism and its dispose-all commodity culture.

Both conservatives and futurists, Lasch believes, miss the point. The problem today is neither the acquisitive self nor the person pursuing nonmaterialistic self-fulfillment, but social conditions which produce someone wholly lacking a core self (or what I have called soul). While organizational and technological changes since 1920 have given the ascendent class of managers and technocrats a heady sense of power and control, for the great mass of the population it has meant the opposite— the loss of opportunities to gain a solid sense of self through practical, self-reliant activity. The consumer-citizen is essentially passive, a spectator rather than a participant-actor. Hence the growing sense of powerlessness, victimhood, and a mythology of government and big business as conspiracies. Where there should be inner gravity, a "felt core" of identity providing a basis for independence, identity is felt to be cosmetically put on for the eyes of others. We are back, in fact, to Joan Didion's image of an insubstantial self lacking coherent narrative line or durability, and for whom the external world is reduced to flash pictures on a cutting-room floor. The absence of firm self-organization leaves a vacuum wide open to the tyranny of inner compulsions and grandiose, free-floating fantasies fed by advertising hype and the promised wonders of painless advances in science—space travel, biological engineering, computer wizardry.

THE PROBLEM OF NARCISSUS

Apollo and Dionysius within us, order and chaos, pull in opposite directions. We desire both to stand out and to belong. Psychoanalytic theory grounds these twin motives in primary narcissism, that is, in an infant's sense of omnipotence and symbiotic fusion. The self, Kierkegaard argued in *Sickness Unto Death*, ([1849] 1954: 162) consists in a dialectical movement between expansive possibility and limiting necessity; it "is the conscious synthesis of infinitude and finitude." At both extremes lies despair: on the finite side, a desperate narrowness, emasculation, dumb submission, a failure to venture at all; on the other side, a disease of the grandiose imagination that, plunging into the infinite, volatilizes feeling, will, and knowledge. The first indicates a loss of primitiveness, being "ground smooth," a forgetfulness of one's own true name. I have called it soullessness, a lack of inner depth. The second is soulless in a different way, expressed in the absence of containment, a lack of boundaries, the inability to obey or submit to limits and necessity in oneself. It is the nemesis of the eternal youth.

Clinically, the second kind of soullessness describes Narcissus. The narcissist has failed to negotiate an early stage of psychosocial development, the travail of separation from the mother. The constitutional weakness here is an inability to sustain "object relations"—with the stubborn material world, resistant other persons, or one's own fixations. Narcissus drowns in his own reflection because he fails to recognize it as a reflection, because he lacks the concept of the difference between himself and his surroundings, self and not-self. And insofar as the distinction between self and not-self underlies all others—between generations, sexual differences, and the difference between life and death—impairment at this level is fundamental and (because preverbal) has defied standard psychoanalytic treatment. The person has to regrow a self—differentiated but not utterly disjunct from Mother Earth. If this does not happen, a person may well surrender to imperious longings, either for undifferentiated fusion states or for absolute autonomy.

The memory of embryonic and infantile bliss, in other words, lies behind the heroic *causa sui* project of denying dependency and becoming totally self-sufficient. As Lasch puts it, the party of ego's technological enterprise of achieving absolute independence of nature embodies the "solipsistic" side of narcissism. The desire for mystical union, however, falls into the trap of narcissism's other side. Lasch worries that the consciousness movement overreacts to the technocratic solipsism that gives will-power a bad name. But purposeful mastery of nature becomes patho-logical, Lasch argues, not when it compensates for earlier losses, but only when it denies, under the pretense of omnipotence, that there were any losses to begin with. Besides, the renunciation of purposive will is not a happy alternative. The movement, Lasch fears, is oblivious that its pro-motion of ecstatic union with nature ministers to the symbiotic, self-obliterating side of narcissism. In fact, both sides represent denials of dependency and reject psychological maturation. Narcissus and Pro-metheus are brothers under the skin.

FUSION STATES?

Behaviorally, the narcissist does not have the stomach for conflict and tension. He or she is thus prey to grandiose, solipsistic fantasies—fanta-sies constantly fueled by mass culture, mass media, and mass-produced objects which the consumer has had no part in making. The problem is not selfishness but the loss of self, an inner emptiness which easily gives up on managing infernal external reality and turns to a survivalist culture of self-management. This can masquerade as concern for the life of the spirit. Grail questers of this type can't stand anything like the trials of that tantric, alchemical descent into the nether world that I referred to in chapter 6. Quite the opposite, they pursue the quick-fix, short-cut tran-scendence, Freud's "nirvana principle" of complete cessation of tension, desire, and purposeful activity; that is, homeostasis, perfect equilibrium, a form of death—or what the Western ascetical tradition condemns as quietism. The narcissist scorns both the body's longings and death, in effect regressing to an embryonic state in which death and exertion have no meaning.

But wait a minute. Narcissism cannot be used as the background for Lasch's reading, and in my judgment misreading, of Norman O. Brown's *Love's Body*. Throughout that work, Brown polemicizes against a litera-list's univocal reading of texts and the world, calling repeatedly for multi-dimensional, symbolic understanding. Declaiming against the same pas-sive spectator-consumer stance that Lasch deplores, Brown calls for a "resurrection of the body," which Lasch proceeds to understand univocal-ly and literalistically as a celebration of raw instinct and feeling over intellect. Brown speaks (1966: 253–54) of "Pentecostal freedom," a "uni-ty which is impersonal or supra-personal." Any Catholic ought to under-stand what follows:

Fusion: the distinction between inner self and outside world, between subject and object, overcome. To the enlightened man, the universe becomes his body. "You never enjoy the world aright till the Sea itself floweth in your veins, till you are clothed with the heavens and crowned with the stars." *Anima est quodammodo omnia . . .* what happens to the person's own body is identified with what happens in the universe.

The doctrine of the Eucharist, if not Prigogine's thermodynamics and Bohm's holographic world, should give some inkling of what Brown means; however, Lasch knows only one kind of fusion state, Freud's equilibrium of death, and obviously that's the way he reads Brown. But Brown is not glorifying a diffuse, animistic oral consciousness; he is telling of its recapitulation at a higher level, freely—as the immediately following passages declare (1966: 254, 254, 255):

> Civilized objectivity is non-participating consciousness, consciousness as separation, as dualism, distance, definition; as property and prison; consciousness ruled by negation . . . the death instinct. Symbolical consciousness, the erotic sense of reality, is a return to the principle of ancient animistic science, mystical participation, but now for the first time freely; instead of religion, poetry.

> The goal can only be conscious magic . . . conscious mastery of these fires. And dreaming while awake.

> To become conscious of our participation in the creation of the phenomenal world is to pass from passive experience—perceptions as impressions on a passive mind—to conscious creation, and creative freedom.

I could be wrong, but I think Brown is speaking of that ontological revolution we addressed in chapter 5, where first-millennium B.C. religions recovered the divine bloodline of an oral consciousness in a free mode—and moved culture decisively from the passive to the active voice.

THE DIVIDED MIND

The only mature way out of the impasse of our divided nature, Lasch argues, is through the creation of cultural objects, "transitional objects" in D. H. Winnicott's sense, that simultaneously restore a sense of connection with mother and Mother Nature and enable us to assert our mastery without denying our dependence on mothers and nature. Cultural objects, that is, are like the child's teddy bears and blankets, surrogates for mother, to be played with as ways of maintaining that primal connection without which work turns empty and coldly meaningless. Childhood is outgrown because the aura of the child's transitional objects is diffused over the entire cultural field. Separation from mother constitutes a painful loss, and exposes us to the fear of death. But fear of death need not be paralyzing (the despair of finitude) or feed grandiose fantasies of invulnerability (despair of infinity) if, as children, we learn to *actively contribute* to that external, durable, and reassuring world of human artifact, association, and memory that both transcends the self and constitutes the primal connection on a new basis—one that enables the tension between self and not-self to be maintained even while it allows an interplay between subject and object. Organizing itself around practical activity—the crucial third pole in this case—the self doesn't melt into its environment, losing all sense of boundary and limitation; on the other hand, it is not cut off, utterly abandoned to its own devices. (In more analytic form, this is the point I was making in connection with my "murmuring" meditation in chapter 6.)

In this understanding, Lasch argues, the realm of work can retain the spirit of a child's imaginative play. At the same time, just as Aristotle believed, practical activity can contribute to internal goods, to the formation of virtues—competence, responsibility, a sane self-reliance. The intermediate world of purposeful work, now so often overwhelmed by machines and big institutions, Lasch maintains, is what binds people to nature as loving caretakers. The whole argument points up the inherent menace of living in a prefabricated commodity world designed to inflate desire and appeal to inner fantasy, but that we seldom had any performative role in making ourselves. The result is that as the reality of a common, durable, public world begins to fade, the fear of separation and death intensifies—and proportionately, so does the need for fantastic illusions. Ending his book with a message uttered earlier in this century by Lutheran theologian Reinhold Niebuhr, Lasch insists that there is no real freedom without recognition of our divided self's "uneasy conscience." In addition to restoring that intermediate realm of practical, virtue-building work, he thinks we might do well to recover the Judeo-Christian dialectic of conscience—that is, the critical awareness, showing up as guilt, of the gulf between aspiration and performance. Writes Lasch (1984: 20):

> Selfhood is the painful awareness of the tension between our unlimited aspirations and our limited understanding, between our original intimations of

immortality and our fallen state, between oneness and separation. . . . Neither Prometheus nor Narcissus will lead us out of our present predicament. Brothers under the skin, they will only lead us further down the road on which we have already traveled much too far.

Granted, too far. We are balancing acts, dissipative structures. But Lasch's moral exhortation has all the weaknesses of the genre—it offers unforgiving goals without a word about the means of relieving guilt or acquiring the spirited energy to attain the goals. The thing turns into a rule book's dead letter, which leaves the gulf between aspiration and performance exactly where it was before the edifying lecture. Once again we find ourselves stalemated by a dualism. Lasch's moralism is a little like trying to build a thermodynamic engine without a reservoir or a means of circulating energy. The recommendation of reversion to the Judeo-Christian ethic rings a bit hollow when, as I suggested in the case of Norman O. Brown, Lasch can't seem to comprehend what the mystical core of the Judeo-Christian tradition might mean. If I am right in what I tried to say in Part II of this book, what many jaded Westerners rediscovered through their pilgrimages to the East was actually the reservoir and circulatory system of the Judeo-Christian tradition from which a Cartesian-Newtonian mind-set had cut us off.

THE QUESTION STANDS

Do I mean to deny, then, that the consciousness movement harbors many with a survivalist mentality? Hardly. In fact, there is not much doubt that the movement has provided a refuge for minimal selves—sometimes one that heals, sometimes one that reinforces the condition. In an increasingly self-critical movement, however, the issue has not been overlooked. Jack Engler, a clinical psychologist at Harvard and a teacher of Theravada Buddhist "insight" meditation, comments (1984: 35) on his meditation students:

> In many students I see a particular vulnerability and disturbance in their sense of identity and self-esteem. . . . This is particularly true of two major groups who become interested in Buddhism and appear at retreats: those in late adolescence and those entering or passing through the mid-life transition. Individuals in these two groups often seem attracted to Buddhist practice as a short-cut solution to the developmental tasks appropriate and necessary to their stage of the life cycle. The Buddhist teaching that I neither have

nor am an enduring self is often misinterpreted to mean that I do not need to struggle with the tasks of identity formation or with finding out who I am, what my capabilities are, what my needs are, what my responsibilities are, how I am related to other selves, and what I should or could do with my life. The *anatta* (no-self) doctrine is taken to justify their premature abandonment of essential psychosocial tasks.

Freely admitted, the minimal self Lasch worries about forms a "sizable subgroup" in many a meditation hall. No surprise. If Lasch is at all accurate in his analysis of trends in American cultural formation (or deformation), all our institutions and social movements will have members of a narcissistic type.

Let me take up Jack Engler's analysis of the problem from the point of view of Theravada Buddhism's discipline of self-transcendence. Since Buddhism probably presents the most radical Eastern version of abolishing "self," clarifying what this does *not* mean — namely, destroying "ego strength" in the Western sense — may allay fears that Eastern spirituality is antithetical to Western. Conversely, some understanding of the Buddhist path may offer insight into Christian mysticism's doctrine of dying to the self, which suffers from similar misunderstanding. The fact is that both Buddhism and Christianity, having developed during and after the period of the heroic priest-king, *presuppose* a developed self. Undoing the tyranny of ego requires trial in the outer world, if you will, that ego-strength and "street smarts" have already been won. If the heroic ordeals of Lasch's divided self are not the last word, this tensional stage cannot be bypassed. You could put it this way: the prelude to Kierkegaard's leap of faith involves living with, and containing, the tensions Lasch speaks of, whereas the wisdom of that faith, if and when grace breaks through, is typically comprehensible only in the second half of life — after we have despaired of serving either the self or its rule books and a genuine inner journey begins. Meditation is then relevant.

TYPES OF MEDITATION: PRIEST, PROPHET, MONK

Theravada "insight" (or *vipassana*) meditation represents one type, the "negative way," among three modal forms of meditation which correspond to three distinct but complementary spiritual paths, all of which aim to transform or transcend the kind of selfhood whose main preoccupation is its own importance or heroic immortality project. The fundamental misconception is to take these procedures individualistically, as an instance of the solipsistic self's navel gazing. Though carried out in private or in small groups, the act is essentially public; what meditators dwell upon, if they know what they are doing, is the city and the cosmos in which they are implicated—which runs through their open, thermodynamic body-systems. The inwardness of meditative disciplines have to be seen in this open-ended context—and as openers, even when the initial move is to shut out traffic noise.

These different methods aim at widening the gyre of life, as we put it in discussing psychedelics in chapter 3, from that of a lifetime to the span of history and history's meaning. Or, in terms of the different time frames I referred to in chapter 5, these ways are designed to move one from heroic time into the pilgrim time frame, and perhaps beyond that to an apocalypse which blows—and reveals—the whole show in every breath that is taken.

The Way of Forms or Concentration

This path is favored by religions which highlight divine incarnation and has been dominant in the West since Augustine's *credo ut intelligam*—"I believe in order to understand." It may be called the way of forms or of crystallized wisdom. The basic dictum is: "Here is the truth; assimilate it, make it yours" (see Naranjo and Ornstein, 1971: 129; see also pp. 19–74). This path is hieratic and concentrative, paradigmatically the way of the priest, of formal cult and ritual action. The destination is set forth in advance of the journey. One is directed to trust *on faith* that the symbol or model is reliable—that others have been this way before and it works. One can therefore "sacrifice" one's narrow self (let the "seed" die) to the symbol, with the result that in projecting oneself into it or assimilating it, the wayfarer finds his or her own deepest reality and center—as in Paul's "not me, but Christ in me" or Islam's *fan-f'illah* (extinction into God).

Here, in the first instance at least, the meditator dwells upon an externally given symbolic object (an image or icon of God, koan, mantra, parable, mandala symbol, etc.) to which she is receptive, and with which she identifies. Attention is *restricted* from manifold sensory inputs so that the mind arrives at a one-pointedness or is absorbed in the object of focus (*samadhi* or the Christian "unitive" way). Again, the principle is that of poetic synecdoche, that any part, even a grain of sand, can stand for the whole. Or, as David Bohm would have it, that material reality is holographic; the implicate order is to some degree present in every detail of the explicate dimension. The medium is not necessarily the message, but it does communicate. The most pedestrian images of the world, Aquinas thought, were the most apt for representing God—just because there was less danger that way of confusing the representation with what it ultimately represented.

The way of forms is the method of traditional piety, devotion, or "religion" in the sense of the virtue of "yoking" to some symbol of ultimate reality—with the result that one becomes a confluent channel of that reality. In some measure, of course, the aim of selfless identification is utterly familiar, for it underlies all aesthetic experience, all genuine human empathy, all knowing "from within"—all instances which relativize and temporarily overcome the subject-object distinction.

The Way of Surrender and Expression

If the way of forms stresses tradition and is Apollonian, this next approach ostensibly represents the Dionysian antithesis: "The truth lies within you, and you can find it only by forgetting the ready-made answers." The path of highly individualized *vocation*, it is paradigmatically the way of the shaman, the prophet, the inspired artist, and of charismatic ecstasy and enthusiasm. Meditation in this line seeks to attune the individual "to an inner form or a formless depth out of which a personal form emerges—in imagery, thoughts, gestures, feelings, or, above all, as an attitude toward the situation at the moment" (Naranjo and Ornstein, 1971: 17). The meditator surrenders expectations, preconceptions, and prescribed modes of response, seeking to become receptive to the unfolding of a deeper spontaneity and richer expression. Though on the surface this approach may appear (to Apollonian or traditionalist minds) as anarchic, properly understood, it gives rise to novel, more appropriate forms. It ought to be seen in terms of Victor Turner's liminal "anti-structure"—out of which arise more complex forms to contain the burgeoning energies of a culture. Understandably, this path will tend to surface and assume special importance in periods of cultural ferment when the "way of forms" is experienced as ossified (e.g., late Roman Empire, sixteenth-century Europe).

Clearly, with all its methods of deconditioning, lifting inhibitions, and tapping spontaneity, the human potential and consciousness movements were drawn especially to the expressive path. What was often misunderstood, in the sixties anyway, was that this path can be hazardous to the health when taken in isolation, or if separated from the normal social ties and ethical prescriptions which surrrounded its use by Sufi mystics, Eastern Orthodox hesychasts, and in Hindu and Buddhist Tantrism. Patanjali's yoga is representative in this respect: its meditative practices, of whatever kind, *presuppose* right conduct—nonviolence, not lying, no stealing, no possessiveness, and no sexual misconduct (equivalents of the Mosaic commandments). The classic text in Christianity on this point is doubtless Paul's lecture (1 Cor. 11–14) to the charismatic Corinthians regarding spiritual gifts ("faith, hope, and love; and the greatest of these is love"). The big trouble with the early days of the consciousness movement was that its notion of the individual owed entirely too much to the standard liberal conception of the solo self—who could presumptively go about fulfilling itself independent of social relations and community.

Though overtly antithetical and often in conflict historically, the way of forms and the way of expression should be seen dialectically and as converging. If pursued consistently, surrendering to inner imagery—for instance, as in the Jungian practice of "active imagination"—will usually lead, at a certain depth, to the emergence of collective patterns in which all people tacitly share (the "symbolic" level of psyche referred to in chapter 3). As Jung was fond of pointing out, these patterns are often reminiscent of the universal mythic forms mediated by traditional religions. Conversely, at some point or other, all of the mythic archetypes of the way of forms originated in the spontaneous experience of some charismatic figure like Moses, the Buddha, Jesus, or Mohammed. Moreover, in all of the great traditions stemming from these figures both approaches, of forms and expression, can be found in different mixes appropriate to different circumstances. (At a certain stage in the contemplative life, John of the Cross insists, meditating on the Bible can be a positive obstacle; prayer becomes spontaneous, passes into the expressive mode.) Apparently it is only the narrowly sectarian spirit which finds these two approaches incompatible.

The Negative Way

The third approach, of which the Buddhist insight method is an example, consists of a self-emptying process that relies upon attention to breathing. It is also the traditional path of negative (or apophatic) Christian mystical theology (John of the Cross's dark night of the soul being paradigmatic). Again, though overtly different from concentrative and expressive ways, it is actually the inner secret of their achievement. Thus the precondition for becoming one with an object of meditation is a still, undistracted mind. The mind must get out of its own way, in a sense eliminate itself, be empty, in order that its field be filled with the object contemplated. As for the expressive way, allowing inner experience to arise on its own supposes that one has let go of control, habits, preconceptions, expectations, and filtering defenses. In this sense, for their efficacy, both concentrative and expressive ways require the kind of renunciation or selfless presence-in-absence which the practice of the negative way instills. Starting from three different points, these three paths converge toward unity. Plunging into formlessness, the Buddhist comes to realize that a radiant lotus blooms even from an open sewer—the thesis of the way of forms.

Without adverting to it explicitly, we have encountered the negative path before—by discussing (in chapter 6) the superconductive mind required for tantric descent. All that I said there applies here. Par excellence, the archetype is the cloistered monk or nun. The cloister need not be taken literally. Basically, it is a condition of uninhibited awareness and attention, a metaphorical cloister which spells an identity free of attachment to possessions, title, or the compulsive need to horde attention. The paradox: emptiness of self-seeking (or the renunciation of the need to succeed) is the condition and ground of fullness. Nothing is to get in the way of the mind's clarity; not being anything itself, the mind can become all things, dwelling in swamps and funks as well as ecstasies without getting lost in them. Buddhists call this elusive mode of being and being aware "right mindfulness." In the Theravada tradition, mindfulness involves *vipassana*, the practice of "clear apprehension" or insight—which is designed to lead the meditator experientially to the recognition of the impermanence of all things (*anicca*), the cause of suffering (*dukkha*) as the separate self, and impersonality (*anatta*) as deliverance from suffering.

The assumption behind insight meditation is that, normally, our experience of the world is impoverished, masked by simplified labels, and distorted by preconceptions and expectations which have the effect of tying us either to the past or to anxieties about the future. The present opportunity typically eludes us. The practice aims to clean or purify the mind of such contamination by temporarily stilling its conceptualizing activity and automatic emotional reactions. One cultivates nonattachment toward internal and external perceptions alike, and of the most ordinary, this-worldly kind. Contrary to the restrictive method of the way of forms, attention is *expanded*—gradually—to as many mental and physical states as possible. The meditator develops the habit of "bare attention" to whatever is there in consciousness, usually beginning with sensory physical states, then working on to feelings and thoughts. The idea is simply to be a witness to such states—without censorship, judgment, or interpretation. No subject is taboo or too trivial to merit attention. On the other hand, the meditator is not to seek gratification in wishes, impulses, desires, or striving; no acting out, abreaction, or cathartic discharge is to be allowed. Just sit there and take it—without clinging to anything. You have to have the capacity to step back while experiencing, to become a dispassionate witness—in order to open up the gamut of experience in all its complexity. In order to be free, not the plaything of moods, set ideas, or circumstances. That is, the practice aims to free the individual from uncontrolled states of mind which "take over" or compulsively "drive" us.

Christopher Lasch and a lot of other people (including many overtly "religious" people) confuse the attitudes of detachment and equanimity with emotional coldness, depersonalization, and austere withdrawal from action in the world (thus Lasch's reading of Doris Lessing). But a refusal to identify oneself with accumulated "things" or with performance roles, in short, a measure of nonattachment, is the source of the ability to stand on one's own. Similarly, the ability to stand above moods and whims, to accept pain and frustration rather than avoid them, is the source of that independence from others which is the precondition for genuine relationships. More, if the negative way of nonattachment—to ecstasies as well as depressions—is the secret backbone of the two other approaches, then Lasch's principle objection to Eastern spiritual practice is misplaced. For what else is this nonattachment but critical distance, an empty space in which to experience the tension between what is and what might be? It means having a conscience. Together, the three meditative ways aim at clear-sightedness, an unconflicted sense of inward flow, an enhancement of energy; but such extensions of normal range will very likely only intensify the sense of how much "more" the world could be than it reveals.

Insight meditation can drive you almost mad in the very real process of relieving you of extra psychological poundage. I once spent ten days in retreat at the Insight Meditation Center in Barre, Massachusetts, where Jack Engler has been an instructor. As the days wore on, I think every psychosomatic pain in my body must have surfaced, as well as many of the demons and monsters closeted away in my life history. The whole point is to disidentify and see through the illusion of object-constancy—and it isn't easy being that permissively empty. Narcissistic personality types can't pull it off. The thing requires what is called ego strength.

SOMEBODY BEFORE BEING NOBODY

The first thing to see about insight meditation is that a person with poorly developed object relations can't do it. To practice this method and achieve its aims, Jack Engler submits (1984: 43), "it is developmentally necessary to acquire a cohesive and integrated self first." Engler and other insight meditation teachers have observed that many Americans have great trouble, to put it mildly, in following this path, and as a rule fail to progress in the practice as rapidly as do our counterparts in Burma or Thailand. Americans tend to get sidetracked with strong transference relations to the teacher, or get absorbed in the content of awareness rather than attending to the process—the always changing stream of sensations, feelings, images, and thoughts.

The problem will be compounded where the meditator exhibits the fluid boundaries of a narcissistic or borderline personality disorder—and where, therefore, inner and outer are not well defined. It means that the person is extremely vulnerable to violent mood swings, which cannot be differentiated from an objective world—now felt as magically all-good and beneficent, now turning malevolent, frustrating, all-bad. Such a person cannot be expected to sustain the insight practice: to distance, detach, tolerate painful affects, and endure postponed gratification and conflict. Nor will a weak ego be able to contain itself when powerful primitive drives begin to surface. As I say from personal experience, such upsurges of affect and memory (right out of Stanislav Grof's hellish and purgatorial matrices) do come. For the method *unstructures* consciousness, takes the lid off. At that juncture, the narcissist's automatic response will probably be to bury itself in some fusion state, or resort to primitive defense mechanisms—denial, projection, exaggerated idealization, and splitting. As Engler puts it, "you have to be somebody before you can be nobody."

What, then, about that "sizable subgroup" attracted to Buddhist disciplines who suffer from narcissistic deficits, who therefore have the greatest difficulty objectifying or decathecting. This is the second point. Engler is forthright. Insight methods are not designed to cure such problems and are probably "contraindicated." They are being used to avoid adolescent and mid-life developmental tasks. For in cases of weak ego structure, a method which unstructures habits of mind will only reinforce the pathology—and as Lasch suspects, dissolve all tension. The narcissistic meditator will simply lose himself or herself in a stream of fantasies or merge into undifferentiated chaos which then may be mistaken for nirvana. The object, however, is to contain the chaos. Oceanic merger, unfairly identified as "oriental mysticism," is what Ken Wilber—and the consciousness movement at large—have come to call *prepersonal*, as contrasted to a *transpersonal* and genuinely transformative experience of breaking into a new level of consciousness (see Wilber, 1980: 8, 50). The point is that Buddhism is simply not interested in a regressive state of inert, thermic equilibrium or what Kierkegaard termed the volatilized "despair of infinity."

As Engler concedes, Theravada Buddhism is not much concerned about this whole level of pathology. Its concern is rather with problems of rigid overidentification, with *fixations*. Thus where the problem is *changeability*, the kind of protean instability characteristic of poor identity formation or borderline personality problems, the Theravada tradition has very little to say. The way of forms may do better. For concentrative meditation offers a therapeutic structure to adhere to; it provides supportive boundaries, structures, forms of "ego ideal" that may nurture a regrowing of ego. But the best treatment is probably a new and different kind of sustained relationship with a therapist or friend—the kind of relationship which narcissistic people were unable to achieve during the early developmental crisis when the capacity for object relations normally occurs. In effect, the friend or therapist becomes the meditative object of concentration and assimilation, a surrogate for parents who couldn't live up to that function.

There is a general principle of distinction at stake in the above discrimination. Where Western psychotherapy focuses on remedies for failing to develop a self, and thus works back to untie knots in family relations, as a general rule *spiritual* disciplines focus on the troubled sequel to the constellation of the self. The requirement of a certain maturity is especially evident in the case of the expressive and negative paths, less so with the way of forms. For the adult who follows any of the three ways or a combination of them, the focal disabilities relate to a loss of connection and wider belongingness, or simply to a vast inhibition of possible creative power.

BEYOND FIXATION

Insight meditation is an "uncovering technique" analogous to psychoanalysis. Strictly speaking, there is no term in Buddhist psychology for "meditation." The word used for that body of practices which we would call meditation is *bhavana*, or "development." The central concern is fixation or arrested growth. The basic principle of growth, as Engler puts it (1984: 26), is "that all psychological growth comes about by being able to renounce outworn, infantile ties to objects and to give up or modify self-representations that have become restrictive, inadequate or outgrown." If Hinduism in its mothering aspect focuses on beginnings, Buddhist practice focuses on endings. The regular practice of insight meditation releases a flood of object-loss, reminds you of all those separations, farewells, losses, small deaths still buried in your deep tissue. In fact, the practice asks you to anticipate the final surrender of your whole life involved in physical death. Curious: If Stanislav Grof is right about the death-rebirth struggle of the third perinatal matrix, Buddhist practice heads us toward that final decompression-release which constitutes the matrix of authentic Christianity. Curious: Buddhism begins to look like covert pentecostalism. In the first instance, however, the practice is time for mourning, for letting go of whatever your identity has been fixed upon and which blocks change. It's Good Friday.

The practice is to be understood in terms of where the self gets stuck. The self evolves correlatively, I have been saying throughout these pages, with changing images of the objective world. Psychoanalytic object relations theory and Buddhist psychology define self in ways which highlight the correlation. Acquiring a self in both perspectives is a process of synthesis and adaptation between inner life and external reality which eventually coalesce in a feeling of personal sameness and continuity. Gradually, one differentiates a cohesive schema of internalized images, a self-representation, from internalized images of objects. What Buddhism stresses here is that the solidity of self-representation stems from identifying with (or clinging to) putatively solid objects. For both Buddhist and modern psychology, then, the sense of "I," of personal unity, sameness, and continuity over time, place, and different states of consciousness, is not innate, but a developmental phenomenon. It is viewed, as Jack Engler says (1984: 29),

> as *evolving developmentally out of our experience of objects and the kinds of interactions we have with them.* In other words, the "self" is literally *constructed* out of our experience with the object world. The "self" which we take to be "me" . . . is an internalized image, a composite representation, constructed by a selective and imaginative "remembering" of past encounters with significant objects in our world. In fact, the self . . . is *actually being constructed anew from moment to moment.*

"Moment to moment"—this is where Buddhist psychology becomes radical, step by step unraveling the socialization and self-formation process. Bare awareness functions to disclose to the meditator the total impermanence of self and objects—not discursively, as a doctrine, but as a concrete experience. By attending closely to the flow of sensation, feeling, imagery, and thought it is brought home to a meditator that selfhood is not given or fixed, but constructed moment by moment, as it were, out of the radically contingent quantum pulsations of energy. The practice retraverses, as Engler says (1984: 46), *"the key stages in the representational process* which yields individual self and object representations only as the end products of a very long and complex reworking of stimulus information."* At ground zero of perception, then, there is only physical event and an awareness, moment by discontinuous moment, such that, strictly speaking, there are *"no constant endproducts of representation; there is only a continual process of representing"* (1984: 46). As insight practice is honed and refined, as the mind is cleared of afflictions, it functions somewhat like an electron microscope—focusing attention freshly on each momentary micro throb emerging from nothing and vanishing again. "What the meditator is actually experiencing," if he or she reaches the goal, remarks Engler (1984: 46), "is the temporal nature of perception prior to pattern recognition." Without passing out, in other words, you recapitulate ontogeny and if possible phylogeny as well, descending again into the primeval *tehom*. The postulate is that this death to self is implicitly present in every now—with each emptying of the breath.

In order to see the point of such practice, you have to understand where adult development reaches a point of arrest and the active process of self and object representation gives way to routine, turns passive, and begins to atrophy. Buddhism recognizes two distinct levels of psychoneurosis (or suffering) that need to be addressed. The first is roughly familiar to Western psychology. The process by which a person arrives at a stable self-representation involves a dual strategy of identifications and repressions. We step into a preformed inheritance, a set of transference objects consisting in the main of a linguistic culture which includes some specific paradigm of an ideal self—hero of great deeds, mystic, knight, gentleman, self-made man, and so on. In the first instance, we have no more choice over the cultural legacy than we do about our biological parents. And the assimilation, as Ernest Becker argued, is also one of self-mutilating introjection. Whatever is inconsistent with the consolidated self-image is split off and condemned to death; repressed, it forms the "shadow" side Jung focused on; or it begets the suffering due to conflicts between the ego and instinctual wish that Freud held to be "everyday unhappiness" and the incurable price of civilization. Insight meditation is preoccupied with the second go-around as a conscious adult, and the chance arising *after* we have more or less unquestioningly absorbed our cultural patrimony and constellated a self in some variant indigenous form. The re-traversal of the socialization process is meant to loosen inflexible intra-psychic structures, enable the integration of lost aspects of the self, and open up the possibility of real choice in the matter of a tradition.

But Buddhism recognizes a second level of dis-ease and agony that the secular West almost wholly ignores or believes unrelievable. It has to do with patterns of automatic repression, aversion, and avoidance of objects which threaten self-image; or on the other side, with equally compulsive patterns of attraction for objects which gratify self-image. Instead of responding adaptively and creatively to events and altered circumstances, we resist, block, and deny the actual flow of experience. Psychoanalysis and current theory of emotion take the ego's striving for maximized pleasure and maneuvering to evade pain as part of the human condition. According to this view, we have no option but to respond to sensations of pain and pleasure by avoidance and attraction, and little choice over the cultural conditioning which governs our interpretations of "good" and "bad" sensations.

Not so, says Buddhism; human instinct is incredibly plastic. From the meditative standpoint, our bondage to the thirsts and desires triggered by ideational systems need not lie beyond our control. On the contrary, affect is implicitly self-induced — by its links to the anything but inevitable construction of self-image and object-representation. What passes for fateful instinct, from this perspective, derives from the constructed habit of clinging to our precious self-image or this or that object. Our driven-ness represents a vain effort to achieve homeostasis or to ward off death. But if the linkage between drive and ego has been made up, imaginally constructed, it can also be undone, reimagined — and voluntarily assumed. The practice of bare awareness aims to disconnect the automatic nervous system's control of response to pain and pleasure, and even more, to disconnect organismic responses from preset cultural ideas. The objective, so far as possible, is regenerative in the most radical sense — to posit an unconditioned condition of being and doing in the world.

FREEDOM AND NECESSITY

The subtle objective can easily be misunderstood. The Buddhist tradition bears no animus against resistance to injustice. What this tradition questions, even for a just cause, is the inner quality of the doer. The issue is whether the action is truly free. In this regard, Buddhism has a much wider notion of what potentially lies within our voluntary control than does most modern Western psychology. And Western psychology, failing to notice how grounded Buddhist meditation practice is in physical sensation and the ordinary details of life, misconstrues the self-emptying process as nihilistic—as a way of jumping out of one's skin or rejecting biological and cultural inheritance. Quite the opposite. In chapter 3, in telling of my LSD experience, I mentioned that quite the most beneficial impact of recovering from the amnesia I experienced was the uncanny sense that "this time around" I had a choice, that I could say yes or no to my own narrative line—even to those elements of it like parents or being in a body or living at this particular juncture in history, which otherwise, to my everyday mind, appeared quite outside my will. At the time, this experience puzzled me deeply. But now I understand; it is just this sort of release from being lost in one's story line that the practice of meditative nonattachment is designed to effect. It creates an opening, an infinitesmal gap between mind and sensation, mind and feeling, mind and grabby idea—and through this clearing, this silent nowhere, one can step willingly but not blindly into body, accept parents and trials, embrace the opportunity of one's time.

The negative way's sweeping policy of disidentification offers a way of turning Kierkegaard's necessity into main chance. Norman O. Brown rhapsodizes (1966: 260), but his point about the value of clearing sclerotic mental circuits is clear:

> Freedom is instability; the destruction of attachments; the ropes, the fixtures, fixations, that tie us down.

> Empty words; dissolve the solid meanings. To dissipate the gravity, the darkness of matter, let the light in. To illuminate and ventilate, let words be filled with light and air: spirit. Let there be light. Love without attachment is light. Consciousness penetrates the darkness; consciousness is an opening or void.

> Admit the void; accept loss forever. . . . Wisdom is mourning; blessed are they that mourn.

The meditative disconnection is provisional and tactical, a way of clearing mindful space for a willing acceptance of biological rootedness, the vagaries and limits of one's parentage and cultural tradition, and the opportunities of one's limited moment in time. Each of these spheres is rendered all the more precious and urgent by the immediate death in the letting go of each breath. Instead of being condemned to the human condition of being a symbolic animal, either its unwilling victim or driven to escape earthiness by pretending to be god or angel, one could positively will it—gladly. At the same time, the gap of mindful space offers a point of resistance, space for refusal; neither biology nor cultural tradition need settle destiny. The idea, asserts Engler (1984: 51), is *"to set ego and object relations development in motion again."*

Admit the void, the silence, the great absence—as when a loved one dies, as when you yourself have to relinquish your hold on everything as you die. The surprise is that self-negation opens the circuits again, releases deep breathing, a rush of imagination, new words and meanings. In this condition, something other than biology and sociology moves destiny. Neither Father-God of sky nor Mother-God of the underground, the Buddha called it the Unborn, Unoriginated, Uncreated, Unformed—something wholly in the active voice, unnameable, featureless like the wind. This is a doctrine of *pneuma*, the wind that blows where it will, whose sound you hear but cannot tell where it comes from or where it is going.

EX NIHILO:
THE BEGINNINER'S MIND

There is more at stake in the negative way than mere reconciliation with the personal past, social setting, or with biological necessity. The negative way's return to that elemental moment before pattern recognition, to the formless larval state of the primeval waters, internalizes the first chapter of the Book of Genesis. The method, which Christians refer to as the path of *kenosis* or self-emptying, bears on the secret of creativity, a full-hearted engagement in the present. The meditator closes in on the nothingness, the heart of darkness both within and without, and takes it in; the nothingness occurs in every now as a phase in a cycle of death and life, neither of which is to be denied. Beseiged by demons, the Buddha touches earth and laughs. The Kabbalist and Teresa of Avila dance. John of the Cross incants erotic poetry, rewrites the *Song of Songs*.

This brings us full circle to the recognition, accented in contemporary physics as well, that I called the ontological revolution of first-millennium B.C. religion: the shift from a passive to an active voice in shaping creation. The Buddhist perspective adds its own special light to the idea that we have a creative relationship to nature, that life invites us to invent our world—*poiēsis* in the radical sense. What shall we breathe into it? Merely our small personalities? Or something more? The secret of the something more lies, as it does for Christianity, in learning to accept death. Apparently thrown here by fate without proper instructions, we drift like the Heideggerian self who has "forgotten Being." Retracing the process of representation, this time around consciously, is the way to "remember Being." It leads to a second birth, a draft of life that exceeds the big breath you took on your first day. No extreme austerities are required. The Buddha tried extreme asceticism, as he had tried self-indulgence, and neither worked. Call it surpassing yourself, transpersonal, transcendence in the strictly spiritual sense, the great breakthrough, whatever—what is clear is that the decompression-release, the death of self Buddhists have in mind is not meant to be an out-of-this-world event. Return from the dead, from formless *tehom*, is to occur in this world. At the same time, return from the dead opens up a kingdom not of this world, whose meaning does not lie in loquacity but rests between the words, in the silence beyond reach of literalist explication. The style is reticent, quiet, because first of all it is the telling language of the body. In the last of the famous Zen ox-herding pictures describing the whole process—after both ox and self are forgotten, after the return to the Source—the enlightened one returns to the marketplace in order to bring withered trees to bloom—"muddied and dust-covered, how broadly he grins!" (See Kapleau, 1967: 301–11). The message is made flesh in the belly's laughter.

"What is always speaking silently," says Norman O. Brown (1966: 265), "is the body." Jesus is silent before Pilate. A mere look is enough to set the apostle Peter weeping that, out of fear of death, he had denied what his heart had heard—that the human body's emptiness, its soul-space, enjoys the capacity to freely receive an infinite breath, the voice of Being. Brown's final chapter of *Love's Body* is titled "Nothing." Ironically, the key to the great beginning, a second genesis, rests there. As he writes (1966: 262),

> The obstacle to incarnation is our horror of the void. Instead of vanity, emptiness. Being found in the shape of a human being, he emptied himself.

> A pregnant emptiness. Object-loss, world-loss, is the precondition for all creation. Creation is in or out of the void; *ex nihilo*.

> Creation out of nothing. . . . Imagination is a better artist than imitation; for where one carves only what she has seen, the other carves what she has not seen; that never was on sea or land.

Creation out of nothing. Time and space are integrated into that ultimate pointlike unity, *bindu*: point, dot, zero, drop, germ, seed, semen.

Our valleys and depressions, it would seem, fall at the peak of an infinite inhalation at the brink of bursting forth again. At the abyss, await the next big breath, the moment of release. The void, our time of abhorrent need, of the Hindu's *kali yuga*, is the black hole through which, from the mystical standpoint, immeasurable fullness catches our breath, draws us home to the fullness of time's meaning.

Brown refers to the Buddhist *bindu* or primal point. "It is the point," said the late Lama Govinda, "from which inner and outer space have their origin and in which they become *one* again." Strikingly, medieval Jewish Kabbalist contemplatives also speak of experiencing a flame of light, a primal point or seed erupting at the bottoming-out darkness of their meditative breath (see Scholem [1941] 1961: 205–86). As the thirteenth-century *Book of Splendor* saw primordial genesis:

> In the beginning, when the will of the King began to take effect . . . a dark flame sprang forth from the innermost recess of the mystery of the Infinite, *En Sof*, like a fog which forms out of the formless. . . . In the innermost center of the flame a well sprang forth from which flames poured. . . . The well broke through . . . [and] a hidden supernal point shone forth.

The Kabbalist mystics, like Buddhists, experienced the Creator-Beginner as an unknowable "Nothing" from which all beginnings take their start. How does the Infinite create? By voiding or emptying itself—in the exodus of breath. The whole of creation, the sixteenth-century Isaac Luria claimed, happens as an event within the no-thingness of the Infinite, as a gigantic process of inhalation and exhalation. In this sense, the creative dialectic of being and nonbeing was conceived as interior to Being itself, the void in God constituting space for creation as an outpouring of divine glory, the *Shekhinah*. With every breath, God loses himself in creation—and the earthen vessels break. This is the context of Ilya Prigogine's talmudic citation, "Let's hope it works!"

Twenty-six attempts preceded the current cosmos. The honor and terror of a human being consists in the power to retard or accelerate the process of at-onement, the recovery of the Creator's diffused glory and the remarriage of heaven and earth. The Creator takes chances. Whenever something genuinely new enters the world, said the Kabbalist masters, an opportunity exists to catch the Creator in act, through a crack in beings and Being itself. We miss the cracks, the open moments of nothingness tacitly present in every letting go of our breath—because we mistake a beginning for death. The Kabbalist contemplative's breathing exercises were an acceleration of the process of at-onement. Contemplation was understood as the mystery of conjunction, an experience of direct participation in the Beginner's creative act and glory, the first day of creation in every moment.

But this insight is not confined to Kabbalists and Buddhists. Participatory breathing of this sort once told Thomas Aquinas's fellow Dominican and greatest heir, Meister Eckhart (1260–1328), that God's eternal rhythm of self-emptying was the measure of the world's fullness (see Fox, 1980: 166–290). Again, God-process and cosmic-process are at bottom one. Godhead inhales: it is an act of drawing in, filling with infinite glory. And exhales: an act of release, letting go, abysmal emptying. In the theogonic process itself, fullness empties and emptiness fills; God's exit is God's entry into his own infinite Being. And into the world as well. Creation from this vantage point is the void, self-negation in God, which God fills and informs. Like the Buddhist and the Kabbalist, Eckhart is caught by this breath of life when he himself empties, releases all holding patterns. He coined the word *Galassenheit*, "releasement" or letting go, and it's the key to God's nature, the world's, and our own (see Woods, 1986: 119–27; Tobin, 1986: 89–146). The only difference Eckhart could see between himself and a stone or a grasshopper, which were equally the voice of God, was the privilege he had of becoming conscious of the process with every breath he took. Meister Eckhart consequently speaks of not being shut out in any way from an eternal breathing process; God's ground is his own (see Fox, 1980: 226–30; 292–303). That awareness more than condensed time and human history into the compass of a single lifetime; it brought the end-time of eternity into the immediate present, and revealed that, like God's exit and entry into himself, every human going out into the temporal world could mean an entry into God's fullness and a new beginning. Emptiness was Eckhart's formula for renaissance.

"You'd be amazed," an Israeli physiotherapist once told me when I was tied in knots, "what a difference it makes to breathe." She was right. To illuminate the process of the negative way, consult the experience of your own breathing when coordinated asymmetrically with another's breathing opposite you—so that you are breathing in when they are breathing out, and they are breathing out when you are breathing in. It will tell you, on the one hand, that the sustenance of your own life depends on the rhythm of letting go and filling, and that the relative fullness of life hangs on the depth of your exiting breath, the death in every now. Your exit is your entry into life. On the other hand, your emptiness at the bottom of your breath creates the receptacle to take in your partner's expansive exhalation (or word); and vice versa, the other's self-emptying creates space for your entry. If both of you are full of yourselves (information-tight, with no chaotic emptiness), no exchange, no metamorphosis will occur; the giving and receiving depends on that act of self-nullification and silence. The vacuum, the ground zero present in every exiting breath, is the implicit third in any act of communication—a clearing, a listening space, an opening for communion. Wherever two are gathered, there is a third.

ELEVEN

Jean Houston's Ritual Theater

Everything in creation is dependent on method, including the points of intersection between this world and the next. . . . The method merely differs according to the different sphere. The higher one goes, the more rigorous and precise it becomes. It would be strange, indeed, if the order of material things were to reflect more of divine wisdom than that of spiritual things. The contrary is true.

Simone Weil

*Then to the elements
Be free, and fare thou well!*

Prospero, *The Tempest*

The consciousness movement dawned during the Vietnam War, hardly a time when God's command to "fill the earth and subdue it" (Gen. 1:28) seemed like a bright idea. A good part of the movement has wanted to repudiate that commission, or at least has felt very ambivalent about it—as if the Bible were endorsing superpowers and the Promethean self. In this respect, Christopher Lasch is on target in his criticism that many New Agers have confused Lockean individualism with the Western tradition itself. I have been focusing on another side of the movement whose journeys inward and East have been concerned to "remember" in a more radical, almost Augustinian sense. For them, the American Dream is less a consumer paradise and more the prospect and promise of a New Jerusalem, a "city on a hill," a *novus ordo saeculorum*. The old eschatological itch is very much alive. No longer quite the quick-change artists of the sixties, the Aquarian conspirators of the eighties are still engaged in some great "evolutionary leap forward."

Such leaps require inner tuning, spiritual discipline. Major American cities today are therapeutic shopping malls, world-religions bazaars. Looking through New York City's Open Center catalogue, for instance, one encounters weekends with Iroquois sacred fire keepers, talks by Tibetan lama Tara Tulku Rimpoche and the Sufi Vilayat Khan, M. Scott Peck and Brother David Steindl-Rast on Christian spirituality, Gary Zukav on the new physics and self-knowledge. The workshop bill of fare offers Zen drawing, Gabrielle Roth's dance-movement, Elizabeth Cogburn's Ameroindian ritual, aikido, ancient Hawaiian problem-solving methods, Chinese medicine, psychic healing, massage, poetry readings, Gurdjieff work, seminars on the nuclear arms race, nutrition, "A Course in Miracles," women and power, humanistic management practice, and sacred geometry and architecture. Esalen has clearly moved to the East coast. Another nearby growth center which opens for the summer, the Omega Institute in Rhinebeck, New York, specializes in transforming politics, business, and the social order in general. A Pandora's box? A snare for the curious? A table of *hors d'oeuvres* always less than a real meal?

In the mid-seventies, the answer to both questions might have been yes. But today, in the eighties? My impression is that the economic slump of the late seventies winnowed out most fair-weather dilettantes, and that those who keep places like Open Center and Omega in business tend to be serious seekers after something "more" than the relative success and recognition they have already achieved in the marketplace and/or through raising families. It's sometimes articulated as transition to a second career, a search for another dimension to life, or straightforwardly as spiritual hunger. To my own thinking, the whole phenomenon is part of a long-term quest for a larger context of meaning that various secular ideologies, from Marx to Nietzsche to Freud, have been unable to supply because they are essentially negative, better at rationalizing frustration and dis-ease than at providing access to the energy of renewal. I realize that one's analysis of central issues in this regard will depend on where you are on the economic totem pole, that bread and a bit of social justice can take priority if you're on the bottom—and I hardly want to suggest that a passion for social justice is antithetical to the spirited life. But for people of my stratum in late twentieth-century America, I think that Otto Rank, Roberto Assagioli, and Ira Progoff (1973) had it right: the central psychological problem of our times, at least for the affluent West, lies in the repression, not of sex, but of spiritual capacity. Another way to phrase the issue would be to say that the unfinished task is still to fill the vacuum left in the Western psyche when traditional religion lost its hold.

If this is so, then the major issue is a practical one: how to give people

access to the means, procedures, and disciplines by which creative spiritual energies can be experienced first-hand and released. This larger cultural task was what Rank had in mind in his call to move "beyond psychology"—where "psychology" largely meant curing familial problems and
returning the client to everyday unhappiness. Providing the means for
spiritual regeneration and a larger public purpose was also the project of
Abraham Maslow's (1968; 1971) "third force" psychology. What does
that look like in the eighties? Places like the Open Center and the Omega
Institute provide one indication; the unostentatious, patient work of the
Insight Meditation Center in Barre, Massachusetts, or the Tibetan Buddhist Naropa community in Boulder, Colorado provide another. Still
another, more showy, would be the work of Jean Houston—and in a very
self-conscious way, her work relates to the theme of what we are to make
of the world or breathe into it.

STATE OF THE ART

Jean Houston reaches an audience difficult to classify that is somewhere
between those served by places like Open Center and those who have
settled down to a particular spiritual discipline and tradition. In the rest
of this chapter, I will give an exposition of Houston's eclectic methods—
as a prime example of the current state of the art in the consciousness
movement. In chapter 3 I discussed her pioneer work in LSD research,
and I mentioned that *Mind Games*, a book she coauthored in the early
seventies with her husband Robert Masters, charted a set of spiritual
exercises and rituals for exploring the various levels of psyche and spirit.
Since that time Houston has continued to develop her ritual approach,
drawing from the repositories of world religions. In terms of the categories presented in the last chapter, the spiritual path she exposes mixes the
"way of form" with the "expressive way." It's almost Confucian: life is a
great ceremony—and Houston's rites of passage, in her own jazzy, Prigo-
ginian style, attempt to empower people with such an outlook.

A former president of the Association for Humanistic Psychology, and
sometimes known as "the human potential movement from the neck up,"
Jean Houston has been something of an academic gypsy. At one time or
another she has taught at Columbia, the New School, Hunter College,
Marymount College (Tarrytown), and the University of California. Like
many another former Esalen star, these days she is an international circuit rider offering weekend introductory workshops (mere "tastes" as it

were) and, more seriously, extended programs stretched over one to three years. The extended programs are commonly held in settings, such as a YMCA camp in Port Jervis or a former Biddle mansion in Tarrytown, New York, where maximum use can be made of the environment (some rites call for "baptisms" in lakes or swimming pools, or all-night marathons in the woods). They usually involve a few adjutant leaders, and include at least one sound technician to handle the music (a very big feature). The weekend affairs are priced around $195, the extended programs anywhere from $2,000 to $2,500 per year for the three-year training. In one year-long training titled "The Mystery School" which I participated in from 1984 to 1985, approximately one-third of the 160 people attending were on scholarship. If the latter was any index, the age spread of a Houston congregation stretches from the early twenties to people in their seventies, but with the largest number middle-aged. The background of the participants also runs the gamut, from nuns and ministers to church- and synagogue-goers to the religiously unaffiliated. From the very nature of the case, such a diverse audience requires an ecumenical approach, a tantric weaving — and gets it.

Others than Jean Houston could represent the current, ongoing movement I have been tracing since Mother Esalen gave permission, but I know of few others who better signify the state of the art in the eighties: the passage beyond a narrow human potentials approach to a transpersonal one, a wide-ranging appropriation of method, incorporation of the revisioned cosmology — and more attention to the sociology of spiritual life. By the latter I mean that Houston, like many other leaders of the movement, is aware of the fallacies of the one-shot "high." Wherever she travels these days, she tries to leave behind her some kind of network organization where people can continue to join each other in spiritual work and find mutual support.

A TIME OF PARENTHESIS

In her attitude toward time and history, Houston's approach represents a decidedly activist, Western synthesis. It is informed by a sense of *kairos*, an acute feeling for the challenge and opportunity of the moment. As Houston (1980: 5–6) writes,

> The age we live in is shivering amidst the tremors of ontological breakdown.
> It's all shifting: the moral mandates; the structural givens, the standard-brand

governments, religions, economics, the very consensual reality is breaking down. . . . The world by which we understood ourselves . . . is a world that no longer works. It is a world whose lease has run out, whose paradigms are eroding . . . .

There is a lag between the end of an age and the discovery of that end. We are the children of the lag, the people of the time of parenthesis — and there is no juicier time to be alive.

This is Houston's way of making Victor Turner's point: that our world exists in a liminoid, in-between state of flux. She would like to seize the moment and turn it into another renaissance.

To counter strategies of defeat, to move forward, Houston's solution is to awaken the full complement of the human, to complicate the psyche we bring to bear on the world. A recent book (Houston, 1982) captures the range. It's chapters treat the following topics: awakening the body; awakening the senses; awakening the brain; awakening memory; awakening your evolutionary history; the art of high practice; the creative realms of inner space; and finally, a new natural philosophy. This expansiveness aims at changing the world — first of all by amplifying and charging the human instrument. Unless the human instrument is tuned up, her rationale goes, it is unlikely we will breathe anything beneficial into the worlds we create. Modern historical scholarship, she thinks, places our generation in a unique position with regard to human history. We ought to be able to reflect consciously on the nature of historical happening, and to learn from the failures of nerve and interruptions in cultural development. We have reached the point, she says, "where we can choose to become the co-trustees of the evolutionary process."

BECOMING ALL THINGS

Nothing in Houston's repertoire is more central than the art of "active imagination." That means that most rediscover the child's (and oral person's) capacity to become what it beholds — and imagine anything, from rabbits to mad queens, from "inside." And in an exemplaristic way, as an image of the whole.

The assumption behind active imagination is Coleridge's, and it underlies all meditation of the "way of form" type: when the imagination confronts any alien thing, it can become "esemplastic," and coalesce with it. In this way, a stone can be endowed with life and allowed to stir the heart and mind. Conversely, returning to the object itself, a particular sky, moon, tree, or an animal can be transformed into a concrete universal, an image of the cosmos. The object thus becomes transfigured into a Platonic exemplar full of power. Take the following exercise, for instance (Houston, 1980: 101–102):

> Gather all participants around an absolutely splendid log, a regular "Ancient of Days.". . . Have the members of the group call out spontaneously what they see in the log—eyes, owls, faces, fish.
>
> After a while, ask them to look with a deeper level of themselves and try to perceive mythic and symbolic patterns in the log. Many will see myths unfolding: Buddha meditating, Christ on the cross, heroic battles, meetings of the gods, mandalas, death and resurrection, the story of evolution, partings, passages. . . .
>
> Finally, have the participants look at the log for the patterns and possibilities of their own lives. . . .
>
> Divide the group into partners. Each pair . . . finds a similarly potent object of nature. They sit in front of it, reflecting on it, as they breathe deeply . . . so that they feel a flow-through and deep continuity . . . [allowing] themselves to become what they behold.
>
> Both partners will now speak for several minutes as the object, with the wisdom and knowing of the object, using the pronoun *I*. . . . [Then] they will talk about some particular problem, question, exploration, or concern of their human lives . . . in terms of the patterns they see in the natural object they have just become.

The sample above probably illustrates fairly well the tone many transpersonalist group leaders have learned to adopt for a pluralistic, nonsectarian audience—evocative yet not imposing, respectful of whatever the participant's experience may be. At the same time, it shows the several levels which a Houston exercise addresses—both "mythic and symbolic" and "some particular problem, question, exploration or concern," which strikes a Freudian note.

All the while, however, the child-play of flowing into nature has the larger purpose of enhancing the capacity for world-building or creative cultural activity. As I noted in the last chapter, the whole second-nature world of cultural artifact which surrounds us derives from a prior primal unity with the environment that is prefigured in the child's capacity to identify with what it is not. The child imaginatively acts out what is foreign, thereby transforming it, giving it a cultural meaning. "World-building," says Houston (1982: 86), whether it be art, industry, or communications networks, is the necessary outgrowth of this special sensitivity and playful genius of the child. These extensions become the prostheses of ourselves, the further organization of nature's materials that transforms Nature itself. Because of our prolonged childhood, with its extended allowance for the plasticity and playfulness of our perception and thought, we are able to become co-evolutionists and weave new threads into the fabric of reality.

This is Houston's way of talking of H. D. Winnicott's "transitional objects." To lose that sense of symbiosis and the imagination that goes with it, argues Houston, is to lose a sense of creative "entelechy," one's place and call in the scheme of things. Heady stuff. All the more important, then, to keep one's feet on the ground. Which is part of what Houston's body work is about.

PRIMING THE NEURAL SYSTEM AND THE KINESTHETIC BODY

Without engaging distorted nerves and musculature, Houston believes, words engage too little of our being. She and her husband Robert Masters discovered, she says, "that you cannot have a successful and permanent extension of mental, psychological, and spiritual capacity without working toward an enhancement of physiological capacity." Thus, Houston maintains that "the key to transpersonal realities [lies] in the expansion of physical awareness" (Houston, 1982: xix).

At any Houston program these days, then, before working to join archetypal, mythic material to personal story, it is obligatory to engage in body work of some form—to "awaken the body and the senses," and to keep one's Jungian feet on the ground. Participants may be encouraged to dance to Jewish folk music or African tom-toms, or led through the gentle Feldenkrais movements (similar to those infants make), or put through one of the physical exercises which Robert Masters, who specializes in "psychophysical reeducation," has devised (collected in Masters and Houston, 1978). The presupposition is that the refinement of perception underlies acute conception. Wordsworth was wrong: the "celestial light" of the child's sensory-motor stage is not inexorably outgrown and dimmed with age.

In this regard, Houston focuses on overcoming a negative neurological representation of the body—by reimagining what she calls the "kinesthetic body." (I have referred to kinesthesia on several occasions, in regard to the more active sensory-motor modes of an oral sensorium, and I can now clarify the meaning. It also relates to what medieval thinkers spoke of as "interior senses.") Relying on the neurosurgeon Wilder Penfield's thesis that our awareness of different parts of the body is often misaligned with their actual size and function due to the fact that the representation is governed by their use and misuse in interpreting the environment, Houston focuses on reconstructing a whole 'body image" without inhibited, frozen, or occluded parts. The kinesthetic body, then, is the body of an enlivened muscular imagination. In terms of all I have said in Part II about literacy's effect in centering the Western sensorium on sight, activating the kinesthetic body in effect redistributes sensorial power throughout the physical system. A first step in deposing ego tyranny, reconstructing the kinesthetic body restores economic democracy at the psychophysical level.

One exercise in the repertoire begins this way (Houston, 1982: 15–16):

> Stand comfortably, with your knees relaxed and your eyes closed. Focus on your breathing as a way of directing your attention inward. . . .
> Scan your body . . . particularly your shoulders and neck area.
> Raise your *real* right arm and stretch, sensing the shifting alignment of the muscles all over your body. . . . Feel the stretch of your fingers, your arm, your shoulders, your torso. Now, with equal awareness, lower your arm.
> Repeat this several times.
> Now stretch your *kinesthetic* right arm [i.e., in imagination only], allowing yourself to experience this as vividly as possible.
> Stretch your *real* right arm, then your *kinesthetic* arm.
> Alternate. . . .
> Now, with your *real* body, make a fencing lunge to the right. . . . Repeat. . . . Now lunge to the right with your *kinesthetic* body.

And so on with other body parts and movements. At one level, such imaginative rehearsal can be applied to overcoming a "sense of local incompetence" and enhancing practical skills required for tennis, swimming, or dancing—or any activity requiring physical skill. Exercises of this type merge in Houston's work with others bearing on "fine-tuning" the senses, hearing, taste, touch, sight, smell, and "sixth sense." She will take people on an imaginative journey through their blood vessels, for instance, and have them cleanse the doors of each of these senses, reexperiencing bouts of sensuous pleasure with each (e.g., nursing a baby, the touch and smell of clean sheets, listening to the ocean, the quiet of snowfall, etc.)—or perhaps listening to music synesthetically, with their whole body. The idea is multipurpose: to get around the fixated personality or ego, to heighten physical alacrity and perceptual acuity, and thus contribute to the "detrivialization of the commonplace."

A variety of exercises also aim at augmenting memory. In one of these, for instance, Houston adapts neuropsychologist Paul McLean's studies of the triple-brain (i.e., obsessive-compulsive reptilian brain, the emotive limbic system, the calculating mammalian brain). The exercise recapitulates phylogeny: people squirm on the floor like fish, belly-crawl like amphibians and reptiles, hop about on all fours behaving (and sounding) like lemurs, monkeys, and great apes—and finally take on Neanderthalers and early humans.

Other workouts concentrate on the brain's fluency at processing information in different ways. The overemphasis on analytic reason (or left-hemisphere dominance) is counteracted by teaching people to "talk" to the brain, actively recruiting its dormant aesthetic powers. For instance, in one exercise, Houston (1982: 65) instructs participants with their eyes closed to move first the right eye, and then separately the left, in various directions:

> Keeping eyes closed and relaxed, imagine the images that will be suggested as vividly as possible. Don't strain.
> On the left side of your brain, imagine the number 1.
> And on the right side the letter A. . . .
> On the left side the number 2. . . .
> And on the right side the letter B. . . .
> Rest for a minute. . . . Now reverse the process. . . .
> Continuing . . . on the left side of your brain, imagine a festive outdoor scene with a big picnic and fireworks.
> On the right image a couple getting married. . . .
> On the left is an atom.
> On the right is a galaxy.
> On the left are fruit trees bearing new blossoms.

And so on. My favorite example of such efforts to extend neurological capacity is an exercise designed to teach a serial thinker to think, do, and imagine several different things at once. Houston calls it "multitracking," an excerpt from which goes like this (Houston, 1982: 73–74):

> Stand up and make sure you have enough room to move freely. Get centered and balanced.

Let your head and shoulders move from left to right together in an even swinging movement. . . . Now . . . in opposite directions from each other. . . .

Now let your head go right and your face go left.

Now reverse and let your head go left and your face go right.

Keep on doing this, reversing the order each time.

Add a little jog and snap your fingers. At the same time move your hands in circles.

And hum "Yankee Doodle Dandy"!

And, simultaneously, think about a hive of bees, a spiral staircase, and a bowl of Jell-O.

Stop and rest. . . .

If this doesn't get you going, the laughter will.

THE IMAGINAL BODY

The enhancement of physical mobility and sensitivity also has to do with subtle matters such as overcoming writing blocks and virtues such as courage and gracefulness in general. Though Houston seems to me to get her history of medieval philosophy quite wrong (in general, she seems partial to gnostic haters of matter, I think, because they were so persecuted), in practice and intention she reaches back to medieval spiritual alchemy's dissatisfaction with the church's version of that ascension theology and transcendental denial which we observed in India. But the context is even broader.

As I proposed (chapter 5), the revision of an earlier, almost dualistic other-wordliness and asceticism of withdrawal marked almost all the great first-millennium B.C. religions in the course of time. More or less, they all move from a world-denying sense of transcendence to a sense of divine immanence and incarnation—the history of Hinduism from Upanishads to Krishna and Rama epics is representative. The development shows up in those contemplative traditions which envision a subtle, "spiritual body": ancient Egypt's *haidu* body, Buddhism's "diamond body," Sufism's "man of light," the Kabbala's *Adam Kadmon*, and the Eastern Orthodox Christianity with its notion of "divinization." Sufi teachers, among others, note the close correlations between flexible body parts and the psychospiritual dimension. Consider, for example, these correlations (see Lilly and Hart, 1975: 342–44):

Hearing and perception—inner meaning
Nose—recognition of possibilities
Liver—assimilation or internalization
Colon, bladder, and kidneys—elimination of memories and ideas
Genitals—orientation
Thighs and upper arms—capacity and character
Knees and elbows—charism or the ability to influence others
Calves and forearms—means for action
Feet and hands movement toward goals

Consciously, Houston operates out of this nondualist tradition, building up slowly from the kinesthetic body to a "new myth of the body" akin both to the Christian resurrected body and the Sufi "body of light." Influenced by Islamic scholar Henry Corbin's studies of the latter (see Corbin, 1978), Houston calls it the "imaginal" (or ideal) body.

Depending on the context, exercises in the imaginal body usually involve a detailed scanning of one's "real" body, then proceed to place an "ideal body" (Houston, 1982: 24)

> so that you can "see" the back of it and jump into it. How does it feel? If it doesn't feel comfortable, jump out quickly. Adjust those parts, or even the whole image if necessary, to be more realistic. Again, put it in front of you and jump into it. Continue to do this. . . . Begin to move in this body, allowing the knowing of it to be integrated into your patterns of standing and walking, of sitting and dancing.

The reader unfamiliar with imagination in this sense may dismiss such play as dabbling in impotent fantasy. That would be a mistake, the kind of mistake the literalistic mind makes—for whom energy and instinct is dead and dumb, mere "id." In sequence with exercises which enhance breathing and release physical energy, imaginal exercises represent a way of charging the body with lightness and "vital spirit." They transform dumb energy, give it voice. Reimagining the body in this way, and jumping into it, usually has psychophysical effects which exercitants can test out for themselves. Of course there are limits; one does not alter the physical habits of a lifetime overnight—especially after forty.

In most Houston programs, exercises in trying on an imaginal body arise in the context in which exercitants are being simultaneously acclimated to "body wisdom" by other meditative exercises wherein participants expand their body image by incorporating archetypal figures of both history and fiction. It's Houston's version of the "communion of saints." The whole program here, obviously, is far more active and constructive than the Buddhist way of receptive attention. In fact, it's the other side of deconstruction, or retraversing the representational process—an invitation, within limits, to reconstruct one's body- and self-image. The catch, as I observed in the last chapter in connection with the role of "negative" detachment for the concentrative and expressive ways, is that unless one distances oneself from old body-mind habits, a new way of imagining oneself is unlikely to take hold. In this regard, the negative way, or something like "bare awareness" meditation, could use more play in Houston's work than it receives.

PREPARING FOR RESURRECTION

"What do you do," Houston asks, "*after* the resurrection?" She means that we're so obsessively and narrowly goal oriented that should some great awakening occur, we fall apart or revert, unable to manage living at a new plane of being. It's the problem of America's occasional "mystics" who can't stand intensity. The question then becomes: What have you done to prepare, to stand "too much," to contain the event should the "kingdom come"? About the "coming" itself, about inspiration in the strict sense, there is no telling, only silence. Houston is fond of citing Mozart on the "flow" of musical ideas: "I cannot account for it," wrote Mozart, "*Whence* or *how* they come, I know not; nor can I force them." Yet he could describe something of the setting: "when I am, as it were, completely myself, entirely alone, and of good cheer—say traveling in a carriage, or walking after a good meal, or during the night when I cannot sleep." Soul work is about such settings and preliminaries, as well as something like the athlete's conditioning.

Following her earlier LSD research, Houston's assumption is that in the process of expansion, one will pass through the fourfold hierarchy of soul—sensory, recollective-analytic, mythic-ritual, and integral-religious levels. All of her programs reflect this structure. A person can extend from immediacy to a sense of the whole lifetime, from lifetime to a sense of place in history—and possibly into the sphere of the great "I AM," God's time. But if the latter dimension is to be reached, a certain amount of "bridging" is required. That includes any unfinished business left over from Oedipal struggles; much of Houston's psychodrama is taken up with this Freudian domain. As an older tradition would have put it, genuine transcendence requires careful "ascent," a methodical movement from "gross" perceptions to "subtle."

THIS-IS-ME, WE ARE, I AM

Negatively, this ascesis focuses on dismantling the literalist mind; positively, it consists of developing a symbolic consciousness. The thing can be read as a practical application of one of Norman O. Brown's dicta (Brown, 1966: 223):

> Literalism makes the world of abstract materialism; of dead matter; of the human body as dead matter. Literalism kills everything, including the body. . . Literalism makes a universe of stone, and men astonished, petrified. . . The incarnation of symbols gives us a new heart, a heart for the first time human, a heart for the first time, or is it the second time, made of flesh.

In a journal interview, Houston speaks of her typology of psyche in more familiar terms as the realms of "THIS-IS-ME, WE ARE, AND I AM." By the first, she means the self of Freud's "everyday unhappiness." If this were all there were to us, Houston thinks, "we would never have gotten out of the cave." There would be "no poetry, no art, no religion, and very little creativity in general." Beneath this level of the liberal Lockean self, however, lies the connective tissue of the mythic-ritual level, the "WE ARE" (Houston, 1981: 41):

> This is the realm of the symbols, the images, the myths, the archetypes. I call it the WE ARE because it is so plentiful — it is the place of the self where the self joins its polyphrenic possibilities. The gods and godlings are part of it — what the Asians refer to as the *yidams*, which are essentially personified rivers to the Source. They are the human form of the gods — Jesus, Krishna, Buddha, Zoroaster — the semi-historical beings elevated to godhood with whom we feel a loving resonance and with whose numinous power we can identify, who evoke us to become what we can be. The WE ARE is also the place of the great archetypal myths and legends, the place of death and resurrection, of rites of passage, of the great transitional themes . . . . The WE ARE provides the patterns of connection by which we access the potencies of Being.

It is under the heading of the WE ARE that Houston programs spend a great deal of time training the imagination as an ontological faculty for exploring and envisioning the real at a deeper level. Programs are often organized around some classic myth or archetypal, historical figure. She will focus, say, on the Amor and Psyche legend, or Odysseus's journey. Other favorites are the first chapters of Genesis, Dante's descent into purgatory and hell, the grail legend, the Egyptian Isis-Osiris myth, the Gospel infancy narratives, the story of the Buddha's enlightenment, or Rumi the Persian's love affair with Shamsoddin. In conjunction with such storytelling, Houston will lecture on both the historical background of the tales and their contemporary application. She will then devise ritual enactments whereby participants weave these larger motifs into their personal histories (Houston, 1981: 39):

> The great stories of transformation light up like a force field anyone who comes within their province because they're part of your own transpersonal structure. Take Dante's *Divine Comedy* or *The Odyssey* or any of the great heroes' journeys, for example. In each of these, the personal-particular of your own individual tale joins the personal-universal of the larger mythos. You're carried not only by your own story but also by everyone's story, and thus you become Everyman and Everywoman.

Participants will be invited, for instance, to find the guiding Virgils or Beatrices in their own life, the wounds of a fisher-king, or to descend into the frozen hells they have known—to remember and truly experience these events. The point will be to dramatize such events against the background of Dante's journey, Parsifal's, or Rumi's. History and myth are acted out liturgically—in a way not dissimilar to the way in which a participant in the Catholic Mass is supposed to allow Christ's passion story to interpenetrate his or her own story. (The decisive difference here is that in a Houston ritual everyone is priest.) This "collective" level of psyche is above all the soul's social dimension, not simply connecting with our contemporaries but with the past. It is a genealogical link across time.

In this regard, Houston would awaken her audience to a symbolic historical consciousness, what the Sufis call the *mundus imaginalis* (imaginal world). She tries to bring home to a typically ahistorical American audience that myth and history still run in their veins, and can be empowering. Psyche and history must be joined, she thinks, by dancing or enacting history ritually (Houston, 1980: 16–17):

> I propose that, instead of regarding history horizontally, we look at it vertically and mythically. We view it not as empirical data to be plotted and

graphed, but as something to be done and danced and encountered in our depths—a living metaphor that gives us both music and the clues to play the great game of Lost and Found in the maze of time and meaning. . . .The metaphoric mode demands a symbolic use of the historical material, and when history is treated mythically it gains in usefulness and creative energy what it may lose in provable facts.

Classic soul-journey tales like Odysseus's or the grail story, then, are used as a vehicle for what I have called a "thickening" of a person's sense of history—and one's role in time. Take Parsifal's story: at one point, participants in this program will be led to remember both the power and recklessness of their own naïve departures into the social world; at other junctures, they will recall their missed opportunities due to the inhibitions of a conventional education; at other moments to recollect times of mourning, wasteland, ordeal, and pitched battle. By turns, they identify with Parsifal and the other players in the drama, in effect retrieving (or "fishing" for) disowned, forgotten parts of themselves, turning points, and open moments.

The movement into time's plots, according to Houston, is crucial for complicating psychological awareness. Rather than looking "at" history from outside, as a series of names and dates, mythic motifs such as the grail provide ways of *entering into* history's labyrinths at a deep level. The aim is to free the individual from the "tyranny of the personal," to "congregationalize the heart" by introducing it to aristocratic company. In this way, Houston tries to midwife a kind of second birth for her audience, into a larger sociotemporal order—a "larger ecology of Being." The human race has passed through four stages, she tells her audiences: tribal, primitive existence; the age of heroic cultures; the inward turn of the ascetical era; and the individualist-humanistic stage of modern times. That whole movement is somehow ingrained in us. We are now implicated in the turmoil of a fifth epoch, she claims, that of the "post-individual"—where subtle depths of spirit will be as important as control over the external world.

Establishing continuity with the myths of the past, moving from the personal-particular to the personal-universal, however, is only the first step in the process. To Houston's thinking it serves as transition to something more—the "I AM."

Beyond and within personal history and collective archetype is a deeper unfolding—God as the Unity of Being. "Beneath and yet surrounding the other two realms is the I AM, which is Being itself, pure potency, a realm of organicity, of love, of the very stuff of reality." The "I" is not to be confused with the "I" of the human ego. What Houston has in mind, rather, is the "I AM that I AM" spoken at the theophany of Sinai. This takes some working up to. Houston (1980: 42) writes:

> For most of us, it's too great a leap from THIS-IS-ME "lensed" reality to the Unity of Being. . . . From the THIS-IS-ME perspective, many of us tend to need the archetypal amplification of our personal-particular drawn into the personal-universal of the WE ARE. In our state of extension by virtue of identity with one or another of our "inner crew" of the WE ARE, we're able to receive the full numinous presence of the I AM. The I AM floods into the WE ARE, priming and juicing these great archetypal patterns—these *yidams*—with its power, and then, in more human form, these archetypal stories and storied beings of the soul give inspiration to the creative life of THIS-IS-ME. This is the healing of the whole.

The overall aim, then, cannot be understood except in a theological sense, but it is a theology imagined on the wider base of a soul that is recognized as polycentric. Instead of being frozen into a single persona, a participant in a Houston program is invited to exercise flexibility—acting out a protean capacity to take on different faces, including those of gods, animals, vegetables, and minerals. As my last chapter suggested, this may *not* be what a narcissistic personality, already too protean, really needs, and I do not recommend Houston work-outs for Christopher Lasch's "minimal selves." But for those suffering from rigid self-image or an "uptight" theology, these rights may be just what is needed. Houston (1980: 43) says:

> I don't believe you can have a decent new psychology until you re-vision theology on a much broader basis. Theological dictums are crucial to the psyche. It's only when you have a real ecological and *sacred* sense of what the human being is in all his or her dimensions—his or her polytheistic dimensions as well—that you can have a psychology capable of addressing soul. . . . Otherwise you merely have a rather happy upward-and-onward but tenderminded enthusiasm, or a version of "humanistic psychology" that has skipped the great middle ground.

The allusion to the soul's "polytheistic dimensions" refers to the more complicated psyche which surfaces in the course of overthrowing the dominance of a one-sided ego. This reference shows Houston's debt to the "polytheistic" archetypal psychology of James Hillman. The "great middle ground" refers to Plato's "metaxy," that sphere of soul in which the

Christian Aristotelianism of Aquinas's type discerned a kind of primal bonding, a "natural desire" or entelechy for participation in God—or "pure act." In Houston's view "primal bonding" is not enough. In order for the "possible human" to release, primal bonding must undergo a break and transformation.

BETRAYAL AND SUFFERING

When Jean Houston takes up the Christ story, you can never exactly tell what will happen. My impression is that her interpretation changes from year to year as she wrestles with it, as she does with other great archetypal figures. But one fairly constant use she makes of it is to lead people to reassess the gains implicit in their wounds and betrayals.

Her interpretation owes much to James Hillman (1975a: 63–81, esp. 68–70). Thus she makes much of the primal bonding the Gospels portray Jesus having with God the Father ("I and the Father are one") as an exemplification of the heroic masculine mystique (see chapter 2 in connection with Ernest Becker's critique of the heroic ego). In Jesus' case, this masculine mystique shows itself, Hillman thinks, in "the fearless safety of the miracle preacher." The absolute surety of the father-connection renders him invulnerable, but to a Jungian eye the dark side of such strength very likely manifests itself in distrust of the feminine element. That's the situation until the betrayals of the Passion begin to mount up: Judas's, the sleeping disciples', Peter's, and the ultimate one on the cross, "My God, my God, why have you forsaken me?" As the relationship of primal trust is being broken, Hillman points out, an extraordinary constellation of anima symbolism grows proportionately: the washing of the feet; the commandment to love; the agony at Gethsemane; the garden; the cup; the barren women on the way to Golgotha; the warning of Pilate's wife; nakedness and weakness; the Marys around the cross; the wounded side; and finally the discovery of the risen Christ by women. Only when the invulnerable hero dies to his primal father-bond, pierced in the side, does love flow, is the complete man born. As Hillman (1975a: 70) puts it,

It would seem that the message of love, the Eros mission of Jesus, carries its final force only through the betrayal and crucifixion. For at the moment when God lets him down, Jesus becomes truly human, suffering the human tragedy, with his pierced and wounded side from which flows the water and blood, the released fountain of life, feeling, and emotion.

When Houston draws the moral, the value of suffering comes across this way (Houston, 1981: 40):

> This is also true of ourselves. It is only when we lose our sense of intimate and absolute linkage with the other, be it mother or father or family or ideology—when we feel ourselves betrayed to the very deeps and in that terrible wounding we are thrust out into the world—that we really begin to grow, often bleeding and grieving all the way. The complete being, the possible human, as with Jesus, is the godly man, the manly god. God grows by becoming human, and man grows by having the aspirations of God, the archetypes of God in himself.

None of this would happen without the wounding. Houston (1981: 40) continues:

> By the betrayal, you have been provoked into extending your psyche in the world. You become more complex by the wounding. In the wounding is the entry of the gods, the entry of the More, insights that were not there before. The resolution of betrayal and the coming of extended consciousness often takes time . . . as you begin to become aware of what those insightful patterns are, you have grown into wisdom, love, and forgiveness. Jesus becomes a god of love after his betrayal.

Houston wants to serve as a catalyst for considerably more than Christopher Lasch has in mind when he recommends recovering the Judeo-Christian tradition. When Lasch calls for a Judeo-Christian sense of the self, all he can think of is the acquisition of a conflicted moral "conscience," which may well be neither forgiving nor energizing. What Jean Houston focuses on, in contrast, is the means of getting in on the Big Act which Aquinas understood as the *verbum cordis* ("word of the heart"). I suspect that such a word, especially when actually experienced in the energetic mode of the archaic "word of power," as Houston understands it, may be a good deal more productive than guilt.

THE NEW NATURAL THEOLOGY

The Judeo-Christian "mood" of a Houston program is no accident. Her reference to the "I AM" of Sinai is explicit. Which doesn't mean an unecumenical spirit; for her God of Sinai obviously lets his sun shine, and rain fall, on Hindus, Buddhists, Druids, and Sufis among others. On the one hand, the ambience she creates in one of her instantly invented sacred spaces is full of talk of cross-connections, open options and possibilities. The mood, that is, is subjunctive, and to a considerable extent this mood is created by body-work. On the other hand, that subjunctive atmosphere is usually quickly succeeded by the imperative mood — or rather by evocative rhetoric and exercises which set people hunting for a ground swell of command, a sense of summons, "must be," or world-building willing. She calls it a search for a basic sense of "entelechy" or "creative intention." She wants people to bring to awareness something like the call of Isaiah or Ezekiel. Such momentum, says Houston (1980: 86–87),

> [is] often carried in the surge of an *entelechy* — a kind of structured dynamic energy rising from a source that contains all codings. It is the entelechy of an acorn to be an oak. . . . It is the entelechy of you and me to be God only knows what. When experienced. . . it provides a momentum for change and unfolds as a creative, transforming energy which charges one's life with growth and meaning.

A typical "creative intention" exercise will often be primed with lectures on the new "natural philosophy" of David Bohm and Ilya Prigogine. The exercise part might go something like this. Participants will be invited to wander about outdoors for twenty minutes, pondering what it is important to be, do, become, or "explicate." "The intention is looking for you, too. Be open to it, " Houston will advise. Then, gathering together again, a group is asked to begin with a repetitive mantra, a humming chant (Houston, 1982: 206–10):

> Now put forth your creative intention . . . mmmmmm . . . literally into every cell of your being. A very subtle "hmmmmm" sound. . . . Let a kind of delicious rippling wave of frequencies hum throughout your being . . . your body, your protein structure, your cells, your atoms, your mind, the force fields around you, the creative intention moving as waves. . . . You and all the waves are one with your creative intention . . . mmmmmmmm. . . .
> Let it all rise in you, getting more and more complex. Deepen with it and let the passion of implicate for explicate and explicate for implicate go back and forth in resonance . . . mmmmmm. . . . Every part of your being is all Being, you are incarnate *bodhisattva*, God-manifest in self . . . mmmmmmmm. . . . Let yourself show it, the hologram knowing the Hologram, the union with the Source. . . .
> Put forth your creative intention — and be it! Send it throughout the entire order of Being. . . . Use your hands [and arms] . . . as branches and again

send out your creative intention . . . [to] find a further nexus of connection with the world out there, with thoughts becoming substance and aspiration moving to manifestation.

"The news from the deeps," remarks Houston of those who are able to temporarily release from cultural inhibitions, "is very good." It informs us that creative work and expression are "natural," built in, and not merely personal. Regarding any revelatory "calls" that come, she is quick to insist (Houston, 1982: 163–64):

> To be meaningful, the connection to the extant cultural forms must, of course, be present! There must be a common language or symbol system if the expression is not to be purely personal or perversely autistic.

Houston takes the social reconnection very seriously. In the last several years she has expended a great deal of energy setting up a new local networking arrangement, known as "The Possible Society," which tries to tap into the interests and skills of different professions for the purpose of collaborative social action and service of one sort or another. Like the groups devoted to inner work which she has encouraged to materialize around the country, all these various network groups are autonomous or "self-organizing."

POLYTHEISM?

The preceding work, like the negative way, is likely to release the underground aspects of the self, unfamiliar barbarians and ghosts in the closet, unrecognized conflicts, influxes of monstrous psychic energies difficult to channel. The self's multidimensionality explodes—and more than the self—and it's likely to blow one's cool. For Houston the "more than the self" part is where "polytheistic psychology" comes in. Naming the beasts, goblins, and witches that emerge gives a way of establishing a relationship to anonymous, raw energy rather than being strung out by it, or disowning the potential in it. James Hillman (1975: 26) defines a polytheistic psychology as

> the inherent dissociability of the psyche and the location of consciousness in multiple figures and centers. A psychological polytheism provides archetypal containers for differentiating our fragmentation and . . . offers another perspective to pathology.

Polycentricity offers "another perspective" to that of ego or even super-ego. Rather than trying to restore order by encouraging the executive ego to reclaim totalitarian control, a "polycentric" psychology points out that ego itself is typically under the sway of some single archetypal energy: Jewish Mother, Jealous Wife, Benign Neglecter, Super Salesman, Outsider, Eternal Youth, Sacred King, Dragon Slayer, Great Lover, Good Soldier, Self-Sacrificer, and so on. It is a "monotheism of consciousness" in this sense, and the plea for recognition of other relatively autonomous complexes in the psyche, which stands behind the polemic against legitimizing the imperial ego with monotheistic religious props. The caution here, of extreme importance, I think, is that one must avoid invoking the One prematurely or precipitously — lest what you get is nothing but a blown-up image of your ego or your father's. Or some spurious cultural ideal.

As the author of the medieval *Cloud of Unknowing* says, God is enshrouded, and the human mind draws a blank. Severed from this mystical, apophatic wisdom, Christians often fall into the trap Hillman points to. Both individually and institutionally, deity has often been invoked to support the restoration of the *ancien régime* of one-dimensional ego tyranny — just when an underground society of barbarian selves begins to appear on the streets. As the political alternative would be to give the masses in revolt responsible social roles in public life, so at the psychological level the idea is to provide amplified containers for potentially explosive energy.

Why call this underground rabble "gods"? In chapter 3, I cited Carl Jung: "To serve a mania is detestable and undignified, but to serve a god is full of meaning." Partly it is a conceit, and partly it is to disabuse us of the conceit that the ego "owns" or possesses the authority and fecundity of these powers as if they were personal property. Archetypal psychology suggests, rather, that their "otherness" must be respected; and that the key to making them allies is to regard oneself as their channel or circuit of manifestation. Just as likely to be pathologically twisted as the dominant ego type, each of these manic energies requires a narrative line for working through its protest marches, adolescence, and gradual maturation. Essentially, the storehouse of world mythology, heroic saga, tragedy and comedy is just that, a way out of the maelstrom, to the calm eye of the storm. I am not sure that Hillman thinks there is a calm eye of the storm; he sometimes sounds as if he is opting for psychological pluralism *tout court*.

For Houston, however, the I AM signals both the unity of Being and the psychic unity of the human race — perhaps an elusive goal but nevertheless there. Riotous psychic energy, properly channeled, can serve as a "bridge" to higher synthesis and manifestation. This is also the idea in Roberto Assagioli's psychosynthesis method. However muddied our various faces may be, potentially, they are the many faces of the Source—and possible manifestations of divine virtue and glory if, instead of denying them, we can discover their virtue or specific strengths. The polytheism here is thus provisional, and a matter of containing and cultivating explosive energy—which otherwise is merely dissipated or lost through repression. Houston's organization of most of her programs around mythic themes and stories is her way of channeling, providing archetypal containers, forms for a process of "higher genesis."

Objections on behalf of orthodox monotheists to the "new polytheism," at least understood in Houston's sense, strike me as a case of mistaken identity. It is an example of passing up that opportunity (chaos-riddled at first) for real understanding and compassion for others. The titans and demons one discovers in oneself—bound to rocks in the Caucasus or banished to hell—represent a good portion of the rest of the bound and gagged human race, and earth itself groaning, nested within one's own being. Descending into one's own hell, loosing one's own bonds—not alone but in the company of others who have trod there and returned to tell the tale—these are the crooked way to swallow the earthly city which, in the Krishna and Christ mythos, God swallows. In this sense, polycentric archetypal psychology is the necessary detour one takes to *communitas*.

SYNCRETISM?

What may trouble the religiously orthodox reader of my presentation of Jean Houston's work may be something else altogether. I mean the appearance of theological promiscuity, the heresy of eclecticism or syncretism. If anything, my exposition has underplayed the way in which she draws from the treasure of world religions, featuring the mysteries of Eleusis one week, Celtic religion the next, and the saga of the Buddha the following. Can this be anything but an indiscriminate jumble of heterogeneous pieces, or worse, some kind of synthesis which levels out unique differences? It would take another book to answer this question properly, but some comments are in order.

If there is a weakness in Houston's universalism, I suspect it lies in the direction of her failure to take the full measure of the differences among the great world religions—and a propensity at times to be somewhat careless of historical detail. However, I have tried, I hope fairly and accurately, to anticipate the objection of indiscriminant eclecticism by suggesting that Houston's architectonic is that of the Judeo-Christian tradition, broadly conceived. However critical she may be of that tradition—and she definitely is—it provides an inclusive frame that is remarkably hospitable to the truth and meaning of other spiritual paths. At the same time, those other paths, recognized in their own right, have obviously contributed to her insight into the Western tradition which she espouses in a most catholic, inclusive form. Suffice it to say, whatever problems I may have with Houston on the score of interpreting the Judeo-Christian tradition—and there are some—I applaud the effort to understand that tradition in relation to world religions.

The time is past when I can present myself as a Christian without placing my faith in the context of Hinduism, Buddhism, African and Oceanic religion, Taoism and Confucianism. God is great and one, and the plenitude and diversity of creation, most notably the many-colored cloak worn by the human race, expresses that greatness. Not only that, I have been unable to understand my own tradition until I see it through the eyes of strangers. It is like the Hasidic story Martin Buber told of the impoverished Rabbi Eisik of Cracow. He had a recurrent dream that if he would travel to Prague, there, underneath a bridge leading to the royal castle he would find a buried treasure. So he set out on the journey to Prague. Finding the bridge guarded night and day by sentries, the rabbi was afraid to dig beneath it. Finally, one day, the captain of the guard took notice of the rabbi and asked him if he had lost something. Eisik explained his dream, at which the captain scoffed, saying that no rational man believed in dreams. Why the captain himself had had a repeated dream, that if he went to Cracow he would find treasure hidden behind the stove in the home of a certain rabbi named Eisik. Silly. So Rabbi Eisik returned to Cracow, dug into the wall behind his stove, and found the treasure which ended his poverty.

This was the favorite story of the great Hindologist Heinrich Zimmer, who drew the moral: treasure is always in front of our noses, close to home, in our own being in fact, if we know how to dig for it. But in order to realize that, we have to journey far, to a strange land, and hear the meaning of our inner journey from "a stranger, of another faith and another race." The way to Catholic Tantrism is like that.

TWELVE

End Notes

Remain faithful to the earth; but the earth has no other refuge except to become invisible in us.

Norman O. Brown

Things fall apart. Within limits, I am glad they do. Somewhere in the late sixties, my world came apart; the bottom dropped out of nearly all my settled theological doctrines. The political disturbances of the period coincided with the opening of my church's windows, letting in fresh air, street noise, instability, and the void. The Catholic church had switched identifying metaphors (always a sign of sea change in sensibility) from fortress and mother to pilgrim and people-on-the-move, from bank depository to seeker and learner. After four centuries of Counter-Reformation defensiveness and a classically minded ahistoricism in doctrine, the church had decided to assimilate the prophetic spirit of the Protestant Reformation and the critical spirit of the Enlightenment—all in the space of a decade. A bit much. Overnight, we Catholics had to adjust to a church that had itself become, like all secular culture, a nonequilibrium system. Even for those of us who welcomed the challenge, it's been a shock—rather like learning the trick of dying and rising again.

The painful wrench of unanticipated losses, the street noise, and the void—none of that can be denied. I thought I was prepared; I was not. My secure liberal Catholic identity cracked, began to dissipate, to leak like a sieve. There were times when every step I took toward an altar to celebrate Mass met resistance, as if I were conducting an event in the dark, perhaps underneath the sea, and when every word and gesture during the course of that rite seemed utterly unfamiliar and weird, as if I were uttering a language I did not know. For a while there, the Christian tradition became as alien to me as the unconscious is alien, as silent

308

nature is alien. Yet it was with the sense that, at a wholly nonverbal, physiological level, I was rooted in those strange, subterranean parts. Like the unconscious and silent nature, my Christianity went underground, became an untold story.

The sense of strangeness took some getting used to. In retrospect I am grateful—for the sense of being lost, caught out in the deep, in unknown waters, and over my head. Conscious estrangement restored a sense of profound personal ignorance, and got me moving on a pilgrimage into the unknown. (Never again, after India, would the Christian idea of accomplishing the human project in the space of a single lifetime seem anything less than startling.) It was not a matter of denying my tradition so much as asking myself how much of it I can personally stand behind, really *mean*, put my body into. Or to put the matter in another form: when was the last time I heard the message of an angel, mothered God, gave birth by the Holy Spirit? If I was supposed to be able to pass along a blessing rather than a curse, much less preach or teach about the difference, I'd better have some fresh experience of blessing, something I could testify to, celebrate, give away.

Estrangement was a blessing. It meant taking nothing for granted, starting from scratch. The formulas of my youth became esoteric, hidden, a set of koans. What is the sound of one hand clapping? The meaning of the nonsense syllable *Mu*? How does one get the goose out of a bell jar without breaking any glass? The parabolic story of Jesus of Nazareth, the Catholic liturgy, became as enigmatic as these Zen koans. Koans are not answers but questions, the kind of question you have to step into and identify with in order to solve. They bring ordinary imagination and reason to the edge of dispair; and over the edge, into the unimaginable. You *become* the imprisoned goose, the bell jar, the sound of a hand cupping for air in the void. That is, you become the joke on your solemn, rational mind—until it bursts. Until, with patience and persistence—as if your life depended on it—you get the joke, until the irony, then the flow of lyric laughter comes.

You have to travel far and hear the meaning of the journey from a stranger, perhaps from a Israeli physiotherapist, a clairvoyant Californian, a Sufi clown, or a reincarnate Tibetan wise man. Spirit is like the wind; you never know where it's coming from or when. Strictly speaking, you can do nothing about it—except to prepare a vessel and let it happen. For me, the consciousness movement provided an experimental laboratory in preparing the vessel; it gave answers to the *how to let it happen* question. It provided *means*—ways of learning to listen, breathe, taste, touch, and move in new ways. It reanimated the contemplative tradition, provided rites of initiation, pilgrim routes, ways of inquiring, and mixed company (often hilarious) along the way. When I traveled to Esalen, to the East, and around the American consciousness circuit, I was seeking out conversation partners, people who might know a thing or two about Mosaic theophanies, prophetic calls, or annunciations of virgin births— not in some bygone time but in the here and now. I was trying to crack the koans of my own tradition, trying to unveil what the Semitic heritage knew as *kabod*, the true weight, glory, and greatness of God hidden in our bone marrow and tissue. As a Jesuit who had spent the better part of a lifetime in school, I was not about to renounce libraries and my addiction to reading as part of my search, but God knows, more than talk and bibliotherapy I needed body-work, psychodrama, and sheer silence—so that I could unlearn my own character-armor and insularity, so that I could begin again to learn, as I found in India, that Earth is expectant, heavy with child, longing to blaze with fire.

What I wanted was firsthand experience, not of the first coming but of the second—Pentecostal firewater. At first, the search took me away from my own community and tradition, to other paths and doctrines. Roberto de Nobili and Matteo Ricci, Renaissance Jesuits who absorbed the wisdom of Hindu and Chinese culture, would have understood. Ignatius of Loyola, the founder of my order, though no ecumenist, would at least have understood the drive for firsthand experience. For it was not formal learning at Barcelona, Acalá, or the University of Paris which gave Ignatius his fundamental vision of "finding God in all things." Nor was it the Bible. Rather, it was the mystical insights into creation and the Trinity that this ex-courtier had as an untutored hermit in a cave. "The things he saw strengthened him then," he wrote of himself in the third person ([1731] 1974:39), "gave him such strength in his faith that he often thought to himself: if there were no Scriptures to teach us these matters of the faith, he would be resolved to die for them, only because of what he had seen." I wanted to "see" like that, and the consciousness movement was at hand, a place to start.

Of course there were problems and, for a Catholic, frictions. Medieval pilgrimages followed relatively well-marked routes to a predetermined sacred destination. For Americans, it is largely otherwise; in a culture formed by Protestantism, which had repudiated the wisdom of the contemplative, monastic tradition, the geography is unmarked. To be a spiritual pilgrim in this country means, for most, to enter a wilderness where trial is by error. The consciousness movement was messy, anarchic, and wildly experimental; it collected masterminds and camp followers hell-bent to make as many mistakes as they could as rapidly as possible. Even if movement leaders had been acquainted with monasticism, however, it was of limited use as a model. No one was particularly interested in a reclusive, cloistered existence; the challenge was to discover a secular spirituality, contemplative disciplines appropriate for highly mobile politicians, business people, and professionals who had worlds to manage. The challenge, which had actually been part of the Western agenda since the sixteenth century, was to cultivate contemplatives-in-action.

In its early incarnation, the movement was not immune (nor was I) to the error of making personal enlightenment appear as an end in itself, independent of wider social obligations. It tended to foster a solipsistic spirituality of the "alone to the Alone." In retrospect, I am grateful for the internal resistance my Catholicism put up to such Neoplatonism. The bond between God and the soul may well be permanent, a given; that's not only the doctrine of the Upanishads but the assertion of John of the Cross and Meister Eckhart as well. But between the mystical soul and its *realization* of direct communion with God, a Catholic sensibility will place the stumbling block of the church itself, symbol of the complicated, fractious, anything-but-perfect human community in time. It's a reminder that salvation or enlightenment is no solo event, that disclosing the glory that hides in us must pass *through* the conflicts and complications, the mess and mud, of history. Two-way ladders between heaven and earth, wrestling matches with anonymous angels, even mountains of transfiguration—such things happen; and I've known their analogues. But they don't conclude the mission so much as gird you for the next meeting. When it works, a Catholic eschatology bars quick-fix transcendence and gnostic escapes from the wounded body of this world.

In the sixties and seventies, most Americans set out on the grail quest as if it were a spare-time, leisure activity. The fact is that in articulating the spiritual quest, we are hampered by a speech impediment, a language which inevitably distorts what we do with our solitude. For as social critics Robert Bellah and his colleagues recently put it in *Habits of the Heart* (1985), the "first language" that is available to us is that of utilitarian effectiveness or expressive individualism; "second languages," say of the biblical tradition or the civic virtues of the republican tradition, tend to get lost, especially in public discourse. The distortion, even when far more is at stake, is that the quest for spiritual goods takes on the appearance of a private affair, basically emotional, idiosyncratic, and quite separate from one's ordinary work, civic duties, and responsibilities to children. (It often seemed as if the movement, with its anti-institutional bias, had forgotten children altogether, and would therefore vanish as a social force with the next, uninstructed generation.) The result was crippling, a prescription for inanition. It meant that the movement tended to fragment into a complex of "lifestyle enclaves" (Bellah, 1985: 71–75), sequestered from the turbulent public arena, withdrawn into small circles of like-minded seekers, pursuing endless self-examination and hot-house soul-searching. The atmosphere would grow thick, bloodlessly stale, and self-congratulatory. Understandably, critics of the consciousness movement wonder if it did not buy "psychological sophistication at the price of moral impoverishment" (Bellah, 1985:139).

There is no denying this part of the story. Expurgated versions of oriental mysticism offered little correction. Uprooted from their proper cultural and social contexts, Hinduism and to a lesser extent Buddhism were air-brushed clean of their rich sense of the demonic in life. The American market for spiritual wisdom, it was thought, could not stand too much reality and wanted things simple, wanted to "feel good," wanted (literally) to "profit" from sensational parapsychological experiences — and the demand was filled in due course, with much spiritual junk food that dulled the hunger for the real thing. In this respect, there was a strong gnostic element in the movement, an unacknowledged flight from time, partisan politics, and the messy conflicts among particular communities of memory and hope. Members of the consciousness movement often overlooked their economically advantaged position in society, forgot the forgotten, and converted spiritual work into a more subtle method of upward mobility. Or, bewitched by grandiose plans for the future, many had little time or patience for the next, halting step in bringing that future about. The followers of G. I. Gurdjieff had a good maxim: that if you can't learn how to care for a plant, you're probably not up to caring for another human being, much less the planet. It was a maxim frequently ignored in practice.

All this is true enough, yet only part of the story. The movement also collected fast learners, and in my estimation their disillusionment with a succession of gurus and regimes of guaranteed enlightenment is more significant in the end than the initial infatuations were. If old forms and certainties dissolved during this period, so did most of the new Aquarian certainties and panaceas. People found themselves returned to the street noise, the hollowness of the secular city, and the void; but perhaps, if disillusionment did not turn bitter, the next venture for wisdom would be a little more patient and discriminating. If you didn't give up the struggle, the plot often thickened.

The data of science became matter for meditation. The archeological dig into the individual psyche transmuted into a search for ancestors, roots, a sense of genealogy, wider belonging, and larger obligation — to the bacteria that swim in our cells no less than to the past and future generations of people who swim in our genetic structure, memories, and imaginations. None of this was simple. In its own way, the movement wrote the obituary of the insulated Cartesian self and of nature as wholly independent of mind. It began to dawn on American individualists that we are radically social beings; that you cannot get your own act together without working at the same time to heal the divisions of the planet. There is no solo liberation.

Nature and history congregate in each of us as in a city, a place of opportunity, a second chance. As with all fresh visions occurring in a transitional, subjunctive time period, the first form of this vision was aesthetic. The moral implications and a deepening respect for the world's wisdom traditions would come later. The vision was that our native field does not stop with ourselves, familial relations, or the human race. Psychologically, we know well enough, we can shut down, close our borders, turn to stone. But physiologically, we are unstable, open systems, energy lines, magnetic fields, flow-through and flow-together charts that moment by moment unify streams of influence from all over the cosmos as well as from our proximate neighbors. Like subatomic wave-particles, we unconsciously spread out and gather together. We are the voice of the hurricane, sheafs, bouquets of time, places of assembly, transformers of dissonant noise into order. If this be good news, it is also disturbing, a challenge.

The good news may be thought to enter at a different level, a kind of background music difficult to hear through the din of groaning nature and society. The intention of the whole, says David Bohm, is hologrammatically coded in every fragment, analogous to the way in which DNA programs reside in every cell. If this is true, the body is silent metaphor, habitation of soul, a reservoir of prophetic dreams, our depth probe into the abyss of God's will. To become even slightly aware of this dimension of body, as it were its vertical axis in the *mysterium tremendum*, may be good news indeed, and a different kind of gravity than we customarily attend to. But if you keep in mind the horizontal and lateral connections to nature and society in addition to the vertical axis, what you get is not likely to be an unalloyed peak experience. On the contrary, what you get is likely to be a tug of war, the body in pain, stretched out, cruciform upon the world. All that openness you've cultivated exposes you to the tension, lets in the conflict, the agonies and loss of the ages as well as the desire of the everlasting hills. Maybe not exactly what you bargained for. Can you still sing out while tied to a withered tree of life? Does the sun shine even here, at the heart of darkness in this world? Is it so? And do you rise up to greet it with song?

To many of my fellow pilgrims, it no longer appeared exotic or strange to imagine that the Ultimate Surd, the original Dispatcher, circulates in our common blood like some kind of high energy "morphic resonance." The language might differ from mine, come in Taoist, Hindu, Sufi, or modern scientific idioms, but the movement provided a network of people for whom the world had begun to appear as it did for the author of John's Gospel. Things fall apart; they also re-form, come alive.

"In the beginning was the Word: the Word was with God and the Word was God. He was with God in the beginning. Through him all things came to be" (John 1: 1–3). If you were to view the cosmos as the prologue to John's Gospel does, as if from a satellite, you would *hear* the Creator speaking into the heart of every element in it, the signal vibrating there like the radiation left over from the Big Bang. The Word of God, said the second-century Ignatius of Antioch, is the *bythos* of nature, nature's depth, and he recognized that depth, as did the early disciples, sounding in the voice of Jesus of Nazareth, like the eternal longing of the hills. To properly imagine John's prologue these days, you have to put yourself in astronomical time, where two thousand years is nothing. Where, comparatively, the Jesus-event might just as well have occurred seconds ago, and we haven't yet begun to figure it out. You would have to think of viewing evolution through a time-lapse film, as a process of gradual awakening to another dawn, another genesis. The Big Bang, the condensation of gas clouds into galaxies, the formation of biospheres, the emergence of life, self-consciousness—all these metamorphoses would appear as stages in the transformation of matter, the glory of God gradually surfacing, blooming forth from mud like one of the Buddha's apocalyptic lotuses—right through the middle of your being. The creation remains unfinished, indeed frustrated, until the hidden sound of the great Dispatcher erupts in our throats, reaches our tongues. This, I began to understand again, was my unfinished story, and at that a collective one, the secret of the Big Bang's exhale and inhale, the mystery hidden from eternity.

"I am in my Father and you in me and I in you" (John 14:20). On first hearing, the "I am" sayings of John's Gospel sound like telexes from another planet in a foreign tongue, but from John's perspective they code a message of premonition and of promise latent from the outset in the condensed star gas upon which we stand. In fact, wherever one encounters "I am" sayings, it's a social category, an invitation to participate in a metaphoric sign; one is meant to pass over into the other, to become all that Christ is—shepherd, angry prophet, door, living water, light, temple, way, truth, vine, bread, wine, one with the ultimate surd, the Father. The images are experientially accurate. The movements of Spirit do not come with the labels "God" or "Christ," much less "Brahman" or "Shiva," attached. They come as light, breath, underground rivers of water, doors opening, fresh wind and rain, the ripening rhythms of life. And the passage is not necessarily blissfully peaceful; John's Gospel is one long series of crises, of worlds put in question by a man born ahead of his time.

The prefigural first coming is critical—as any new discovery in science or human affairs will be. But breakthroughs, be they Christ's or Einstein's, are otiose unless repeatable, unless recurrent, unless they open a way. The second coming, the reincarnation of a seminal crystallization, is crucial. Meister Eckhart, I found, was not impressed by the notion that God became man, uniting the divine energy with the human, unless he himself, and indeed every creature including grasshoppers, got in on that action. My sentiments exactly. "How would it avail me," Eckhart asked (in Fox, 1980: 199), "if I had a brother who was a rich man and I were a poor man? How would it avail me if I had a brother who was a wise man and I were a fool?" The question posed by the Jesus-koan, then, is this: what moves, perhaps like a whisper, underneath the surface of our lives and in the events of our time?

"What is life?" Eckhart asks (Colledge and McGinn, 1981: 187), and answers: "It flows without any medium from God into the soul. . . . God's being is my life. If my life is God's being, then God's existence must be my existence and God's is-ness is my is-ness, neither less nor more." Jesus is not to be shelved on a museum pedestal, nor is God. We are all in on the act. Eckhart continues:

"The Word was with God" (John 1:1). It was wholly equal, and it was close beside, not beneath there or above there, but just equal. . . . So should the just soul be equal with God and close beside God, equal beside him, not beneath or above.

"Not beneath or above," but equal. No longer servants but friends, peers. Take and eat; swallow it whole, apocalypse now. We may hold back, but God holds nothing back.

What happens if we let go, release all our holding patterns? You are that—*tat tvam asi*. Eckhart calls it the "birth of the Son in the soul," something God can't help doing if we give in to his love. Eckhart's language is unequivocal:

> The Father gives birth to his Son in eternity, equal to himself. . . . It was the same in the same nature. Yet I say more: He has given birth to him in my soul. Not only is the soul with him, and equal with it, but he is in it, and the Father gives his Son birth in the soul in the same way as he gives him birth in eternity, and not otherwise. He must do it whether he likes it or not. The Father gives birth to his Son without ceasing; and I say more. He gives me birth, me, his Son and the same Son. I say more: He gives birth not only to me, his Son, but he gives birth to me as himself and himself as me and to me as his being and nature. In the innermost source, there I spring out in the Holy Spirit, where there is one life and one being and one work. [Colledge and McGinn, 1981: 187–88]

"He must do it." One life, one being, one work. Strong stuff. This is a monk speaking, but no recluse; a man whose experience tells him that every venture out into the world is equivalently an entry into God. What kind of God? A God, I think, who pours himself out, whose body is broken and distributed to a broken world. Purists, escapists, idealists, and uninvolved experts—like myself in various disguises—get no comfort here. Finally, Eckhart is incorrigibly Catholic; he moves toward God through this messy world.

And so do I. Learn to release, let go, says Eckhart; it's the basic rule for good sex as for meditation and the higher reaches of prayer. Yet I resist, hold on, invariably imagining that if I let go, I'll be surrendering the world I've carefully built up to some other hero's monopoly politics, a divine corporate raider perhaps. Letting go would spell nullification, death (maybe just what I need). I am deterred by the stone of stumbling Christianity throws in the way of mystical quantum leaps. God is personal, we insist, or at least not less than personal. And that complicates matters, constitutes a severe test—because it implicates God, literally buries God, in the tangled history of one's relations with persons and groups of persons, particularly in intense family politics. It's as if to say that there's no direct way to recover an existential realization of your permanent union with the Ground of Being except by indirection; until you work through all those complicated and highly charged involvements with fathers, mothers, sisters, brothers, close friends, colleagues, competitors, and more remote bureaucrats and institutions. They are the major media as well as the biggest obstacle, the conduits through which the river of life flows and dams up in your own body-mind, delaying that rebirth Eckhart speaks of. So they provide the major subject of ongoing work, the heart of my asceticism.

It's like clearing a channel through the main street of a city, a city rather like New York or Bombay, full of all kinds. The open invitation to the thirsty at the close of the book of Revelation is to drink from a river, the nonstop river of life that flows through the main street of a very peculiar city. Peculiar cities, like New York or Bombay, I like. "Then the angel showed me the river of life . . . flowing crystal-clear down the middle of the city street" (Rev. 22: 1–2). Occasionally, I've heard from that angel, and seen the sight for sore eyes. And I drink, freely. This story is to be continued.

Bibliography

Anderson, Walter Truett. 1983. *Upstart Spring: Esalen and the American Awakening*. Reading, MA: Addison-Wesley.

Assaglioli, Roberto. 1965. *Psychosynthesis*. New York: Viking Press.

Auerbach, Erich. [1946] 1968. *Mimesis: The Representation of Reality in Western Literature*. Translated by Willard Trask. Princeton: Princeton University Press.

Barfield, Owen. [1929] 1973. *Poetic Diction: A Study in Meaning*. Middletown, CT: Wesleyan University Press.

_____. [1944] 1966. *Romanticism Comes of Age*. London: Rudolph Steiner Press.

_____. 1965. *Saving the Appearances*. New York: Harcourt Brace & World.

_____. 1967. *Speaker's Meaning*. Middletown, CT: Wesleyan University Press.

_____. 1981. *History, Guilt, and Habit*. Middletown, CT: Wesleyan University Press.

Barrow, John D., and Frank J. Tipler. 1986. *The Anthropic Cosmological Principle*. New York: Oxford University Press.

Bates, Harvey. 1977. "Letters from Ernest: Correspondence between Ernest Becker and a Protestant Campus Pastor." *Christian Century* (9 March): 217–27.

Becker, Ernest. 1973. *The Denial of Death*. New York: Free Press.

_____. 1975. *Escape from Evil*. New York: Free Press.

Bellah, Robert N. 1970. *Beyond Belief*. New York: Harper & Row.

Bellah, Robert N., Richard Madsen, William M. Sullivan, Ann Swidler, and Steven M. Tipton. 1985. *Habits of the Heart: Individualism and Commitment in American Life*. Berkeley: University of California Press.

Berger, Peter L., and Thomas Luckmann. 1967. *The Social Construction of Reality: A Treatise in the Sociology of Knowledge*. Garden City, NY: Doubleday, Anchor Press.

319

The Bhagavad Gita. 1964. Edited and translated by Franklin Edgerton. New York: Harper Torchbooks.

Bohm, David. 1951. *Quantum Theory*. New York: Prentice-Hall.

_____. 1957. *Causality and Chance in Modern Physics*. London: Routledge & Kegan Paul.

_____. 1973. "Quantum Theory as an Indication of a New Order in Physics, Part B. Implicate and Explicate Order in Physical Law." *Foundation Physics* 3(2): 139–68.

_____. 1978. "The Enfolding-Unfolding Universe: A Conversation with David Bohm." *Re-Vision* 1(3/4): 24–51.

_____. 1980. *Wholeness and the Implicate Order*. London/Boston: Routledge & Kegan Paul.

_____. 1985. "Hidden Variables and the Implicate Order" and "Fragmentation and Wholeness in Religion and in Science." *Zygon: Journal of Religion and Science* 20(2): 111–33. (Under the title "David Bohm's Implicate Order: Physics, Philosophy, and Theology," the entire issue is devoted to Bohm's theory. See pp. 107–220.)

Boman, Thorlief. 1960. *Hebrew Thought Compared with Greek*. Philadelphia: Westminster Press.

Briggs, John P., and F. David Peat. 1984. *Looking Glass Universe: The Emerging Science of Wholeness*. New York: Simon & Schuster.

Brown, Norman O. 1959. *Life Against Death: The Psychoanalytic Meaning of History*. New York: Alfred A. Knopf.

_____. 1966. *Love's Body*. New York: Random House, Vintage Books.

Buddhist Scriptures. 1959. Selected and translated by Edward Conze. Harmondsworth, England: Penguin Books.

Campbell, Jeremy. 1982. *Grammatical Man: Information, Entropy, Language, and Life*. New York: Simon & Schuster.

Capra, Fritjof. 1975. *The Tao of Physics: An Exploration of the Parallels Between Modern Physics and Eastern Mysticism*. Boulder, CO: Shambhala.

Chesterton, G. K. *Orthodoxy*. [1908] 1959. Garden City, NY: Doubleday, Image Books.

Clecak, Peter. 1983. *America's Quest for the Ideal Self: Dissent and Fulfillment in the 60s and 70s*. New York: Oxford University Press.

Cochrane, Charles Norris. [1940] 1968. *Christianity and Classical Culture: A Study of Thought and Action from Augustus to Augustine*. New York: Oxford University Press.

Colledge, Edmund, and Bernard McGinn, translators. 1981. *Meister Eckhart: The Essential Sermons, Commentaries, Treatises, and Defense*. Ramsey, NJ: Paulist.

Collingwood, R. G. 1960. *The Idea of Nature.* New York: Oxford University Press.

Corbin, Henry. 1969. *Creative Imagination in the Sufism of Ibn 'Arabi.* Translated by Ralph Manheim. Princeton: Princeton University Press.

_____. 1978. *The Man of Light in Iranian Sufism.* Translated by Nancy Pearson. Boulder, CO: Shambhala.

Cornford, Francis. 1957. *From Religion to Philosophy: A Study in the Origins of Western Speculation.* New York: Harper Torchbooks.

D'Allonnes, Olivier Revault. 1984. *Musical Variations of Jewish Thought.* Translated by Judith L. Greenberg. New York: George Braziller.

Didion, Joan. 1979. *The White Album.* New York: Simon & Schuster.

Dumont, Louis. 1970. *Homo Hierarchicus: The Caste System and Its Implications.* Translated by Mark Saintsbury. Chicago: University of Chicago Press.

Engler, Jack. 1984. "The Therapeutic Aims in Psychotherapy and Meditation: Developmental Stages in the Representation of Self." *The Journal of Transpersonal Psychology.* 16(1): 25–61.

Eiseley, Loren. 1975. *All the Strange Hours: The Excavations of a Life.* New York: Charles Scribner's Sons.

Eliade, Mircea. 1958. *Patterns of Comparative Religion.* New York: Sheed & Ward.

_____. 1961. *The Sacred and the Profane: The Nature of Religion.* New York: Harper Torchbooks.

_____. 1977. *The Myth of the Eternal Return, or Cosmos and History.* Princeton: Princeton University Press.

Ferguson, Marilyn. 1981. *The Aquarian Conspiracy: Personal and Social Transformation in the 1980s.* Los Angeles: Jeremy P. Tarcher.

Feyerabend, Paul. 1978. *Against Method: Outline of an Anarchistic Theory of Knowledge.* London: Verso.

Fox, Matthew, ed. 1980. *Breakthrough: Meister Eckhart's Creation Spirituality in New Translation.* Garden City, NY: Doubleday, Image Books.

Freud, Sigmund. 1962. *Civilization and Its Discontents.* New York: W. W. Norton.

Frye, Northrup. 1973. *The Critical Path: An Essay on the Social Context of Literary Criticism.* Bloomington: Indiana University Press.

_____. 1982. *The Great Code: The Bible and Literature.* New York: Harcourt Brace Jovanovich.

Gennep, Arnold van. [1908] 1960. *The Rites of Passage.* Chicago: University of Chicago Press.

Gerhart, Mary, and Allan Russell. 1984. *The Metaphoric Process: The*

Creation of Scientific and Religious Understanding. Fort Worth, TX: Christian University Press.

Greeley, Andrew M., and William C. McCready. 1976. *The Ultimate Values of the American Population.* Beverly Hills, CA: Sage Publications.

Grinspoon, Lester, and James B. Bakalar. 1979. *Psychedelic Drugs Reconsidered.* New York: Basic Books.

Grof, Stanislav. 1976. *Realms of the Human Unconscious: Observations from LSD Research.* New York: E. P. Dutton.

———. 1977. "Perinatal Roots of Wars, Totalitarianism, and Revolutions: Observations on LSD Research." *Journal of Psychohistory* 4(3): 269–308.

———, ed. 1984. *Ancient Wisdom and Modern Science.* Albany: State University of New York Press.

———. 1985. *Beyond the Brain: Birth, Death, and Transcendence in Psychotherapy.* Albany: State University of New York Press.

Grof, Stanislav, and Joan Halifax. 1977. *The Human Encounter with Death.* New York. E. P. Dutton.

Harding, Esther. 1963. *Psychic Energy: Its Source and Its Transformation.* Princeton: Princeton University Press.

Havelock, Eric A. 1963. *Preface to Plato.* Cambridge, MA: Harvard University Press, Belknap Press.

———. 1982. *The Literate Revolution in Greece and Its Cultural Consequences.* Princeton: Princeton University Press.

Heard, Gerald. 1963. *The Five Ages of Man: The Psychology of Human History.* New York: Julian Press.

Herbert, Nick. 1985. *Quantum Reality: Beyond the New Physics.* Garden City, NY: Doubleday, Anchor Press.

Hillman, James. 1967. *Insearch: Psychology and Religion.* New York: Charles Scribner's Sons.

———. 1975a. *Loose Ends.* Zurich: Spring Publications.

———. 1975b. *Re-Visioning Psychology.* New York: Harper & Row.

Hocart, A. M. 1954. *Social Origins.* London: Franklin Watts.

———. 1969. *Kingship.* London: Oxford University Press.

———. 1970. *Kings and Councilors.* Chicago: University of Chicago Press.

Houston, Jean. 1980. *Lifeforce: The Psycho-Historical Recovery of the Self.* New York: Delacorte Press.

———. 1981. "On Therapeia" (interview by Jane Prettyman). *Dromenon* 3(3): 37–41.

_____. 1982. *The Possible Human: A Course in Extending Your Physical, Mental, and Creative Abilities*. Los Angeles: Jeremy P. Tarcher.

Huizinga, J. [1924] 1954. *The Waning of the Middle Ages*. New York: Doubleday, Anchor Press.

Ignatius Loyola. [1731] 1974. *The Autobiography of St. Ignatius Loyola*. Edited by John C. Olin and translated by Joseph F. O'Callaghan. New York: Harper Torchbooks.

Jacoby, Russell. 1975. *Social Amnesia: A Critique of Contemporary Psychology from Adler to Laing*. Boston: Beacon Press.

James, William. [1903] 1919. *The Varieties of Religious Experience*. London: Longmans Green.

Jantsch, Erich. 1980. *The Self-Organizing Universe*. Oxford/New York: Pergamon Press.

Jaynes, Julian. 1976. *The Origins of Consciousness in the Breakdown of the Bicameral Mind*. Boston: Houghton Mifflin.

The Jerusalem Bible. 1966. Garden City, NY: Doubleday.

Jung, C. G. 1965. *Memories, Dreams, Reflections*. Edited by Aniela Jaffe and translated by Richard and Clara Winston. New York: Vintage Books.

Kaufmann, Walter. 1954. *The Portable Nietzsche*. New York: Viking Press.

Kapleau, Philip. 1967. *The Three Pillars of Zen*. Boston: Beacon Press.

Kierkegaard, Søren. [1849] 1954. *Fear and Trembling and Sickness unto Death*. Translated by Walter Lowrie. New York: Doubleday, Anchor Press.

Kuhn, Thomas S. 1962. *The Structure of Scientific Revolutions*. Chicago: University of Chicago Press.

Lannoy, Richard. 1971. *The Speaking Tree: A Study of Indian Culture and Society*. New York: Oxford University Press.

Lao Tzu. *Tao Te Ching*. 1963. Translated by D. C. Lau. Baltimore: Penguin Books.

Lasch, Christopher. 1978. *The Culture of Narcissism: American Life in an Age of Diminishing Expectations*. New York: W. W. Norton.

_____. 1984. *The Minimal Self: Psychic Survival in Troubled Times*. New York: W. W. Norton.

Lilly, John. 1972. *The Center of the Cyclone: An Autobiography of Inner Space*. New York: Julian Press.

Lilly, John, and Joseph E. Hart. 1975. "The Arica Training." In *Transpersonal Psychologies*, edited by Charles Tart. New York: Harper & Row. Pp. 329–51.

Lingis, Alphonso. 1983. *Excesses: Eros and Culture*. Albany: State University of New York Press.

Lord, Albert B. 1960. *The Singer of Tales*. Cambridge, MA: Harvard University Press.

Lovelock, James E. 1982. *Gaia: A New Look at Life on the Earth*. New York: Oxford University Press.

Lovejoy, Arthur O. [1936] 1969. *The Great Chain of Being: A Study of the History of an Idea*. New York: Harper Torchbooks.

Lovin, Robin W., and Frank E. Reynolds, eds. 1985. *Cosmogony and Ethical Order: New Studies in Comparative Ethics*. Chicago: University of Chicago Press.

Lowen, Alexander. 1969. *The Betrayal of the Body*. New York: Collier Books.

_____. 1973. *Depression and the Body: The Biological Basis of Faith and Reality*. Baltimore: Penguin.

McLean, Paul D. 1973. *A Triune Concept of the Brain and Behavior*. Toronto: University of Toronto Press.

The Mahabharata. 1973. Translated by J. A. B. van Buitenen. 3 vols. Chicago: University of Chicago Press.

Malcolm X, with Alex Haley. 1966. *The Autobiography of Malcolm X*. New York: Grove Press.

Marcuse, Herbert. 1964. *One Dimensional Man: Studies in the Ideology of Advanced Industrial Society*. Boston: Beacon Press.

Maslow, Abraham. 1968. *Toward a Psychology of Being*. Princeton: Van Nostrand Reinhold.

_____. 1971. *The Farther Reaches of Human Nature*. New York: Viking Press.

Masters, Robert E. L., and Jean Houston. 1966. *Varieties of Psychedelic Experience*. New York: Delta Books.

_____. 1972. *Mind Games: The Guide to Inner Space*. New York: Delta Books.

_____. 1978. *Listening to the Body: The Psychophysical Way to Health and Awareness*. New York: Delacorte Press.

Mauss, Marcel. [1925] 1967. *The Gift: Forms and Functions of Exchange in Archaic Societies*. New York: W. W. Norton.

Mead, Sidney E. 1963. *The Lively Experiment: The Shaping of Christianity in America*. New York: Harper & Row.

Merton, Thomas. 1973. *The Asian Journal of Thomas Merton*. Edited by Naomi Burton, Brother Patrick Hart, and James Laughlin. New York: New Directions Press.

Metzner, Ralph, ed. 1968. *The Ecstatic Adventure*. New York: Macmillan.

Monod, Jacques. 1972. *Chance and Necessity*. New York: Vintage Books.

Montagu, Ashley. 1971. *Touching: The Human Significance of the Skin*. New York: Columbia University Press.

Moreno, Jacob Levy. 1966. *Psychodrama: Collected Papers, Foundations of Psychotherapy, Action-Therapy and Principles of Practice*. 3 vols. Beacon, NY: Beacon House.

Murphy, Michael. 1972. *Golf in the Kingdom*. New York: Viking Press.

_____. 1977. *Jacob Atabet: A Speculative Fiction*. Milbrae, CA: Celestial Arts.

Naipaul, V. S. 1978. *India: A Wounded Civilization*. New York: Vintage Books.

Naisbitt, John. 1982. "John Naisbitt Monitors a Changing America." *The Tarrytown Letter* (April): 1–3, 11.

Naranjo, Claudio. 1973. *The One Quest*. New York: Viking Press.

Naranjo, Claudio, and Robert E. Ornstein. 1971. *On the Psychology of Meditation*. New York: Viking Press.

Neumann, Erich. [1954] 1973. *The Origins and History of Consciousness*. Princeton: Princeton University Press.

_____. 1976. *The Child*. Translated by Ralph Mannheim. New York: Harper & Row.

O'Flaherty, Wendy Doniger. 1980. "Inside and Outside the Mouth of God: The Boundary between Myth and Reality." *Daedalus* 109(2): 93–125.

Onians, Richard B. 1951. *The Origin of European Thought about the Body, the Mind, the Soul, the World*. New York: Arno Press.

Ong, Walter J. 1977. *Interfaces of the Word: Studies in the Evolution of Consciousness and Culture*. Ithaca: Cornell University Press.

_____. 1981. *The Presence of the Word: Some Prolegomena for Cultural and Religious History*. Minneapolis: University of Minnesota Press.

_____. 1982. *Orality and Literacy: The Technologizing of the Word*. New York: Metheun.

Otto, Rudolph. 1957. *The Idea of the Holy*. Translated by John W. Harvey. London: Oxford University Press.

Patanjali. 1969. *How to Know God: The Yoga Aphorisms of Patanjali*. Translated by Swami Praghavanda and Christopher Isherwood. New York: Mentor Books.

Parry, Milman. 1971. *The Making of Homeric Verse: The Collected*

Papers of Milman Parry. Edited by Adam Parry. Oxford: Clarendon Press.

Peacocke, Arthur. 1984a. *Intimations of Reality: Critical Realism in Science and Religion*. Notre Dame: University of Notre Dame Press.

————. 1984b. "Thermodynamics and Life," in *Zygon: Journal of Religion and Science* 19(4): 389–432.

Perls, F[rederick] S. [1947] 1969. *Ego, Hunger, and Aggression*. New York: Vintage.

————. 1971a. *Gestalt Therapy Now*. New York: Harper Colophon.

————. 1971b. *Gestalt Therapy Verbatim*. New York: Bantam Books.

Preller, Victor. 1967. *Divine Science and the Science of God: A Reformulation of Thomas Aquinas*. Princeton: Princeton University Press.

Pribram, Karl H. 1971. *Language and the Brain*. Englewood Cliffs, NJ: Prentice-Hall.

————, ed. 1976. *Central Processing of Sensory Input*. Cambridge: MIT Press.

————. 1978. "What the Fuss Is All About." *Re-Vision* 1(3/4): 8–13.

Prigogine, Ilya. 1980. *From Being to Becoming: Time and Complexity in the Physical Sciences*. San Francisco: W. H. Freeman.

————. 1984. "The Rediscovery of Time." *Zygon* 19(4): 433–37. (Under the title "Order and Disorder: Thermodynamics, Creation, and Values," the entire issue focuses on Prigogine's work. See pp. 389–505.)

Prigogine, Ilya, and Isabelle Stengers. 1984. *Order Out of Chaos: Man's New Dialogue with Nature*. New York: Bantam Books.

Progoff, Ira. [1959] 1973. *Depth Psychology and Modern Man*. New York: McGraw-Hill.

Rahula, Walpola. 1975. *What the Buddha Taught*. New York: Grove Press.

Ramayana. 1975. Edited and translated by C. Rajagopalachari. Bombay: Bharatiya Vidya Bhavan.

Rank, Otto. 1929. *The Trauma of Birth*. New York: Harcourt Brace.

————. [1932, 1936] 1959. *The Myth of the Birth of the Hero and Other Writings*. Edited by Philip Freund. New York: Vintage Books.

————. [1941] 1958. *Beyond Psychology*. New York: Dover.

Ricoeur, Paul. 1969. *The Symbolism of Evil*. Translated by Emerson Buchanan: Boston: Beacon Press.

The Rig Veda: An Anthology. 1981. Selected and edited by Wendy Doniger O'Faherty. Harmondsworth, England: Penguin Books.

Rothenberg, Jerome, and Diane Rothenberg. 1983. *Symposium of the Whole: A Range of Discourse toward an Ethnopoetics*. Berkeley: University of California Press.

St. John of the Cross. 1973. *The Collected Works of St. John of the Cross.* Translated by Kieran Kavanaugh and Otilio Rodriguez. Washington, D.C.: Institute of Carmelite Studies.

Sagan, Carl. 1978. *Broca's Brain.* New York: Random House.

Scholem, Gershom G. [1941] 1961. *Major Trends in Jewish Mysticism.* New York: Schocken Books.

Schuon, Frithjof. [1948] 1975. *The Transcendental Unity of Religions.* Translated by Peter Townsend. New York: Harper Torchbooks.

Schur, Edwin. 1976. *The Awareness Trap: Self-Absorption Instead of Social Change.* New York: McGraw-Hill.

Schutz, William. 1967. *Joy: Expanding Human Awareness.* New York: Grove Press.

Serres, Michel. 1982. *Hermes: Literature, Science, Philosophy.* Edited by Josue V. Harari and David F. Bell. Baltimore: Johns Hopkins University Press.

Sheldrake, Rupert. 1981. *The New Science of Life: The Hypothesis of Formative Causation.* Los Angeles: Jeremy P. Tarcher.

_____. 1981. "Special Issue: 'A New Science of Life.'" *Brain/Mind Bulletin* 6(3): 1–4.

Smith, Huston. 1965. *The Religions of Man.* New York: Harper Perennial Library.

_____. 1976. *Forgotten Truth: The Primordial Tradition.* New York: Harper & Row.

_____. 1981. *Beyond the Post-Modern Mind.* New York: Crossroad.

Snell, Bruno. 1982. *The Discovery of Mind in Greek Philosophy and Literature.* New York: Dover.

Sutich, A. J. 1969. "Some Considerations Regarding Transpersonal Psychology," in *The Journal of Transpersonal Psychology* 1(1): 11–20.

Suzuki, Daisetz T. 1971. *Mysticism: Christian and Buddhist.* New York: Harper Perennial Library.

Suzuki, Shunryu. 1970. *Zen Mind, Beginner's Mind: Informal Talks in Zen Meditation.* New York: John Weatherhill.

Tart, Charles T., ed. 1975. *Transpersonal Psychologies.* New York: Harper & Row.

Tobin, Frank. 1986. *Meister Eckhart: Thought and Language.* Philadelphia: University of Pennsylvania Press.

Tocqueville, Alexis de. [1850] 1944. *Democracy in America.* Edited by Bradley Phillips and translated by Henry Reeve. 2 vols. New York: Random House.

Toulmin, Stephen. 1983. *The Return to Cosmology: Postmodern Science and the Theology of Nature.* Berkeley: University of California Press.

_____. 1984. "Cosmology as Science and as Religion." In *On Nature*, edited by Leroy S. Rouner. Notre Dame, IN: University of Notre Dame.

Turner, Victor. [1969] 1974. *Dramas, Fields, and Metaphors: Symbolic Action in Human Society.* Ithaca: Cornell University Press.

_____. [1974] 1977. *The Ritual Process: Structure and Anti-Structure.* Ithaca, NY: Cornell University Press.

Turner, Victor, and Edith Turner. 1978. *Image and Pilgrimage in Christian Culture: Anthropological Perspectives.* New York: Columbia University Press.

Underhill, Evelyn. [1911] 1958. *Mysticism: A Study of the Nature and Development of Man's Spiritual Consciousness.* New York: Mentor Books.

The Upanishads. 1965. Translated by Juan Mascaro. Baltimore: Penguin Books.

Watson, Lyall. 1979. *Lifetide: The Biology of the Unconscious.* New York: Simon & Schuster.

Wilber, Ken. 1977. *The Spectrum of Consciousness.* Wheaton, IL: Quest Books.

_____. 1980. *The Atman Project: A Transpersonal View of Human Development.* Wheaton, IL: Theosophical Publishing House.

_____. 1981. *Up From Eden: A Transpersonal View of Human Evolution.* Garden City: Doubleday, Anchor Press.

_____, ed. 1982. *The Holographic Paradigm and Other Paradoxes: Exploring the Leading Edge of Science.* Boulder, CO: Shambhala.

Wheelwright, Philip. 1968. *Metaphor and Reality.* Bloomington: Indiana University Press.

Whitehead, Alfred North. [1925] 1958. *Science and the Modern World.* New York: Mentor Books.

_____. 1933. *Adventures of Ideas.* New York: Macmillan.

Whyte, Lancelot Law. 1950. *The Next Development of Man.* New York: Mentor Books.

_____. [1960] 1978. *The Unconscious Before Freud.* New York: St. Martin's Press.

Woods, Richard. 1986. *Eckhart's Way.* Wilmington, DE: Michael Glazier.

Yankelovich, Daniel. 1981. *New Rules: Searching for Self-Fulfillment in a World Turned Upside Down.* New York: Random House.

Young, Louise B. 1986. *The Unfinished Universe.* New York: Simon & Schuster.

Zaehner, R. C. 1961. *Mysticism Sacred and Profane*. New York: Oxford University Press.

_____. 1962. *Hinduism*. Oxford: Oxford University Press.

Zukav, Gary. 1979. *The Dancing Wu Li Masters: An Overview of the New Physics*. New York: William Morrow.

Index

Absolute space, Newton, 198
Acoustic space, 107–109
"Active imagination," 289
Adams, Ansel, 9
Adler, Alfred, 56
Adorno, Theodor, 7
Albert the Great, 112, 124
Allport, Gordon, 56
Alpert, Richard, 62, 65
American Psychological Association (APA), 208
Analogous concept, examples of, 241–242
Anderson, Walter Truett, 14
Anima mundi, 139, 166
Anthropic principle, 230
Arica method, 20
Aristotle, 31, 100, 103, 107, 258
Arya Samaj, 155
Aspect, Alain, 214
Assagioli, Roberto, 16, 50, 56, 286
Association of Humanistic Psychology, 37, 287
Association of Transpersonal Psychology, 37
Atlan, H., 237
Augustine, Saint, 32, 111, 187, 204, 269
Aurobindo, Shri, 8, 160
Australian Aborigine culture, 128
Ayer, A. J., 43

Bacon, Francis, 31
Bakalar, James B., 58
Barfield, Owen, 34, 35, 46, 111, 117, 142
Barth, Karl, 119
Bateson, Gregory, 9, 47, 66
Baudelaire, 29
Beatitudes, 22
Becker, Ernest, 48–50, 67, 92, 96, 99, 117, 131, 132, 146, 163, 277, 301
"Being psychology," 56
Bell, John Stewart, 212–213
Bellah, Robert N., 35, 144, 145, 311
Bell's Theorem, 213–214
Belousov-Zhabotinsky reaction, 241, 246

Benjamin, Walter, 7
Berger, Peter L., 47
Bergson, Henri, 189
Berkeley, Bishop, 159
Bernstein, Jeremy, 215
Besso, Michele, 230
Bhagavad Gita, 102, 123, 145, 160
Bhakti, 92, 96, 124, 149, 154
    antiintellectualism, 157
Bible, 119, 135, 136, 140, 143, 159, 204
Bioenergetics, 13
Biological birth, 73, 74–75
Birth, 78–81
Black age (*kali yuga*), 151, 152
Black Panthers, 30
Blake, William, 39, 185
Bloch, Ernst, 26
Bob and Carol and Ted and Alice, 13
Body work, 10
Body wrestling, 13
Boehme, Jacob, 172, 184
Bohm, David, 204, 209–211, 214, 215, 216, 217, 218, 219, 221, 222, 223, 224, 225, 226–227, 233, 236, 247, 249, 251, 269, 303, 313
Bohr, Neils, 203, 204, 234
Boltzmann, Ludwig, 191, 192, 231, 234, 238
    Darwin and, 245
Brahmo Samaz, 155
Breath, exodus of, 282–283
Brecht, Bertolt, 11
Breuer, Josef, 67
Bridges, Harry, 9
Broglie, Louis de, 210
Brooks, Charles, 10
Brothers Karamazov, 173
Brown, George, 7
Brown, Joseph Epes, 87
Brown, Norman O., 9, 48, 257, 259, 264, 267, 279, 281, 297, 308
Brownian motion, 191, 200, 235
Buber, Martin, 11, 169, 307
Bultmann, Rudolph, 65

Burn-out, 33

Calvin, John, 185
Calvinist predestinationism, 185
Campbell, Joseph, 9
Capra, Fritjof, 208
Carnot, Nicholas Leonard Sadi, 190
Caste, 91, 154
Catholic Left, 16
Chance and necessity, 242–245
Chesterton, G. K., 55, 99, 138, 148
Chew, Geoffrey, 210
Christianity, 138, 142, 268
Church, Frederick, 236
Church of the God of Prophecy, 8
Civil religion, 35
Clausius, Rudolph, 190, 234, 244
Clausner, John, 213
Cobbs, Price, 7
COEX systems, 67
Cognitive dissonance, 26–54
Communitas, 20, 146
    liminal, 54, 60–61
    and structure, 18–19
Complementarity, principle of, 203
Confucianism, 18
Consciousness
    altered states of, 37
    contradictory, 143
    expansion of, 76
    history of, 42, 45
    as part of nature, 46
    symbolic, developing, 297–302
Consciousness movement, 88, 92, 285,
    311
    momentum, 258
"Consciousness revolution," 5, 9
Corbin, Henry, 295
"Cosmic anonymous" state, 129
"Cosmic computer," 51
"Cosmic plasma," 215
Cosmology, 27, 80, 136
    joyous, 38–40
    oral, 133
Cox, Harvey, 65
Creative science, 167
Crick, Francis, 196
Crystallized wisdom, 269–270
Currie, Rob, 92
Cybernetic physics, 234

D'Allones, Olivier Revault, 140, 141
Darwin, Charles, 186

Boltzmann and, 245
Dass, Ram, 62
Dayananda, Swami, 155
Death-rebirth struggle, 78–81
Decentralization, 99, 134
Deliverance/resurrection. See Birth
Depersonalization, 62
Desai, Anita, 159
Descartes, René, 13, 106, 180
Development, psychosynthesis approach
    to, 16
Didion, Joan, 26, 29, 30, 31, 83, 262
Dirac, Paul, 202
Disinherited mind, 33
Divided mind, 265–267
Divine emanation, doctrine of, 41
DNA, 235, 250, 313
Donne, John, 179
Double-helix DNA molecule, 195, 196
Dukkha, 64
Durkheim, Emile, 19
Dylan, Bob, 3

Eckhart, Meister, 172, 283, 311, 315, 316
Eddington, Arthur S., 229
Ego death, 78
Ego psychology, 56
Einstein, Albert, 198–203, 207, 212, 220,
    229
Eiseley, Loren, 186–189, 192–193, 252
Eliade, Mircea, 14, 81, 87, 100, 152
Eliot, T. S., 257
"Empirical metaphysics," 56
Encounter groups, interracial, 7
Engler, Jack, 267, 268, 273, 274–280
Enlightenment, 47, 104
Enlightenment epistemology, 30
Entropy, 190–192, 247, 248
    barrier, 243
    and information, 234–238
Epic period, 123
EPR experiment, 211–214
Erhart, Werner, 15, 25
Erickson, Milton K., 81
Erikson, Erik, 75, 89
Erosion, thermodynamic law of, 244
Esalen Institute, 3–25, 53, 82, 310
Esalen's law, 10
Eucharist, doctrine of, 265
Everett, Hugh, 203
Evolution, 42, 45
Evolution by natural selection, Darwin's,
    233

Evolutionary memories, 66–71
Ex nihilo, 280–284
Extended family, 154

Fadiman, James, 38
Feldenkrais, Moshe, 11
Ferguson, Marilyn, 27
Feuerbach, Ludwig, 41, 120
Feyerabend, Paul, 194
Feynman, Richard, 206
Fifth International Conference of Transper-
   sonal Psychology, 208
Final surd, 251, 252–253
"Flower children," 7, 37, 65, 88
Force fields, four fundamental, 207
Four-stage ideal typology, 65–72
Frankfurt School, 7
Freedman, Stuart, 213
Freedom and necessity, 278–280
Freud, Sigmund, 6, 11, 22, 41, 55, 66,
   163, 277
Fromm, Erich, 6, 10, 56
Fry, Christopher, 26, 36
Frye, Northrop, 83, 135, 160
Functional integration, 11
Future, 245–247

Gabor, Dennis, 220
Gadamer, Hans-Georg, 29, 163
Gai-fu-Feng, 11
Gandhi, Mohandas (Mahatma), 124, 155,
   156, 160
Genetic coding, 195
Gestalt Prayer, 12
Gestalt therapy, 7, 8, 10, 13
Gindler, Elsa, 10
Ginsberg, Allen, 38, 88
God-as-Mother, 71, 76
Goldstein, Kurt, 10, 11
Golf in the Kingdom, 9
Goodman, Paul, 9
Gravity, law of, 207
Great Chain of Being, 89, 215, 224, 225
Greeley, Andrew, 61
Gregory of Nyssa, 121
Griffith, Bede, 196
Grinspoon, Lester, 58
Grof, Stanislav, 57, 58, 62, 63, 65, 67, 68,
   69, 72–74, 82, 84, 125, 193, 276
Gropius, Walter, 11
"Growth centers," 4
Growth movement, 6
Guilt, 92–93

Gurdjieff, G. I., 20, 312

Havelock, Eric, 106
Hayakawa, S. I., 9
Heard, Gerald, 8, 34
Heider, John, 14
Heisenberg, Werner, 202, 203, 211, 214,
   224, 231, 234
Hell and damnation, 76–77
Heraclitus, 102, 116
"Hermeneutics of restoration," 163
Heschel, Abraham Joshua, 148
Heteronomy, 222
"High noon" showdowns, 13
Hillman, James, 34, 152, 170, 300, 304,
   305
Hinduism, 92, 93, 94–95, 150
   bhakti, 92, 98, 124, 149, 154
   central myth of, 116
   classic, 123–124
   medieval, 124
   modern, 124–127
   ociology of dependency, 153–155
   Upanishadic, 157
Hocart, A. M., 98
Holography, 220–222
Holomovement, 211, 233
Holonomic mind, 225–228
Holonomic paradigm of mind and matter,
   209
Honomics, 206–228
Horkheimer, Max, 7
Horney, Karen, 6, 56
Houston, Jean, 61, 62, 63, 65, 67, 72, 74,
   81, 84, 287–307
Howard, Jane, 15
Hubbard, Ron, 25
Huizinga, J., 157
Human identity, transformation of, 143
Human potential movement, 9, 34
Human potential psychology, 28
Humanistic medicine, 7
Husband and wife, affective relations
   between, 155
Huxley, Aldous, 8, 39, 58, 62
Hyperspace, 202

Ichazo, Oscar, 20, 25
Ignatius of Loyola, 81
Imaginal body, 294–296
India, 85–176
Inequality, 129
Information, defined, 234

Inner space skills, 81
Insight Meditation Center (Barre,
    Massachusetts), 273, 287
Islamic Sufi tradition, 20

James, William, 39, 40, 55, 62
Jantsch, Erich, 199
Jehovah, 120
Jesus, 55
John of the Cross, 62, 118, 280, 311
"Joint family," 154
Joseph Atabet, 9
Joyce, James, 116, 236
Jung, Carl, 50, 56, 117, 125, 271

Kabbalist, 280, 282, 283
Kairos, 5, 14, 83, 161, 288
Kant, Immanuel, 40, 41, 44, 47, 105, 106,
    120
Kerouac, Jack, 38
Kierkegaard, Soren, 122, 257, 263, 279
Kinesthetic body, 291–294
Koyre, Alexander, 188
Kubrick, Stanley, 23, 58
Kuhn, Thomas S., 47, 194, 195

Labor pains, 78
Laing, Ronald, 53
Lannoy, Richard, 160
Lasch, Christopher, 33, 83, 259, 260, 261,
    263, 264, 265, 266, 268, 273, 285,
    300
Lashley, Karl, 226
Late Darsana period, 124
Law of entropy, 229
Law of Karma, 68, 123
Law of Manu, 91, 123, 127, 132, 134,
    154
Law of mass action, 230
Lawrence, D. H., 103
Leary, Timothy, 39, 62, 65
Leon, Moses de, 184
Leonard, George, 7, 9, 36, 40, 81
Lessing, Doris, 260
Levy-Bruhl, Lucien, 102
Libido, 55, 95, 171
Lienhardt, Godfrey, 128
Lilly, John, 51, 52, 67, 76, 77, 88, 193
Liminality, 16–19
    permanent, 19
Linear nature, 104
Literacy, 100, 101–104, 108
Local causality, doctrine of, 207

Love's Body, 259, 264, 281
Lowen, Alexander, 13
Luckmann, Thomas, 47
Luria, A. R., 129
Luther, Martin, 93
d-Lysergic acid (LSD), 39, 41, 51, 52, 56,
    57, 58, 59, 62, 279
    research, 296

McCready, William, 61
McLean, Paul, 293
Macrocosm, 35
Malcolm X, 18, 19
Manifest Destiny, 30
Mannheim, Karl, 47
Many worlds hypothesis, 203
Mao Zedong, 160
Marcuse, Herbert, 105
Marin, Peter, 15
Marx, Karl, 7, 29, 41
Maryland Psychiatric Center, 57
Maslow, Abraham, 6, 9, 10, 12, 13, 14,
    15, 35, 37, 48, 56, 287
Maslow, Bertha, 10
Masters, Robert, 61–63, 65, 67, 72, 74,
    81, 84, 287, 291
Matrix mechanics, 202
Maturana, Humberto, 242
Mauss, Marcel, 96
Maxwell, James Clerk, 211
May, Rollo, 9, 13
"Me generation," 93
Mead, Sidney E., 36
Meditation, 270
    insight, 38, 272, 274, 275–278
    types of, 268–275
Merton, Thomas, 174
Mescaline, 56
Miller, Stuart, 7, 15
Mills, C. Wright, 140
Mind, as virgin, 167
Minimal self, 261–262
Misplaced concreteness, 43–46
Mitchell, Basil, 90
Monod, Jacques, 43, 193
Montagu, Ashley, 9
Moreno, Jacob Levy, 11, 12
Morgenrath, Selig, 4, 15
Morley, Michelson, 201
Morphogenetic fields, 196–198
Mother-religion, 148–176
Mother-son affective bonding, 155
Mousike, 106

Müller, Max, 110
Multiple time, 122–127
Murphy, Gardner, 9
Murphy, Michael, 8, 9, 12, 15, 16, 24
Mystical journey, Western three-stage distinction of, 52
Mysticism vs. physics, 214–217

Naipaul, V. S., 150, 164
Naisbitt, John, 262
Naranjo, Claudio, 20, 21
Narcissism, 257–284
Narcissists and mediators, 257–284
Narcissus, problem of, 263–264
National Training Laboratory, 12
Natural theology, new, 302–304
Nature
    linear, 104
    link to, 42–46
    physical, 113
Nature mysticism, 71
Naylor, Gloria, 155
Negative way, 271–273, 280–281
Negentropy, 248, 249
Neumann, Erich, 129
Neurological capacity, extension of, 293
New Testament, 136, 138
New Science of Life, 196
Newton, Huey, 30
Newton, Isaac, 119, 185, 186, 189–192, 195, 202, 206
Niebuhr, Reinhold, 266
Nietzsche, Friedrich Wilhelm, 60
Nobili, Roberto de, 310
Nonequilibrium thermodynamics, 204
Novus ordo saecularum, 5, 30
Nudity, 13

Omega Institute, 286, 287
On the Psychology of Meditation, 20
One Quest, The, 20
Ong, Walter J., 102, 108, 118, 134
Ontological revolution, 139
Open, nonequilibrium systems, 239
Open Center, 286, 287
Oral culture, 99–103, 109, 120, 139
Oral tradition, 87–115
Order through fluctuation, 238–240
Ornstein, Robert, 20
Orr, Leonard, 15
Oxymorons, 22

Paganism, 142, 146

Paradigm shifts in natural science, 194–196
    liminoid periods of, 197
Passivity, 154
Patanjali, 81
Paul, Saint, 107
Pauling, Linus, 9
Peacocke, Arthur, 241, 248
Peak experience, 173
Penfield, Wilder, 226, 292
Percy, Walker, 3, 88
Perinatal matrix, 73
    first, 125
    fourth, 127
    second, 193
Perls, Frederick (Fritz), 3, 10, 11, 12, 13, 14, 15, 20
Philosophical rationalism, 55
"Phylogenetic" experience, 68
Physical awareness, expansion of, 291
Pike, Bishop James, 9
Planck, Max, 198, 199, 201, 235
    constant of quantum action, 208, 230
Pneuma, doctrine of, 280
Pneumatic energy, 59
Podolsky, Boris, 212
Polanyi, Michael, 47
Pollock, Jackson, 236
Polonnaruwa Buddha, 174
Polytheism, 304 306
Popper, Karl, 232
Possible Society, The, 304
Prefiguration, 135
Pribram, Karl, 226
Price, Richard, 8, 10, 24
Prigogine, Ilya, 204, 233, 238, 239, 241, 242, 244, 245, 247, 248, 249, 257, 303
Primal bond, 168–169
Primal scream, 13
Primitive myth, 128
Progoff, Ira, 286
Psychedelic drugs, 13, 39, 40, 51, 56, 57
Psychedelic Drugs Reconsidered, 58
Psychedelic experience, 61–65
Psychodrama, 7, 11, 13
Psychosynthesis exercises, 13
Puranic age, 123
Purgatory. *See* Labor pains

Quantum physics, 207–211

Radix therapy, 22
Rajneesch, Baghwan, 25

Ramakrishna, Sri, 124
Ramus, Peter, 118
Rank, Otto, 48, 49, 56, 286, 287
Ray, Satyajit, 159
Reality, 46–48
    social construction of, 47
Rebellion against caste rules, 155–156
Reich, Wilhelm, 11, 23
Relativity, theory of, 200, 207
Representations in vector form, 202
Ricci, Matteo, 310
Richard, Mira, 9
Ricoeur, Paul, 93, 127, 216
Rig Veda Period, 123
Ritual
    age of, 96
    centralization of, 131
Robinson, John A., 65
Role models, 158–160
Rolph, Ida, 11
Rosen, Nathan, 212
Roth, Gabrielle, 11
Rousseau, Jean Jacques, 32
Roy, Ram Mohen, 124, 155
Rushdie, Salmon, 150, 159
Russell, Bertrand, 210

Sadism, 78
Sagan, Carl, 73
Sakharov, Andre, 230
San Francisco State riots, 30
Satir, Virginia, 9
Schrüodinger, Erwin, 191, 202
Schrüodinger equations, 231
Schutz, Will, 12, 13, 14, 82
Science, and humanities, 247–248
Science of death, 188–192
Scientism, 55
Scientology, 25
Script culture, 101
Secularization, 107
Seekers After Truth, 21
Self
    rebuilding of, 33
    release of, 129
Self-actualizers, 10
Self-awareness, 88
Self-diminishment, 50
Self-emptying, 280
Selfhood, 128, 161, 266
Self-realization, 48–50, 53, 93
Self-reliance, 154
Self-renunciation, 171

Self-sacrifice, 126
Selver, Charlotte, 10
Sen, Keshub Chander, 124
Sensitivity sessions, 12, 13
"Sensory awareness" exercises, 10
Separation, sense of, 118
Serres, Michel, 179, 189, 229, 237, 249, 250, 251, 252
Shannon, Claude, 236, 237
Sheldrake, Rupert, 196, 219
Shrinkage of the self, 48
Simon, Pierre, 185
Sirag, Saul-Paul, 206
Sirius (dog star), 228, 240
Slate's Hot Springs, 8
Smith, Huston, 39, 40, 41, 46, 51, 56, 62, 65
Snow, C. P., 28, 181
Snyder, Gary, 38
Social amnesia, 6
Social order, objectification of, 144
Sociology of dependency, 153–155
Soledad prison, 30
Solipsism, 29
Song of Songs, 162
Soul, 169–170
Sound, kinetics of, 109–110
Space-time, Einstein's, 227
Spiegelberg, Frederic, 8
Spiritual capacity, repression of, 286
Sports Center in San Francisco, 9
Stanford University, 8
Stanner, E. H., 128
Stapp, Henry, 208
Structure, evolution of, 242
Sufis, 298
Sufism, 124, 294
Sullivan, Harry Stack, 56
Superconductivity, 241
Superquantum potential, 219, 223
Sutich, Anthony, 39, 208
Sutra Period, 123
Suzuki, Shunryu, 38
Symbolic universe, 110–115
Syncretism, 306–307

Tagore, Devendranath, 124
Tagore, Rabindranath, 155
Tantric yoga, 170–173
Tao Te Ching, 139
Tate, Sharon, murders, 30
Teresa of Avila, 62, 280
T-groups, 12, 13

Theilhard de Chardin, Pierre, 121, 182
Theravada Buddhism, 38, 267–268, 274–280
Thermodynamics, 186, 229–254
    first law of, 190
    nonequilibrium, 204
    second law of, 190, 243
Thomas, Dylan, 87
Thomas Aquinas, 105, 107, 108, 112, 113, 114, 124, 258
Tibetan Vajrayana Buddhism, 38
Tillich, Paul, 5, 9, 11
Time, 245–247
Tocqueville, Alexis de, 26, 33, 258
Toffler, Alvin, 262
Tolstoy, Leo, 92
Toulmin, Stephen, 28
Toynbee, Arnold, 9
Training groups. *See* T-groups
Transcendental denial, 151–153
Transpersonal psychology, 37–38, 56
Trust exercises, 13
Turgenev, Ivan, 32
Turner, Victor, 17, 18, 29, 54, 146, 270, 289
Two cultures, 181–182
Typology
    aesthetic-sensory level, 66
    integral-religious level, 66 67
    recollective-analytic level, 66–67
    symbolic level, 67–71

Universalism, 306
Upanishads, 97, 123, 142, 150, 151–152, 158

van Gennep, Arnold, 17

Verela, Francisco, 242
von Helmholz, Heinrich, 190
von Neumann, John, 212, 218

Watson, James, 196
Watts, Alan, 8, 10, 39, 50, 90, 151
Wave-form quantum laws of motion, 202
Way of expression, 270–271
Way of forms, 269–270
Way of surrender, 270–271
Weil, Kurt, 11
Welty, Eudora, 29
Wheeler, John A., 202, 215, 258
Wheelwright, Philip, 201
White Album, The, 26
Whitehead, Alfred North, 41, 42, 43, 65, 137, 148, 179, 200, 210, 228, 251, 253
Whyte, Lancelot Law, 43, 49, 233
Wiener, Norbert, 236, 237
Wilber, Ken, 120, 208, 215, 216, 223, 224, 275
Winnicott, H. D., 291
Womb experience, 75
Wordsworth, William, 55

Xenophanes, 214

Yankelovich, Daniel, 27, 259
Yeats, W. B., 55, 116

Zaehner, R. C., 58
"Zen boom," 38
Zen Buddhism, 164, 179
Zen Center, San Francisco, 38
Zimmer, Heinrich, 91, 307
Zukav, Gary, 208